The Lady of the Castle visits Sir Gawain

(See p. viii)

SIR GAWAIN & The Green Knight

Edited by

J. R. R. TOLKIEN

&

E. V. GORDON

OXFORD
At the Clarendon Press

OXFORD UNIVERSITY PRESS
AMEN HOUSE, E.C. 4
London Edinburgh Glasgow New York
Toronto Melbourne Cape Town Bombay
Calcutta Madras
GEOFFREY CUMBERLEGE
PUBLISHER TO THE UNIVERSITY

FIRST PUBLISHED 1925
REPRINTED WITH CORRECTIONS 1930
1936, 1946

PRINTED IN GREAT BRITAIN

PREFACE

THE first endeavour of this edition has been to provide the student with a text which, treating the unique manuscript with all due respect, is yet pleasant for the modern reader to look at, and is free (as are few Middle English texts) from a litter of italics, asterisks, and brackets, the trail of the passing editor. The second has been to provide a sufficient apparatus for reading this remarkable poem with an appreciation as far as possible of the sort which its author may be supposed to have desired. Much of the literature that begins to gather about *Sir Gawain and the Green Knight*, though not without interest, has little bearing on this object, and many of the theories held, or questions asked, about the poem have here been passed over or lightly handled—the nature and significance of the 'test'; the sources, near and remote, of the story's elements and details; the identity, character, life, and other writings of the author (who remains unknown); his immediate motive in writing this romance; and so on.

On the other hand, the more linguistic part of the apparatus, which is principally directed towards determining, as precisely as possible, the meaning of the author's actual words (in so far as the manuscript is fair to him), is in proportion more extensive. The glossary, for instance, bulks unusually large. But to a certain extent the author has made this inevitable. While a full glossary is still essential for students of any Middle English text that merits a close and scholarly attention, the vocabulary and idiom of *Sir Gawain* deserve as much as even Chaucer's best work (which has not received it) a full and careful analysis—one even fuller and more careful than has here been possible. The language is idiomatic, and the vocabulary rich. There are approximately[1] as many distinct individual words as there are lines in the poem: a new word for every line.

Our thanks are due to Mr. J. F. Sharpe for his kindness in answering questions concerning the geography of lines 696–700; to Mr. C. T. Onions for his help on several points, and for his constant interest; to Mr. K. Sisam for personal advice and help; to Sir Walter Napier for the loan of the late Professor Napier's notes. The general debt of a pupil, still freshly remembering Napier's skill in the elucidation of the difficult language of the poems of this manuscript, is thus greatly increased. Though not much of the present edition is derived directly from this source, it is noteworthy that many of the suggestions made independently by others are there found anticipated but unpublished.

J. R. R. T.
E. V. G.

[1] Words about 2690; lines 2530.

INTRODUCTION

The Manuscript.

THE manuscript is a small quarto on vellum (7 × 5 in.) in the Cotton Collection in the British Museum—MS. Nero A. x. It contains three other poems, known as *Pearl*, *Purity* (or *Cleanness*), and *Patience*. They are all written in the same small sharp hand which has been dated about 1400. The ink has faded considerably, and some lines were blotted against the opposite page when the manuscript was written, so that it is not easy to read. The first transcribers deserve great credit for their care and accuracy, as evidenced in Madden's *Syr Gawayne* and Morris's *Early English Alliterative Poems.*

It was discovered by Mr. J. P. Gilson of the British Museum that this manuscript appears in a catalogue of the library of Henry Savile (1568–1617) of Banke, Yorkshire,[1] whence no doubt Sir Robert Cotton obtained it. It is now bound with two Latin tracts which are distinct manuscripts; when in Savile's possession it does not seem to have been bound with any other manuscript, and the present binding was probably executed for Sir Robert Cotton.

The four poems are crudely illustrated in colour, but the illustrations are somewhat rubbed and indistinct. There are four illustrations to *Pearl*, two to

[1] See preface to Sir I. Gollancz's edition of *Patience.*

Purity, two to *Patience*, and four to *Sir Gawain*. The first of the illustrations to *Sir Gawain* shows Gawain taking the axe from King Arthur, and also the beheading scene before the dais, with the Green Knight holding up his severed head; all this is combined in one picture. The second (which is the clearest, and is reproduced as frontispiece) shows the lady's stealthy visit to Sir Gawain; above the picture is written (in a different hand from that of the copyist)

> Mi minde is mukul on on þat wil me noȝt amende
> Sum time was trewe as ston & fro scham couþe hir defende.

These lines have no relevance to the situation in the poem. The third illustration shows Sir Gawain and the Green Knight at the Green Chapel; it is very indistinct. The fourth pictures Gawain's return to Arthur.

The four main divisions of the poem are indicated by large ornamental coloured capitals. Smaller coloured capitals without ornament occur at the beginning of lines 619, 1421, 1893, 2259.

It is not known where the manuscript was written, but as the Lancashire character of the language is perfectly preserved, it is likely that the copying as well as the composition belongs to Lancashire.

The Story.

A summary of the story of *Sir Gawain* at this point may be a convenience:

King Arthur held court at Camelot in Christmas season. On New Year's Day he kept his vow not to begin the feast on such a high day before he had seen a marvel. As he waited, a horseman came riding into the hall, a Green Knight on a green horse; even the knight's hair and skin were green. Without

The Beginning of the Text

MS. Cotton Nero A. x. folio 91 a

dismounting, the Green Knight issued a challenge, that any of Arthur's knights should strike him a blow with the huge axe which he carried, and receive from him a blow in return in a year's time. The court was astounded and silent, and the Green Knight laughed aloud. In anger then Arthur seized the axe and was about to strike, when Gawain arose and asked that the adventure might be his. With a single stroke Gawain sent the green head rolling on the floor; but the knight lifted it up, and it opened its eyes and moved its lips, adjuring Gawain to meet the knight in a year's time at the Green Chapel. With that the headless knight leaped on his horse and rushed out of the hall.

After the autumn court on All Saints' Day, Gawain set out from Camelot to search for the Green Chapel. He rode north through Wales and over the Dee, and still his quest was not achieved. On Christmas Eve he came upon a castle in the midst of a wild forest, and there got lodging. The lord of the castle entertained him nobly. He was entertained also by the ladies of the castle, the lord's fair wife, who was more beautiful than Guinevere, Gawain thought, and an ancient dame as hideous as the other was fair. Gawain stayed over St. John's day (Dec. 27), and then would have departed to continue his quest, but the lord assured him that the Green Chapel was not two miles away, and bade him stay till New Year's morning.

On each of the intervening three days the lord proposed a merry bargain, that they should exchange in the evening whatever fortune they achieved during the day. The lord went forth at daybreak to the chase, while Gawain lay late abed to rest. Now Gawain was visited thrice secretly by the lady, who made offers of her love, but Gawain protested his unworthiness and evaded her offers without the discourtesy of a direct refusal. On each occasion she kissed him (once, twice, three times [1]), and the kisses he rendered faithfully to the lord, who each evening presented his kill to Gawain.

On the third day the lady offered him love-tokens. Her girdle of green silk, she said, had such virtue that none could be wounded who wore it. Gawain thought of the Green Knight's axe, to be wielded on the morrow, and when she pressed the girdle on him he yielded, and promised to conceal it from her lord.

In the morning he rode over the hills to a wild valley where he found the Green Chapel—no ordinary chapel, but a hollow green mound. There came the Green Knight with an axe even bigger than before. Gawain made ready to take the blow, but

[1] ll. 1306, 1505 and 1555, 1868–9.

shrank a little as he saw the blade descend; the knight withheld his axe and reproached him. Again the knight made a feint with the axe; but at the third time he let it wound Gawain's neck slightly. Gawain sprang up more than a spear length, and made ready to defend himself, but the Green Knight leaned upon his axe and spoke merrily to him. He knew all about the temptations of the lady; he was no other than the lord of the castle. He had made two feints at Gawain for the two days when he had resisted temptation and faithfully paid up the kisses. He had nicked Gawain's neck at the third stroke because he had not been perfect in troth, but had concealed the girdle. The name of the Green Knight was Bercilak de Hautdesert, the ancient dame at his castle was Morgan la Fay, who had wrought the whole enchantment to frighten Guinevere and shame Arthur's court. Gawain's virtue had defeated her purpose.

Though praised by the Green Knight, Gawain felt himself greatly shamed. The green girdle he kept and wore as a baldric in token of his fault. Now he took his way back to Arthur's court, where he was comforted; the lords and ladies of the Round Table ever after wore a green baldric in honour of Gawain's great loyalty.

This is a story shaped with a sense of narrative unity not often found in Arthurian romance. Most of the Arthurian romances, even the greatest of them, such as the French *Perlesvaus*, or Malory's *Morte Darthure* (which is much better knit than its French originals), are rambling and incoherent. It is a weakness inherited from the older Celtic forms, as we may see in the Welsh Mabinogion, stories told with even greater magic of style and even less coherence than the French and English compilations. Instead of the usual multitude of adventures *Sir Gawain* has only two, and they are neatly linked by making the outcome of the beheading game dependent on the result of the temptation. The motive for the peculiar challenge and enchantment has been thought insufficient:[1] but Morgan's hatred of the Round Table

[1] Kittredge, *Gawain*, pp. 132, 136.

is quite enough to account for the Green Knight's quest. We may imagine that she could do no more than put Arthur's knights to the test, in spite of all her magic, the powers of evil being unable to harm them while they remained virtuous. The beheading game was a way of drawing a knight to her castle and disposing of him if he failed in the test of loyalty and chastity; she hoped also that the sight of the beheading would frighten Guinevere.[1] There was a more vital reason for it in other stories of beheading—it was usually a means of disenchantment—but the reasons for its presence in this story are good enough.

The story is an excellent one for the purposes of the romancer. It has all the traditional elements which medieval authors had learned to excel in treating—marvellous adventure, courtly life, knightly love-making. It was, moreover, a story to call forth all that humanity which was the greatest virtue of the medieval romancer—a virtue which is usually overlooked. *Sir Gawain* is as human as Chaucer or Shakespeare or any modern romance. In spite of this humanity, it must not be forgotten that magic is a fundamental element in the plot. The same power protects the Green Knight in Arthur's hall and his lady in the castle.

The History of the Legend.[2]

The story of *Sir Gawain* consists of two main adventures, the first (occupying the first and fourth divisions of the poem) of the Green Knight's challenge and the ensuing beheading match, the second (in the

[1] As apparently it did; cf. Arthur's words, line 470; also 2460.
[2] For detailed analysis, see Kittredge's study of Gawain.

second and third divisions) of the temptation of Sir Gawain at the castle. These two adventures are found separately in other romances, in forms recognizably similar; they exist in the combined form only in *Sir Gawain* and two later English poems which are closely related to it. Both adventures derive ultimately from Celtic legend.

The Celtic form of the adventure of the challenge is exemplified in *The Champion's Bargain*, an episode in the Middle Irish romance *Bricriu's Feast*,[1] preserved in a manuscript dating from about 1100. The story itself must be at least a century older. In the Irish version the challenge has already a developed literary form and contains all the essential details of the later versions. An interesting feature which only the Irish story and *Sir Gawain* have in common is that *three* blows are aimed at the hero when it is the challenger's turn to strike.

From a Celtic version the story of the challenge passed into French, but through what channel is impossible to discover. There is nothing to show whether the immediate Celtic source was Welsh, Cornish, or Breton.[2]

[1] *Fled Bricrend,* ed. with translation by G. Henderson, Irish Text Society, 1899.

[2] According to Miss Weston (in her *Legend of Sir Perceval*, Vol. I, Chap. 12, II, p. 25), the chief source of Gawain legend in French was a lost *Geste de Gauvain* composed by the Welsh romancer Bleddri, who is quoted as an authority who 'knew all the gestes and tales of the British kings and nobles' in several French romances. Even greater importance is claimed for Bleddri as a source of Arthurian romance in France by Loomis, *Mod. Lang. Notes*, xxxix. 319. For an identification of this shadowy romancer (whose works do not exist) see *Revue Celtique*, xxxii. 5. There is no evidence to connect the story of *Sir Gawain and the Green Knight* with Bleddri. One French version of the challenge, *Le Livre de Caradoc*, forms part of a work which quotes Bleheris as authority, but the Caradoc episode is almost certainly not from the same source as the rest of the romance.

The existing French versions of the challenge are these:

(C) *Le Livre de Caradoc*, forming part of the first continuation (by Wauchier de Denain) of the unfinished *Perceval* of Chrestien de Troyes. It has been edited by Potvin in *Perceval le Gallois*, Mons, 1866, vol. iii, pp. 117 ff. There is a prose version also in the Old French prose *Perceval*, printed at Paris in 1530.

(M) *La Mule sanz Frain*, by Paien de Maisieres, ed. Orlowski, *La Demoiselle à la Mule*, Paris, 1911; and by R. T. Hill, Baltimore, 1911.

(P) In *Perlesvaus*, a prose romance, ed. Potvin, vol. i.

(H) *Gawain et Humbaut*, ed. Stürzinger and Breuer, Dresden, 1914, Gesellschaft für romanische Literatur, xxxv.

These romances all date from the thirteenth century. Only in M and H is Gawain the hero. They resemble the English *Sir Gawain* closely, especially C, but none of them is the immediate source. Professor Kittredge has assumed that the English poet found the story in a related French romance, now lost. The existence of such an original cannot be proved, and has been questioned:[1] the Celtic legend might have passed into currency in the north-west of England without the assistance of a French version. But it is evident that the author of *Sir Gawain* was in some degree dependent on French romance; his insistence on the courtliness of his characters belongs to French

[1] By Frl. von Schaubert, *Englische Studien*, lvii. 394.

tradition;[1] the influence of French idiom is traceable, as in the expressions *cros kryst* 762, *for alle lufeȝ* 1786; further, the correspondence with the French analogues is often detailed.[2] On the whole, Kittredge's assumption of a French original (which we may call *g*) seems justified.

It is to be observed that no one of the French versions is derived from another, and at least two more lost romances linking their tradition must be assumed. One of these (O) is the work of the poet who first put the story into French, the other (R) was a retelling of O.

The nearest analogue to the adventure of the temptation is the English *Carl of Carlisle*, composed in the fifteenth century. A parallel episode in the French romance *Le Chevalier a l'Epee* (E) shows that the *Carl* too is based on a French original, which was very near to the version of the temptation in *g*, in which (it is assumed) the two adventures were first combined.

There are two later English versions of the combined plot, namely, *The Turk and Gawain* (T) and *The Green Knight* (K). Both are preserved in the Percy Folio Manuscript (written *c.* 1650). T is probably a debased form of another romance derived from *g*. The story of K is almost identical with that of *Sir Gawain*; the very wording of passages in *Sir Gawain* is echoed, and details are reproduced which were probably not in the French original (*g*). K is therefore a condensed form of the English *Sir Gawain*.

The reconstruction of such literary relations is necessarily uncertain, but if our analyses and assump-

[1] See especially note to 1979.
[2] See the note on 'guisarme', 288, and to 2274.

tions are correct, the descent of the legend is expressed in the following table:—

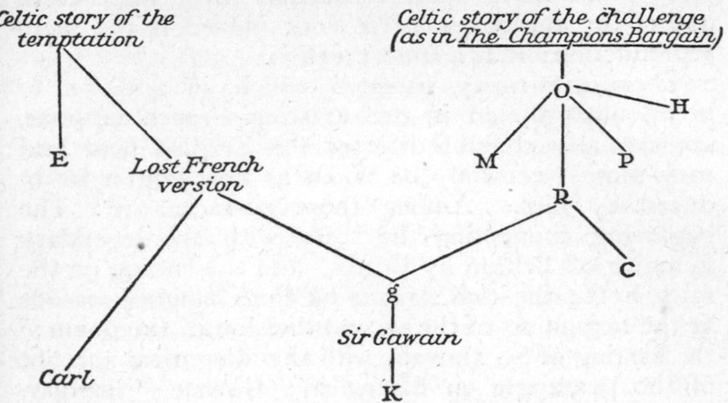

Treatment of the Source.

What is common to *Sir Gawain* and the French analogues may be taken to have passed through the lost French original. There is little in the action of *Sir Gawain* which is not also found in these analogues: hence it appears that in relating the story the English poet followed his source closely, as he promised to do:

> I schal telle hit astit, as I in toun herde.

The author of *Sir Gawain* appreciated the aims and virtues of French romance as few English romancers did. His poem is as human, as skilfully diversified, and at all times as courtly as the best French romance. In these very qualities he probably surpassed his original, as he undoubtedly surpassed the existing romances of the beheading and temptation. He has, further, a special gift for description, and has elaborated the whole setting with a richness of detail unusual in French romance. He handles the story with a moral sensitiveness not to be matched in any of the analogues. His work indeed is not mere reproduction: it is a fresh creation.

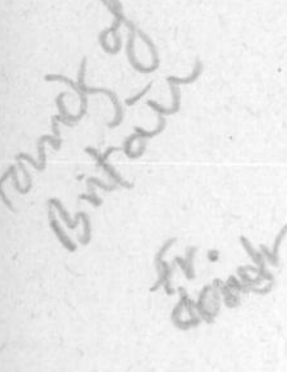

There are many passages which, in addition to being unparalleled in the existing French versions, are specially characteristic of the English poet and may almost certainly be taken as new matter introduced by him. Among these passages are: The beginning connecting the story with the legendary founding of Britain by Brutus,[1] and the ending on the same note; the two stanzas on the changing seasons at the beginning of the second division of the poem;[2] the arming of Sir Gawain, with the allegorical account of the pentangle on his shield; Gawain's itinerary, and the description of Bercilak's castle; the descriptions of the three hunts;[3] the winter weather and landscape in the last division of the poem.

It is doubtful how much of Bercilak's explanation of his quest as the Green Knight is due to the English poet; probably the figure of the enchantress who was responsible for the whole plot is old, but her identification with Morgan la Fay the invention of the English poet.[4]

[1] Cf. the beginning of *St. Erkenwald.*

[2] Though it is recognized that the beginning of the divisions of a romance with lines of lyrical tone as in these two stanzas is an imitation of French convention. The same sort of lyrical introductions is found in the romances of *Kyng Alysaunder* and *Arthour and Merlin*, and in the *mansǫnguar* of Icelandic rímur.

[3] See note to 1133.

[4] Kittredge (p. 134) is of the opinion that the enchantress herself was introduced by the English poet. But where there is enchantment an enchantress is likely to be one of the earliest developments of the story. In *Le Livre de Caradoc* and in *Diu Krone* (the Middle High German romance which contains a version of the *Mule sanz Frain* story) there is an enchanter. The old and withered enchantress is a

Though the story is taken from a French source, in style the poem is a culmination of Middle English alliterative tradition; the poet draws freely on the traditional stock of words and phrases. He does not appear to be indebted to any particular alliterative poem which is still extant. The parallels with the work of other poets are merely conventional or fortuitous. He has, however, made use of phrases and descriptive details from poems that appear to be earlier productions of his own,[1] notably in his description of Arthur's New Year's Feast (114 ff.), which resembles closely the description of Belshazzar's feast in *Purity* (1401 ff.), and in the description of Bercilak's castle, where he repeats phrases used in *Purity* to describe the 'aþel vessel' brought into Belshazzar's feast.

The Author and his Work.

The identity of the author of *Sir Gawain* is unknown. There is no good evidence for ascribing the poem to Huchown,[2] or to Strode (whom Sir I. Gollancz suggested as its author), and *a priori* probability is strongly against either of them.

Sir Gawain is closely related in language and

conventional figure of French romance (see Kittredge, p. 134, and Madden's *Syr Gawayne*, note to 2460), and is more likely to have been introduced by a French poet.

[1] See notes to ll. 790, 796, 802.

[2] The ascription was first made by Guest, who was followed by many Scottish scholars. The hollowness of their case is shown by MacCracken, Publ. M. L. Ass., 1910. The only specific evidence for this ascription is that at the head of *Sir Gawain* a fifteenth-century hand has written 'Hugo de', but there is no reason why this should have any reference to Huchown; there were more Hugos than one. The one poem which may reasonably be ascribed to Huchown, *The Pistill of Susan*, is obviously not by the author of *Sir Gawain*.

style to the other three poems in the same manuscript. As has been noted (p. xvii), there are descriptive passages of some length in *Sir Gawain* and *Purity* of striking similarity, containing whole lines that are almost identical. *Sir Gawain* is most closely connected with *Purity*, but there are many links with the other two poems also. It is usually assumed from the unity of dialect, the numerous verbal and stylistic parallels found in these poems, and from their being copied together in one manuscript, that they are all by one author. The arguments are not conclusive, but the assumption withstands all tests so well that most of those who have worked over the poems in detail have been convinced that they are all by one author.

It has been suggested that *St. Erkenwald* also is by this poet, and there is, undeniably, a strong similarity between its workmanship and that of the four poems in MS. Cotton Nero A. x. The similarity is not so close as between the four poems themselves, however, and the ascription of *St. Erkenwald* to the same poet must be regarded as very dubious.

The other poems show a considerable variety of form and subject. *Patience* relates in a lively manner the story of Jonah and how he learned his lesson of patience. The poet's descriptive talent is not even baffled by the interior of the whale: it is as picturesque as the landscapes of *Sir Gawain*. *Purity* retells three more biblical stories illustrating the value of chastity and God's punishment of impurity—the destruction of Sodom and Gomorrah, the Deluge, and the fall of Belshazzar. *Purity* is inferior to *Patience* and *Sir Gawain* in narrative art, but the poet was not the man to miss the descriptive opportunities of the flood and Belshazzar's feast. *Patience* and *Purity* are written in alliterative lines arranged in quatrains, though the quatrain system here and there breaks down. *Pearl* is an elegy on the poet's little daughter, who died in her second year. One day he fell asleep by her grave and his 'spirit sprang in space' to Elysian fields. By the bank of a celestial stream he met his daughter, now a queen of heaven. She told him of the heavenly bliss and showed him the vision of the heavenly city. Written in stanzas of twelve four-stress lines (which fall into quatrains within the stanzas), *Pearl* is swifter and more lyrical in movement than any other of the poet's work. He is here more personal and impassioned than in the other poems, both in sorrow for the loss of his daughter and in the fire of his religious feeling. He does not always maintain complete mastery over the difficult combination of alliteration with a complicated rhyme-scheme, yet in spite of its inequality the poem is as fine of its kind as *Sir Gawain*.

There are indications[1] that *Patience* and *Purity* were composed before *Sir Gawain*. It is further noteworthy that the quatrain arrangement which runs through *Patience* and *Purity* is found also in *Pearl*, but not in *Sir Gawain*; this may be taken as an indication that the other three poems were produced in sequence, and *Sir Gawain* last, but it is certainly nothing more than an indication.

The homiletic character of *Patience* and *Purity*, the theology of *Pearl*, the moral earnestness of *Sir Gawain*, all suggest that the author might have been a priest. Certainly he had an ecclesiastical education, but his familiarity with courtly life, and his delight in it, make it doubtful whether he was a priest. We know from *Pearl* that he had a daughter, but that is not decisive: he may for instance have been ordained later in life.

[1] They are summarized by Menner in his edition of *Purity*, xxvii ff.

He was well informed concerning the worldly life of noblemen, but even if he was a priest, he may well have been chaplain in a nobleman's household, or himself of noble birth and polite education. In *Sir Gawain* he shows detailed and even technical knowledge of hunting; of the service in a nobleman's household; of the latest castle architecture of the time; of the armour and gear of a knight. In *Patience* he uses readily enough the right terms for the parts of a ship. He has plenty of book learning too: we know that he read the Latin of the Vulgate, in *Purity* he cites Clopingel's *Roman de la Rose*, and has clearly availed himself of the French text of Mandeville's Travels. *Sir Gawain* illustrates further his reading of French. Perhaps the only safe conclusion to be drawn about the poet from his poems is that he was a man of learning and genius.

Date.

Sir Gawain cannot be dated precisely. An attempt has been made to date it from a supposed connexion with the Order of the Garter; but such a connexion is very doubtful, and even if it were admitted it would prove only that the poem was composed after 1345, the probable date of the Order's foundation.[1] Costume, armour, and architecture described in the poem point to a date towards the end of the fourteenth century. They show the love of elaborate decoration which marks the later Middle Ages—the end of the fourteenth and the fifteenth century. More precisely the details

[1] I. Jackson (*Anglia*, xxxvii. 395) dates *Sir Gawain* precisely 1362, when Edward III's son Lionel became Duke of Clarence; but there is no evidence that the poem was connected with that occasion. In *Sir Gawain* the title *Duke of Clarence* is derived from French Arthurian romance. See 552 note.

which indicate such a date are: the ornamental peitrel of the Green Knight's horse, hung with pendants 168; and that of Gringolet 601; the square-toed *sabatounȝ* worn by Gawain 574; the fret worn by the lady 1738; the numerous pinnacles of the castle 796. See the notes on these passages.

The only feature of the language of the poem which gives any indication of the date of composition is the pronunciation of final unaccented *-e*. The rhymes show an inconsistent pronunciation. In 413 *to þe: soþe*, 2355 *waþe: ta þe*, the final *-e* of *soþe* (dat.) and of *waþe* (ON. *váði*) was certainly pronounced, and from the regularity of rhymes of words in *-e* throughout the poem it appears that *-e* of the infinitive, of the indic. and subj. pl., of the pa. t. of weak verbs, and of the pl. of adjectives was usually pronounced. On the other hand there are rhymes showing that final *-e* was sometimes dropped; for example:

> *payne* (infin.) 1042 rhyming with *Gawayn*;
> *fayn* (adj. pl.) 840: *Gawayn*;
> *to graunte* 1841: *seruaunt*;
> *myȝt* (pa.t.) 201: *lyȝt*.

Evidently final *-e* was in process of being dropped; but as verse usage is more conservative than colloquial speech, final *-e* in the poet's spoken dialect may have been comparatively rare. The chronology of the loss of final unaccented *-e* is not known certainly, but the process seems to have been complete by *c*. 1400, to judge from the spelling of the Ireland MS. and the metre of *The Destruction of Troy*.

The criteria, such as they are, point to a date in the last quarter of the fourteenth century, the latest possible date being determined by that of the manuscript, *c*. 1400. The most definite indication that the poem cannot be earlier than the last quarter of the century is in the *sabatounȝ* which Gawain wore. Even in the last quarter of the century they were not yet in ordinary use.

Dialect.

Morris, in his second edition of the *Early English Alliterative Poems* in 1869, expressed the opinion that the dialect of these poems and of *Sir Gawain* was that of Cheshire or Lancashire. Such indications of dialect as can be discovered tend to confirm Morris's opinion. The language of the poems as preserved closely resembles that of the romances in the Ireland MS., which there is reason to believe was written at Hale in south-west Lancashire, not many years earlier than 1413.[1] This resemblance, however, only goes to show that the dialect of the copyist was of Lancashire. As evidence of the dialect of the original form of the poem we have:

(1) The local knowledge shown by the author. In 691–702 of *Sir Gawain* he seems to show detailed knowledge of the geography of North Wales and Wirral. As the places he mentions cannot be identified, his knowledge is not certain, but undoubtedly he speaks of the natural features of these parts as if they were familiar to him. See the note on 691 ff.

(2) The evidence of vocabulary, which is slight. A large number of words used in the poem are characteristic of northern and north Midland dialects, but very few can be localized in a limited area. There are, however, two words of which the localization is significant: *kay* 422, found only in Lancashire and

[1] See *Three Metrical Romances*, ed. Robson, pp. xxxvii–xlv.

Cheshire dialects ; *misy* 749, modern *mizzy*, restricted to south Lancashire dialects.

(3) The alliteration : it is notable that in *Sir Gawain* *wh* (= OE. *hw*) alliterates with original *w*, in contrast to such a poem as *The Destruction of Troy*, in which *wh* (= OE. *hw*) alliterates with *qu* (= OE. *cw*). Yet *The Destruction of Troy* is probably north-west Midland: the general character of its language in the extant copy is confirmed by the occurrence of the west Midland form *hom*, 'them', in alliteration. The alliteration of *wh* and *w* in *Sir Gawain* indicates that it was composed further south than *The Destruction of Troy*. The line between the different developments of OE. *hw* which made possible these different types of alliteration seems to have been roughly the valley of the Ribble. Thus local names originally beginning with *hw-* written down at Cockersand or Furness are spelt *qu-*, whereas such local names written at Lancaster, Whalley, and elsewhere south of the Ribble are spelt *wh-*, *w-*. This difference may be followed in the selection of medieval spellings of place-names in Ekwall's *Place-Names of Lancashire*, if care is taken to distinguish the place where the forms were written down.

(4) The rhymes. The general character of the dialect forms, as proved by rhymes, is Midland, with an intermixture of northern forms, such as might be expected of a Midland dialect bordering on the northern dialect area. The following forms are characteristically northern or north Midland:

Imper. sg. and pres. indic. 2 sg. in *-es*, *-eȝ*, as in *slokes* 412, *cnokeȝ* 414, rhyming with *he strokes*.

Pres. indic. pl. in *-es*: *þay hyȝes* 1351, rhyming with *þyȝes*.

Pres. part. in *-ande*: *laȝande* 1207, rhyming with *in blande*, *hande*.

OE. *ā* remains: *hame* 1534, rhyming with *game*; and 2451, rhyming with *name*, *tame*; *waþe*, 2355, rhyming with *scaþe*.

There are also forms proved by rhyme which are specially characteristic of the north-west Midlands, namely:

(i) *ó* + *ng* pronounced as [*ung*]: *stronge* 34, *longe* 36, rhyming with *tonge*. (N. W. Mid. and West Riding.)

(ii) OE. *āw* remains *aw*, and does not become *ow*, as elsewhere in the Midlands: *knowe* 1645 rhyming with *lawe* and *drowe* (with scribal *ow* for etymological *aw*).

(iii) Shortened forms of *take*: *ta þe* 2357, rhyming with *waþe*; including a form with *ǭ*: *tone* 2158 (rhyming with *grone*) which is not found in Northern or the other Midland dialects.

On the whole the evidence points to south Lancashire rather than Cheshire as the home of the dialect.

SELECT BIBLIOGRAPHY

EDITIONS.

Syr Gawayne, ed. Sir F. Madden, for the Bannatyne Club, 1839. A diplomatic text. Other Middle English romances which have Gawain as their hero are included. The only edition with full notes.

Sir Gawayne and the Green Knight, ed. R. Morris, for the E.E.T.S., 1864. Corrects some of the errors of Madden's text. There are a few notes and a glossary (incomplete, of little value). Text revised by Sir I. Gollancz, 1897 and 1912.

Lines 2069–2488, excellently ed. K. Sisam in *Fourteenth Century Verse and Prose*, with glossary by J. R. R. Tolkien, Oxford, 1921.

Editions of the other poems ascribed to the author of *Sir Gawain*.

Early English Alliterative Poems, ed. R. Morris for the E.E.T.S., 1867, revised 1869; contains *Pearl*, *Cleanness* (*Purity*), and *Patience*. Good text, the apparatus somewhat out of date.

Pearl, ed. Osgood, Boston, 1906.
ed. Sir I. Gollancz, with metrical translation, London, 1891; revised edition, together with Boccaccio's *Olympia*, 1921.

Purity, ed. R. J. Menner, Yale Univ. Press, 1920.
ed. Sir I. Gollancz, as *Cleanness*, London, 1922. The glossary and illustrative texts have not yet appeared.

Patience, ed. Sir I. Gollancz, London, 1913.
ed. H. Bateson, Manchester Univ. Press, 1912, 2nd edition, 1915.

Saint Erkenwald, ed. C. Horstmann, in *Altenglische Legenden* (*Neue Folge*), Heilbronn, 1881 (text only).
ed. Sir I. Gollancz, London, 1922.

FACSIMILE.

Pearl, Cleanness, Patience, and Sir Gawain, reproduced in facsimile from MS. Cotton Nero A. x. in the British Museum, with an introduction by Sir I. Gollancz, E.E.T.S., 1923. The introduction contains a list of the textual emendations proposed.

BIBLIOGRAPHICAL.

A Manual of the Writings in Middle English, by J. E. Wells, Yale Univ. Press, 1916; supplements, 1919, 1923. For bibliography of the Middle English texts referred to in this edition.

La Littérature Française au Moyen Age, by Gaston Paris, 5th edition, Paris, 1914. For history and bibliography of Old French romances.

LITERARY HISTORY AND THE ANALOGUES.

A Study of Gawain and the Green Knight, by G. L. Kittredge, Harvard Univ. Press, 1916.

The Mabinogion, medieval Welsh romances translated by Lady Charlotte Guest, reprinted with notes by A. Nutt, 3rd edition, 1910; translated Ellis and Lloyd, Oxford, 1929. French translation by J. Loth, *Les Mabinogion*, 2nd edition, Paris, 1912.

Historia Regum Britanniae, by Geoffrey of Monmouth, ed. Giles, London, 1844; ed. San Marte (A. Schulz), Halle, 1854; translated by S. Evans, Everyman Library, 1912. It is the origin or earliest record of much Arthurian matter.

For bibliography of the Irish and French analogues of *Sir Gawain*, see pp. xii and xiii, and the bibliography in Kittredge's study.

THE HISTORICAL SETTING.

Accessible medieval hunting treatises useful for the interpretation of the hunting descriptions 1139 ff. are:

The Art of Hunting, ed. Sir H. Dryden, 1843, and re-edited by Alice Dryden, Northampton, 1908. It contains: Twici's *Le Art de Venerie* (in Anglo-Norman; Twici was huntsman to Edward II); a fifteenth-century translation of Twici entitled *The Craft of Venery*, and a translation in modern English of the thirteenth century French poem *La Chace dou Cerf*.

The Master of Game. The oldest hunting treatise in English, written between 1406 and 1413 by Edward, second duke of York. Ed. W. A. Baillie Grohman, Edinburgh, 1904; 2nd (modernized) edition, London, 1909.

The Boke of Saint Albans. Treatises on hunting, hawking, and coat-armour, traditionally ascribed to Dame Juliana Berners or Barnes. Printed at St. Albans, 1486, and ed. in facsimile by W. Blades, 1901.

The Noble Art of Venerie or Hunting, usually ascribed to George Turberville. Printed in London, 1576, and reprinted in the Oxford Tudor and Stuart Library, 1908. It is almost entirely a translation of the 1573 edition of Du Fouilloux's *La Venerie* (first published 1562; based on earlier French treatises).

For study of costume:

Planché's *Cyclopædia of Costume*, Vol. I. *Dictionary*, Vol. II. *A General History of Costume in Europe*, London, 1876–9. Useful illustrations.

Enlart, C. *Le Costume*, forming Vol. III of his *Manuel d'Archéologie Française*, Paris, 1916. Relates primarily to French costume.

On castle architecture:

Thompson, A. Hamilton. *Military Architecture in England during the Middle Ages*, Oxford, 1912.

LANGUAGE.

Morris, R. Preface to his second edition of *Early English Alliterative Poems*, E.E.T.S., 1869. Morris's views on the dialect of the poems were sound.

Knigge. *Die Sprache des Dichters von Sir Gawain, und der sogen. Early English Alliterative Poems*, Marburg, 1885. Now somewhat out of date, but still useful.

TEXT.

Knott's collation of Morris and Gollancz's text, published in Modern Language Notes, XXX. 102, is important.

Gollancz, Introduction to the Facsimile of the MS. (see above).

METRE.

Luick, K., in Paul's *Grundriss der germanischen Philologie*, 2nd edition, Vol. II, Part 2, pp. 181 ff.

DICTIONARIES.

A New English Dictionary on Historical Principles, ed. Sir J. A. H. Murray, H. Bradley, W. A. Craigie, C. T. Onions, Oxford, 1888–. Quoted as NED.

THE TEXT

THE spelling of the manuscript is reproduced, except for corrections of scribal errors. Emendations are indicated by footnotes, where the original forms of the manuscript are quoted. No emendations have been made on metrical grounds; the details of the original metrical form are too uncertain. Contractions have been expanded without notice. There can be no doubt of the interpretation of any of them except ꝙ, expanded in this text as *quoþ*, in previous editions as *quod*; the word is nowhere written in full in the manuscript, but cf. *coþe* 776. Words which stand divided in the manuscript, such as *in noȝe* 514, have been joined without indication of the manuscript division. The long *i* of the manuscript is printed as *j* except in *Iwis* and the pronoun *I*. Capital letters are used as in modern English, and the editors are responsible also for the punctuation. The only diacritic that has been added is an acute accent to mark an unaccented *e* when it stands for etymological *i* or OFr. *é*, as in *meré* 'merry', *bewté* 'beauty'.

Since the last edition of *Sir Gawain* was published, Dr. Knott has pointed out the textual value of the 'offset'. When the manuscript was written the leaves were closed together before the ink was dry, with the result that here and there it stuck to the opposite page and left words illegible in their original position. By examining the offsets with a mirror, Dr. Knott recovered some of the illegible letters. These offsets the present editors have examined again, and have confirmed most of Knott's readings; a few have not been accepted. The whole text has been collated with the manuscript and some new readings obtained.[1]

[1] The most important are;
1334 lere *for* bere
1442 grym*me* *for Knott's* gryndre.

SIR GAWAYN

AND

ÞE GRENE KNYȜT

I

f. 91a

SIÞEN þe sege and þe assaut watȝ sesed at Troye,
Þe borȝ brittened and brent to brondeȝ and askeȝ,
Þe tulk þat þe trammes of tresoun þer wroȝt
Watȝ tried for his tricherie, þe trewest on erthe:
Hit watȝ Ennias þe athel and his highe kynde,
Þat siþen depreced prouinces, and patrounes bicome
Welneȝe of al þe wele in þe West Iles.
Fro riche Romulus to Rome ricchis hym swyþe,
With gret bobbaunce þat burȝe he biges vpon fyrst,
And neuenes hit his aune nome, as hit now hat;
Ticius to Tuskan and teldes bigynnes,
Langaberde in Lumbardie lyftes vp homes,
And fer ouer þe French flod Felix Brutus
On mony bonkkes ful brode Bretayn he setteȝ
wyth wynne,
Where werre and wrake and wonder
Bi syþeȝ hatȝ wont þerinne,
And oft boþe blysse and blunder
Ful skete hatȝ skyfted synne.

Ande quen þis Bretayn watȝ bigged bi þis burn rych,
Bolde bredden þerinne, baret þat lofden,

In mony turned tyme tene þat wroȝten.
Mo ferlyes on þis folde han fallen here oft
Þen in any oþer þat I wot, syn þat ilk tyme.
Bot of alle þat here bult of Bretaygne kynges
Ay watȝ Arthur þe hendest, as I haf herde telle.
Forþi an aunter in erde I attle to schawe, f. 91b
Þat a selly in siȝt summe men hit holden,
And an outtrage awenture of Arthureȝ wondereȝ.
If ȝe wyl lysten þis laye bot on littel quile,
I schal telle hit astit, as I in toun herde,
with tonge,
As hit is stad and stoken
In stori stif and stronge,
With lel letteres loken,
In londe so hatȝ ben longe.

Þis kyng lay at Camylot vpon Krystmasse
With mony luflych lorde, ledeȝ of þe best,
Rekenly of þe Rounde Table alle þo rich breþer,
With rych reuel oryȝt and rechles merþes.
Þer tournayed tulkes by tymeȝ ful mony,
Justed ful jolilé þise gentyle kniȝtes,
Syþen kayred to þe court caroles to make.
For þer þe fest watȝ ilyche ful fiften dayes,
With alle þe mete and þe mirþe þat men couþe avyse;
Such glaum ande gle glorious to here,
Dere dyn vpon day, daunsyng on nyȝtes,
Al watȝ hap vpon heȝe in halleȝ and chambreȝ
With lordeȝ and ladies, as leuest him þoȝt.
With alle þe wele of þe worlde þay woned þer samen,
Þe most kyd knyȝteȝ vnder Krystes seluen,
And þe louelokkest ladies þat euer lif haden,
And he þe comlokest kyng þat þe court haldes;
For al watȝ þis fayre folk in her first age,
on sille,

41 by: y *rubbed, former edd.* bi. 43 make: *ake* rewritten.
46 glaumande *MS.*

þe hapnest vnder heuen,
Kyng hyȝest mon of wylle;
Hit were now gret nye to neuen
So hardy a here on hille.

Wyle Nw Ȝer watȝ so ȝep þat hit watȝ nwe cummen,
þat day doubble on þe dece watȝ þe douth serued,
Fro þe kyng watȝ cummen with knyȝtes into þe halle,
þe chauntré of þe chapel cheued to an ende.
Loude crye watȝ þer kest of clerkeȝ and oþer,
Nowel nayted onewe, neuened ful ofte; f. 92[a]
And syþen riche forth runnen to reche hondeselle,
Ȝeȝed ȝeres-ȝiftes on hiȝ, ȝelde hem bi hond,
Debated busyly aboute þo giftes;
Ladies laȝed ful loude, þoȝ þay lost haden,
And he þat wan watȝ not wrothe, þat may ȝe wel trawe.
Alle þis mirþe þay maden to þe mete tyme;
When þay had waschen worþyly þay wenten to sete,
þe best burne ay abof, as hit best semed,
Whene Guenore, ful gay, grayþed in þe myddes,
Dressed on þe dere des, dubbed al aboute,
Smal sendal bisides, a selure hir ouer
Of tryed tolouse, of tars tapites innoghe,
þat were enbrawded and beten wyth þe best gemmes
þat myȝt be preued of prys wyth penyes to bye,
in daye.
þe comlokest to discrye
þer glent with yȝen gray,
A semloker þat euer he syȝe
Soth moȝt no mon say.

Bot Arthure wolde not ete til al were serued,
He watȝ so joly of his joyfnes, and sumquat childgered:
His lif liked hym lyȝt, he louied þe lasse
Auþer to longe lye or to longe sitte,

58 werere *MS.* 88 longe (*1st*): lenge *MS.*

So bisied him his ȝonge blod and his brayn wylde.
And also an oþer maner meued him eke
Þat he þurȝ nobelay had nomen, he wolde neuer ete
Vpon such a dere day, er hym deuised were
Of sum auenturus þyng an vncouþe tale,
Of sum mayn meruayle, þat he myȝt trawe,
Of alderes, of armes, of oþer auenturus,
Oþer sum segg hym bisoȝt of sum siker knyȝt
To joyne wyth hym in iustyng, in jopardé to lay,
Lede lif for lyf, leue vchon oþer,
As fortune wolde fulsun hom, þe fayrer to haue.
Þis watȝ kynges countenaunce where he in court were,
At vch farand fest among his fre meny
in halle. f. 92[b]
Þerfore of face so fere
He stiȝtleȝ stif in stalle,
Ful ȝep in þat Nw Ȝere
Much mirthe he mas with alle.

Thus þer stondes in stale þe stif kyng hisseluen,
Talkkande bifore þe hyȝe table of trifles ful hende.
There gode Gawan watȝ grayþed Gwenore bisyde,
And Agrauayn a la dure mayn on þat oþer syde sittes,
Boþe þe kynges sistersunes and ful siker kniȝtes;
Bischop Bawdewyn abof bigineȝ þe table,
And Ywan, Vryn son, ette with hymseluen.
Þise were diȝt on þe des and derworþly serued,
And siþen mony siker segge at þe sidbordeȝ.
Þen þe first cors come with crakkyng of trumpes,
Wyth mony baner ful bryȝt þat þerbi henged;
Nwe nakryn noyse with þe noble pipes,
Wylde werbles and wyȝt wakned lote,
Þat mony hert ful hiȝe hef at her towches.
Dayntés dryuen þerwyth of ful dere metes,
Foysoun of þe fresche, and on so fele disches

95 Of (*1st*): Of of *MS.* 113 wit *MS.*

Þat pine to fynde þe place þe peple biforne
For to sette þe sylueren þat sere sewes halden
on clothe.
Iche lede as he loued hymselue
Þer laght withouten loþe;
Ay two had disches twelue,
Good ber and bryȝt wyn boþe.

Now wyl I of hor seruise say yow no more,
For vch wyȝe may wel wit no wont þat þer were.
An oþer noyse ful newe neȝed biliue,
Þat þe lude myȝt haf leue liflode to cach;
For vneþe watȝ þe noyce not a whyle sesed,
And þe fyrst cource in þe court kyndely serued,
Þer hales in at þe halle dor an aghlich mayster,
On þe most on þe molde on mesure hyghe;
Fro þe swyre to þe swange so sware and so þik,
And his lyndes and his lymes so longe and so grete,
Half etayn in erde I hope þat he were, f. 93a
Bot mon most I algate mynn hym to bene,
And þat þe myriest in his muckel þat myȝt ride;
For of bak and of brest al were his bodi sturne,
Both his wombe and his wast were worthily smale,
And alle his fetures folȝande, in forme þat he hade,
ful clene;
For wonder of his hwe men hade,
Set in his semblaunt sene;
He ferde as freke were fade,
And oueral enker grene.

Ande al grayþed in grene þis gome and his wedes:
A strayt cote ful streȝt, þat stek on his sides,
A meré mantile abof, mensked withinne
With pelure pured apert, þe pane ful clene
With blyþe blaunner ful bryȝt, and his hode boþe,

124 sylueN*er MS.* 144 Bot *MS.*

Þat watȝ laȝt fro his lokkeȝ and layde on his schulderes;
Heme wel-haled hose of þat same grene,
Þat spenet on his sparlyr, and clene spures vnder
Of bryȝt golde, vpon silk bordes barred ful ryche,
And scholes vnder schankes þere þe schalk rides;
And alle his vesture uerayly watȝ clene verdure,
Boþe þe barres of his belt and oþer blyþe stones,
Þat were richely rayled in his aray clene
Aboutte hymself and his sadel, vpon silk werkeȝ,
Þat were to tor for to telle of tryfles þe halue
Þat were enbrauded abof, wyth bryddes and flyȝes,
With gay gaudi of grene, þe golde ay inmyddes.
Þe pendauntes of his payttrure, þe proude cropure,
His molaynes, and alle þe metail anamayld was þenne,
Þe steropes þat he stod on stayned of þe same,
And his arsounȝ al after and his aþel sturtes,
Þat euer glemered and glent al of grene stones;
Þe fole þat he ferkkes on fyn of þat ilke,
          sertayn,
     A grene hors gret and þikke,
     A stede ful stif to strayne,
     In brawden brydel quik—
     To þe gome he watȝ ful gayn. f. 93b

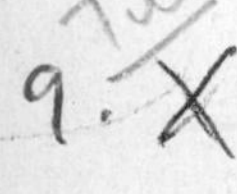

Wel gay watȝ þis gome gered in grene,
And þe here of his hed of his hors swete.
Fayre fannand fax vmbefoldes his schulderes;
A much berd as a busk ouer his brest henges,
Þat wyth his hiȝlich here þat of his hed reches
Watȝ euesed al vmbetorne abof his elbowes,
Þat half his armes þer-vnder were halched in þe wyse
Of a kyngeȝ capados þat closes his swyre;
Þe mane of þat mayn hors much to hit lyke,
Wel cresped and cemmed, wyth knottes ful mony
Folden in wyth fildore aboute þe fayre grene

168 *second* þe: pe *MS.*   182 as: as as *MS.*

Ay a herle of þe here, an oþer of golde ;
Þe tayl and his toppyng twynnen of a sute,
And bounden boþe wyth a bande of a bryȝt grene,
Dubbed wyth ful dere stoneȝ, as þe dok lasted,
Syþen þrawen wyth a þwong a þwarle knot alofte,
Þer mony belleȝ ful bryȝt of brende golde rungen.
Such a fole vpon folde, ne freke þat hym rydes,
Watȝ neuer sene in þat sale wyth syȝt er þat tyme,
        with yȝe.
    He loked as layt so lyȝt,
    So sayd al þat hym syȝe ;
    Hit semed as no mon myȝt
    Vnder his dynteȝ dryȝe.

Wheþer hade he no helme ne hawbergh nauþer,
Ne no pysan ne no plate þat pented to armes,
Ne no schafte ne no schelde to schwue ne to smyte,
Bot in his on honde he hade a holyn bobbe,
Þat is grattest in grene when greueȝ ar bare,
And an ax in his oþer, a hoge and vnmete,
A spetos sparþe to expoun in spelle, quoso myȝt.
Þe hede of an elnȝerde þe large lenkþe hade,
Þe grayn al of grene stele and of golde hewen,
Þe bit burnyst bryȝt, wyth a brode egge
As wel schapen to schere as scharp rasores.
Þe stele of a stif staf þe sturne hit bi grypte,
Þat watȝ wounden wyth yrn to þe wandeȝ ende, f. 94ª
And al bigrauen with grene in gracios werkes ;
A lace lapped aboute, þat louked at þe hede,
And so after þe halme halched ful ofte,
Wyth tryed tasseleȝ þerto tacched innoghe
On botounȝ of þe bryȝt grene brayden ful ryche.
Þis haþel heldeȝ hym in and þe halle entres,
Driuande to þe heȝe dece, dut he no woþe,
Haylsed he neuer one, bot heȝe he ouer loked.

203 hawbrgh *MS.* 216 gracōs *MS.*

Þe fyrst word þat he warp, 'Wher is', he sayd,
'Þe gouernour of þis gyng? Gladly I wolde
Se þat segg in syȝt, and with hymself speke
raysoun.'
To knyȝteȝ he kest his yȝe,
And reled hym vp and doun;
He stemmed, and con studie
Quo walt þer most renoun.

Ther watȝ lokyng on lenþe þe lude to beholde,
For vch mon had meruayle quat hit mene myȝt,
Þat a haþel and a horse myȝt such a hwe lach,
As growe grene as þe gres and grener hit semed,
Þen grene aumayl on golde glowande bryȝter.
Al studied þat þer stod, and stalked hym nerre
Wyth al þe wonder of þe worlde what he worch schulde.
For fele sellyeȝ had þay sen, bot such neuer are;
Forþi for fantoum and fayryȝe þe folk þere hit demed.
Þerfore to answare watȝ arȝe mony aþel freke,
And al stouned at his steuen and stonstil seten
In a swoghe sylence þurȝ þe sale riche;
As al were slypped vpon slepe so slaked hor loteȝ
in hyȝe—
I deme hit not al for doute,
Bot sum for cortaysye—
Bot let hym þat al schulde loute
Cast vnto þat wyȝe.

Þenn Arþour bifore þe hiȝ dece þat auenture byholdeȝ,
And rekenly hym reuerenced, for rad was he neuer,
And sayde, 'Wyȝe, welcum iwys to þis place,
Þe hede of þis ostel Arthour I hat; f. 94b
Liȝt luflych adoun and lenge, I þe praye,
And quat-so þy wylle is we schal wyt after.'
'Nay, as help me,' quoþ þe haþel, 'he þat on hyȝe
syttes,

236 lowande *MS.*

To wone any quyle in þis won, hit watȝ not myn ernde;
Bot for þe los of þe, lede, is lyft vp so hyȝe,
And þy burȝ and þy burnes best ar holden,
Stifest vnder stel-gere on stedes to ryde,
Þe wyȝtest and þe worþyest of þe worldes kynde,
Preue for to play wyth in oþer pure laykeȝ,
And here is kydde cortaysye, as I haf herd carp,
And þat hatȝ wayned me hider, iwyis, at þis tyme.
Ȝe may be seker bi þis braunch þat I bere here
Þat I passe as in pes, and no plyȝt seche;
For had I founded in fere in feȝtyng wyse,
I haue a hauberghe at home and a helme boþe,
A schelde and a scharp spere, schinande bryȝt,
Ande oþer weppenes to welde, I wene wel, als;
Bot for I wolde no were, my wedeȝ ar softer.
Bot if þou be so bold as alle burneȝ tellen,
Þou wyl grant me godly þe gomen þat I ask
bi ryȝt.'
Arthour con answare,
And sayd, 'Sir cortays knyȝt,
If þou craue batayl bare,
Here fayleȝ þou not to fyȝt.'

'Nay, frayst I no fyȝt, in fayth I þe telle,
Hit arn aboute on þis bench bot berdleȝ chylder.
If I were hasped in armes on a heȝe stede,
Here is no mon me to mach, for myȝteȝ so wayke.
Forþy I craue in þis court a Crystemas gomen,
For hit is Ȝol and Nwe Ȝer, and here ar ȝep mony:
If any so hardy in þis hous holdeȝ hymseluen,
Be so bolde in his blod, brayn in hys hede,
Þat dar stifly strike a strok for an oþer,
I schal gif hym of my gyft þys giserne ryche,
Þis ax, þat is heué innogh, to hondele as hym lykes,
And I schal bide þe fyrst bur as bare as I sitte. f. 95a

282 so: fo. *MS.* 283 gomen: gome̅ *MS.*

If any freke be so felle to fonde þat I telle,
Lepe ly3tly me to, and lach þis weppen,
I quit-clayme hit for euer, kepe hit as his auen,
And I schal stonde hym a strok, stif on þis flet;
Elle3 þou wyl di3t me þe dom to dele hym an oþer barlay,
And 3et gif hym respite,
A twelmonyth and a day;
Now hy3e, and let se tite
Dar any herinne o3t say.'

If he hem stowned vpon fyrst, stiller were þanne
Alle þe heredmen in halle, þe hy3 and þe lo3e.
Þe renk on his rouncé hym ruched in his sadel,
And runischly his rede y3en he reled aboute,
Bende his bresed bro3e3, blycande grene,
Wayued his berde for to wayte quo-so wolde ryse.
When non wolde kepe hym with carp he co3ed ful hy3e,
Ande rimed hym ful richley, and ry3t hym to speke:
'What, is þis Arþure3 hous,' quoþ þe haþel þenne,
'Þat al þe rous rennes of þur3 ryalmes so mony?
Where is now your sourquydrye and your conquestes,
Your gryndellayk and your greme, and your grete wordes?
Now is þe reuel and þe renoun of þe Rounde Table
Ouerwalt wyth a worde of on wy3es speche,
For al dares for drede withoute dynt schewed!'
Wyth þis he la3es so loude þat þe lorde greued;
Þe blod schot for scham into his schyre face and lere;
He wex as wroth as wynde,
So did alle þat þer were.
Þe kyng as kene bi kynde
Þen stod þat stif mon nere,

312 grydel layk *MS.*

Ande sayde, 'Haþel, by heuen, þyn askyng is nys,
And as þou foly hatȝ frayst, fynde þe behoues.
I know no gome þat is gast of þy grete wordes;
Gif me now þy geserne, vpon Godeȝ halue,
And I schal bayþen þy bone þat þou boden habbes.'
Lyȝtly lepeȝ he hym to, and laȝt at his honde. f. 95b
Þen feersly þat oþer freke vpon fote lyȝtis.
Now hatȝ Arthure his axe, and þe halme grypeȝ,
And sturnely stureȝ hit aboute, þat stryke wyth hit þoȝt.
Þe stif mon hym bifore stod vpon hyȝt,
Herre þen ani in þe hous by þe hede and more.
Wyth sturne schere þer he stod he stroked his berde,
And wyth a countenaunce dryȝe he droȝ doun his cote,
No more mate ne dismayd for hys mayn dinteȝ
Þen any burne vpon bench hade broȝt hym to drynk
of wyne.
Gawan, þat sate bi þe quene,
To þe kyng he can enclyne,
'I beseche now with saȝeȝ sene
Þis melly mot be myne.'

'Wolde ȝe, worþilych lorde,' quoþ Wawan to þe kyng,
'Bid me boȝe fro þis benche, and stonde by yow þere,
Þat I wythoute vylanye myȝt voyde þis table,
And þat my legge lady lyked not ille,
I wolde com to your counseyl bifore your cort ryche.
For me þink hit not semly, as hit is soþ knawen,
Þer such an askyng is heuened so hyȝe in your sale,
Þaȝ ȝe ȝourself be talenttyf to take hit to yourseluen,
Whil mony so bolde yow aboute vpon bench sytten,
Þat vnder heuen, I hope, non haȝerer of wylle,
Ne better bodyes on bent þer baret is rered.
I am þe wakkest, I wot, and of wyt feblest,
And lest lur of my lyf, quo laytes þe soþe,
Bot for as much as ȝe ar myn em I am only to prayse,

343 Gawan *MS.*

No bounté bot your blod I in my bodé knowe;
And syþen þis note is so nys, þat noȝt hit yow falles,
And I haue frayned hit at yow fyrst, foldeȝ hit to me,
And if I carp not comlyly, let all þis cort rych
bout blame.'
Ryche togeder con roun,
And syþen þay redden alle same
To ryd þe kyng wyth croun,
And gif Gawan þe game.

Þen comaunded þe kyng þe knyȝt for to ryse; f. 96a
And he ful radly vpros, and ruchched hym fayre,
Kneled doun bifore þe kyng, and cacheȝ þat weppen;
And he luflyly hit hym laft, and lyfte vp his honde,
And gef hym Goddeȝ blessyng, and gladly hym biddes
Þat his hert and his honde schulde hardi be boþe.
'Kepe þe, cosyn,' quoþ þe kyng, 'þat þou on kyrf sette,
And if þou redeȝ hym ryȝt, redly I trowe
Þat þou schal byden þe bur þat he schal bede after.'
Gawan gotȝ to þe gome with giserne in honde,
And he baldly hym bydeȝ, he bayst neuer þe helder.
Þen carppeȝ to Sir Gawan þe knyȝt in þe grene,
'Refourme we oure forwardes, er we fyrre passe.
Fyrst I eþe þe, haþel, how þat þou hattes,
Þat þou me telle truly, as I tryst may.'
'In god fayth,' quoþ þe goode knyȝt, 'Gawan I hatte,
Þat bede þe þis buffet, quat-so bifalleȝ after,
And at þis tyme twelmonyth take at þe an oþer
Wyth what weppen so þou wylt, and wyth no wyȝ elleȝ
on lyue.'
Þat oþer onswareȝ agayn,
'Sir Gawan, so mot I þryue,
As I am ferly fayn
Þis dint þat þou schal dryue.'

384 so: fo *MS.*

'Bigog,' quoþ þe grene knyȝt, 'Sir Gawan, me lykes
Þat I schal fange at þy fust þat I haf frayst here.
And þou hatȝ redily rehersed, bi resoun ful trwe,
Clanly al þe couenaunt þat I þe kynge asked,
Saf þat þou schal siker me, segge, bi þi trawþe,
Þat þou schal seche me þiself, where-so þou hopes
I may be funde vpon folde, and foch þe such wages
As þou deles me to-day bifore þis douþe ryche.'
'Where schulde I wale þe,' quoþ Gauan, 'where is þy place?
I wot neuer where þou wonyes, bi hym þat me wroȝt,
Ne I know not þe, knyȝt, þy cort ne þi name.
Bot teche me truly þerto, and telle me howe þou hattes,
And I schal ware alle my wyt to wynne me þeder,
And þat I swere þe for soþe, and by my seker traweþ.' f. 96b
'Þat is innogh in Nwe Ȝer, hit nedes no more,'
Quoþ þe gome in þe grene to Gawan þe hende,
'Ȝif I þe telle trwly, quen I þe tape haue
And þou me smoþely hatȝ smyten, smartly I þe teche
Of my hous and my home and myn owen nome,
Þen may þou frayst my fare and forwardeȝ holde;
And if I spende no speche, þenne spedeȝ þou þe better,
For þou may leng in þy londe and layt no fyrre— bot slokes!
Ta now þy grymme tole to þe,
And let se how þou cnokeȝ.'
'Gladly, sir, for soþe,'
Quoþ Gawan; his ax he strokes.

The grene knyȝt vpon grounde grayþely hym dresses,
A littel lut with þe hede, þe lere he discouereȝ,
His longe louelych lokkeȝ he layd ouer his croun,
Let the naked nec to þe note schewe.
Gauan gripped to his ax, and gederes hit on hyȝt,
Þe kay fot on þe fold he before sette,
Let hit doun lyȝtly lyȝt on þe naked,

Þat þe scharp of þe schalk schyndered þe bones,
And schrank þurȝ þe schyire grece, and scade hit in twynne,
Þat þe bit of þe broun stel bot on þe grounde.
Þe fayre hede fro þe halce hit to þe erþe,
Þat fele hit foyned wyth her fete, þere hit forth roled;
Þe blod brayd fro þe body, þat blykked on þe grene;
And nawþer faltered ne fel þe freke neuer þe helder,
Bot styþly he start forth vpon styf schonkes,
And runyschly he raȝt out, þere as renkkeȝ stoden,
Laȝt to his lufly hed, and lyft hit vp sone;
And syþen boȝeȝ to his blonk, þe brydel he cachcheȝ,
Steppeȝ into stelbawe and strydeȝ alofte,
And his hede by þe here in his honde haldeȝ;
And as sadly þe segge hym in his sadel sette
As non vnhap had hym ayled, þaȝ hedleȝ he were in stedde.
He brayde his bluk aboute,
Þat vgly bodi þat bledde; f. 97ᵃ
Moni on of hym had doute,
Bi þat his resounȝ were redde.

For þe hede in his honde he haldeȝ vp euen,
Toward þe derrest on þe dece he dresseȝ þe face,
And hit lyfte vp þe yȝe-lyddeȝ and loked ful brode,
And meled þus much with his muthe, as ȝe may now here:
'Loke, Gawan, þou be grayþe to go as þou hetteȝ,
And layte as lelly til þou me, lude, fynde,
As þou hatȝ hette in þis halle, herande þise knyȝtes;
To þe grene chapel þou chose, I charge þe, to fotte
Such a dunt as þou hatȝ dalt—disserued þou habbeȝ—
To be ȝederly ȝolden on Nw Ȝeres morn.
Þe knyȝt of þe grene chapel men knowen me mony;
Forþi me for to fynde if þou fraysteȝ, fayleȝ þou neuer

432 ruyschly *MS.* 438 he: ho *MS.*; were: we *MS.*

Þerfore com, oþer recreaunt be calde þe behoueus.'
With a runisch rout þe rayneʒ he torneʒ,
Halled out at þe hal dor, his hed in his hande,
Þat þe fyr of þe flynt flaʒe fro fole houes.
To quat kyth he becom knwe non þere,
Neuer more þen þay wyste fram queþen he watʒ wonnen.
What þenne?
Þe kyng and Gawen þare
At þat grene þay laʒe and grenne,
Ʒet breued watʒ hit ful bare
A meruayl among þo menne.

Þaʒ Arþer þe hende kyng at hert hade wonder,
He let no semblaunt be sene, bot sayde ful hyʒe
To þe comlych quene wyth cortays speche,
'Dere dame, to-day demay yow neuer;
Wel bycommes such craft vpon Cristmasse,
Laykyng of enterludeʒ, to laʒe and to syng,
Among þise kynde caroles of knyʒteʒ and ladyeʒ.
Neuer þe lece to my mete I may me wel dres,
For I haf sen a selly, I may not forsake.'
He glent vpon Sir Gawen, and gaynly he sayde,
'Now sir, heng vp þyn ax, þat hatʒ innogh hewen';
And hit watʒ don abof þe dece on doser to henge, f. 97b
Þer alle men for meruayl myʒt on hit loke,
And bi trwe tytel þerof to telle þe wonder.
Þenne þay boʒed to a borde þise burnes togeder,
Þe kyng and þe gode knyʒt, and kene men hem serued
Of alle dayntyeʒ double, as derrest myʒt falle;
Wyth alle maner of mete and mynstralcie boþe,
Wyth wele walt þay þat day, til worþed an ende
in londe.
Now þenk wel, Sir Gawan,
For woþe þat þou ne wonde
Þis auenture for to frayn
Þat þou hatʒ tan on honde.

II

THIS hanselle hatȝ Arthur of auenturus on fyrst
In ȝonge ȝer, for he ȝerned ȝelpyng to here.
Thaȝ hym wordeȝ were wane when þay to sete wenten,
Now ar þay stoken of sturne werk, stafful her hond.
Gawan watȝ glad to begynne þose gomneȝ in halle,
Bot þaȝ þe ende be heuy, haf ȝe no wonder;
For þaȝ men ben mery in mynde quen þay han mayn drynk,
A ȝere ȝernes ful ȝerne, and ȝeldeȝ neuer lyke,
Þe forme to þe fynisment foldeȝ ful selden.
Forþi þis Ȝol ouerȝede, and þe ȝere after,
And vche sesoun serlepes sued after oþer:
After Crystenmasse com þe crabbed lentoun,
Þat frayst eȝ flesch wyth þe fysche and fode more symple;
Bot þenne þe weder of þe worlde wyth wynter hit þrepeȝ,
Colde clengeȝ adoun, cloudeȝ vplyften,
Schyre schedeȝ þe rayn in schowreȝ ful warme,
Falleȝ vpon fayre flat, flowreȝ þere schewen,
Boþe groundeȝ and þe greueȝ grene ar her wedeȝ,
Bryddeȝ busken to bylde, and bremlych syngen
For solace of þe softe somer þat sues þerafter bi bonk;
And blossumeȝ bolne to blowe
Bi raweȝ rych and ronk,
Þen noteȝ noble innoȝe
Ar herde in wod so wlonk. f. 98a

After, þe sesoun of somer wyth þe soft wyndeȝ,
Quen Ȝeferus syfleȝ hymself on sedeȝ and erbeȝ;
Wela wynne is þe wort þat waxes þeroute,
When þe donkande dewe dropeȝ of þe leueȝ,
To bide a blysful blusch of þe bryȝt sunne.
Bot þen hyȝes heruest, and hardenes hym sone,

Warneȝ hym for þe wynter to wax ful rype ;
He dryues wyth droȝt þe dust for to ryse,
Fro þe face of þe folde to flyȝe ful hyȝe ;
Wroþe wynde of þe welkyn wrasteleȝ with þe sunne,
Þe leueȝ lancen fro þe lynde and lyȝten on þe grounde,
And al grayes þe gres þat grene watȝ ere ;
Þenne al rypeȝ and roteȝ þat ros vpon fyrst,
And þus ȝirneȝ þe ȝere in ȝisterdayeȝ mony,
And wynter wyndeȝ aȝayn, as þe worlde askeȝ,
    no fage,
  Til Meȝelmas mone
  Watȝ cumen wyth wynter wage ;
  Þen þenkkeȝ Gawan ful sone
  Of his anious uyage.

Ȝet quyl Al-hal-day with Arþer he lenges ;
And he made a fare on þat fest for þe frekeȝ sake,
With much reuel and ryche of þe Rounde Table.
Knyȝteȝ ful cortays and comlych ladies
Al for luf of þat lede in longynge þay were,
Bot neuer þe lece ne þe later þay neuened bot merþe :
Mony ioyleȝ for þat ientyle iapeȝ þer maden.
For aftter mete with mournyng he meleȝ to his eme,
And spekeȝ of his passage, and pertly he sayde,
'Now, lege lorde of my lyf, leue I yow ask ;
Ȝe knowe þe cost of þis cace, kepe I no more
To telle yow teneȝ þerof, neuer bot trifel ;
Bot I am boun to þe bur barely to-morne
To sech þe gome of þe grene, as God wyl me wysse.'
Þenne þe best of þe burȝ boȝed togeder,
Aywan, and Errik, and oþer ful mony,
Sir Doddinaual de Sauage, þe duk of Clarence, f. 98b
Launcelot, and Lyonel, and Lucan þe gode,
Sir Boos, and Sir Byduer, big men boþe,

531 sage *MS.*

And mony oþer menskful, with Mador de la Port.
Alle þis compayny of court com þe kyng nerre
For to counseyl þe knyȝt, with care at her hert.
Þere watȝ much derue doel driuen in þe sale,
Þat so worthé as Wawan schulde wende on þat ernde,
To dryȝe a delful dynt, and dele no more
wyth bronde.
Þe knyȝt mad ay god chere,
And sayde, 'Quat schuld I wonde?
Of destinés derf and dere
What may mon do bot fonde?'

He dowelleȝ þer al þat day, and dresseȝ on þe morn,
Askeȝ erly hys armeȝ, and alle were þay broȝt.
Fyrst a tulé tapit tyȝt ouer þe flet,
And miche watȝ þe gyld gere þat glent þeralofte;
Þe stif mon steppeȝ þeron, and þe stel hondeleȝ,
Dubbed in a dublet of a dere tars,
And syþen a crafty capados, closed aloft,
Þat wyth a bryȝt blaunner was bounden withinne.
Þenne set þay þe sabatounȝ vpon þe segge foteȝ,
His legeȝ lapped in stel with luflych greueȝ,
With polayneȝ piched þerto, policed ful clene,
Aboute his kneȝ knaged wyth knoteȝ of golde;
Queme quyssewes þen, þat coyntlych closed
His thik þrawen þyȝeȝ, with þwonges to tachched;
And syþen þe brawden bryné of bryȝt stel ryngeȝ
Vmbeweued þat wyȝ vpon wlonk stuffe,
And wel bornyst brace vpon his boþe armes,
With gode cowters and gay, and gloueȝ of plate,
And alle þe godlych gere þat hym gayn schulde
þat tyde;
Wyth ryche cote-armure,
His gold sporeȝ spend with pryde,
Gurde wyth a bront ful sure
With silk sayn vmbe his syde.

When he watȝ hasped in armes, his harnays watȝ ryche: f. 99a
Þe lest lachet oþer loupe lemed of golde.
So harnayst as he watȝ he herkneȝ his masse,
Offred and honoured at þe heȝe auter.
Syþen he comeȝ to þe kyng and to his cort-fereȝ,
Lacheȝ lufly his leue at lordeȝ and ladyeȝ;
And þay hym kyst and conueyed, bikende hym to Kryst.
Bi þat watȝ Gryngolet grayth, and gurde with a sadel
Þat glemed ful gayly with mony golde frenges,
Ayquere naylet ful nwe, for þat note ryched;
Þe brydel barred aboute, with bryȝt golde bounden;
Þe apparayl of þe payttrure and of þe proude skyrteȝ,
Þe cropore and þe couertor, acorded wyth þe arsouneȝ;
And al watȝ rayled on red ryche golde nayleȝ,
Þat al glytered and glent as glem of þe sunne.
Þenne hentes he þe helme, and hastily hit kysses,
Þat watȝ stapled stifly, and stoffed wythinne.
Hit watȝ hyȝe on his hede, hasped bihynde,
Wyth a lyȝtly vrysoun ouer þe auentayle,
Enbrawden and bounden wyth þe best gemmeȝ
On brode sylkyn borde, and bryddeȝ on semeȝ,
As papiayeȝ paynted pernyng bitwene,
Tortors and trulofeȝ entayled so þyk
As mony burde þeraboute had ben seuen wynter in toune.
    Þe cercle watȝ more o prys
    Þat vmbeclypped hys croun,
    Of diamaunteȝ a deuys
    Þat boþe were bryȝt and broun.

Then þay schewed hym þe schelde, þat was of schyr gouleȝ
Wyth þe pentangel depaynt of pure golde hweȝ.
He braydeȝ hit by þe bauderyk, aboute þe hals kestes,

591 oþer: ou*er* *MS.*

Þat bisemed þe segge semlyly fayre.
And quy þe pentangel apendeȝ to þat prynce noble
I am intent yow to telle, þof tary hyt me schulde:
Hit is a syngne þat Salamon set sumquyle
In bytoknyng of trawþe, bi tytle þat hit habbeȝ,
For hit is a figure þat haldeȝ fyue poynteȝ, f. 99^b
And vche lyne vmbelappeȝ and loukeȝ in oþer,
And ayquere hit is endeleȝ; and Englych hit callen
Oueral, as I here, þe endeles knot.
Forþy hit acordeȝ to þis knyȝt and to his cler armeȝ,
For ay faythful in fyue and sere fyue syþeȝ
Gawan watȝ for gode knawen, and as golde pured,
Voyded of vche vylany, wyth vertueȝ ennourned
in mote;
Forþy þe pentangel nwe
He ber in schelde and cote,
As tulk of tale most trwe
And gentylest knyȝt of lote.

Fyrst he watȝ funden fautleȝ in his fyue wytteȝ,
And efte fayled neuer þe freke in his fyue fyngres,
And alle his afyaunce vpon folde watȝ in þe fyue woundeȝ
Þat Cryst kaȝt on þe croys, as þe crede telleȝ;
And quere-so-euer þys mon in melly watȝ stad,
His þro þoȝt watȝ in þat, þurȝ alle oþer þyngeȝ,
Þat alle his fersnes he feng at þe fyue joyeȝ
Þat þe hende heuen quene had of hir chylde;
At þis cause þe knyȝt comlyche hade
In þe more half of his schelde hir ymage depaynted,
Þat quen he blusched þerto his belde neuer payred.
Þe fyft fyue þat I finde þat þe frek vsed
Watȝ fraunchyse and felaȝschyp forbe al þyng,
His clannes and his cortaysye croked were neuer,
And pité, þat passeȝ alle poynteȝ, þyse pure fyue

629 emdeleȝ *MS.* 634 verertueȝ *MS.* 646 fersnes, feng: forsnes, fong *MS.*

Were harder happed on þat haþel þen on any oþer.
Now alle þese fyue syþeȝ, for soþe, were fetled on þis
knyȝt,
And vchone halched in oþer, þat non ende hade,
And fyched vpon fyue poynteȝ, þat fayld neuer,
Ne samned neuer in no syde, ne sundred nouþer,
Withouten ende at any noke aiquere, I fynde,
Whereeuer þe gomen bygan, or glod to an ende.
Þerfore on his schene schelde schapen watȝ þe knot
Ryally wyth red golde vpon rede gowleȝ,
Þat is þe pure pentaungel wyth þe peple called f. 100[a]
with lore.
Now grayþed is Gawan gay,
And laȝt his launce ryȝt þore,
And gef hem alle goud day,
He wende for euer more.

He sperred þe sted with þe spureȝ and sprong on his way,
So stif þat þe ston-fyr stroke out þerafter.
Al þat seȝ þat semly syked in hert,
And sayde soþly al same segges til oþer,
Carande for þat comly: 'Bi Kryst, hit is scaþe
Þat þou, leude, schal be lost, þat art of lyf noble!
To fynde hys fere vpon folde, in fayth, is not eþe.
Warloker to haf wroȝt had more wyt bene,
And haf dyȝt ȝonder dere a duk to haue worþed;
A lowande leder of ledeȝ in londe hym wel semeȝ,
And so had better haf ben þen britned to noȝt,
Hadet wyth an aluisch mon, for angardeȝ pryde.
Who knew euer any kyng such counsel to take
As knyȝteȝ in cauelaciounȝ on Crystmasse gomneȝ!'
Wel much watȝ þe warme water þat waltered of yȝen,
When þat semly syre soȝt fro þo woneȝ
þad daye.

658 fayld: f *and* d *rewritten*. 659 nouþ . r *MS.*
660 aiquere I: jquere *MS.* 683 caueloun3 *MS.*

He made non abode,
Bot wyȝtly went hys way;
Mony wylsum way he rode,
Þe bok as I herde say.

Now rideȝ þis renk þurȝ þe ryalme of Logres,
Sir Gauan, on Godeȝ halue, þaȝ hym no gomen þoȝt.
Oft leudleȝ alone he lengeȝ on nyȝteȝ
Þer he fonde noȝt hym byfore þe fare þat he lyked.
Hade he no fere bot his fole bi frytheȝ and douneȝ,
Ne no gome bot God bi gate wyth to karp,
Til þat he neȝed ful neghe into þe Norþe Waleȝ.
Alle þe iles of Anglesay on lyft half he haldeȝ,
And fareȝ ouer þe fordeȝ by þe forlondeȝ,
Ouer at þe Holy Hede, til he hade eft bonk
In þe wyldrenesse of Wyrale; wonde þer bot lyte
Þat auþer God oþer gome wyth goud hert louied. f. 100b
And ay he frayned, as he ferde, at frekeȝ þat he met,
If þay hade herde any karp of a knyȝt grene,
In any grounde þeraboute, of þe grene chapel;
And al nykked hym wyth nay, þat neuer in her lyue
Þay seȝe neuer no segge þat watȝ of suche hweȝ
of grene.
Þe knyȝt tok gates straunge
In mony a bonk vnbene,
His cher ful oft con chaunge
Þat chapel er he myȝt sene.

Mony klyf he ouerclambe in contrayeȝ straunge,
Fer floten fro his frendeȝ fremedly he rydeȝ.
At vche warþe oþer water þer þe wyȝe passed
He fonde a foo hym byfore, bot ferly hit were,
And þat so foule and so felle þat feȝt hym byhode.
So mony meruayl bi mount þer þe mon fyndeȝ,
Hit were to tore for to telle of þe tenþe dole.

697 noghe *MS.* 705 clapel *MS.*

Sumwhyle wyth wormeȝ he werreȝ, and with wolues als,
Sumwhyle wyth wodwos, þat woned in þe knarreȝ,
Boþe wyth bulleȝ and bereȝ, and boreȝ oþerquyle,
And etayneȝ, þat hym anelede of þe heȝe felle ;
Nade he ben duȝty and dryȝe, and dryȝtyn had serued,
Douteles he hade ben ded and dreped ful ofte.
For werre wrathed hym not so much, þat wynter was wors,
When þe colde cler water fro þe cloudeȝ schadde,
And fres er hit falle myȝt to þe fale erþe ;
Ner slayn wyth þe slete he sleped in his yrnes
Mo nyȝteȝ þen innoghe in naked rokkeȝ,
Þer as claterande fro þe crest þe colde borne renneȝ,
And henged heȝe ouer his hede in hard iisse-ikkles.
Þus in peryl and payne and plytes ful harde
Bi contray cayreȝ þis knyȝt, tyl Krystmasse euen,
al one ;
Þe knyȝt wel þat tyde
To Mary made his mone,
Þat ho hym red to ryde
And wysse hym to sum wone. f. 101a

Bi a mounte on þe morne meryly he rydes
Into a forest ful dep, þat ferly watȝ wylde,
Hiȝe hilleȝ on vche a halue, and holtwodeȝ vnder
Of hore okeȝ ful hoge a hundreth togeder ;
Þe hasel and þe haȝþorne were harled al samen,
With roȝe raged mosse rayled aywhere,
With mony bryddeȝ vnblyþe vpon bare twyges,
Þat pitosly þer piped for pyne of þe colde.
Þe gome vpon Gryngolet glydeȝ hem vnder,
Þurȝ mony misy and myre, mon al hym one,
Carande for his costes, lest he ne keuer schulde
To se þe seruyse of þat syre, þat on þat self nyȝt

727 schadden *MS.* 732 iisse *altered in MS. from* ysse.
734 caryeȝ *MS.* 751 seruy *MS.*

Of a burde watȝ borne oure baret to quelle ;
And þerfore sykyng he sayde, ‘I beseche þe, lorde,
And Mary, þat is myldest moder so dere,
Of sum herber þer heȝly I myȝt here masse,
Ande þy matyneȝ to-morne, mekely I ask,
And þerto prestly I pray my pater and aue
and crede.’
He rode in his prayere,
And cryed for his mysdede,
He sayned hym in syþes sere,
And sayde ‘Cros Kryst me spede!’

Nade he sayned hymself, segge, bot þrye,
Er he watȝ war in þe wod of a won in a mote,
Abof a launde, on a lawe, loken vnder boȝeȝ
Of mony borelych bole aboute bi þe diches :
A castel þe comlokest þat euer knyȝt aȝte,
Pyched on a prayere, a park al aboute,
With a pyked palays pyned ful þik,
Þat vmbeteȝe mony tre mo þen two myle.
Þat holde on þat on syde þe haþel auysed,
As hit schemered and schon þurȝ þe schyre okeȝ ;
Þenne hatȝ he hendly of his helme, and heȝly he þonkeȝ
Jesus and sayn Gilyan, þat gentyle ar boþe,
Þat cortaysly had hym kydde, and his cry herkened.
f. 101[b]
‘Now bone hostel,’ coþe þe burne, ‘I beseche yow ȝette!’
Þenne gerdeȝ he to Gryngolet with þe gilt heleȝ,
And he ful chauncely hatȝ chosen to þe chef gate,
Þat broȝt bremly þe burne to þe bryge ende
in haste.
Þe bryge watȝ breme vpbrayde,
Þe ȝateȝ wer stoken faste,
Þe walleȝ were wel arayed,
Hit dut no wyndeȝ blaste.

774 say *MS.* 777 gedereȝ *MS.*

Þe burne bode on bonk, þat on blonk houed,
Of þe depe double dich þat drof to þe place;
Þe walle wod in þe water wonderly depe,
Ande eft a ful huge heȝt hit haled vp on lofte
Of harde hewen ston vp to þe tableȝ,
Enbaned vnder þe abataylment in þe best lawe;
And syþen garyteȝ ful gaye gered bitwene,
Wyth mony luflych loupe þat louked ful clene:
A better barbican þat burne blusched vpon neuer.
And innermore he behelde þat halle ful hyȝe,
Towres telded bytwene, trochet ful þik,
Fayre fylyoleȝ þat fyȝed, and ferlyly long,
With coruon coprounes craftyly sleȝe.
Chalkwhyt chymnees þer ches he innoȝe
Vpon bastel roueȝ, þat blenked ful quyte;
So mony pynakle payntet watȝ poudred ayquere,
Among þe castel carneleȝ clambred so þik,
Þat pared out of papure purely hit semed.
Þe fre freke on þe fole hit fayr innoghe þoȝt,
If he myȝt keuer to com þe cloyster wythinne,
To herber in þat hostel whyl halyday lested,
        auinant.
    He calde, and sone þer com
    A porter pure plesaunt,
    On þe wal his ernd he nome,
    And haylsed þe knyȝt erraunt.

'Gode sir,' quoþ Gawan, 'woldeȝ þou go myn ernde
To þe heȝ lorde of þis hous, herber to craue?'
'Ȝe, Peter,' quoþ þe porter, 'and purely I trowee f. 102[a]
Þat ȝe be, wyȝe, welcum to won quyle yow lykeȝ.'
Þen ȝede þat wyȝe aȝayn swyþe,
And folke frely hym wyth, to fonge þe knyȝt.
Þay let doun þe grete draȝt and derely out ȝeden,
And kneled doun on her knes vpon þe colde erþe

795 towre *MS.*   803 iñghe *MS.*   813 trowoe *MS.*

To welcum þis ilk wyȝ as worþy hom þoȝt;
Þay ȝolden hym þe brode ȝate, ȝarked vp wyde,
And he hem raysed rekenly, and rod ouer þe brygge.
Sere seggeȝ hym sesed by sadel, quel he lyȝt,
And syþen stabeled his stede stif men innoȝe.
Knyȝteȝ and swyereȝ comen doun þenne
For to bryng þis buurne wyth blys into halle;
Quen he hef vp his helme, þer hiȝed innoghe
For to hent hit at his honde, þe hende to seruen;
His bronde and his blasoun boþe þay token.
Þen haylsed he ful hendly þo haþeleȝ vchone,
And mony proud mon þer presed þat prynce to honour.
Alle hasped in his heȝ wede to halle þay hym wonnen,
Þer fayre fyre vpon flet fersly brenned.
Þenne þe lorde of þe lede louteȝ fro his chambre
For to mete wyth menske þe mon on þe flor;
He sayde, 'Ȝe ar welcum to welde as yow lykeȝ;
Þat here is, al is yowre awen, to haue at yowre wylle
and welde.'
'Graunt mercy,' quoþ Gawayn,
'Þer Kryst hit yow forȝelde;'
As frekeȝ þat semed fayn
Ayþer oþer in armeȝ con felde.

Gawayn glyȝt on þe gome þat godly hym gret,
And þuȝt hit a bolde burne þat þe burȝ aȝte,
A hoge haþel for þe noneȝ, and of hyghe eldee;
Brode, bryȝt, wat; his berde, and al beuer-hwed,
Sturne, stif on þe stryþþe on stalworth schonkeȝ,
Felle face as þe fyre, and fre of hys speche;
And wel hym semed, for soþe, as þe segge þuȝt,
To lede a lortschyp in lee of leudeȝ ful gode.
Þe lorde hym charred to a chambre, and chefly cumaundeȝ f. 102b
To delyuer hym a leude, hym loȝly to serue;

850 clesly *MS.*

And þere were boun at his bode burneȝ innoȝe,
Þat broȝt hym to a bryȝt boure, þer beddyng watȝ noble,
Of cortynes of clene sylk wyth cler golde hemmeȝ,
And couertoreȝ ful curious with comlych paneȝ,
Of bryȝt blaunmer aboue enbrawded bisydeȝ,
Rudeleȝ rennande on ropeȝ, red golde ryngeȝ,
Tapiteȝ tyȝt to þe woȝe of tuly and tars,
And vnder fete, on þe flet, of folȝande sute.
Þer he watȝ dispoyled, wyth specheȝ of myerþe,
Þe burn of his bruny, and of his bryȝt wedeȝ.
Ryche robes ful rad renkkeȝ hym broȝten,
For to charge, and to chaunge, and chose of þe best.
Sone as he on hent, and happed þerinne,
Þat sete on hym semly wyth saylande skyrteȝ,
Þe ver by his uisage verayly hit semed
Welneȝ to vche haþel, alle on hwes,
Lowande and lufly alle his lymmeȝ vnder,
Þat a comloker knyȝt neuer Kryst made
hem þoȝt.
Wheþen in worlde he were,
Hit semed as he moȝt
Be prynce withouten pere
In felde þer felle men foȝt.

A cheyer byfore þe chemné, þer charcole brenned,
Watȝ grayþed for Sir Gawan grayþely with cloþeȝ,
Whyssynes vpon queldepoyntes þat koynt wer boþe;
And þenne a meré mantyle watȝ on þat mon cast
Of a broun bleeaunt, enbrauded ful ryche
And fayre furred wythinne with felleȝ of þe best,
Alle of ermyn inurnde, his hode of þe same;
And he sete in þat settel semlych ryche,
And achaufed hym chefly, and þenne his cher mended.

862 hem *MS.* 865 hyn *MS.* 872 myȝt *MS.*
874 fyȝt *MS.* 877 þa *MS.* 881 in erde *MS.*
883 cefly *MS.*

Sone watȝ telded vp a tabil on tresteȝ ful fayre,
Clad wyth a clene cloþe þat cler quyt schewed,
Sanap, and salure, and syluerin sponeȝ.
Þe wyȝe wesche at his wylle, and went to his mete. f. 103a
Seggeȝ hym serued semly innoȝe
Wyth sere sewes and sete, sesounde of þe best,
Double-felde, as hit falleȝ, and fele kyn fischeȝ,
Summe baken in bred, summe brad on þe gledeȝ,
Summe soþen, summe in sewe sauered with spyces,
And ay sawes so sleȝe þat þe segge lyked.
Þe freke calde hit a fest ful frely and ofte
Ful hendely, quen alle þe haþeles rehayted hym at oneȝ
as hende:
'Þis penaunce now ȝe take,
And eft hit schal amende.'
Þat mon much merþe con make,
For wyn in his hed þat wende.

Þenne watȝ spyed and spured vpon spare wyse
Bi preué poynteȝ of þat prynce, put to hymseluen,
Þat he beknew cortaysly of þe court þat he were,
Þat aþel Arthure þe hende haldeȝ hym one,
Þat is þe ryche ryal kyng of þe Rounde Table,
And hit watȝ Wawen hymself þat in þat won sytteȝ,
Comen to þat Krystmasse, as case hym þen lymped.
When þe lorde hade lerned þat he þe leude hade,
Loude laȝed he þerat, so lef hit hym þoȝt,
And alle þe men in þat mote maden much joye
To apere in his presense prestly þat tyme,
Þat alle prys and prowes and pured þewes
Apendes to hys persoun, and praysed is euer,
Byfore alle men vpon molde his mensk is þe most.
Vch segge ful softly sayde to his fere:
'Now schal we semlych se sleȝteȝ of þeweȝ
And þe teccheles termes of talkyng noble,

884 tabil: tapit *MS.* 893 sleȝeȝ *MS.*

Wich spede is in speche vnspurd may we lerne,
Syn we haf fonged þat fyne fader of nurture.
God hatȝ geuen vus his grace godly for soþe,
Þat such a gest as Gawan grauntеȝ vus to haue,
When burneȝ blyþe of his burþe schal sitte
and synge.
In menyng of manereȝ mere
Þis burne now schal vus bryng, f. 103b
I hope þat may hym here
Schal lerne of luf-talkyng.'

Bi þat þe diner watȝ done and þe dere vp,
Hit watȝ neȝ at þe niyȝt neȝed þe tyme.
Chaplayneȝ to þe chapeles chosen þe gate,
Rungen ful rychely, ryȝt as þay schulden,
To þe hersum euensong of þe hyȝe tyde.
Þe lorde loutes þerto, and þe lady als,
Into a cumly closet coyntly ho entreȝ.
Gawan glydeȝ ful gay and gos þeder sone;
Þe lorde laches hym by þe lappe and ledeȝ hym to sytte,
And couþly hym knoweȝ and calleȝ hym his nome,
And sayde he watȝ þe welcomest wyȝe of þe worlde;
And he hym þonkked þroly, and ayþer halched oþer,
And seten soberly samen þe seruise quyle.
Þenne lyst þe lady to loke on þe knyȝt,
Þenne com ho of hir closet with mony cler burdeȝ.
Ho watȝ þe fayrest in felle, of flesche and of lyre,
And of compas and colour and costes, of alle oþer,
And wener þen Wenore, as þe wyȝe þoȝt;
He ches þurȝ þe chaunsel to cheryche þat hende.
An oþer lady hir lad bi þe lyft honde,
Þat watȝ alder þen ho, an auncian hit semed,
And heȝly honowred with haþeleȝ aboute.
Bot vnlyke on to loke þo ladyes were,
For if þe ȝonge watȝ ȝep, ȝolȝe watȝ þat oþer;

930 claplayneȝ *MS.*

Riche red on þat on rayled ayquere,
Rugh ronkled chekeȝ þat oþer on rolled;
Kerchofes of þat on, wyth mony cler perleȝ,
Hir brest and hir bryȝt þrote bare displayed,
Schon schyrer þen snawe þat schedeȝ on hilleȝ;
Þat oþer wyth a gorger watȝ gered ouer þe swyre,
Chymbled ouer hir blake chyn with chalkquyte vayles,
Hir frount folden in sylk, enfoubled ayquere,
Toret and treieted with tryfleȝ aboute,
Þat noȝt watȝ bare of þat burde bot þe blake broȝes, f. 104[a]
Þe tweyne yȝen and þe nase, þe naked lyppeȝ,
And þose were soure to se and sellyly blered;
A mensk lady on molde mon may hir calle,
for Gode!
Hir body watȝ schort and þik,
Hir buttokeȝ balȝ and brode,
More lykkerwys on to lyk
Watȝ þat scho hade on lode.

When Gawayn glyȝt on þat gay, þat graciously loked,
Wyth leue laȝt of þe lorde he went hem aȝaynes;
Þe alder he haylses, heldande ful lowe,
Þe loueloker he lappeȝ a lyttel in armeȝ,
He kysses hir comlyly, and knyȝtly he meleȝ.
Þay kallen hym of aquoyntaunce, and he hit quyk askeȝ
To be her seruaunt sothly, if hemself lyked.
Þay tan hym bytwene hem, wyth talkyng hym leden
To chambre, to chemné, and chefly þay asken
Spyceȝ, þat vnsparely men speded hom to bryng,
And þe wynnelych wyne þerwith vche tyme.
Þe lorde luflych aloft lepeȝ ful ofte,
Mynned merthe to be made vpon mony syþeȝ,
Hent heȝly of his hode, and on a spere henged,
And wayued hom to wynne þe worchip þerof,
Þat most myrþe myȝt meue þat Crystenmas whyle—

956 scheder *MS.* 958 mylkquyte *MS.* 967 bay *MS.*

'And I schal fonde, bi my fayth, to fylter wyth þe best,
Er me wont þe wede with help of my frendeȝ.'
Þus wyth laȝande loteȝ þe lorde hit tayt makeȝ,
For to glade Sir Gawayn with gomneȝ in halle
þat nyȝt,
Til þat hit watȝ tyme
Þe lord comaundet lyȝt;
Sir Gawen his leue con nyme
And to his bed hym diȝt.

On þe morne, as vche mon myneȝ þat tyme
Þat dryȝtyn for oure destyné to deȝe watȝ borne,
Wele waxeȝ in vche a won in worlde for his sake;
So did hit þere on þat day þurȝ dayntés mony:
Boþe at mes and at mele messes ful quaynt f. 104b
Derf men vpon dece drest of þe best.
Þe olde auncian wyf heȝest ho sytteȝ,
Þe lorde lufly her by lent, as I trowe;
Gawan and þe gay burde togeder þay seten,
Euen inmyddeȝ, as þe messe metely come,
And syþen þurȝ al þe sale, as hem best semed,
Bi vche grome at his degré grayþely watȝ serued.
Þer watȝ mete, þer watȝ myrþe, þer watȝ much ioye,
Þat for to telle þerof hit me tene were,
And to poynte hit ȝet I pyned me parauenture.
Bot ȝet I wot þat Wawen and þe wale burde
Such comfort of her compaynye caȝten togeder
Þurȝ her dere dalyaunce of her derne wordeȝ,
Wyth clene cortays carp closed fro fylþe,
Þat hor play watȝ passande vche prynce gomen,
in vayres.
Trumpeȝ and nakerys,
Much pypyng þer repayres;
Vche mon tented hys,
And þay two tented þayres.

987 wedeȝ *MS.* 992 lord: kyng *MS.*
996 þat: þ *illegible.* 1014 þat: & *MS.*

Much dut watȝ þer dryuen þat day and þat oþer,
And þe þryd as þro þronge in þerafter;
Þe ioye of sayn Joneȝ day watȝ gentyle to here,
And watȝ þe last of þe layk, leudeȝ þer þoȝten.
Þer wer gestes to go vpon þe gray morne,
Forþy wonderly þay woke, and þe wyn dronken,
Daunsed ful dreȝly wyth dere caroleȝ.
At þe last, when hit watȝ late, þay lachen her leue,
Vchon to wende on his way þat watȝ wyȝe stronge.
Gawan gef hym god day, þe god mon hym lachcheȝ,
Ledes hym to his awen chambre, þe chymné bysyde,
And þere he draȝeȝ hym on dryȝe, and derely hym
þonkkeȝ
Of þe wynne worschip þat he hym wayued hade,
As to honour his hous on þat hyȝe tyde,
And enbelyse his burȝ with his bele chere.
'Iwysse sir, quyl I leue, me worþeȝ þe better
Þat Gawayn hatȝ ben my gest at Goddeȝ awen fest.' f. 105a
'Grant merci, sir,' quoþ Gawayn, 'in god fayth hit is
yowreȝ,
Al þe honour is your awen—þe heȝe kyng yow ȝelde!
And I am wyȝe at your wylle to worch youre hest,
As I am halden þerto, in hyȝe and in loȝe,
bi riȝt.'
Þe lorde fast can hym payne
To holde lenger þe knyȝt;
To hym answareȝ Gawayn,
Bi non way þat he myȝt.

Then frayned þe freke ful fayre at himseluen
Quat derue dede had hym dryuen at þat dere tyme
So kenly fro þe kyngeȝ kourt to kayre al his one,
Er þe halidayeȝ holly were halet out of toun.
'For soþe, sir,' quoþ þe segge, 'ȝe sayn bot þe trawþe,

1030 þe: þ *MS.* 1032 þat: & *MS.*
1037 nerci *MS.* 1044 answreȝ *MS.*

A heʒe ernde and a hasty me hade fro þo woneʒ,
For I am sumned myselfe to sech to a place,
I ne wot in worlde whederwarde to wende hit to fynde.
I nolde bot if I hit negh myʒt on Nw Ʒeres morne
For alle þe londe inwyth Logres, so me oure lorde help!
Forþy, sir, þis enquest I require yow here,
Þat ʒe me telle with trawþe if euer ʒe tale herde
Of þe grene chapel, quere hit on grounde stondeʒ,
And of þe knyʒt þat hit kepes, of colour of grene.
Þer watʒ stabled bi statut a steuen vus bytwene
To mete þat mon at þat mere, ʒif I myʒt last;
And of þat ilk Nw Ʒere bot neked now wonteʒ,
And I wolde loke on þat lede, if God me let wolde,
Gladloker, bi Goddeʒ sun, þen any god welde!
Forþi, iwysse, bi ʒowre wylle, wende me bihoues,
Naf I now to busy bot bare þre dayeʒ,
And me als fayn to falle feye as fayly of myyn ernde.'
Þenne laʒande quoþ þe lorde, 'Now leng þe byhoues,
For I schal teche yow to þat terme bi þe tymeʒ ende,
Þe grene chapayle vpon grounde greue yow no more;
Bot ʒe schal be in yowre bed, burne, at þyn ese,
Quyle forth dayeʒ, and ferk on þe fyrst of þe ʒere,
And cum to þat merk at mydmorn, to make quat yow likeʒ f. 105b
in spenne.
Dowelleʒ whyle New Ʒeres daye,
And rys, and raykeʒ þenne,
Mon schal yow sette in waye,
Hit is not two myle henne.'

Þenne watʒ Gawan ful glad, and gomenly he laʒed:
'Now I þonk yow þryuandely þurʒ alle oþer þynge,
Now acheued is my chaunce, I schal at your wylle
Dowelle, and elleʒ do quat ʒe demen.'
Þenne sesed hym þe syre and set hym bysyde,

1053 ne *supplied*. 1069 þa terme *MS*.

Let þe ladieȝ be fette to lyke hem þe better.
Þer watȝ seme solace by hemself stille;
Þe lorde let for luf loteȝ so myry,
As wyȝ þat wolde of his wyte, ne wyst quat he myȝt.
Þenne he carped to þe knyȝt, criande loude,
'Ȝe han demed to do þe dede þat I bidde;
Wyl ȝe halde þis hes here at þys oneȝ?'
'Ȝe, sir, for soþe,' sayd þe segge trwe,
'Whyl I byde in yowre borȝe, be bayn to ȝowre hest.'
'For ȝe haf trauayled,' quoþ þe tulk, 'towen fro ferre,
And syþen waked me wyth, ȝe arn not wel waryst
Nauþer of sostnaunce ne of slepe, soþly I knowe;
Ȝe schal lenge in your lofte, and lyȝe in your ese
To-morn quyle þe messequyle, and to mete wende
When ȝe wyl, wyth my wyf, þat wyth yow schal sitte
And comfort yow with companyny, til I to cort torne;
        ȝe lende,
    And I schal erly ryse,
    On huntyng wyl I wende.'
    Gauayn granteȝ alle þyse,
    Hym heldande, as þe hende.

'Ʒet firre,' quoþ þe freke, 'a forwarde we make:
Quat-so-euer I wynne in þe wod hit worþeȝ to youreȝ,
And quat chek so ȝe acheue chaunge me þerforne.
Swete, swap we so, sware with trawþe,
Queþer, leude, so lymp lere oþer better.'
'Bi God,' quoþ Gawayn þe gode, 'I grant þertylle,
And þat yow lyst for to layke, lef hit me þynkes.' f. 106ª
'Who bryngeȝ vus þis beuerage, þis bargayn is maked':
So sayde þe lorde of þat lede; þay laȝed vchone,
Þay dronken and daylyeden and dalten vntyȝtel,
Þise lordeȝ and ladyeȝ, quyle þat hem lyked;
And syþen with frenkysch fare and fele fayre loteȝ
Þay stoden and stemed and stylly speken,

1092 ȝowe *MS.*

Kysten ful comlyly and kaȝten her leue.
With mony leude ful lyȝt and lemande torches
Vche burne to his bed watȝ broȝt at þe laste,
        ful softe.
    To bed er ȝet þay ȝede,
    Recorded couenauntez ofte;
    Þe olde lorde of þat leude
    Cowþe wel halde layk alofte.

III

FUL erly bifore þe day þe folk vprysen,
Gestes þat go wolde hor gromeȝ þay calden,
And þay busken vp bilyue blonkkeȝ to sadel,
Tyffen her takles, trussen her males,
Richen hem þe rychest, to ryde alle arayde,
Lepen vp lyȝtly, lachen her brydeles,
Vche wyȝe on his way þer hym wel lyked.
Þe leue lorde of þe londe watȝ not þe last
Arayed for þe rydyng, with renkkeȝ ful mony;
Ete a sop hastyly, when he hade herde masse,
With bugle to bent-felde he buskeȝ bylyue.
By þat any daylyȝt lemed vpon erþe,
He with his haþeles on hyȝe horsses weren.
Þenne þise cacheres þat couþe cowpled hor houndeȝ,
Vnclosed þe kenel dore and calde hem þeroute,
Blwe bygly in bugleȝ þre bare mote;
Braches bayed þerfore and breme noyse maked;
And þay chastysed and charred on chasyng þat went,
A hundreth of hunteres, as I haf herde telle,
        of þe best.
    To trystors vewters ȝod,
    Couples huntes of kest;

1129 her (*1st*): he *MS*.   1137 þat þat *MS*.

Þer ros for blasteȝ gode f. 106b
Gret rurd in þat forest.

At þe fyrst quethe of þe quest quaked þe wylde;
Der drof in þe dale, doted for drede,
Hiȝed to þe hyȝe, bot heterly þay were
Restayed with þe stablye, þat stoutly ascryed.
Þay let þe hertteȝ haf þe gate, with þe hyȝe hedes,
Þe breme bukkeȝ also with hor brode paumeȝ;
For þe fre lorde hade defende in fermysoun tyme
Þat þer schulde no mon meue to þe male dere.
Þe hindeȝ were halden in with hay! and war!
Þe does dryuen with gret dyn to þe depe sladeȝ;
Þer myȝt mon se, as þay slypte, slentyng of arwes—
At vche wende vnder wande wapped a flone—
Þat bigly bote on þe broun with ful brode hedeȝ.
What! þay brayen, and bleden, bi bonkkeȝ þay deȝen,
And ay rachches in a res radly hem folȝes,
Huntereȝ wyth hyȝe horne hasted hem after
Wyth such a crakkande kry as klyffes haden brusten.
What wylde so atwaped wyȝes þat schotten
Watȝ al toraced and rent at þe resayt,
Bi þay were tened at þe hyȝe and taysed to þe wattreȝ;
Þe ledeȝ were so lerned at þe loȝe trysteres,
And þe grehoundeȝ so grete, þat geten hem bylyue
And hem tofylched, as fast as frekeȝ myȝt loke,
Þer ryȝt.
Þe lorde for blys abloy
Ful oft con launce and lyȝt,
And drof þat day wyth joy
Thus to þe derk nyȝt.

Þus laykeȝ þis lorde by lynde-wodeȝ eueȝ,
And Gawayn þe god mon in gay bed lygeȝ,
Lurkkeȝ quyl þe daylyȝt lemed on þe wowes,

1179 Gawayn: G. *MS.*

Vnder couertour ful clere, cortyned aboute;
And as in slomeryng he slode, sleȝly he herde
A littel dyn at his dor, and derfly vpon;
And he heueȝ vp his hed out of þe cloþes,
A corner of þe cortyn he caȝt vp a lyttel, f. 107a
And wayteȝ warly þiderwarde quat hit be myȝt.
Hit watȝ þe ladi, loflyest to beholde,
Þat droȝ þe dor after hir ful dernly and stylle,
And boȝed towarde þe bed; and þe burne schamed,
And layde hym doun lystyly, and let as he slepte;
And ho stepped stilly and stel to his bedde,
Kest vp þe cortyn and creped withinne,
And set hir ful softly on þe bed-syde,
And lenged þere selly longe to loke quen he wakened.
Þe lede lay lurked a ful longe quyle,
Compast in his concience to quat þat cace myȝt
Meue oþer amount—to meruayle hym þoȝt,
Bot ȝet he sayde in hymself, 'More semly hit were
To aspye wyth my spelle in space quat ho wolde.'
Þen he wakenede, and wroth, and to hir warde torned,
And vnlouked his yȝe-lyddeȝ, and let as hym wondered,
And sayned hym, as bi his saȝe þe sauer to worthe,
with hande.
Wyth chynne and cheke ful swete,
Boþe quit and red in blande,
Ful lufly con ho lete
Wyth lyppeȝ smal laȝande.

'God moroun, Sir Gawayn,' sayde þat gay lady,
'Ȝe ar a sleper vnslyȝe, þat mon may slyde hider;
Now ar ȝe tan astyt! Bot true vus may schape,
I schal bynde yow in your bedde, þat be ȝe trayst':
Al laȝande þe lady lanced þo bourdeȝ.
'Goud moroun, gay,' quoþ Gawayn þe blyþe,

1199 in *illegible*. 1208 gay: fayr *MS*.
1213 gay, ay *blurred; only room for two letters*.

'Me schal worþe at your wille, and þat me wel lykeȝ,
For I ȝelde me ȝederly, and ȝeȝe after grace,
And þat is þe best, be my dome, for me byhoueȝ nede':
And þus he bourded aȝayn with mony a blyþe laȝter.
'Bot wolde ȝe, lady louely, þen leue me grante,
And deprece your prysoun, and pray hym to ryse,
I wolde boȝe of þis bed, and busk me better,
I schulde keuer þe more comfort to karp yow wyth.'
'Nay for soþe, beau sir,' sayd þat swete, f. 107b
'Ȝe schal not rise of your bedde, I rych yow better,
I schal happe yow here þat oþer half als,
And syþen karp wyth my knyȝt þat I kaȝt haue;
For I wene wel, iwysse, Sir Wowen ȝe are,
Þat alle þe worlde worchipeȝ quere-so ȝe ride;
Your honour, your hendelayk is hendely praysed
With lordeȝ, wyth ladyes, with alle þat lyf bere.
And now ȝe ar here, iwysse, and we bot oure one;
My lorde and his ledeȝ ar on lenþe faren,
Oþer burneȝ in her bedde, and my burdeȝ als,
Þe dor drawen and dit with a derf haspe;
And syþen I haue in þis hous hym þat al lykeȝ,
I schal ware my whyle wel, quyl hit lasteȝ,
with tale.
Ȝe ar welcum to my cors,
Yowre awen won to wale,
Me behoueȝ of fyne force
Your seruaunt be, and schale.'
'In god fayth,' quoþ Gawayn, 'gayn hit me þynkkeȝ,
Þaȝ I be not now he þat ȝe of speken;
To reche to such reuerence as ȝe reherce here
I am wyȝe vnworþy, I wot wel myseluen.
Bi God, I were glad, and yow god þoȝt,
At saȝe oþer at seruyce þat I sette myȝt
To þe plesaunce of your prys—hit were a pure ioye.'
'In god fayth, Sir Gawayn,' quoþ þe gay lady,

1214 your*r MS.*

'Þe prys and þe prowes þat pleseȝ al oþer,
If I hit lakked oþer set at lyȝt, hit were littel daynté;
Bot hit ar ladyes innoȝe þat leuer wer nowþe
Haf þe, hende, in hor holde, as I þe habbe here,
To daly with derely your daynté wordeȝ,
Keuer hem comfort and colen her careȝ,
Þen much of þe garysoun oþer golde þat þay hauen.
Bot I louue þat ilke lorde þat þe lyfte haldeȝ,
I haf hit holly in my honde þat al desyres,
þurȝe grace.'
Scho made hym so gret chere,
Þat watȝ so fayr of face, f.108a
Þe knyȝt with speches skere
Answared to vche a cace.

'Madame,' quoþ þe myry mon, 'Mary yow ȝelde,
For I haf founden, in god fayth, yowre fraunchis nobele;
And oþer ful much of oþer folk fongen hor dedeȝ,
Bot þe daynté þat þay delen for my disert nysen;
Hit is þe worchyp of yourself, þat noȝt bot wel conneȝ.'
'Bi Mary,' quoþ þe menskful, 'me þynk hit an oþer;
For were I worth al þe wone of wymmen alyue,
And al þe wele of þe worlde were in my honde,
And I schulde chepen and chose to cheue me a lorde,
For þe costes þat I haf knowen vpon þe, knyȝt, here,
Of bewté and debonerté and blyþe semblaunt,
And þat I haf er herkkened and halde hit here trwee,
Þer schulde no freke vpon folde bifore yow be chosen.'
'Iwysse, worþy,' quoþ þe wyȝe, 'ȝe haf waled wel better,
Bot I am proude of þe prys þat ȝe put on me,
And, soberly your seruaunt, my souerayn I holde yow,
And yowre knyȝt I becom, and Kryst yow forȝelde.'
Þus þay meled of muchquat til mydmorn paste,
And ay þe lady let lyk as hym loued mych;

1255 þat: þat þat *MS.* 1262 aswared *MS.*
1281 as hym: ahȳ *MS.*

Þe freke ferde with defence, and feted ful fayre.
'Þaȝ I were burde bryȝtest', þe burde in mynde hade,
'Þe lasse luf in his lode'—for lur þat he soȝt
boute hone,
Þe dunte þat schulde hym deue,
And nedeȝ hit most be done.
Þe lady þenn spek of leue,
He granted hir ful sone.

Þenne ho gef hym god day, and wyth a glent laȝed,
And as ho stod, ho stonyed hym wyth ful stor wordeȝ:
'Now he þat spedeȝ vche spech þis disport ȝelde yow!
Bot þat ȝe be Gawan, hit gotȝ in mynde.'
'Querfore?' quoþ þe freke, and freschly he askeȝ,
Ferde lest he hade fayled in fourme of his castes;
Bot þe burde hym blessed, and bi þis skyl sayde:
'So god as Gawayn gaynly is halden, f. 108b
And cortaysye is closed so clene in hymseluen,
Couth not lyȝtly haf lenged so long wyth a lady,
Bot he had craued a cosse, bi his courtaysye,
Bi sum towch of summe tryfle at sum taleȝ ende.'
Þen quoþ Wowen: 'Iwysse, worþe as yow lykeȝ;
I schal kysse at your comaundement, as a knyȝt falleȝ,
And fire, lest he displese yow, so plede hit no more.'
Ho comes nerre with þat, and cacheȝ hym in armeȝ,
Louteȝ luflych adoun and þe leude kysseȝ.
Þay comly bykennen to Kryst ayþer oþer;
Ho dos hir forth at þe dore withouten dyn more;
And he ryches hym to ryse and rapes hym sone,
Clepes to his chamberlayn, choses his wede,
Boȝeȝ forth, quen he watȝ boun, blyþely to masse;
And þenne he meued to his mete þat menskly hym
keped,
And made myry al day, til þe mone rysed,
with game.

1286 sclulde *MS.* 1304 so: fo *MS*

Watȝ neuer freke fayrer fonge
Bitwene two so dyngne dame,
Þe alder and þe ȝonge;
Much solace set þay same.

And ay þe lorde of þe londe is lent on his gamneȝ,
To hunt in holteȝ and heþe at hyndeȝ barayne;
Such a sowme he þer slowe bi þat þe sunne heldet,
Of dos and of oþer dere, to deme were wonder.
Þenne fersly þay flokked in folk at þe laste,
And quykly of þe quelled dere a querré þay maked.
Þe best boȝed þerto with burneȝ innoghe,
Gedered þe grattest of gres þat þer were,
And didden hem derely vndo as þe dede askeȝ;
Serched hem at þe asay summe þat þer were,
Two fyngeres þay fonde of þe fowlest of alle.
Syþen þay slyt þe slot, sesed þe erber,
Schaued wyth a scharp knyf, and þe schyre knitten;
Syþen rytte þay þe foure lymmes, and rent of þe hyde,
Þen brek þay þe balé, þe bauleȝ out token,
Lystily forlancyng, and lere of þe knot; f. 109[a]
Þay gryped to þe gargulun, and grayþely departed
Þe wesaunt fro þe wynt-hole, and walt out þe gutteȝ;
Þen scher þay out þe schuldereȝ with her scharp knyueȝ,
Haled hem by a lyttel hole to haue hole sydes.
Siþen britned þay þe brest and brayden hit in twynne,
And eft at þe gargulun bigyneȝ on þenne,
Ryueȝ hit vp radly ryȝt to þe byȝt,
Voydeȝ out þe avanters, and verayly þerafter
Alle þe rymeȝ by þe rybbeȝ radly þay lance;
So ryde þay of by resoun bi þe rygge boneȝ,
Euenden to þe haunche, þat henged alle samen,
And heuen hit vp al hole, and hwen hit of þere,
And þat þay neme for þe noumbles bi nome, as I trowe,
bi kynde;

1315 watȝ: w[t] *MS.* 1333 bauleȝ: baleȝ *MS.* 1344 So: fo *MS.*

Bi þe byȝt al of þe þyȝes
Þe lappeȝ þay lance bihynde;
To hewe hit in two þay hyȝes,
Bi þe bakbon to vnbynde.

Boþe þe hede and þe hals þay hwen of þenne,
And syþen sunder þay þe sydeȝ swyft fro þe chyne,
And þe corbeles fee þay kest in a greue;
Þenn þurled þay ayþer þik side þurȝ bi þe rybbe,
And henged þenne ayþer bi hoȝes of þe fourcheȝ,
Vche freke for his fee, as falleȝ for to haue.
Vpon a felle of þe fayre best fede þay þayr houndes
Wyth þe lyuer and þe lyȝteȝ, þe leþer of þe pauncheȝ,
And bred baþed in blod blende þer-amongeȝ.
Baldely þay blw prys, bayed þayr rachcheȝ,
Syþen fonge þay her flesche, folden to home,
Strakande ful stoutly mony stif moteȝ.
Bi þat þe daylyȝt watȝ done þe douthe watȝ al wonen
Into þe comly castel, þer þe knyȝt bideȝ
ful stille,
Wyth blys and bryȝt fyr bette.
Þe lorde is comen þertylle;
When Gawayn wyth hym mette,
Þer watȝ bot wele at wylle.

Thenne comaunded þe lorde in þat sale to samen alle
þe meny, f. 109b
Boþe þe ladyes on loghe to lyȝt with her burdes
Bifore alle þe folk on þe flette, frekeȝ he beddeȝ
Verayly his venysoun to fech hym byforne,
And al godly in gomen Gawayn he called,
Techeȝ hym to þe tayles of ful tayt bestes,
Scheweȝ hym þe schyree grece schorne vpon rybbes.
'How payeȝ yow þis play? Haf I prys wonnen?

1357 aþer *MS.* 1369 lorde: e *partly erased.*
1376 Gaway *MS.*

Haue I þryuandely þonk þurȝ my craft serued?'
'Ȝe iwysse,' quoþ þat oþer wyȝe, 'here is wayth fayrest
Þat I seȝ þis seuen ȝere in sesoun of wynter.'
'And al I gif yow, Gawayn,' quoþ þe gome þenne,
'For by acorde of couenaunt ȝe craue hit as your awen.'
'Þis is soth,' quoþ þe segge, 'I say yow þat ilke:
Þat I haf worthyly wonnen þis woneȝ wythinne,
Iwysse with as god wylle hit worþeȝ to ȝoureȝ.'
He hasppeȝ his fayre hals his armeȝ wythinne,
And kysses hym as comlyly as he couþe awyse:
'Tas yow þere my cheuicaunce, I cheued no more;
I wowche hit saf fynly, þaȝ feler hit were.'
'Hit is god,' quoþ þe god mon, 'grant mercy þerfore.
Hit may be such, hit is þe better, and ȝe me breue wolde
Where ȝe wan þis ilk wele bi wytte of yorseluen.'
'Þat watȝ not forward,' quoþ he, 'frayst me no more—
For ȝe haf tan þat yow tydeȝ, trawe ȝe non oþer—
ȝe mowe.'
Þay laȝed, and made hem blyþe
Wyth loteȝ þat were to lowe;
To soper þay ȝede as-swyþe,
Wyth dayntés nwe innowe.

And syþen by þe chymné in chamber þay seten,
Wyȝeȝ þe walle wyn weȝed to hem oft,
And efte in her bourdyng þay bayþen in þe morn
To fylle þe same forwardeȝ þat þay byfore maden:
Wat chaunce so bytydeȝ hor cheuysaunce to chaunge,
What nweȝ so þay nome, at naȝt quen þay metten.
Þay acorded of þe couenaunteȝ byfore þe court alle;
Þe beuerage watȝ broȝt forth in bourde at þat tyme, f. 110a
Þenne þay louelych leȝten leue at þe last,
Vche burne to his bedde busked bylyue.

1386 þat: & *MS.*; wonnen *supplied.* 1389 he: ho *MS.*
1394 yor-: hor *MS.* 1406 Wat: þat *MS.*

Bi þat þe coke hade crowen and cakled bot þryse,
Þe lorde watȝ lopen of his bedde, þe leudeȝ vch one;
So þat þe mete and þe masse watȝ metely delyuered,
Þe douthe dressed to þe wod, er any day sprenged,
to chace;
Heȝ with hunte and horneȝ
Þurȝ playneȝ þay passe in space,
Vncoupled among þo þorneȝ
Racheȝ þat ran on race.

Sone þay calle of a quest in a ker syde,
Þe hunt rehayted þe houndeȝ þat hit fyrst mynged,
Wylde wordeȝ hym warp wyth a wrast noyce;
Þe howndeȝ þat hit herde hastid þider swyþe,
And fellen as fast to þe fuyt, fourty at ones;
Þenne such a glauer ande glam of gedered rachcheȝ
Ros, þat þe rochereȝ rungen aboute;
Huntereȝ hem hardened with horne and wyth muthe.
Þen al in a semblé sweyed togeder,
Bitwene a flosche in þat fryth and a foo cragge;
In a knot bi a clyffe, at þe kerre syde,
Þer as þe rogh rocher vnrydely watȝ fallen,
Þay ferden to þe fyndyng, and frekeȝ hem after;
Þay vmbekesten þe knarre and þe knot boþe,
Wyȝeȝ, whyl þay wysten wel wythinne hem hit were,
Þe best þat þer breued watȝ wyth þe blodhoundeȝ.
Þenne þay beten on þe buskeȝ, and bede hym vpryse,
And he vnsoundyly out soȝt seggeȝ ouerþwert;
On þe sellokest swyn swenged out þere,
Long sythen fro þe sounder þat wiȝt forolde.
For he watȝ breme, bor alþer grattest,
Ful grymme quen he gronyed, þenne greued mony,

1412 croweȝ *MS.*
1433 Þay *from offset.*
1435 wythinne: wytinne *MS.*
1440 fro: for *MS.*
1441 breme *blotted and illegible*; bor: hor *MS.* now (*h* prob. [damaged *b*).
1442 ful grymme *prob. reading of offset.*

For þre at þe fyrst þrast he þryȝt to þe erþe,
And sparred forth good sped boute spyt more.
Þise oþer halowed hyghe! ful hyȝe, and hay! hay! cryed,
Haden horneȝ to mouþe, heterly rechated;
Mony watȝ þe miyry mouthe of men and of houndeȝ f. 110b
Þat buskkeȝ after þis bor with bost and wyth noyse to quelle.
Ful oft he bydeȝ þe baye,
And maymeȝ þe mute inn melle;
He hurteȝ of þe houndeȝ, and þay
Ful ȝomerly ȝaule and ȝelle.

Schalkeȝ to schote at hym schowen to þenne,
Haled to hym of her areweȝ, hitten hym oft;
Bot þe poynteȝ payred at þe pyth þat pyȝt in his scheldeȝ,
And þe barbeȝ of his browen bite non wolde,
Þaȝ þe schauen schaft schyndered in peceȝ;
Þe hede hypped aȝayn were-so-euer hit hitte.
Bot quen þe dynteȝ hym dered of her dryȝe strokeȝ,
Þen, braynwod for bate, on burneȝ he raseȝ,
Hurteȝ hem ful heterly þer he forth hyȝeȝ,
And mony arȝed þerat, and on lyte droȝen.
Bot þe lorde on a lyȝt horce launces hym after,
As burne bolde vpon bent his bugle he bloweȝ,
He rechated, and rode þurȝ roneȝ ful þyk,
Suande þis wylde swyn til þe sunne schafted.
Þis day wyth þis ilk dede þay dryuen on þis wyse,
Whyle oure luflych lede lys in his bedde,
Gawayn grayþely at home, in gereȝ ful ryche of hewe.
Þe lady noȝt forȝate,
Com to hym to salue;

1443 þre at: þre a *from offset*. 1444 sparred *possible reading aided by offset* (previously read *sped him*). 1445 Þise oþer *from offset*.
1457 browen: browe *MS*. 1466 rode: od *illegible*.

Ful erly ho watȝ hym ate
His mode for to remwe.

Ho commes to þe cortyn, and at þe knyȝt totes.
Sir Wawen her welcumed worþy on fyrst,
And ho hym ȝeldeȝ aȝayn ful ȝerne of hir wordeȝ,
Setteȝ hir sofly by his syde, and swyþely ho laȝeȝ,
And wyth a luflych loke ho layde hym þyse wordeȝ:
'Sir, ȝif ȝe be Wawen, wonder me þynkkeȝ,
Wyȝe þat is so wel wrast alway to god,
And conneȝ not of compaynye þe costeȝ vndertake,
And if mon kennes yow hom to knowe, ȝe kest hom of your mynde; f. 111[a]
Þou hatȝ forȝeten ȝederly þat ȝisterday I taȝtte
Bi alder-truest token of talk þat I cowþe.'
'What is þat?' quoþ þe wyghe, 'Iwysse I wot neuer;
If hit be sothe þat ȝe breue, þe blame is myn awen.'
'Ȝet I kende yow of kyssyng,' quoþ þe clere þenne,
'Quere-so countenaunce is couþe quikly to clayme;
Þat bicumes vche a knyȝt þat cortaysy vses.'
'Do way,' quoþ þat derf mon, 'my dere, þat speche,
For þat durst I not do, lest I denayed were;
If I were werned, I were wrang, iwysse, ȝif I profered.'
'Ma fay,' quoþ þe meré wyf, 'ȝe may not be werned,
Ȝe ar stif innoghe to constrayne wyth strenkþe, ȝif yow lykeȝ,
Ȝif any were so vilanous þat yow devaye wolde.'
'Ȝe, be God,' quoþ Gawayn, 'good is your speche,
Bot þrete is vnþryuande in þede þer I lende,
And vche gift þat is geuen not with goud wylle.
I am at your comaundement, to kysse quen yow lykeȝ,
Ȝe may lach quen yow lyst, and leue quen yow þynkkeȝ,
in space.'
Þe lady louteȝ adoun,
And comlyly kysses his face,

1484 kennes: *catchword* & if mon kēneȝ.

Much speche þay þer expoun
Of druryes greme and grace.

'I woled wyt at yow, wyȝe,' þat worþy þer sayde,
'And yow wrathed not þerwyth, what were þe skylle,
Þat so ȝong and so ȝepe as ȝe at þis tyme,
So cortayse, so knyȝtyly, as ȝe ar knowen oute—
And of alle cheualry to chose, þe chef þyng alosed
Is þe lel layk of luf, þe lettrure of armes;
For to telle of þis teuelyng of þis trwe knyȝteȝ,
Hit is þe tytelet token, and tyxt of her werkkeȝ,
How ledes for her lele luf hor lyueȝ han auntered,
Endured for her drury dulful stoundeȝ,—
And after wenged with her walour and voyded her care,
And broȝt blysse into boure with bountees hor awen—
And ȝe ar knyȝt comlokest kyd of your elde,
Your worde and your worchip walkeȝ ayquere, f. 111b
And I haf seten by yourself here sere twyes,
Ȝet herde I neuer of your hed helde no wordeȝ
Þat euer longed to luf, lasse ne more;
And ȝe, þat ar so cortays and coynt of your hetes,
Oghe to a ȝonke þynk ȝern to schewe
And teche sum tokeneȝ of trweluf craftes.
Why! ar ȝe lewed, þat alle þe los weldeȝ?
Oþer elles ȝe demen me to dille your dalyaunce to herken?
For schame!
I com hider sengel, and sitte
To lerne at yow sum game;
Dos, techeȝ me of your wytte,
Whil my lorde is fro hame.'

'In goud fayþe,' quoþ Gawayn, 'God yow forȝelde!
Gret is þe gode gle, and gomen to me huge,
Þat so worþy as ȝe wolde wynne hidere,

1508 woled: ed *probably rewritten.* 1513 lellayk *MS.*
1514 For: or *illegible.* 1516 ledes: edes *illegible*; for: r *illegible.*

And pyne yow with so pouer a mon, as play wyth your
knyȝt
With anyskynneȝ countenaunce, hit keuereȝ me ese;
Bot to take þe toruayle to myself to trwluf expoun,
And towche þe temeȝ of tyxt and taleȝ of armeȝ
To yow þat, I wot wel, weldeȝ more slyȝt
Of þat art, bi þe half, or a hundreth of seche
As I am, oþer euer schal, in erde þer I leue,
Hit were a folé felefolde, my fre, by my trawþe.
I wolde yowre wylnyng worche at my myȝt,
As I am hyȝly bihalden, and euermore wylle
Be seruaunt to yourseluen, so saue me dryȝtyn!'
Þus hym frayned þat fre, and fondet hym ofte,
For to haf wonnen hym to woȝe, what-so scho þoȝt elleȝ;
Bot he defended hym so fayr þat no faut semed,
Ne non euel on nawþer halue, nawþer þay wysten
bot blysse.
Þay laȝed and layked longe;
At þe last scho con hym kysse,
Hir leue fayre con scho fonge
And went hir waye, iwysse.

Then ruþes hym þe renk and ryses to þe masse,
And siþen hor diner watȝ dyȝt and derely serued. f. 112a
Þe lede with þe ladyeȝ layked alle day,
Bot þe lorde ouer þe londeȝ launced ful ofte,
Sweȝ his vncely swyn, þat swyngeȝ bi þe bonkkeȝ
And bote þe best of his bracheȝ þe bakkeȝ in sunder
Þer he bode in his bay, tel bawemen hit breken,
And madee hym mawgref his hed for to mwe vtter,
So felle floneȝ þer flete when þe folk gedered.
Bot ȝet þe styffest to start bi stoundeȝ he made,
Til at þe last he watȝ so mat he myȝt no more renne,
Bot in þe hast þat he myȝt he to a hole wynneȝ
Of a rasse bi a rokk þer renneȝ þe boerne.
He gete þe bonk at his bak, bigyneȝ to scrape,

Þe froþe femed at his mouth vnfayre bi þe wykeȝ,
Whetteȝ his whyte tuscheȝ; with hym þen irked
Alle þe burneȝ so bolde þat hym by stoden
To nye hym on-ferum, bot neȝe hym non durst
for woþe;
He hade hurt so mony byforne
Þat al þuȝt þenne ful loþe
Be more wyth his tusches torne,
Þat breme watȝ and braynwod bothe,

Til þe knyȝt com hymself, kachande his blonk,
Syȝ hym byde at þe bay, his burneȝ bysyde;
He lyȝtes luflych adoun, leueȝ his corsour,
Braydeȝ out a bryȝt bront and bigly forth strydeȝ,
Foundeȝ fast þurȝ þe forth þer þe felle bydeȝ.
Þe wylde watȝ war of þe wyȝe with weppen in honde,
Hef hyȝly þe here, so hetterly he fnast
Þat fele ferde for þe freke, lest felle hym þe worre.
Þe swyn setteȝ hym out on þe segge euen,
Þat þe burne and þe bor were boþe vpon hepeȝ
In þe wyȝtest of þe water; þe worre hade þat oþer,
For þe mon merkkeȝ hym wel, as þay mette fyrst,
Set sadly þe scharp in þe slot euen,
Hit hym vp to þe hult, þat þe hert schyndered,
And he ȝarrande hym ȝelde, and ȝed ouer þe water
ful tyt.
A hundreth houndeȝ hym hent, f. 112b
Þat bremely con hym bite,
Burneȝ him broȝt to bent,
And doggeȝ to dethe endite.

There watȝ blawyng of prys in mony breme horne,
Heȝe halowing on hiȝe with haþeleȝ þat myȝt;
Brachetes bayed þat best, as bidden þe maystereȝ

1580 and *upplied.* 1583 luslych *MS.*
1588 frekeȝ *MS.* 1595 ȝed ouer: ȝedoū *MS.*

Of þat chargeaunt chace þat were chef huntes.
Þenne a wyȝe þat watȝ wys vpon wodcrafteȝ
To vnlace þis bor lufly bigynneȝ.
Fyrst he hewes of his hed and on hiȝe setteȝ,
And syþen rendeȝ him al roghe bi þe rygge after,
Braydeȝ out þe boweles, brenneȝ hom on glede,
With bred blent þerwith his braches rewardeȝ.
Syþen he britneȝ out þe brawen in bryȝt brode cheldeȝ,
And hatȝ out þe hastletteȝ, as hiȝtly bisemeȝ;
And ȝet hem halcheȝ al hole þe halueȝ togeder,
And syþen on a stif stange stoutly hem henges.
Now with þis ilk swyn þay swengen to home;
Þe bores hed watȝ borne bifore þe burnes seluen
Þat him forferde in þe forþe þurȝ forse of his honde so stronge.
    Til he seȝ Sir Gawayne
    In halle hym þoȝt ful longe;
    He calde, and he com gayn
    His feeȝ þer for to fonge.

Þe lorde ful lowde with lote—and laȝed myry
When he seȝe Sir Gawayn—with solace he spekeȝ;
Þe goude ladyeȝ were geten, and gedered þe meyny,
He scheweȝ hem þe scheldeȝ, and schapes hem þe tale
Of þe largesse and þe lenþe, þe liþerneȝ alse
Of þe were of þe wylde swyn in wod þer he fled.
Þat oþer knyȝt ful comly comended his dedeȝ,
And praysed hit as gret prys þat he proued hade,
For suche a brawne of a best, þe bolde burne sayde,
Ne such sydes of a swyn segh he neuer are.
Þenne hondeled þay þe hoge hed, þe hende mon hit praysed,
And let lodly þerat þe lorde for to here. f. 113a
'Now, Gawayn,' quoþ þe god mon, 'þis gomen is your awen

1624 Gawayn: G. *MS*

Bi fyn forwarde and faste, faythely ȝe knowe.'
'Hit is sothe,' quoþ þe segge, 'and as siker trwe
Alle my get I schal yow gif agayn, bi my trawþe.'
He hent þe haþel aboute þe halse, and hendely hym kysses,
And eftersones of þe same he serued hym þere.
'Now ar we euen,' quoþ þe haþel, 'in þis euentide
Of alle þe couenauntes þat we knyt, syþen I com hider, bi lawe.'
Þe lorde sayde, 'Bi saynt Gile,
Ȝe ar þe best þat I knowe!
Ȝe ben ryche in a whyle,
Such chaffer and ȝe drowe.'

Þenne þay teldet tableȝ trestes alofte,
Kesten cloþeȝ vpon; clere lyȝt þenne
Wakned bi woȝeȝ, waxen torches;
Seggeȝ sette and serued in sale al aboute;
Much glam and gle glent vp þerinne
Aboute þe fyre vpon flet, and on fele wyse
At þe soper and after, mony aþel songeȝ,
As coundutes of Krystmasse and caroleȝ newe
With al þe manerly merþe þat mon may of telle,
And euer oure luflych knyȝt þe lady bisyde.
Such semblaunt to þat segge semly ho made
Wyth stille stollen countenaunce, þat stalworth to plese,
Þat al forwondered watȝ þe wyȝe, and wroth with himseluen,
Bot he nolde not for his nurture nurne hir aȝayneȝ,
Bot dalt with hir al in daynté, how-se-euer þe dede turned towrast.
Quen þay hade played in halle
As longe as hor wylle hom last,
To chambre he con hym calle,
And to þe chemné þay past.

1639 hent *supplied.*

Ande þer þay dronken, and dalten, and demed eft nwe
To norne on þe same note on Nwe Ȝereȝ euen;
Bot þe knyȝt craued leue to kayre on þe morn,
For hit watȝ neȝ at þe terme þat he to schulde.
Þe lorde hym letted of þat, to lenge hym resteyed, f. 113b
And sayde, 'As I am trwe segge, I siker my trawþe
Þou schal cheue to þe grene chapel þy charres to make,
Leude, on Nw Ȝereȝ lyȝt, longe bifore pryme.
Forþy þow lye in þy loft and lach þyn ese,
And I schal hunt in þis holt, and halde þe towcheȝ,
Chaunge wyth þe cheuisaunce, bi þat I charre hider;
For I haf fraysted þe twys, and faythful I fynde þe.
Now "þrid tyme þrowe best" þenk on þe morne,
Make we mery quyl we may and mynne vpon joye,
For þe lur may mon lach when-so mon lykeȝ.'
Þis watȝ grayþely graunted, and Gawayn is lenged,
Bliþe broȝt watȝ hym drynk, and þay to bedde ȝeden
    with liȝt.
  Sir Gawayn lis and slepes
  Ful stille and softe al niȝt;
  Þe lorde þat his crafteȝ kepes,
  Ful erly he watȝ diȝt.

After messe a morsel he and his men token;
Miry watȝ þe mornyng, his mounture he askes.
Alle þe haþeles þat on horse schulde helden hym after
Were boun busked on hor blonkkeȝ bifore þe halle ȝateȝ.
Ferly fayre watȝ þe folde, for þe forst clenged;
In rede rudede vpon rak rises þe sunne,
And ful clere costeȝ þe clowdes of þe welkyn.
Hunteres vnhardeled bi a holt syde,
Rocheres roungen bi rys for rurde of her hornes;
Summe fel in þe fute þer þe fox bade,
Trayleȝ ofte a traueres bi traunt of her wyles;

1686 Gawayn: G. *MS.* 1690 nnorsel *MS.*
1693 bi forere *MS.* 1700 trayt*e*res *MS.*

A kenet kryes þerof, þe hunt on hym calles ;
His felaȝes fallen hym to, þat ſnasted ful þike,
Runnen forth in a rabel in his ryȝt fare,
And he fyskeȝ hem byfore ; þay founden hym sone,
And quen þay seghe hym with syȝt þay sued hym
fast,
Wreȝande hym ful weterly with a wroth noyse ;
And he trantes and tornayeeȝ þurȝ mony tene greue,
Hauilouneȝ, and herkeneȝ bi heggeȝ ful ofte.
At þe last bi a littel dich he lepeȝ ouer a spenné, f. 114[a]
Steleȝ out ful stilly bi a strothe rande,
Went haf wylt of þe wode with wyleȝ fro þe houndes ;
þenne watȝ he went, er he wyst, to a wale tryster,
þer þre þro at a þrich þrat hym at ones,
al graye.
He blenched aȝayn bilyue
And stifly start on-stray,
With alle þe wo on lyue
To þe wod he went away.

Thenne watȝ hit lif vpon list to lyþen þe houndeȝ,
When alle þe mute hade hym met, menged togeder :
Suche a sorȝe at þat syȝt þay sette on his hede
As alle þe clamberande clyffes hade clatered on hepes ;
Here he watȝ halawed, when haþeleȝ hym metten,
Loude he watȝ ȝayned with ȝarande speche ;
þer he watȝ þreted and ofte þef called,
And ay þe titleres at his tayl, þat tary he ne myȝt ;
Ofte he watȝ runnen at, when he out rayked,
And ofte reled in aȝayn, so Reniarde watȝ wylé.
And ȝe he lad hem bi lagmon, þe lorde and his meyny,
On þis maner bi þe mountes quyle myd-ouer-vnder,
Whyle þe hende knyȝt at home holsumly slepeȝ
Withinne þe comly cortynes, on þe colde morne.

1706 hym : ym *illegible* ; weterly : w *from offset, first* e *illegible*.
1712 to to *MS.*

Bot þe lady for luf let not to slepe,
Ne þe purpose to payre þat pyȝt in hir hert,
Bot ros hir vp radly, rayked hir þeder
In a mery mantyle, mete to þe erþe,
Þat watȝ furred ful fyne with felleȝ wel pured,
No hweȝ goud on hir hede bot þe haȝer stones
Trased aboute hir tressour be twenty in clusteres;
Hir þryuen face and hir þrote þrowen al naked,
Hir brest bare bifore, and bihinde eke.
Ho comeȝ withinne þe chambre dore, and closes hit hir after,
Wayueȝ vp a wyndow, and on þe wyȝe calleȝ,
And radly þus rehayted hym with hir riche wordeȝ,
with chere:
'A! mon, how may þou slepe,
Þis morning is so clere?' f. 114b
He watȝ in drowping depe,
Bot þenne he con hir here.

In dreȝ droupyng of dreme draueled þat noble,
As mon þat watȝ in mornyng of mony þro þoȝtes,
How þat destiné schulde þat day dele hym his wyrde
At þe grene chapel, when he þe gome metes,
And bihoues his buffet abide withoute debate more;
Bot quen þat comly com he keuered his wyttes,
Swenges out of þe sweuenes, and swareȝ with hast.
Þe lady luflych com laȝande swete,
Felle ouer his fayre face, and fetly hym kyssed;
He welcumeȝ hir worþily with a wale chere.
He seȝ hir so glorious and gayly atyred,
So fautles of hir fetures and of so fyne hewes,
Wiȝt wallande joye warmed his hert.
With smoþe smylyng and smolt þay smeten into merþe,
Þat al watȝ blis and bonchef þat breke hem bitwene,
and wynne.

1752 dele hym *supplied*. 1755 com *supplied*.

þay lanced wordes gode,
Much wele þen watȝ þerinne;
Gret perile bitwene hem stod,
Nif Maré of hir knyȝt mynne.

For þat pryncece of pris depresed hym so þikke,
Nurned hym so neȝe þe þred, þat nede hym bihoued
Oþer lach þer hir luf, oþer lodly refuse.
He cared for his cortaysye, lest craþayn he were,
And more for his meschef, ȝif he schulde make synne,
And be traytor to þat tolke þat þat telde aȝt.
'God schylde,' quoþ þe schalk, 'þat schal not befalle!'
With luf-laȝyng a lyt he layd hym bysyde
Alle þe specheȝ of specialté þat sprange of her mouthe.
Quoþ þat burde to þat burne, 'Blame ȝe disserue,
Ȝif ȝe luf not þat lyf þat ȝe lye nexte,
Bifore alle þe wyȝeȝ in þe worlde wounded in hert,
Bot if ȝe haf a lemman, a leuer, þat yow lykeȝ better,
And folden fayth to þat fre, festned so harde
Þat yow lausen ne lyst—and þat I leue nouþe; f. 115[a]
And þat ȝe telle me þat now trwly, I pray yow,
For alle þe lufeȝ vpon lyue layne not þe soþe
for gile.'
Þe knyȝt sayde, 'Be sayn Jon,'
And smeþely con he smyle,
'In fayth I welde riȝt non,
Ne non wil welde þe quile.'

'Þat is a worde' quoþ þat wyȝt, 'þat worst is of alle,
Bot I am swared for soþe, þat sore me þinkkeȝ.
Kysse me now comly, and I schal cach heþen,
I may bot mourne vpon molde, as may þat much louyes.'
Sykande ho sweȝe doun and semly hym kyssed,
And siþen ho seueres hym fro, and says as ho stondes,
'Now, dere, at þis departyng do me þis ese,
Gif me sumquat of þy gifte, þi gloue if hit were,

1770 prynce *MS.*   1799 if: of *MS.*

Þat I may mynne on þe, mon, my mournyng to lassen.'
'Now iwysse,' quoþ þat wyȝe, 'I wolde I hade here
Þe leuest þing for þy luf þat I in londe welde,
For ȝe haf deserued, for soþe, sellyly ofte
More rewarde bi resoun þen I reche myȝt;
Bot to dele yow for druryе, þat dawed bot neked,
Hit is not your honour to haf at þis tyme
A gloue for a garysoun of Gawayneȝ gifteȝ,
And I am here an erande in erdeȝ vncouþe,
And haue no men wyth no maleȝ with menskful þingeȝ;
Þat mislykeȝ me, ladé, for luf at þis tyme,
Iche tolke mon do as he is tan, tas to non ille
ne pine.'
'Nay, hende of hyȝe honours,'
Quoþ þat lufsum vnder lyne,
'Þaȝ I hade noȝt of toureȝ,
Ȝet schulde ȝe haue of myne.'

Ho raȝt hym a riche rynk of red golde werkeȝ,
Wyth a starande ston stondande alofte
Þat bere blusschande bemeȝ as þe bryȝt sunne;
Wyt ȝe wel, hit watȝ worth wele ful hoge.
Bot þe renk hit renayed, and redyly he sayde,
'I wil no gifteȝ for gode, my gay, at þis tyme; f. 115[b]
I haf none yow to norne, ne noȝt wyl I take.'
Ho bede hit hym ful bysily, and he hir bode wernes,
And swere swyfte by his sothe þat he hit sese nolde,
And ho soré þat he forsoke, and sayde þerafter,
'If ȝe renay my rynk, to ryche for hit semeȝ,
Ȝe wolde not so hyȝly halden be to me,
I schal gif yow my girdel, þat gaynes yow lasse.'
Ho laȝt a lace lyȝtly þat leke vmbe hir sydeȝ,
Knit vpon hir kyrtel vnder þe clere mantyle,
Gered hit watȝ with grene sylke and with golde schaped,

1810 tyne *MS.* 1815 oȝt *MS.*
1825 swyfte by: swyftel *MS.* 1830 þat þat *MS.*

Noȝt bot arounde brayden, beten with fyngreȝ ;
And þat ho bede to þe burne, and blyþely bisoȝt,
Þaȝ hit vnworþi were, þat he hit take wolde.
And he nay þat he nolde neghe in no wyse
Nauþer golde ne garysoun, er God hym grace sende
To acheue to þe chaunce þat he hade chosen þere.
'And þerfore, I pray yow, displese yow noȝt,
And letteȝ be your bisinesse, for I bayþe hit yow neuer to graunte ;
I am derely to yow biholde
Bicause of your sembelaunt,
And euer in hot and colde
To be your trwe seruaunt.'

'Now forsake ȝe þis silke,' sayde þe burde þenne,
'For hit is symple in hitself? And so hit wel semeȝ.
Lo ! so hit is littel, and lasse hit is worþy ;
Bot who-so knew þe costes þat knit ar þerinne,
He wolde hit prayse at more prys, parauenture ;
For quat gome so is gorde with þis grene lace,
While he hit hade hemely halched aboute,
Þer is no haþel vnder heuen tohewe hym þat myȝt,
For he myȝt not be slayn for slyȝt vpon erþe.'
Þen kest þe knyȝt, and hit come to his hert,
Hit were a juel for þe jopardé þat hym iugged were,
When he acheued to þe chapel his chek for to fech ;
Myȝt he haf slypped to be vnslayn, þe sleȝt were noble.
Þenne he þulged with hir þrepe and þoled hir to speke, f. 116a
And ho bere on hym þe belt and bede hit hym swyþe—
And he granted—and hym gafe with a goud wylle,
And bisoȝt hym, for hir sake, disceuer hit neuer,
Bot to lelly layne fro hir lorde ; þe leude hym acordeȝ
Þat neuer wyȝe schulde hit wyt, iwysse, bot þay twayne for noȝte ;

1858 myȝ *MS.* 1863 fro : for *MS.*

He þonkked hir oft ful swyþe,
Ful þro with hert and þoȝt.
Bi þat on þrynne syþe
Ho hatȝ kyst þe knyȝt so toȝt.

Thenne lachcheȝ ho hir leue, and leueȝ hym þere,
For more myrþe of þat mon moȝt ho not gete.
When ho watȝ gon, Sir Gawayn gereȝ hym sone,
Rises and riches hym in araye noble,
Lays vp þe luf-lace þe lady hym raȝt,
Hid hit ful holdely, þer he hit eft fonde.
Syþen cheuely to þe chapel choses he þe waye,
Preuély aproched to a prest, and prayed hym þere
Þat he wolde lyfte his lyf and lern hym better
How his sawle schulde be saued when he schuld seye
heþen.
Þere he schrof hym schyrly and schewed his mysdedeȝ,
Of þe more and þe mynne, and merci beseccheȝ,
And of absolucioun he on þe segge calles;
And he asoyled hym surely, and sette hym so clene
As domeȝday schulde haf ben diȝt on þe morn.
And syþen he mace hym as mery among þe fre ladyes,
With comlych caroles and alle kynnes ioye,
As neuer he did bot þat daye, to þe derk nyȝt,
with blys.
Vche mon hade daynté þare
Of hym, and sayde, 'Iwysse,
Þus myry he watȝ neuer are,
Syn he com hider, er þis.'

Now hym lenge in þat lee, þer luf hym bityde!
Ȝet is þe lorde on þe launde ledande his gomnes.
He hatȝ forfaren þis fox þat he folȝed longe;
As he sprent ouer a spenné to spye þe schrewe,
Þer as he herd þe howndes þat hasted hym swyþe, f. 116b

1872 ho: he *MS.*; Gawayn: G. *MS.*

Renaud com richchande þurȝ a roȝe greue,
And alle þe rabel in a res ryȝt at his heleȝ.
Þe wyȝe watȝ war of þe wylde, and warly abides,
And braydeȝ out þe bryȝt bronde, and at þe best casteȝ.
And he schunt for þe scharp, and schulde haf arered;
A rach rapes hym to, ryȝt er he myȝt,
And ryȝt bifore þe hors fete þay fel on hym alle,
And woried me þis wyly wyth a wroth noyse.
Þe lorde lyȝteȝ bilyue, and lacheȝ hym sone,
Rased hym ful radly out of þe rach mouþes,
Haldeȝ heȝe ouer his hede, haloweȝ faste,
And þer bayen hym mony braþ houndeȝ.
Huntes hyȝed hem þeder with horneȝ ful mony,
Ay rechatande aryȝt til þay þe renk seȝen.
Bi þat watȝ comen his compeyny noble,
Alle þat euer ber bugle blowed at ones,
And alle þise oþer halowed þat hade no hornes;
Hit watȝ þe myriest mute þat euer men herde,
Þe rich rurd þat þer watȝ raysed for Renaude saule
with lote.
Hor houndeȝ þay þer rewarde,
Her hedeȝ þay fawne and frote,
And syþen þay tan Reynarde,
And tyruen of his cote.

And þenne þay helden to home, for hit watȝ nieȝ nyȝt,
Strakande ful stoutly in hor store horneȝ.
Þe lorde is lyȝt at þe laste at hys lef home,
Fyndeȝ fire vpon flet, þe freke þer-byside,
Sir Gawayn þe gode, þat glad watȝ withalle,
Among þe ladies for luf he ladde much ioye;
He were a bleaunt of blwe þat bradde to þe erþe,
His surkot semed hym wel þat softe watȝ forred,
And his hode of þat ilke henged on his schulder,
Blande al of blaunner were boþe al aboute.

1906 lacheȝ: cacheȝ *MS.*; hym: by *MS.* 1909 bray *MS.*
1919 Her her *MS.*

He meteȝ me þis god mon inmyddeȝ þe flore,
And al with gomen he hym gret, and goudly he sayde,
'I schal fylle vpon fyrst oure forwardeȝ nouþe,
Þat we spedly han spoken, þer spared watȝ no drynk.' f. 117a
Þen acoles he þe knyȝt and kysses hym þryes,
As sauerly and sadly as he hem sette couþe.
'Bi Kryst,' quoþ þat oþer knyȝt, 'Ȝe cach much sele
In cheuisaunce of þis chaffer, ȝif ȝe hade goud chepeȝ.'
'Ȝe, of þe chepe no charg,' quoþ chefly þat oþer,
'As is pertly payed þe chepeȝ þat I aȝte.'
'Mary,' quoþ þat oþer mon, 'myn is bihynde,
For I haf hunted al þis day, and noȝt haf I geten
Bot þis foule fox felle—þe fende haf þe godeȝ!—
And þat is ful pore for to pay for suche prys þinges
As ȝe haf þryȝt me here þro, suche þre cosses so gode.'
'Inoȝ,' quoþ Sir Gawayn,
'I þonk yow, bi þe rode,'
And how þe fox watȝ slayn
He tolde hym as þay stode.

With merþe and mynstralsye, wyth meteȝ at hor wylle,
Þay maden as mery as any men moȝten—
With laȝyng of ladies, with loteȝ of bordes
Gawayn and þe gode mon so glad were þay boþe—
Bot if þe douthe had doted, oþer dronken ben oþer.
Boþe þe mon and þe meyny maden mony iapeȝ,
Til þe sesoun watȝ seȝen þat þay seuer moste;
Burneȝ to hor bedde behoued at þe laste.
Þenne loȝly his leue at þe lorde fyrst
Fochcheȝ þis fre mon, and fayre he hym þonkkeȝ:
'Of such a selly soiorne as I haf hade here,
Your honour at þis hyȝe fest, þe hyȝe kyng yow ȝelde!
I ȝef yow me for on of youreȝ, if yowreself lykeȝ,
For I mot nedes, as ȝe wot, meue to-morne,

1936 þe *supplied*. 1962 sellyly *MS*.

And ȝe me take sum tolke to teche, as ȝe hyȝt,
Þe gate to þe grene chapel, as God wyl me suffer
To dele on Nw Ȝereȝ day þe dome of my wyrdes.'
'In god fayþe,' quoþ þe god mon, 'wyth a goud wylle
Al þat euer I yow hyȝt halde schal I redé.'
Þer asyngnes he a seruaunt to sett hym in þe waye,
And coundue hym by þe douneȝ, þat he no drechch
had, f. 117b
For to ferk þurȝ þe fryth and fare at þe gaynest
bi greue.
Þe lorde Gawayn con þonk,
Such worchip he wolde hym weue.
Þen at þo ladyeȝ wlonk
Þe knyȝt hatȝ tan his leue.

With care and wyth kyssyng he carppeȝ hem tille,
And fele þryuande þonkkeȝ he þrat hom to haue,
And þay ȝelden hym aȝayn ȝeply þat ilk;
Þay bikende hym to Kryst with ful colde sykyngeȝ.
Syþen fro þe meyny he menskly departes;
Vche mon þat he mette, he made hem a þonke
For his seruyse and his solace and his sere pyne,
Þat þay wyth busynes had ben aboute hym to serue;
And vche segge as soré to seuer with hym þere
As þay hade wonde worþyly with þat wlonk euer.
Þen with ledes and lyȝt he watȝ ladde to his chambre
And blyþely broȝt to his bedde to be at his rest.
Ȝif he ne slepe soundyly, say ne dar I,
For he hade muche on þe morn to mynne, ȝif he wolde,
in þoȝt.
Let hym lyȝe þere stille,
He hatȝ nere þat he soȝt;
And ȝe wyl a whyle be stylle
I schal telle yow how þay wroȝt.

1973 frk *MS.* 1981 aȝay *MS.*

IV

NOW neȝeȝ þe Nw Ȝere, and þe nyȝt passeȝ,
Þe day dryueȝ to þe derk, as dryȝtyn biddeȝ;
Bot wylde wedereȝ of þe worlde wakned þeroute,
Clowdes kesten kenly þe colde to þe erþe,
Wyth nyȝe innoghe of þe norþe, þe naked to tene;
Þe snawe snitered ful snart, þat snayped þe wylde;
Þe werbelande wynde wapped fro þe hyȝe,
And drof vche dale ful of dryftes ful grete.
Þe leude lystened ful wel þat leȝ in his bedde,
Þaȝ he lowkeȝ his liddeȝ, ful lyttel he slepes;
Bi vch kok þat crue he knwe wel þe steuen.
Deliuerly he dressed vp, er þe day sprenged, f. 118ª
For þere watȝ lyȝt of a laumpe þat lemed in his chambre;
He called to his chamberlayn, þat cofly him swared,
And bede hym bryng hym his bruny and his blonk sadel;
Þat oþer ferkeȝ hym vp and feccheȝ hym his wedeȝ,
And grayþeȝ me Sir Gawayn vpon a grett wyse.
Fyrst he clad hym in his cloþeȝ þe colde for to were,
And syþen his oþer harnays, þat holdely watȝ keped,
Boþe his paunce and his plateȝ, piked ful clene,
Þe ryngeȝ rokked of þe roust of his riche bruny;
And al watȝ fresch as vpon fyrst, and he watȝ fayn þenne to þonk;
He hadde vpon vche pece,
Wypped ful wel and wlonk;
Þe gayest into Grece,
Þe burne bede bryng his blonk.

Whyle þe wlonkest wedes he warp on hymseluen—
His cote wyth þe conysaunce of þe clere werkeȝ
Ennurned vpon veluet, vertuus stoneȝ
Aboute beten and bounden, enbrauded semeȝ,

2010 laupe *MS.* 2027 vertuus *MS.*

And fayre furred withinne wyth fayre pelures—
Ȝet laft he not þe lace, þe ladieȝ gifte,
Þat forgat not Gawayn for gode of hymseluen.
Bi he hade belted þe bronde vpon his balȝe hauncheȝ,
Þenn dressed he his drurye double hym aboute,
Swyþe sweþled vmbe his swange swetely þat knyȝt
Þe gordel of þe grene silke, þat gay wel bisemed,
Vpon þat ryol red cloþe þat ryche watȝ to schewe.
Bot wered not þis ilk wyȝe for wele þis gordel,
For pryde of þe pendaunteȝ, þaȝ polyst þay were,
And þaȝ þe glyterande golde glent vpon endeȝ,
Bot for to sauen hymself, when suffer hym byhoued,
To byde bale withoute dabate of bronde hym to were
        oþer knyffe.
    Bi þat þe bolde mon boun
    Wynneȝ þeroute bilyue,
    Alle þe meyny of renoun
    He þonkkeȝ ofte ful ryue.

Thenne watȝ Gryngolet grayþe, þat gret watȝ and
        huge, f. 118b
And hade ben soiourned sauerly and in a siker wyse,
Hym lyst prik for poynt, þat proude hors þenne.
Þe wyȝe wynneȝ hym to and wyteȝ on his lyre,
And sayde soberly hymself and by his soth swereȝ:
'Here is a meyny in þis mote þat on menske þenkkeȝ,
Þe mon hem maynteines, ioy mot þay haue;
Þe leue lady on lyue, luf hir bityde;
Ȝif þay for charyté cherysen a gest,
And halden honour in her honde, þe haþel hem ȝelde
Þat haldeȝ þe heuen vpon hyȝe, and also yow alle!
And ȝif I myȝt lyf vpon londe lede any quyle,
I schuld rech yow sum rewarde redyly, if I myȝt.'
Þenn steppeȝ he into stirop and stydeȝ alofte;
His schalk schewed hym his schelde, on schulder he
        hit laȝt,

Gordeȝ to Gryngolet with his gilt heleȝ,
And he starteȝ on þe ston, stod he no lenger
    to praunce.
  His haþel on hors watȝ þenne,
  Þat bere his spere and launce.
  'Þis kastel to Kryst I kenne':
  He gef hit ay god chaunce.

The brygge watȝ brayde doun, and þe brode ȝateȝ
Vnbarred and born open vpon boþe halue.
Þe burne blessed hym bilyue, and þe bredeȝ passed—
Prayses þe porter bifore þe prynce kneled,
Gef hym God and goud day, þat Gawayn he saue—
And went on his way with his wyȝe one,
Þat schulde teche hym to tourne to þat tene place
Þer þe ruful race he schulde resayue.
Þay boȝen bi bonkkeȝ þer boȝeȝ ar bare,
Þay clomben bi clyffeȝ þer clengeȝ þe colde.
Þe heuen watȝ vp halt, bot vgly þer-vnder;
Mist muged on þe mor, malt on þe mounteȝ,
Vch hille hade a hatte, a myst-hakel huge.
Brokeȝ byled and breke bi bonkkeȝ aboute,
Schyre schaterande on schoreȝ, þer þay doun schowued.
Wela wylle watȝ þe way þer þay bi wod schulden, f. 119[a]
Til hit watȝ sone sesoun þat þe sunne ryses
    þat tyde.
  Þay were on a hille ful hyȝe,
  Þe quyte snaw lay bisyde;
  Þe burne þat rod hym by
  Bede his mayster abide.

'For I haf wonnen yow hider, wyȝe, at þis tyme,
And now nar ȝe not fer fro þat note place
Þat ȝe han spied and spuryed so specially after;
Bot I schal say yow for soþe, syþen I yow knowe,
And ȝe ar a lede vpon lyue þat I wel louy,

Wolde ȝe worche bi my wytte, ȝe worþed þe better.
Þe place þat ȝe prece to ful perelous is halden,
Þer woneȝ a wyȝe in þat waste, þe worst vpon erþe,
For he is stiffe and sturne, and to strike louies,
And more is he þen any mon vpon myddelerde,
And his body bigger þen þe best fowre
Þat ar in Arþureȝ hous, Hestor, oþer oþer.
He cheueȝ þat chaunce at þe chapel grene,
Þer passes non bi þat place so proude in his armes
Þat he ne dyngeȝ hym to deþe with dynt of his honde;
For he is a mon methles, and mercy non vses,
For be hit chorle oþer chaplayn þat bi þe chapel rydes,
Monk oþer masseprest, oþer any mon elles,
Hym þynk as queme hym to quelle as quyk go hym-
seluen.
Forþy I say þe, as soþe as ȝe in sadel sitte,
Com ȝe þere, ȝe be kylled, may þe knyȝt rede,
Trawe ȝe me þat trewely, þaȝ ȝe had twenty lyues
to spende.
He hatȝ wonyd here ful ȝore,
On bent much baret bende,
Aȝayn his dynteȝ sore
Ȝe may not yow defende.

'Forþy, goude Sir Gawayn, let þe gome one,
And gotȝ away sum oþer gate, vpon Goddeȝ halue!
Cayreȝ bi sum oþer kyth, þer Kryst mot yow spede,
And I schal hyȝ me hom aȝayn, and hete yow fyrre
Þat I schal swere bi God and alle his gode halȝeȝ, f. 119b
As help me God and þe halydam, and oþeȝ innoghe,
Þat I schal lelly yow layne, and lance neuer tale
Þat euer ȝe fondet to fle for freke þat I wyst.'
'Grant merci,' quoþ Gawayn, and gruchyng he sayde:
'Wel worth þe, wyȝe, þat woldeȝ my gode,
And þat lelly me layne I leue wel þou woldeȝ.

2105 dy*nn*eȝ *MS.*

Bot helde þou hit neuer so holde, and I here passed,
Founded for ferde for to fle, in fourme þat þou telleȝ,
I were a knyȝt kowarde, I myȝt not be excused.
Bot I wyl to þe chapel, for chaunce þat may falle,
And talk wyth þat ilk tulk þe tale þat me lyste,
Worþe hit wele oþer wo, as þe wyrde lykeȝ
hit hafe.
Þaȝe he be a sturn knape
To stiȝtel, and stad with staue,
Ful wel con dryȝtyn schape
His seruaunteȝ for to saue.'

'Mary!' quoþ þat oþer mon, 'now þou so much spelleȝ,
Þat þou wylt þyn awen nye nyme to þyseluen,
And þe lyst lese þy lyf, þe lette I ne kepe.
Haf here þi helme on þy hede, þi spere in þi honde,
And ryde me doun þis ilk rake bi ȝon rokke syde,
Til þou be broȝt to þe boþem of þe brem valay;
Þenne loke a littel on þe launde, on þi lyfte honde,
And þou schal se in þat slade þe self chapel,
And þe borelych burne on bent þat hit kepeȝ.
Now fareȝ wel, on Godeȝ half, Gawayn þe noble!
For alle þe golde vpon grounde I nolde go wyth þe,
Ne bere þe felaȝschip þurȝ þis fryth on fote fyrre.'
Bi þat þe wyȝe in þe wod wendeȝ his brydel,
Hit þe hors with þe heleȝ as harde as he myȝt,
Lepeȝ hym ouer þe launde, and leueȝ þe knyȝt þere
al one.
'Bi Goddeȝ self,' quoþ Gawayn,
'I wyl nauþer grete ne grone;
To Goddeȝ wylle I am ful bayn,
And to hym I haf me tone.'

Thenne gyrdeȝ he to Gryngolet, and gedereȝ þe
rake, f. 120a

2131 mot *MS.* 2137 & & *MS.*

Schowueȝ in bi a schore at a schaȝe syde,
Rideȝ þurȝ þe roȝe bonk ryȝt to þe dale;
And þenne he wayted hym aboute, and wylde hit hym
þoȝt,
And seȝe no syngne of resette bisydeȝ nowhere,
Bot hyȝe bonkkeȝ and brent vpon boþe halue,
And ruȝe knokled knarreȝ with knorned stoneȝ;
þe skweȝ of þe scowtes skayned hym þoȝt.
þenne he houed, and wythhylde his hors at þat tyde,
And ofte chaunged his cher þe chapel to seche:
He seȝ non suche in no syde, and selly hym þoȝt
Sone, a lyttel on a launde, a lawe as hit were;
A balȝ berȝ bi a bonke þe brymme bysyde,
Bi a forȝ of a flode þat ferked þare;
þe borne blubred þerinne as hit boyled hade.
þe knyȝt kacheȝ his caple, and com to þe lawe,
Liȝteȝ doun luflyly, and at a lynde tacheȝ
þe rayne and his riche with a roȝe braunche.
þenne he boȝeȝ to þe berȝe, aboute hit he walkeȝ,
Debatande with hymself quat hit be myȝt.
Hit hade a hole on þe ende and on ayþer syde,
And ouergrowen with gresse in glodes aywhere,
And al watȝ holȝ inwith, nobot an olde caue,
Or a creuisse of an olde cragge, he couþe hit noȝt deme
with spelle.
'We! Lorde,' quoþ þe gentyle knyȝt,
'Wheþer þis be þe grene chapelle?
Here myȝt aboute mydnyȝt
þe dele his matynnes telle!

'Now iwysse,' quoþ Wowayn, 'wysty is here;
þis oritore is vgly, with erbeȝ ouergrowen;
Wel bisemeȝ þe wyȝe wruxled in grene

2171 were : we *MS.*
2178 þenne : þē. e; n *from offset.*
2179 debatande : *first* e *from offset.*
2180 Hit : h *from offset.*
2182 al *from offset.*
2187 Here : he *MS.*

Dele here his deuocioun on þe deueleȝ wyse.
Now I fele hit is þe fende, in my fyue wytteȝ,
Þat hatȝ stoken me þis steuen to strye me here.
Þis is a chapel of meschaunce, þat chekke hit bytyde!
Hit is þe corsedest kyrk þat euer I com inne!'
With heȝe helme on his hede, his launce in his
honde, f. 120[b]
He romeȝ vp to þe rokke of þo roȝ woneȝ.
Þene herde he of þat hyȝe hil, in a harde roche
Biȝonde þe broke, in a bonk, a wonder breme noyse.
Quat! hit clatered in þe clyff, as hit cleue schulde,
As one vpon a gryndelston hade grounden a syþe.
What! hit wharred and whette, as water at a mulne;
What! hit rusched and ronge, rawþe to here.
Þenne 'Bi Godde' quoþ Gawayn 'þat gere, as I trowe,
Is ryched at þe reuerence me, renk, to mete
bi rote.
Let God worche! "We loo"—
Hit helppeȝ me not a mote.
My lif þaȝ I forgoo,
Drede dotȝ me no lote.'

Thenne þe knyȝt con calle ful hyȝe:
'Who stiȝtleȝ in þis sted me steuen to holde?
For now is gode Gawayn goande ryȝt here.
If any wyȝe oȝt wyl, wynne hider fast,
Oþer now oþer neuer, his nedeȝ to spede.'
'Abyde', quoþ on on þe bonke abouen ouer his hede,
'And þou schal haf al in hast þat I þe hyȝt ones.'
Ȝet he rusched on þat rurde rapely a þrowe,
And wyth quettyng awharf, er he wolde lyȝt;
And syþen he keuereȝ bi a cragge, and comeȝ of a hole,
Whyrlande out of a wro wyth a felle weppen,
A deneȝ ax nwe dyȝt, þe dynt with to ȝelde,
With a borelych bytte bende by þe halme,
Fyled in a fylor, fowre fote large—

2205 as: at *MS.* 2223 with to: w[t]o *MS.*

Hit watȝ no lasse bi þat lace þat lemed ful bryȝt--
And þe gome in þe grene gered as fyrst,
Boþe þe lyre and þe leggeȝ, lokkeȝ and berde,
Saue þat fayre on his fote he foundeȝ on þe erþe,
Sette þe stele to þe stone, and stalked bysyde.
When he wan to þe watter, þer he wade nolde,
He hypped ouer on hys ax, and orpedly stryдeȝ,
Bremly broþe on a bent þat brode watȝ aboute,
on snawe.
Sir Gawayn þe knyȝt con mete, f. 121[a]
He ne lutte hym noþyng lowe;
Þat oþer sayde, 'Now, sir swete,
Of steuen mon may þe trowe'.

'Gawayn,' quoþ þat grene gome, 'God þe mot loke!
Iwysse þou art welcom, wyȝe, to my place,
And þou hatȝ tymed þi trauayl as truee mon schulde,
And þou knoweȝ þe couenaunteȝ kest vus bytwene:
At þis tyme twelmonyth þou toke þat þe falled,
And I schulde at þis Nwe Ȝere ȝeply þe quyte.
And we ar in þis valay verayly oure one;
Here ar no renkes vs to rydde, rele as vus likeȝ.
Haf þy helme of þy hede, and haf here þy pay.
Busk no more debate þen I þe bede þenne
When þou wypped of my hede at a wap one.'
'Nay, bi God,' quoþ Gawayn, 'þat me gost lante,
I schal gruch þe no grwe for grem þat falleȝ.
Bot styȝtel þe vpon on strok, and I schal stonde stylle
And warp þe no wernyng to worch as þe lykeȝ,
nowhare.'
He lened with þe nek, and lutte,
And schewed þat schyre al bare,
And lette as he noȝt dutte;
For drede he wolde not dare.

2240 welcon *MS.* 2247 Haf þy: haf þy þy *MS.*

Then þe gome in þe grene grayþed hym swyþe,
Gedereȝ vp hys grymme tole Gawayn to smyte;
With alle þe bur in his body he ber hit on lofte,
Munt as maȝtyly as marre hym he wolde;
Hade hit dryuen adoun as dreȝ as he atled,
Þer hade ben ded of his dynt þat doȝty watȝ euer.
Bot Gawayn on þat giserne glyfte hym bysyde,
As hit com glydande adoun on glode hym to schende,
And schranke a lytel with þe schulderes for þe scharp yrne.
Þat oþer schalk wyth a schunt þe schene wythhaldeȝ,
And þenne repreued he þe prynce with mony prowde wordeȝ:
'Þou art not Gawayn,' quoþ þe gome, 'þat is so goud halden,
Þat neuer arȝed for no here by hylle ne be vale,
And now þou fles for ferde er þou fele harmeȝ! f. 121b
Such cowardise of þat knyȝt cowþe I neuer here.
Nawþer fyked I ne flaȝe, freke, quen þou myntest,
Ne kest no kauelacion in kyngeȝ hous Arthor.
My hede flaȝ to my fote, and ȝet flaȝ I neuer;
And þou, er any harme hent, arȝeȝ in hert;
Wherfore þe better burne me burde be called þerfore.'
    Quoþ Gawayn, 'I schunt oneȝ,
    And so wyl I no more;
    Bot þaȝ my hede falle on þe stoneȝ,
    I con not hit restore.

Bot busk, burne, bi þi fayth, and bryng me to þe poynt.
Dele to me my destiné, and do hit out of honde,
For I schal stonde þe a strok, and start no more
Til þyn ax haue me hitte: haf here my trawþe.'
'Haf at þe þenne!' quoþ þat oþer, and heueȝ hit alofte,
And wayteȝ as wroþely as he wode were.

2280 q G: *MS.*

He myntez at hym maȝtyly, bot not þe mon ryuez,
Withhelde heterly his honde, er hit hurt myȝt.
Gawayn grayþely hit bydez, and glent with no membre,
Bot stode stylle as þe ston, oþer a stubbe auþer
Þat raþeled is in roché grounde with rotez a hundreth.
Þen muryly efte con he mele, þe mon in þe grene:
'So, now þou hatz þi hert holle, hitte me bihous.
Halde þe now þe hyȝe hode þat Arþur þe raȝt,
And kepe þy kanel at þis kest, ȝif hit keuer may.'
Gawayn ful gryndelly with greme þenne sayde:
'Wy! þresch on, þou þro mon, þou þretez to longe;
I hope þat þi hert arȝe wyth þyn awen seluen.'
'For soþe,' quoþ þat oþer freke, 'so felly þou spekez,
I wyl no lenger on lyte lette þin ernde
    riȝt nowe.'
  Þenne tas he hym stryþe to stryke,
  And frounsez boþe lyppe and browe;
  No meruayle þaȝ hym myslyke
  Þat hoped of no rescowe.

He lyftes lyȝtly his lome, and lette hit doun fayre
With þe barbe of þe bitte bi þe bare nek; f. 122a
Þaȝ he homered heterly, hurt hym no more,
Bot snyrt hym on þat on syde, þat seuered þe hyde.
Þe scharp schrank to þe flesche þurȝ þe schyre grece,
Þat þe schene blod ouer his schulderes schot to þe erþe;
And quen þe burne seȝ þe blode blenk on þe snawe,
He sprit forth spenne-fote more þen a spere lenþe,
Hent heterly his helme, and on his hed cast,
Schot with his schulderez his fayre schelde vnder,
Braydez out a bryȝt sworde, and bremely he spekez—
Neuer syn þat he watz burne borne of his moder
Watz he neuer in þis worlde wyȝe half so blyþe—
'Blynne, burne, of þy bur, bede me no mo!

2291 his: hs *MS.* 2299 Gawayn: G: *MS.*
2304 Riȝt *MS.* 2305 he he *MS.*

I haf a stroke in þis sted withoute stryf hent,
And if þow recheȝ me any mo, I redyly schal quyte,
And ȝelde ȝederly aȝayn—and þerto ȝe tryst—
and foo.
Bot on stroke here me falleȝ—
Þe couenaunt schop ryȝt so,
Fermed in Arþureȝ halleȝ—
And þerfore, hende, now hoo!'

The haþel heldet hym fro, and on his ax rested,
Sette þe schaft vpon schore, and to þe scharp lened,
And loked to þe leude þat on þe launde ȝede,
How þat doȝty, dredles, deruely þer stondeȝ
Armed, ful aȝleȝ: in hert hit hym lykeȝ.
Þenn he meleȝ muryly wyth a much steuen,
And wyth a rynkande rurde he to þe renk sayde:
'Bolde burne, on þis bent be not so gryndel.
No mon here vnmanerly þe mysboden habbeȝ,
Ne kyd, bot as couenaunde at kyngeȝ kort schaped.
I hyȝt þe a strok and þou hit hatȝ, halde þe wel payed;
I relece þe of þe remnaunt of ryȝtes alle oþer.
Iif I deliuer had bene, a boffet paraunter
I couþe wroþeloker haf waret, to þe haf wroȝt anger.
Fyrst I mansed þe muryly with a mynt one,
And roue þe wyth no rof sore, with ryȝt I þe profered
For þe forwarde þat we fest in þe fyrst nyȝt, f. 122[b]
And þou trystyly þe trawþe and trwly me haldeȝ,
Al þe gayne þow me gef, as god mon schulde.
Þat oþer munt for þe morne, mon, I þe profered,
Þou kyssedes my clere wyf—þe cosseȝ me raȝteȝ.
For boþe two here I þe bede bot two bare myntes
boute scaþe.
Trwe mon trwe restore,
Þenne þar mon drede no waþe.

2329 Fermed in, *illegible*: fern, *from offset*.
2337 rykande *MS.* 2339 habbe *MS.*
2344 anger: *doubtful*, ger *perhaps legible*.

At þe þrid þou fayled þore,
And þerfor þat tappe ta þe.

For hit is my wede þat þou wereȝ, þat ilke wouen girdel,
Myn owen wyf hit þe weued, I wot wel for soþe.
Now know I wel þy cosses, and þy costes als,
And þe wowyng of my wyf: I wroȝt hit myseluen.
I sende hir to asay þe, and sothly me þynkkeȝ
On þe fautlest freke þat euer on fote ȝede;
As perle bi þe quite pese is of prys more,
So is Gawayn, in god fayth, bi oþer gay knyȝteȝ.
Bot here yow lakked a lyttel, sir, and lewte yow wonted;
Bot þat watȝ for no wylyde werke, ne wowyng nauþer,
Bot for ȝe lufed your lyf; þe lasse I yow blame.'
Þat oþer stif mon in study stod a gret whyle,
So agreued for greme he gryed withinne;
Alle þe blode of his brest blende in his face,
Þat al he schrank for schome þat þe schalk talked.
Þe forme worde vpon folde þat þe freke meled:
'Corsed worth cowarddyse and couetyse boþe!
In yow is vylany and vyse þat vertue disstryeȝ.'
Þenne he kaȝt to þe knot, and þe kest lawseȝ,
Brayde broþely þe belt to þe burne seluen:
'Lo! þer þe falssyng, foule mot hit falle!
For care of þy knokke cowardyse me taȝt
To acorde me with couetyse, my kynde to forsake,
Þat is larges and lewte þat longeȝ to knyȝteȝ.
Now I am fawty and falce, and ferde haf ben euer
Of trecherye and vntrawþe: boþe bityde sorȝe and care!
I biknowe yow, knyȝt, here stylle, f. 123a
Al fawty is my fare;
Leteȝ me ouertake your wylle
And efte I schal be ware.'

2385 biknowe; *catchword* I beknowe.

Thenn loȝe þat oþer leude and luflyly sayde:
'I halde hit hardily hole, þe harme þat I hade.
Þou art confessed so clene, beknowen of þy mysses,
And hatȝ þe penaunce apert of þe poynt of myn egge,
I halde þe polysed of þat plyȝt, and pured as clene
As þou hadeȝ neuer forfeted syþen þou watȝ fyrst borne;
And I gif þe, sir, þe gurdel þat is golde-hemmed,
For hit is grene as my goune. Sir Gawayn, ȝe maye
Þenk vpon þis ilke þrepe, þer þou forth þryngeȝ
Among prynces of prys, and þis a pure token
Of þe chaunce of þe grene chapel at cheualrous knyȝteȝ.
And ȝe schal in þis Nwe Ȝer aȝayn to my woneȝ,
And we schyn reuel þe remnaunt of þis ryche fest
ful bene.'
Þer laþed hym fast þe lorde
And sayde: 'With my wyf, I wene,
We schal yow wel acorde,
Þat watȝ your enmy kene.'

'Nay, for soþe,' quoþ þe segge, and sesed hys helme,
And hatȝ hit of hendely, and þe haþel þonkkeȝ,
'I haf soiorned sadly; sele yow bytyde,
And he ȝelde hit yow ȝare þat ȝarkkeȝ al menskes!
And comaundeȝ me to þat cortays, your comlych fere,
Boþe þat on and þat oþer, myn honoured ladyeȝ,
Þat þus hor knyȝt wyth hor kest han koyntly bigyled.
Bot hit is no ferly þaȝ a fole madde,
And þurȝ wyles of wymmen be wonen to sorȝe,
For so watȝ Adam in erde with one bygyled,
And Salamon with fele sere, and Samson eftsoneȝ—
Dalyda dalt hym hys wyrde—and Dauyth þerafter
Watȝ blended with Barsabe, þat much bale þoled.
Now þese were wrathed wyth her wyles, hit were a
wynne huge

2390 hardilyly *MS.* 2396 Sir G: *MS.*

To luf hom wel, and leue hem not, a leude þat couþe.
For þes wer forne þe freest, þat folȝed alle þe sele f. 123b
Exellently of alle þyse oþer, vnder heuenryche
þat mused;
And alle þay were biwyled
With wymmen þat þay vsed.
Þaȝ I be now bigyled,
Me þink me burde be excused.

'Bot your gordel' quoþ Gawayn 'God yow forȝelde!
Þat wyl I welde wyth good wylle, not for þe wynne
golde,
Ne þe saynt, ne þe sylk, ne þe syde pendaundes,
For wele ne for worchyp, ne for þe wlonk werkkeȝ,
Bot in syngne of my surfet I schal se hit ofte,
When I ride in renoun, remorde to myseluen
Þe faut and þe fayntyse of þe flesche crabbed,
How tender hit is to entyse teches of fylþe;
And þus, quen pryde schal me pryk for prowes of armes,
Þe loke to þis luf-lace schal leþe my hert.
Bot on I wolde yow pray, displeses yow neuer:
Syn ȝe be lorde of þe ȝonde londe þer I haf lent inne
Wyth yow wyth worschyp—þe wyȝe hit yow ȝelde
Þat vphaldeȝ þe heuen and on hyȝ sitteȝ—
How norne ȝe yowre ryȝt nome, and þenne no more?'
'Þat schal I telle þe trwly,' quoþ þat oþer þenne,
'Bercilak de Hautdesert I hat in þis londe.
Þurȝ myȝt of Morgne la Faye, þat in my hous lenges,
And koyntyse of clergye, bi craftes wel lerned—
Þe maystrés of Merlyn mony ho hatȝ taken;
For ho hatȝ dalt drwry ful dere sumtyme
With þat conable klerk, þat knowes alle your knyȝteȝ
at hame;
Morgne þe goddes
Þerfore hit is hir name:

2426 With wyth *MS.* 2429 G: *MS.* 2448 hatȝ *supplied.*

Weldeȝ non so hyȝe hawtesse
Þat ho ne con make ful tame—

Ho wayned me vpon þis wyse to your wynne halle
For to assay þe surquidré, ȝif hit soth were
Þat rennes of þe grete renoun of þe Rounde Table;
Ho wayned me þis wonder your wytteȝ to reue,
For to haf greued Gaynour and gart hir to dyȝe f. 124a
With glopnyng of þat ilke gome þat gostlych speked
With his hede in his honde bifore þe hyȝe table.
Þat is ho þat is at home, þe auncian lady;
Ho is euen þyn aunt, Arþureȝ half-suster,
Þe duches doȝter of Tyntagelle, þat dere Vter after
Hade Arþur vpon, þat aþel is nowþe.
Þerfore I eþe þe, haþel, to com to þy naunt,
Make myry in my hous; my meny þe louies,
And I wol þe as wel, wyȝe, bi my faythe,
As any gome vnder God for þy grete trauþe.'
And he nikked hym naye, he nolde bi no wayes.
Þay acolen and kyssen and kennen ayþer oþer
To þe prynce of paradise, and parten ryȝt þere
on coolde;
Gawayn on blonk ful bene
To þe kyngeȝ burȝ buskeȝ bolde,
And þe knyȝt in þe enker grene
Whiderwarde-so-euer he wolde.

Wylde wayeȝ in þe worlde Wowen now rydeȝ
On Gryngolet, þat þe grace hade geten of his lyue;
Ofte he herbered in house and ofte al þeroute,
And mony aventure in vale, and venquyst ofte,
Þat I ne tyȝt at þis tyme in tale to remene.
Þe hurt watȝ hole þat he hade hent in his nek,
And þe blykkande belt he bere þeraboute
Abelef as a bauderyk bounden bi his syde,

2461 gopnyng, gomen *MS.*; speked *MS.*: *edd.* spekere.
2472 and kennen *supplied.*

Loken vnder his lyfte arme, þe lace, with a knot,
In tokenyng he watȝ tane in tech of a faute.
And þus he commes to þe court, knyȝt al in sounde.
Þer wakned wele in þat wone when wyst þe grete
Þat gode Gawayn watȝ commen; gayn hit hym þoȝt.
Þe kyng kysseȝ þe knyȝt, and þe whene alce,
And syþen mony syker knyȝt þat soȝt hym to haylce,
Of his fare þat hym frayned; and ferlyly he telles,
Biknoweȝ alle þe costes of care þat he hade,
Þe chaunce of þe chapel, þe chere of þe knyȝt,
Þe luf of þe ladi, þe lace at þe last. f. 124b
Þe nirt in þe nek he naked hem schewed
Þat he laȝt for his vnleute at þe leudes hondes
for blame.
He tened quen he schulde telle,
He groned for gref and grame;
Þe blod in his face con melle,
When he hit schulde schewe, for schame.

'Lo! lorde,' quoþ þe leude, and þe lace hondeled,
'Þis is þe bende of þis blame I bere in my nek,
Þis is þe laþe and þe losse þat I laȝt haue,
Of couardise and couetyse þat I haf caȝt þare;
Þis is þe token of vntrawþe þat I am tan inne,
And I mot nedeȝ hit were wyle I may last;
For non may hyden his harme, bot vnhap ne may hit,
For þer hit oneȝ is tachched twynne wil hit neuer.'
Þe kyng comforteȝ þe knyȝt, and alle þe court als
Laȝen loude þerat, and luflyly acorden
Þat lordes and ladis þat longed to þe Table,
Vche burne of þe broþerhede, a bauderyk schulde haue,
A bende abelef hym aboute of a bryȝt grene,
And þat, for sake of þat segge, in swete to were.
For þat watȝ acorded þe renoun of þe Rounde Table,
And he honoured þat hit hade euermore after,

2491 G: *MS.* 2506 in *supplied.*

As hit is breued in þe best boke of romaunce.
Þus in Arthurus day þis aunter bitidde,
Þe Brutus bokeȝ þerof beres wyttenesse;
Syþen Brutus, þe bolde burne, boȝed hider fyrst,
After þe segge and þe asaute watȝ sesed at Troye,
iwysse,
Mony auntereȝ here-biforne
Haf fallen suche er þis.
Now þat bere þe croun of þorne,
He bryng vus to his blysse! AMEN.

HONY SOYT QUI MAL PENCE.

NOTES

5 *Ennias*: Aeneas. According to a medieval tradition, which began with Dares Phrygius and Dictys Cretensis, the Greeks were enabled to take Troy by the treachery of Aeneas and Antenor. The reference to the trial of Aeneas shows that it was from Guido della Colonna's *Historia Destructionis Troiae* (which is based ultimately on Dares and Dictys) that the author of *Sir Gawayn* derived this tradition. Aeneas was tried for treachery by the Greeks, not by the Trojans, because he had concealed from them Polyxena, through whom Achilles lost his life. 'Greci vero contra Eneam eorum assercionibus impingebant ipsum contra eos s[c]ilicet fregisse fidem rupto sui vinculo iuramenti, ex quo quod Polixenam celaverat ream mortis, cuius occasione magnus Achilles extiterat interfectus. Et ideo communicato consilio Enee exilium indixerunt, ut perpetuo relegaretur a Troia.'—Guido, ed. Strassburg, 1499. See also the English translation of Guido into alliterative verse, *The Gest Historiale of the Destruction of Troy* 12301 ff. Dares merely has: 'Agamemnon iratus Aeneae quod Polyxenam absconderat, cum suis protinus patria excedere iubet. Aeneas cum suis omnibus navibus proficiscitur.'

6 *West Iles*: possibly a reference to the traditional 'three islands of Britain and the three islands adjacent' (teir ynys Prydein ac their rac-ynys, *Kulhwch and Olwen*, 110); defined as Wight, Man, and the Orkneys (Nennius, ch. ii; Welsh Triad, 67).

11 *Ticius*: it is not known who he was. Madden suggests that 'unless Ticius here is a mistake altogether for Antenor, the name may possibly have been derived from Titus Tatius, king of the Sabines, and afterwards colleague of Romulus at Rome'. The parallel of Langaberde suggests that Ticius may be another fictitious descendant of Aeneas, invented to be the eponymous founder of Tuscany.

12 *Langaberde*: the legendary ancestor of the Langobardi or Lombards. He is mentioned as such by Nennius, and represented as the great-grandson of Japhet, and nephew of Brutus the founder of Britain.

13 *Felix Brutus*: according to medieval legend Brutus was grandson of Aeneas and founder of Britain. No other instance of the name Felix being given him is known. It is not likely to be an invention for the sake of alliteration, as the poet could easily have found a suitable English epithet beginning with *f*. His story is first told by Nennius,

who calls him also Bryto (some MSS. Britus): this name probably represents old British *Britto*, 'a Briton'. Nennius says he has heard also of another tradition which makes him the son of Hisicion, who was not of Trojan descent. It looks as if there had been a British tradition of an eponymous founder named Britto, later latinized into Brutus so that descent from the Trojans could be claimed. The Welsh tradition that Britain (Prydein in Welsh) was so called after its conquest by Prydein ab Aedd Mawr may be a reminiscence of the earlier legend.

25 *Bretaygne*: gen. case without ending. This is the Old French form of the name, derived from Latin 'Brittannia'. The original Celtic name was **Pritania*, which is represented to-day by Welsh *Prydain*. Forms with double *t* arose under the influence of *Britto* 'a Briton'. The alternation of *P* and *B* is difficult, but see Morris Jones's *Welsh Grammar*, pp. 5, 157.

26 *Arthur*: the name is direct from Welsh, whereas most of the Arthurian names found in Middle English are derived from Old French sources, though they may be ultimately of Celtic origin. But Arthur in Old French is called *Artu* (nom. *Artus*.) According to some it is a name of Celtic origin, and in a tenth century gloss on Nennius it is interpreted 'ursus horribilis' or 'malleus ferreus', as though it were composed of Welsh elements; but it is just as likely that *Arthur* is a Welsh form of Latin *Artorius*. He is represented by Nennius not as a king, but as *dux bellorum*. He may well have belonged to a romanized British family, as did the other successful leader of the Britons against the Saxons, Aurelius Ambrosius, whose name also appears in a Welsh form, *Emrys*.

If Nennius can be taken as authority, Arthur won twelve great victories over the English; the ninth named by him, the battle of Mount Badon, is undoubtedly historical, and was fought about A.D. 496. Arthur's final battle with Modred on the Camlan is dated by the Annales Cambriae 537, but these annals also date Mount Badon 516, which is certainly too late.

Arthur's activities appear to have been in the north of England, to judge from the battlefields named by Nennius, though they cannot be identified with certainty.

31 The version which the poet here says that he knows is doubtless the lost French romance postulated by Kittredge. See introd, p. xiii.

33 This and the following three lines refer to the present version as it now stands in alliterative verse.

35 *With lel letteres loken*: 'linked with true letters'. This seems to refer to the alliterative staves.

36 'As has long been the custom in the land'—interesting testimony of the continuity of the alliterative tradition.

37 *Camylot*: Malory identifies Camelot with Winchester, and this notion seems to have been usual in the Middle Ages. In Arthurian romances in which Camelot does not appear, Winchester usually takes its place as the first city in Britain. M. Paulin Paris thought that it was the same name as Camulodunum (city of the Celtic god Camulos), and there was an important city of that name on the site of Colchester in Essex. But Camelot is not the form which would normally be developed from Camulodunum: it is rather from a British example of Gaulish *Camulāta*. Others have located Camelot at Cadbury, Somerset, still others at Carlisle. Our poet evidently conceived it to be somewhere in the south of England, see 691, note.

37 *vpon Krystmasse*: as Madden notes, it is stated in the *Roman de Lancelot* that Arthur held court and wore his crown five times a year—Easter, Ascension Day, Pentecost, All Saints, and Noel. Of these festivals Easter was most honoured and Pentecost most joyous.

39 *þe Rounde Table*: there is an account of the founding of the Round Table in Laȝamon's *Brut* (ed. Madden, vol. ii. p. 529, line 22685 ff.). Arthur's guests quarrelled because of the order in which they were placed. Then a 'crafti weorcman' offered to make him a round table, so that all should sit equally high. Sixteen hundred men and more might sit at it. This tradition is also briefly referred to by Wace. But in the *Suite de Merlin* (followed by Malory) it is said that Merlin made the Round Table for Uther, and made it round to symbolize the round world. According to this account only 150 knights could sit at it.

43 *caroles*: dances accompanied by song. Originally the carole was a simple ring-dance, such as is still a popular amusement in the Faroe Islands. In France the primitive form became elaborated into various intricate types, rondel, balade, &c., as early as the twelfth century. For a detailed account, see Jeanroy, *Les Origines de la Poesie Lyrique en France*, Paris, 1889. In the fourteenth century caroles were a fashionable form of entertainment on days of festivity. There is a description of carole-dancing in the romance of *Lanval* 632 ff., in the *Romaunt of the Rose* (Chaucerian translation 743 ff.), and in the prologue to Chaucer's *Legend of Good Women*.

44 *ful fiften dayes*: so, in the *Suite de Merlin*, after Merlin has informed Arthur of his descent, a festival was held which lasted 'quinze jours pleniers'. Cf. *Arthour and Merlin* 3582 'ful fourtenniȝt'.

46 *glaum ande gle*: MS. *glaumande gle*. There is no evidence of a verb formed from Old Norse *glaum* 'a merry noise'. *Glaum ande gle* forms a phrase of the common type of alliterating synonyms; cf. *glam and gle* 1652 and the common *gamen and gle*. The copyist evidently confused the conj. *ande* with the ending of the pres. part., as he did again in 1426.

67 'Cried on high gifts of the New Year, and gave them with their own hands.' The giving of New Year's gifts is mentioned as early as the twelfth century (e.g. by Jocelyn of Brakelonde, *Chronica*, ch. 46) as a custom characteristically English. But precisely in what manner these lords and ladies contended about their gifts, or how the ladies might lose (68–9), is not known.

71 *þe mete tyme*: *N.E.D.* takes this as 'until the fitting time', that is, as long as was fitting. This is possible, but it is more natural to take it as 'until dinner time.'

73 *þe best burne ay abof*: in the description of dinner at Arthur's court the company do not sit at the Round Table, but as in a hall of the author's own time. Here we actually have the graduation according to rank which the Round Table was designed to avoid. See Laȝamon's *Brut*, ed. Madden, 22765 ff. With this passage cf. also *Purity* 114–17.

74 *Guenore*: Guenever, Arthur's queen, Gwenhwyvar of Welsh romance. Guanhumara in the text of Geoffrey of Monmouth is an error due to the misreading and miscopying of *uiu* as *um*: they are almost indistinguishable in some medieval manuscripts. The probable meaning of the name is 'white phantom'. See note on 945.

77 *Tolouse*: see note to 568.

Tars: a rich and costly stuff used in western Europe in the fourteenth and fifteenth centuries in tunics and tapestries. It takes its name from Tharsia where it was made, described by Maundeville as 'the kingdom of Tarse' upon which the land of Cathay 'marcheth toward the west', i.e. Turkestan (*N.E.D.*). One translation of Maundeville speaks of 'clathe of gold or tars', the only definite indication we have of its nature.

88 *longe*: MS. *lenge*; *o* and *e* are distinct in this manuscript, but confusion between them, due probably to their similarity in the exemplar, is frequent. Compare the emendations in ll. 438, 697, 1389, 1872.

90 ff. This custom of Arthur's is mentioned in other romances. That our author got it from his original is indicated by its appearance in the parallel romance *Le Livre de Caradoc*. See also *Le Queste del Saint Graal* (ed. Pauphilet, p. 5) and the corresponding passage in Malory (ed. Sommer, p. 614). Madden quotes another instance of it from the *Roman de Perceval*.

107 Arthur's place was in the middle of the long side of the high table, facing the company. He is standing there in the first of the coloured illustrations in the MS. So also in the romance *Arthour and Merlin* 6511: 'King Arthour sat, wiþouten fable, Midelest at þe heiȝe table.' Guenever would sit next him (73 *grayþed in þe myddes*) on his right. Probably no one sat on the other side of the table. The position in which they sat may be shown thus:

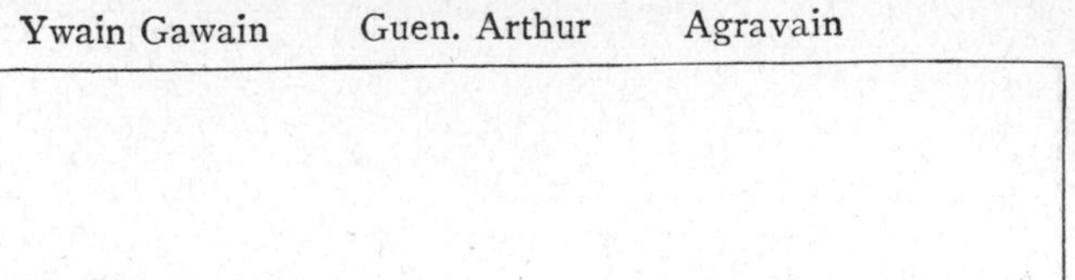

109 *Gawan*: for the other spellings of the name see the Index of Names. Those beginning with *W*- (*Wawan*, &c.) are due to the Welsh and French treatments of the initial *Gw*. In Welsh initial *g* in certain conditions (the so-called soft mutation) was absent, and the forms without *g* were of frequent occurrence. In Celtic names current in Old French this (*g*)*w* was treated like Germanic *w*: in most dialects it appears as *g*(*u*), and *Gauvain* was the normal form of this name. In some northern French dialects, however, Celtic (*g*)*w* and Germanic *w* appeared as *w*, and to some extent also in Anglo-Norman. In the *Brut* of Wace (born in Jersey, and attached to the court of Henry II of England) Gawain's name is spelled *Walwain*; he is

Li quens Walwains
Qui tant fu preudom de ses mains (ll. 9057–8).

In Middle English the variation of *G* and *W* in the name may be due to French influence alone; but in the north-west of England Gawain must have been almost as well known as Arthur, so that his name too may have come direct from Welsh tradition (cf. note to 26).

The true form of the name ends in *-wain*, as do many Celtic names, e.g. Iwain and Agrawain. This ending goes back to Primitive Celtic *ganios*; Iwain (Welsh *Ywein*, *Owein*) is from **Esuganios* (cf. the Gallo-Roman inscription *Esugen*[*ius*]). This ending is clear in the form found in Geoffrey of Monmouth—*Walgainus* (ed. Giles x. 9, 10, 11). The name appears to be an ordinary Celtic type; it is perhaps the same as the latinized Celtic name *Volaginius* found in Tacitus (*Historiae* ii. 75). In Welsh the name is *Gwalchmai*, which has been interpreted 'the hawk of May', but all other traditions (which represent earlier Welsh tradition) agree in following the type ending *-wain*, both Old French and Middle English and William of Malmesbury (who has *Walwen*). The Welsh form is evidently an altered one; cf. the late Welsh treatment of the name *Guingalet* (597 note).

Gawain is said to have been son of Loth, king of Lothian and other Scottish territories. His mother was Arthur's half-sister named Anna by Geoffrey and Belisent in French romances. According to William of Malmesbury Gawain ruled over Walweitha (Galloway).

The oldest tradition of Gawain makes him the greatest of Arthur knights, renowned for courtesy as well as prowess. In the *Mabinogio* (ed. Nutt, p. 116) it is said: 'He was called Gwalchmai because h never returned home without achieving the adventure of which h went in quest. He was the best of footmen and the best of knight He was nephew to Arthur, the son of his sister, and his cousin.' (C *cosyn* 372.) His courtesy is frequently contrasted with the rudeness Kai, in Welsh as well as in English and French romance. In Midd English literature Gawain has the same virtues as in Welsh romanc and his knightly honour and modesty are even more celebrated. Th Middle English romances which have Gawain as their hero are liste in Wells's *Manual of the Writings in Middle English*, pp. 51 ff.

Another tradition of Gawain was developed in romances in whic he was not the central figure. As other heroes of Arthurian legen became celebrated, it was necessary to reduce Gawain's standing make room for them. The oldest romance where the beginning this process can be observed is the Old French *Roman de Merlin*, an it is continued in the *Tristram* and *Lancelot*. Gawain retains h courtesy, but is no longer the chaste knight of the tradition represente by this poem, nor so successful in arms. In Middle English th reduced conception of Gawain appears only in the romances founde on these French versions, i.e. in *Le Morte Arthure* and Malory *Morte d'Arthure*. Tennyson adopted it from Malory, and mak Bedivere condemn him as 'light in life and light in death' when h ghost tries to warn Arthur against fighting next day. Gawain's fam lived longest in north Britain, where to this day Gavin is a favouri baptismal name.

110 *Agrauayn a la dure mayn*: Agrauayn is given a similar appell tion in Chrestien de Troyes' *Perceval*:

> Et li secons est Agrevains.
> Li orguelleus as dures mains.—ed. Potvin, 9509–10.

Hulbert points out that in the Middle High German romance *Parzifal* b Claus Wisse and Philipp Colen he is 'Agrapeus mit der harten hend Agrauayn was Gawain's brother, and his character has suffered fro the same French romancers as did Gawain's. They represent him spying on Lancelot's visits to the queen because he was jealous Lancelot's fame and prowess. They do not even allow him a *du main* in battle. Sir Degrevant of Middle English romance may identical with Agravain, as Halliwell has suggested (*Thorton Romance* p. 289). The English romancer may have taken *degrevauns* in h original to be the hero's name when *d'Egrevauns* was intende A similar addition of *d* is found in *Sir Degare*; the story of t romance which bears his name shows that it ought to be *Egare* (OF *égaré*, 'lost'). If this identification is right, *Sir Degrevant* embodi ie earlier tradition of Agravain and is the only surviving romance ·hich makes him its hero.

112 *Bischop Bawdewyn* ; in the Welsh romances of the *Mabinogion* .rthur has a bishop Bedwini, who is evidently the same person. In ie triads too he is 'chief of bishops in Cornwall'. The Celtic name ;edwini has been assimilated in French romance to the French name ;audwin (from Germanic Baldwini).

113 *ette with hymseluen* : that is, beside Bischop Bawdewyn.

113 *Ywan, Vryn son* : Ywain, son of Urien, well known in Arthurian :gend. Probably they were historical Welsh kings. According to 'aliesin Owein killed Ida, king of Bernicia, who is recorded in the .nglo-Saxon Chronicle as dead in 560. His father Urbgen (Urien) is aid by Nennius to have warred successfully against Ida's son Theoleric, who ruled, it is to be inferred from Nennius, 572–9. Urien .rove the Angles to take refuge in Lindisfarne, but was then murdered ·y a kinsman, Morgant, who was jealous of his success. Owein was .fterwards slain by Theoderic. Urien's kingdom was Reged, which vas perhaps in Cumberland, though there was another district of the ame name in South Wales, including the peninsula of Gower and ›art of Carmarthen. In later legend the southern Reged was the one egarded as his, as we find him called king of Gorre (Gower) in Malory and elsewhere. If Arthur and Ywain were both historical, hey could hardly have been contemporaries, as they are represented n the romances. For the etymology of the name Ywan see the note n *Gawan* 109.

114 ff. Compare the very similar description of Belshazzar's feast in *Purity* 1401 ff.

115 *at þe sidbordeȝ* : the medieval hall was like the dining hall of n Oxford or Cambridge college, with the high table on the dais at one nd, and rows of tables near the long sides of the hall and parallel with hem. These rows were *þe sidbordeȝ*.

118 *nakryn* : gen. pl. of *nakere* (OFr. *nacaire*) 'a drum'. The iom. pl. is *nakerys* 1016. The *-yn* represents the Old English gen. pl. weak) ending *-ena*. Cf. *Purity* 1412 on *blonkken bak* : 1413 *nakeryn noise* ; 1446 *besten blod*.

126–7 'Each knight took ungrudged (*withouten loþe*) what he himself desired.'

137 *on þe most on þe molde* : lit. 'one the largest on the earth'; *on* 'one' strengthening the superlative was a common Middle English construction, and still survived in Shakespeare's time, e.g. *Henry VIII*, II. iv. 48 'one the wisest prince' (Napier).

140–3 'Half a giant on earth I believe he may have been, but at any rate the biggest of men I declare him to be, and withal the shapeliest of figure that might ride.'

144 *Both*: MS. *bot.* The copyist is inclined to drop final *h*, when the next word begins with *h*. Thus we have in the MS. *wit* in line 113, while there is no doubt that the true form of the preposition in this poem is *with*. Napier proposed to emend here to *both* on syntactical grounds, without noticing the scribal treatment of *h* in this position. The required contrast is pointed by *al* = although.

151 *in grene*: green was a fairy colour, and suitable for such a being as this knight, whose Green Chapel was nothing else than a fairy mound; *a balȝ berȝ* 2172.

153 *meré* is 'merry, fair', OE. *myrige*, not 'honourable, splendid' OE. *mǣre*. Cf. 1736, where the decisive spelling *mery mantyle* occurs. So also in *Wars of Alexander* 2864.

160 *scholes*: the explanation adopted in the glossary is that of P. G. Thomas (*Englische Studien*, 47. 312). *scholes* represents OFr *cholet*, a form of *soulet*, a kind of shoe or slipper; at this period it would be a shoe with long pointed toe, such as the Green Knight is seen to be wearing in the illustrations of the manuscript. For the spelling *sch* instead of *ch*, cf. *schere* for *chere* 334, and for the loss of the *t* see the note on *brachetes* 1603. The alliteration of *ch* with *sch* occurs again in 1081. Emerson suggests that *scholes* means 'shoeless'. Cf. ON *skólauss*. Translate then: 'And there he rides with no shoes on his feet.'

165 *to tor for to telle*: an alliterative formula. Compare 719 and *Destruction of Troy* 8717; *William of Palerne* 1428, 5066; *Awntyrs off Arthure* 190. Not only *tor* but the whole phrase may be of Scandinavian origin: compare Old Norse *tortaliðr* 'difficult to tell', and *Fornmanna sǫgur* i. 162: 'Sva miklu fé í gull ok gersimum, at torvelt er mǫrkum at telja.'

168 For illustrations of these pendants see the *Guide to the Mediaeval Room of the British Museum*, 1924, pp. 5 and 6. They were usually enamelled with the arms of the owner.

171 *sturtes*: projections belonging to the gear of the Green Knight's horse, of what kind is uncertain—perhaps part of the saddle-bows. The word is probably from OE. *steort* 'tail'; for the sense 'projection' see *N.E.D.* s.v. *Start* n.

173 *fyn of þat ilke*: 'gay with that same (green).'

186 *capados*: Napier points out that the capados was not a hood (so *N.E.D.*), but a tunic of Cappadocian leather, which buttoned closely at the neck (*closes his swyre*).

211 *grayn*: probably the same word as *grain*='fork, prong' (see *N.E.D.*), from ON. *grein* 'a division'; the spiked shaft of the gisarm is meant (see note to 288).

224 *word þat he warp*: a very old phrase in alliterative use. It occurs in Old English poetry: *Elene* 769 'word aweorpan'; *Exeter Book Gnomic Verses* 191 'Oft hy wordum toweorpað'. It is also in

Old Norse poetry (though it is no longer alliterative in Norse): *Vafþrúðnismál* 7:

> Hvat's þat manna es í mínum sal
> verpumk orði á?

Also *Atlamál* 43. It was evidently a common Germanic phrase. It was frequent in Middle English, e.g. in *St. Katherine* 643, 1325; *Piers Plowman* (A) iv. 142; *Destruction of Troy* 2683; Dunbar's *Twa Mariit Wemen and the Wedo* 150.

257 *won*: 'abode', is probably from ON. *ván* 'hope, expectation'; the sense development in Middle English proceeds from such uses as *konungs var þangat ván* 'there was expectation of the king being there' passing into 'the king was in residence there'; cf. also ON. *allir vánir* 'all the places where one may expect to find a thing or person' (agreeing with the Middle English pl. use as in 685), and mod. Norw. *von* 'haunts of game'. The development was assisted by association and alliteration (as here) with *wunien* 'dwell', but rhymes in good texts show absence of final *-e* and stem vowel *ā*, *ǭ*. Texts that distinguish OE. *o*, *a* before nasal consonants (as *o*) from ON. OE. *ā* (as *a*) offer invariably the form *wane(s)*.

267 *in fere*: probably 'in company', i. e. with a company of fighting men. It is remarkable that in *Rauf Coilȝear* 702 the phrase is used of a knight fighting alone; having been long applied to the company of fighting men the phrase came to mean generally 'in martial fashion', which may be the sense here. But in the phrase *in feir of war* quoted as a parallel by P. G. Thomas (*Eng. Studien* 47. 250) *feir* is a different word = OFr. *afaire*.

288 *giserne*: the gisarm in the Middle Ages differed from the weapon which now goes by that name. Oliver de la Marche, a fifteenth-century French writer, describes it as a combination of battle-axe and dagger. It was probably the ordinary battle-axe with the shaft ending in a spike (*þe grayn* 211). The description of the Green Knight's axe as a *giserne* probably comes direct from the French original: it is a *jusarme* which the hairy *vilain* carries in *La Mule sans Frain*.

296 *barlay*: this word is probably to be identified with *barley* of modern English dialects, now used as a cry to claim a temporary truce in games. Earlier it may have been the cry for truce in battle, cf. Scott's *Waverley*: 'A proper lad of his quarters that will not cry barley in a bruilȝie' (=broil, fight)—quoted in *E.D.D.* The sense here is 'there being no fight, without resistance shown', and Gawain echoes this condition in 384 *wyth no wyȝ elleȝ on lyue*, that is, he will bring no retainers to defend him. The origin of the word is obscure: none of the etymologies which have been suggested are satisfactory.

327 *bayþen*: the infin. of this verb would be *bayþe*, though originally it must have been *bayþene(n)*. Its origin is the Old Norse verb **beiðna*, which appears in Icelandic as *beina* 'to further (a request)'. This verb is related to *beiða* 'to ask' as *greina* to *greiða*. The *-n* suffix was lost in Middle English in this word as it was in *slokes* l. 412 (from ON. *slokna*), no doubt from confusion with the *-n* of the infin. and pres. tense plural, which was often dropped. The phrase *bayþen a bone* is an alliterative formula, cf. Sege of Jerusalem 179 *bayne* (from the later Norse form *beina*) *me my bone*; Lyrics of MS. Harley 2253 (ed. Boddeker 146/35): *Crist, þat bayeþ* (read *bayþeþ* or *bayneþ*) *me my bone.*

352 *haȝerer*: 'fitter, readier'; *haȝer* is the one Scandinavian loanword in Middle English which appears to retain the ending *-r* of the nom. sing. A form representing only the stem *hag-* would be expected. There may have been an analogical declension of Scand. *hagr* in Anglo-Scandinavian after the example of *fagr* 'fair', with gen. **hagrs* instead of *hags*, as though the *r* were part of the stem; *hagr* so declined would regularly give ME. *haȝer*. The tendency to associate *hagr* and *fagr* is illustrated in Modern Icelandic, which has the abstract noun *hegrð* (instead of **hegð*) formed on the analogy of *fegrð* 'fairness'.

372 *on kyrf*: *on* is the preposition. 'Take care, cousin, how you set about your cutting—lit. that you apply (yourself) to cutting—and if you manage him rightly, readily I believe will you endure the blow that he will offer you afterwards.'

424 ff. The original purpose of the beheading was the disenchantment of the strange knight. For parallels see Kittredge's study of Sir Gawain, pp. 200 ff. This purpose has been lost in the development of the story found in this romance. The original disenchantment is preserved in the later and in most ways less original versions *The Carl of Carlisle* and *The Turk and Gawain.*

457 *runisch*: an obscure word peculiar to alliterative verse; it occurs as *runisch*, *renisch* in *Purity* and *Patience*; *renisch* in *Wars of Alexander*. The contexts are not decisive as to its exact senses: 'rough, fierce, horrible' seem most likely. The alternation *u/e* points to earlier *ēo*: cf. ON. *hrjónn* 'rough' and OE. *hrēoh*, *hrēow*. *roynyshe* in *St. Erkenwald* 52 is possibly a form of the same word, but Chaucer's *roi(g)nous* R.R. 988, 6170, and later *roynish* 'coarse, scurvy' are probably not connected.

477 *heng vp þyn ax*: this direction is meant literally, and perhaps figuratively as well: 'Have done with this business'. The use of the expression as a proverb in ME. is clear in *The Owl and the Nightingale* 658; R. of Gloucester's *Chron.* 11771; Böddeker *Alte. Dicht.* p. 134.

492 *ȝelpyng*: boasting, in the sense of vowing a bold undertaking, as do Charlemagne's knights in *Le Pelerinage de Charlemagne.* The next line then means 'Though such words of undertaking were wanting for him'.

531 *no fage*: MS. *no sage.* This emendation was made by C. T. Onions in a letter published in the *Times Literary Supplement* of August 16, 1923, and defended in the issue of September 20. For evidence of the phrase *no fage* in Middle English see these two letters. Various attempts have been made to extract a meaning from the text as it stands in the MS. such as 'as the world requires no wise man (to tell)'—Napier. This interpretation, like the others, is forced. As Onions points out, *as þe worlde askes* is a conventional phrase in Middle English meaning 'as the world requires' in which *askes* does not have an object (as *sage* would be): this phrase occurs e.g. in *Morte Arthure* 2187 and in *Piers Plowman*, Prologue 19.

536 *Al-hal-day*: All Saints Day, November 1. Arthur regularly held his court then, and no doubt Gawain was waiting to attend this function before going on his journey.

551 *Errik*: this is the Celtic name Arrak, probably influenced in its form by English *Eric*, from ON. *Eiríkr.* Errik is identical with Erec of Chrestien de Troyes' *Erec et Enide* and with Arrake fitz Lake in *The Awntyrs of Arthur.* In Chrestien's romance he holds the same place as Geraint ab Erbin in the Welsh romance (Lady Guest's *Mabinogion*, ed. Nutt, 1910, p. 196).

552 *Doddinaual de Sauage*: properly *Dodinal li Sauvage* 'the fierce'. *þe duk of Clarence*: according to *Lestoire de Merlin* and *Le Roman de Lancelot* (the so-called Vulgate versions edited by Dr. Sommer) the duke of Clarence was named Galeshin, cousin, according to the former, brother, according to the latter, of Sir Dodinel. In Malory the duke of Clarence is Chalaunce or Chaleyns. Galeshin is more likely to be the duke our author had in mind, since he names him next to Sir Dodinel.

553 *Launcelot*: Lancelot du Lake, son of King Ban of Benwick. His fame as an Arthurian knight comes from France: he is unknown to Welsh tradition, Geoffrey of Monmouth, or Wace. He is first mentioned by Chrestien of Troyes in his *Erec*, where he says: 'Before all excellent knights Gauvain ought to be named first, and second Erec the son of Lac, and third Lancelot of the Lake.' Later, in *La Chevalier de la Charrette* Lancelot is the chief knight of Arthur's court, and he now appears also as Guinevere's lover. But Lancelot is not Chrestien's creation: there is evidence of an earlier French poem about him which is now lost. It was used by Ulrich von Zatzikhoven for the story of his *Lancelot* (composed early in the thirteenth century).

Lyonel was son of King Bohort of Gannes and Lancelot's cousin.

Lucan was the royal butler, and is usually called *li Bouteillier*; in Malory he is 'Lucan the bottler'.

554 *Boos*: probably identical with Boso, in Geoffrey of Monmouth. He is later called Bors (as in Malory).

Byduer: the same as the Bedivere who in Malory and his source is the sole survivor of Arthur's last battle with Modred on the Camlan. In Welsh legend he is the close friend of Kai; he 'never shrank from any enterprise upon which Kai was bound'. In Geoffrey of Monmouth he and Kai are represented as slain in Arthur's great victory over the Romans. Bedivere first appears as the last survivor of Arthur's knights in the 'Vulgate' Lancelot which Malory used.

555 *Mador de la Port*: this is Mador's usual appellation in romance; no doubt he was Arthur's chief porter. Mador (from Old Celtic *Maturos*) does not appear in Welsh romance, nor in English, except in translation from French.

568 *tulé*: for *tuly*, a term applied to silk, tapestry, &c. of a rich red colour. The stuff is the same as the 'tryed Tolouse' in 77, originally a silk imported from Toulouse; the word was also applied to other stuffs of the same colour.

568 ff. With this description of the arming of Gawain compare the arming of Arthur in *Morte Arthure* 902 ff., and the arming for the tournament in *Clariodus* (quoted by Sir Walter Scott in the notes to his edition of *Sir Tristrem*, p. 269 in the third edition).

Gawain's gear belongs to the latter part of the fourteenth century. The *sabatounȝ* were not much used in England before the end of that century, though the term was used by Robert of Brunne about 1330 in his translation of Wace's *Brut* (Rolls, ed. i. 19926) to render *cauces de fer*, but this is hardly evidence that they were worn in England in his day. The usual protection for the foot then worn by knights was the pointed *solleret*. The elaboration of the *payttrure* and *couertor* also point to the latter end of the century. See note on 1738.

572 *closed aloft*: 'fastened closely around his neck,' cf. 186 note.

574 *foteȝ*: a WMidland dat. pl. with substitution of pl. *-es* for older *-en*, *-e* (OE. *fótum*). Cf. *A. R.* Corpus MS. f. 45 *under hare fotes*, MS. N. *uoten*. But contrast *on his fote* 2229, &c.

596 *conueyed*: 'conducted him on his way', as far as the mounting stage in the castle court.

597 *Gryngolet*: Professor Gollancz thinks that this name belonged originally to the boat of the mythical hero Wade (*Saga-book of the Viking Society*, vol. v, p. 104). But it is found several centuries earlier as the name of Gawain's horse. The earliest authority for Gringalet as the name of Wade's boat is Speght (in his edition of Chaucer, 1598). *Gryngolet* is more probably of Celtic origin, though the Welsh form *Keincaled* appears to be only a late reformation of the

French *Guingalet* under the influence of a false etymology (Welsh *kein* 'fair'; *kaled* 'hard'). The French *Guingalet*, *Gringalet* (with intrusive *r*, as often in the French treatment of Celtic or Germanic *w*) point rather to a name beginning (*g*)*w*-, probably Welsh **Gwyngalet* 'white-hard'.

601 *payttrure*: the usual form of the word is *peitrel*. Here another ending has been substituted. Originally the *peitrel* was a plate of armour protecting the breast of the horse; later it became merely ornamental, as it seems to be here, with its *apparayl*. Cf. l. 168.

602 *couertor*: the rich cloth covering of the horse. Frequently it reached almost to the ground, as in *The Awntyrs off Arthure* 386: His stede with sandelle of Trise (*read* Tarse) was trapput to the hele.

603 *ryche golde nayleȝ*: a specification of *al*. It was all arrayed on a red background, that is, gold nails were studded over it.

606 ff. *stapled stifly, &c.*: staples were used to strengthen the helmet, especially where its parts were joined; the name was also given to the hooks by which the other armour was attached to the helmet. Inside the helmet was padding (*stoffed wythinne*) to take the shock of blows; wound round it, over the *auentayle* or movable mouth-piece, was the *horson* an ornamental band of silk (609–13). Around the upper part of the helmet was the *cercle*, a gold band studded with gems. This rich form of *cercle* is characteristic of the later Middle Ages; cf. *Awntyrs off Arthure* 380, *Morte Arthure* 615.

611 *bitwene* here means 'at intervals (of space)', as also in 791 and 795. This sense, not recorded in dictionaries, is even clearer in *Morte Arthure* 934: Festeneȝ theire faire stedeȝ o ferrum bytwenne.

620 *wyth þe pentangel depaynt*: as Madden points out, though Gawain's arms are described in many romances, there is no authority in any of them for the pentangle as his device. The romances agree in assigning him a shield 'de sinople, a un aigle d'or' or with a lion or gryphon. The pentangle was an ancient symbol of perfection which was used by the Pythagoreans, the Neo-Platonists, and the Gnostics. No doubt the poet came upon a description and interpretation of it in some treatise or commentary of the Alexandrian school, but we have not been able to find his source. He was also acquainted with the popular legends concerning it (629–30). As symbolizing perfection and including most of the virtues it seemed a suitable device for Gawain, and was substituted by the English poet for the usual eagle, lion, or gryphon. Throughout the Middle Ages it was a mystic symbol, and was popularly thought to have power to repel spirits.

625 Solomon's seal was a pentangle in a circle, a symbol still used in synagogues, and in Freemasonry, which is supposed to have had its beginning in the building of the temple by Solomon.

630 *endeles knot*: so-called because its interlacing lines are joined so as to be continuous, and if followed out they bring the tracer back always to the same point, as is described in 657–62. A diagram will make this clear:

632 *in fyue and sere fyue syþeȝ*: 'in five ways, and five times in each way'. Gawain is virtuous in five ways, and in each way with reference to five things, viz. the five wits, the five fingers, the five wounds, the five joys, and five virtues (652–4). Each of these groups is symbolized by a side of the pentangle.

642 *þe fyue woundeȝ*: the five wounds of Christ (in His hands, in His feet, and in His side) are a frequent subject of medieval meditation and devotional verse. There are three poems addressed to the five wounds in the Minor Poems of the Vernon MS. (Part I, pp. 22, 48, 131).

645 *þe fyue ioyeȝ*: celebrated often in medieval literature. Usually they were the joys of Our Lady in the Annunciation, the Nativity, the Resurrection, the Ascension, and the Assumption, though this list is variable. For ME. texts celebrating the five joys, see Wells's *Manual of the Writings in ME.*, p. 536. There is a beautiful description of the joy of the Nativity in *Purity* 1073–88.

649 *hir ymage depaynted*: this is in imitation of the image of the Virgin associated with Arthur. Nennius relates that Arthur bore the image of the Virgin on his shoulders in his eighth battle against the Saxons. William of Malmesbury says he affixed the image to his armour at the battle of Mount Badon. According to Geoffrey of Monmouth it was painted on his shield Pridwen, and 'many a time and oft did it call her back into his memory'. Giraldus Cambrensis says it was fixed on the inside of his shield, so that he might kiss it in battle. It was also on the inside of Gawain's shield that the image was painted, on the upper and larger portion (*þe more half*) above the clasps through which the arm was inserted to hold the shield.

691 ff. The general direction of Gawain's itinerary is clear: since he rode into North Wales, and came 'þurȝ þe ryalme of Logres', a southern locality of Camelot (see note to 37), whence he set out, is to be inferred. His route through North Wales to Wirral presents difficulties. According to 698 he rode east through Carnarvonshire, Denbighshire, and Flintshire, keeping the isles of Anglesey (Anglesey proper, Holy Island, Puffin Island, &c.) on his left. Then he crossed 'the fords by the promontories, over at the Holy Head'. It is not known what fords and promontories are meant, or if the Holy Head was one of these promontories by a ford, or a place farther on. But it seems likely that Gawain was following a known route, since the author refers to '*the* fords by *the* promontories' and expects his audience to know them. The usual route in the Middle Ages may be inferred from the Itinerary of Giraldus Cambrensis and the invasion of Henry II in 1135. *Giraldus* in *Itinerarium Cambriae* (Cap. XI) tells how he proceeded east along the north coast of Wales, crossing the rivers Conwy and Clwyd where they flow into the sea, thence through St. Asaph to Basingwerk, near Holywell, thence along the coast of the estuary of the Dee, crossing the Dee above the estuary, but below Chester. 'The fords by the promontories' probably refers to the crossing of the rivers Conwy and Clwyd, both of which flow into the sea with promontories on either side. On the left bank of the Clwyd near the mouth is a place still called Forydd 'ford'. The Holy Head is where Gawain passed into Wirral, and so would be somewhere on the Dee, between Chester and the estuary. No such place is known there now, nor is there any record of a Holy Head other than Holyhead in Anglesey. Line 698, however, disposes of all possibility that Holyhead in Anglesey may be intended. Another suggestion (Chambers, *Mod. Lang. Rev.* ii. 167) is that Holy Hede is a mistake for Holywell. But Holywell is nearly two miles inland, and is not near a part of the estuary which Gawain could have crossed, especially as it was formerly deeper than it is now.

The possibility that the author's geography was inaccurate and confused must also be considered. He writes, however, as if he knew these parts, using the definite article as though the places were familiar to him: and it is the only part of the itinerary which he chooses to describe in detail. Further, he knew that Anglesey consisted of several islands, and that Wirral was a wilderness. It seems preferable to believe that he knew North Wales and Cheshire well, and that his Holy Head was a place which is no longer known by that name.

691 *Logres*: England south of the Humber (Welsh *Lloegyr*). Geoffrey of Monmouth has a legendary etymology, that it was so-called from the early British king Locrine. The form *Logres* as compared with the Welsh form has the Celtic ending *-es* (*issā*) added.

701 *þe wyldrenesse of Wyrale*: Wirral was made into a forest by Randle Meschines, third earl of Chester, and remained wild as late as the sixteenth century. There was an old saying that

From Blacon Point to Helbree
A squirrel may leap from tree to tree.

709 ff. It has sometimes been assumed that the castle where Gawain harboured and the near-by Green Chapel were in Wirral, but it is clear that a journey of some distance is here described, after Gawain has landed in Wirral. Madden seems to be right in thinking that he rode north into Cumberland and that the forest described 741 ff. is Inglewood Forest. This was the traditional setting for 'awntyrs' of Arthur and his knights; and the mountainous scenery described in the last division of the poem, 2077 ff., is like Cumberland or Westmoreland rather than Wirral. Madden would further identify the Green Chapel with the Chapel of the Grene, which is marked on old maps of Cumberland on a point of land on the western coast, not far from Skinburness. Near it was Volsty (or Vulsty) Castle, where the magic books of the wizard Michael Scott were traditionally supposed to be. A much earlier identification of the castle is found in *The Green Knight* (Percy Folio MS.), a romance which is a condensation of *Sir Gawain and the Green Knight* (see introd., p. xiv). This version may be as old as the fifteenth century. In it, after Gawain and the knight have met at the Green Chapel, they are represented as returning to the knight's castle:

492 To the castle of Hutton can they fare.

There were three Huttons where there was a castle in the Middle Ages: Hutton Bushell, in the North Riding; Hutton, three miles south of Preston, Lancs.; and Hutton-in-the-Forest, about six miles north-west of Penrith, Cumberland. The last is probably the Hutton referred to in *The Green Knight*. For a notice of the remains of the castle there, see Hutchinson's *History of Cumberland*, i. 512. *The Carle of Carlisle* also preserves the general tradition that the scene of the adventure was in Cumberland. But in spite of the precision of *The Green Knight*, it seems unlikely that the author of *Sir Gawain* intended reference to any existing castle in Cumberland: if the castle he describes (785 ff.) actually existed, the style of the architecture shows that it must then have been of comparatively recent building, whereas such a legend would naturally be associated with an old castle.

762 *Cros Kryst me spede*: a common formula of prayer, though usually in the order *Kryst cros, &c.* It was used especially at school, before saying the alphabet, which was arranged on the hornbook in the form of a cross, and called a Christ-cross (see *N.E.D.* s. v.). The order of the words *Cros Kryst* is no copyist's error, for it occurs also in *The Boke of Curtaisve* 144, which is a north-western text like *Sir Gawain*;

it is printed in the E. E. T. S. edition of *The Babees Boke*, ed. Furnivall, 1868. *Cros Kryst* is probably in imitation of OF. *crois Christ*; cf. M. Welsh *croes crist* (Black B. of Carmarthen 82).

774 *Sayn Gilyan*: Gilyan is a variant of Julian. It is St. Julian l'Hospitalier who is thanked by Gawain—appropriately in that he was the patron and protector of travellers, 'qui ab itinerantibus pro inveniendo bono hospitio invocatur'—*L. A.* Knights errant in French romance commonly invoke him, and so also in Chaucer's *House of Fame* 1022:

Seynt Julyan, lo, bon hostell!

According to the legend Julian was of noble birth. As a youth he was inordinately fond of hunting, until it happened that a stag, which he was about to kill, by divine inspiration spoke and said: 'Why do you hunt me, you who will be the slayer of your father and mother?' Julian tried to flee from his fate, but nevertheless afterwards slew his father and mother by mistake. As penance he left his high station and built a hostel by a great river, where he gave lodging to poor travellers and ferried them across. The legend as told in the *Legenda Aurea* (Cap. XXX. i and iv) is an impressive story. There is a Middle English version in *The Early South English Legendary* (ed. Horstmann, p. 256), and a Middle Scottish version in Barbour's *Legendensammlung* (ed. Horstmann, p. 219). The legend has also been artistically retold by Gustave Flaubert.

777 *gerdeȝ*: MS. *gedereȝ*. This emendation was made by Napier, from the analogy of lines 759 and 2062. The copyist's error was in mistaking the position of the contraction for *er* in his exemplar.

790 Similarly in *Purity* the 'aþel vessel' brought out at Belshazzar's feast was (1458–9):

as casteles arayed
Enbaned under batelment wyth bantelles quoynt.

790 *enbaned*: provided with *banteleȝ*, the architectural feature described in *Pearl* 992 f., where they are set as steps at the foot of the wall. Here they are projecting horizontal courses of masonry set near the top of the wall to render assault by means of scaling ladders more difficult. See further *Medium Ævum* II. 184 f.

794 ff. Such elaborate castles with numerous ornamental pinnacles and chimneys rising from bastel roofs began to appear in the last half of the fourteenth century. The poet is evidently describing the latest thing in the castle architecture of his own time.

796–800 Cf. *Purity* 1461–3.

802 Cf. *Purity* 1498 where the 'logges' placed over the dishes of food were

on lofte corven,
Pared out of paper and poynted of golde.

822 *quel*: an unaccented form of *whil*, *quil*; cf. *tel* 1564 for *til*.

845 *beuer-hwed*: in the *Awntyrs of Arthur* 357, Arthur also has a 'beueren berde'.

847 Similarly in *Wars of Alexander* 4922 the sun-god is said to have 'fell face as þe fire'.

849: 'to hold a lordship over good lieges'. *in lee* is an obscure phrase, qualifying *lortschyp*; its sense may be 'in tranquillity, in peace' (*N.E.D.*); or 'in hall', a mere alliterative variation of *in mote*, *on flet*; or 'as protector (of)', parallel to the use of *hleo* in OE. verse as 'lord'. The second of these possibilities seems most likely; cf. the use of the word in l. 1893.

853 *a bryȝt boure*: in *Sir Degrevant* 1425 ff. is an elaborate description of a medieval bower. It had glass windows, tapestries on which the kings famous in romance were pictured, scriptural scenes and figures of holy men carved on the stone of the ceiling and on corbels, and a clock which struck the hours. The bedding was made of the richest materials, as here.

856 *blaunmer* is slightly better as the reading of the MS. than *blaunnier*, as *i* in such an ambiguous position is usually marked as such. Whatever the etymology of the word (it is uncertain—see *N.E.D.* and Kaluza's note to *Libeaus Desconnus* 129 in his edition) there is no doubt that forms ending *-mer* do exist, while the spelling *-nier* is unparalleled and does not accord with any of the etymologies suggested.

864 ff. 'As soon as he took one and was clothed therein, (one) that fitted him well with flowing skirts, the spring-time verily it seemed to each man in his appearance, well-nigh, all his limbs under it glowing and delightful all in colours, &c.' Gawain put on a bright-coloured robe, under which appeared his limbs clad in closer-fitting garments of various colours. The robe was the *bleaunt*, under which were worn surcoat and hose; compare the description of the Green Knight's costume 152 ff., and of Gawain's 1928–31.

879 *bleeaunt*: a brightly coloured silk stuff used especially in tunics and mantles: hence the mantle itself was called a *bleaunt*, as in 1928. It is the same word as OFr. *blialt*, *bliaut*, with the end of the word altered to the common participial ending *-ant*. This process may have been assisted by the fact that in most medieval manuscripts *u* and *n* are indistinguishable. The same fact has also obscured the history of the word, and it is uncertain when the forms with *n* first began to be used. Probably the substitution of the ending *-ant*, *-aunt*, took place in Anglo-Norman, in which it was a common change. Cf. AN. *tyrant* for *tyran*. The form *bliaunt* occurs unambiguously in the Anglo-Norman *Bevis of Hampton* 738 and 745. The form with *n* is further attested by Welsh *bliant*, a loan from Anglo-Norman; *bliant* is

also found in Middle Low German (from Anglo-Norman?), but in other languages, as High German and Icelandic, the form without *n* is borrowed. In Middle English the form with *n* is usual, but the other form also is found, e.g. *blyot* in *The Parlement of Thre Ages* 482.

881 *inurnde*: MS. *in erde*. Sir I. Gollancz emended to *enurnde*. We assume that the copyist had *īur̄de* in his exemplar, and reading it as *in urde* took *urde* as a form of *erde*. Compare the variants *urþe* and *erþe* in *Purity*, of which the *u*-form might have been strange to the copyist's dialect.

884 *telded vp a tabil*: in the Middle Ages the tables were usually not fixed pieces of furniture, as now, but consisted of boards placed on trestles. When the meals were over they were taken away and often hung on the wall of the hall. Not everyone had, like Chaucer's Franklin,

a table dormant in his halle alway
Stod redy covered al the longe day.

893 *sawes so sleȝe*: MS. *sleȝeȝ* is clearly wrong, and the original may well have had *sawseȝ so sleȝe*.

897 *þis penaunce*: when Gawain calls the dinner of fish a feast because it is cooked in so many ways, they remind him that Christmas Eve is a fast day; later he will know a true feast. In John Russel's *Boke of Nurture* (printed with *The Babees Boke*, ed. Furnivall, E.E.T.S. 1868) is described a similarly elaborate fish dinner (p. 166), and the fish *sewes* (p. 171) that were also served, and (p. 173) the sauces used with fish.

916 ff. Gawain was the most famous of knights for courtesy. Chaucer cites him as such in the *Squire's Tale* 89:

This strange knyght . . .
Saleweth kyng and queene and lordes alle
By ordre, as they seten in the halle,
With so heigh reverence and obeisaunce,
As wel in speche as in countenaunce,
That Gawayn, with his olde curteisye,
Though he were comen ageyn out of fairye,
Ne koude hym nat amende with a word.

944 *of alle oþer* is to be construed with *fayrest*—'she was fairest of all'. This illogical construction is not uncommon in Middle English: cf. *Dest. of Troy* 40 *derrist of other* 'more worthy than all others'.

945 *Wenore*: this form as compared with Guenore is explained in the same way as Wawain and Gawain (109 note). Guenever in romances is the standard of beauty: the expression 'fairer than Guenever' was no doubt conventional and may well have been in the French original. Similarly in 'The Lady of the Fountain' (*Mabinogion*, ed. Nutt, 1910,

p. 168), Kynon says of damsels that they are 'more lovely than Gwenhwyvar'. Geoffrey of Monmouth says of Guenever (ix. 9) that 'she surpassed in beauty all the other ladies of the island'. See also 81 ff. of this poem.

965 *for Gode*: the rhyme shows that this is not *for gode* 'for good'; *gode* with tense ō (often spelled *goud*—see glossary) is an impossible rhyme with *brǭde*, whereas a short vowel may rhyme with a long vowel of the same quality in this group of poems: e.g. *nyme* 993 rhyming with *tyme*; *slokes* 412 and *cnokeȝ* 414 rhyming with *strokeȝ*; *upon Pearl* 208 rhyming with *ston*, &c. The *o* was apparently not lengthened in the open syllable of the oblique cases of *God*: cf. *Godde* 2205. The sense here is not 'by God', but rather 'before God (this is true)'.

967 *balȝ*: MS. *bay* is not intelligible here; it could only mean 'bay-coloured'. *lȝ* in MSS. sometimes resembles *y*, when the *l* happens to be written rather short. We assume that the copyist misread *lȝ* as *y* in this instance. Cf. 2032, and, for the alliterative combination *balȝ and brode*, see *Wars of Alexander* 4923, *Parl. of Three Ages* 112.

968–9 'Sweeter to taste was she whom she was leading.' *lyk* has not the modern sense 'lick', but rather 'taste'; cf. *Purity* 1521 'So long likked þise lordes þise likores swete'.

975 'They ask him for (his) acquaintance', that is, 'they desire to become better acquainted with him', *not* 'they claim acquaintance with him'. 'Ask for' is the sense of *callen of* in this poem (see Glossary).

979 Cf. *Morte Arthure* 235 'Thane spyces vnsparyly þay spendyde thereaftyre.' Spiced wine (*piment*) was a favourite drink. The commonest kinds were *hippocras* (see *The Babees Boke*, p. 125) and *clarré*, which was wine, honey, and spices mixed, and then strained clear.

991 Possibly (as suggested by Knott) *knyȝt* should be read, as more likely than *lord* to give rise to the MS. error *kyng*; but *lord* is more than thirty times applied to Sir Bercilak, and alliteration rather than internal rhyme agrees better with the general practice of the poem in the 'wheel'.

1002 The metrical pause falls between *by* and *lent*; *by* thus postponed is accented and independent. This word-order is still a common and a natural one in Middle English quite apart from metrical convenience. It descends from the usual Old English order exemplified in *stodon him twegen weras big*, where *big* is still purely adverbial.

1003 ff.; 'Gawain and the gay lady sat together, even in the middle (of the high table), where the food fittingly came, and then was fairly served through all the hall as best beseemed them, to each man according to his rank.' Gawain and the lady were in the seats of honour in the middle of the high table, where the food was served first. Cf. 73 and note on 107.

1006 *grome* in late Middle English became confused with *gome* 'man', which it eventually replaced; cf. Modern English *bridegroom* and OE. *brydguma.* Here *grome* probably has the sense 'man', though possibly it is 'servant, groom'.

1008–9 '(Such) that it would be very difficult for me to tell of it, even if perchance I took pains to describe it in detail.' *ȝet* 1009 is used in the sense 'though' (see *N.E.D.* s. v. *Yet*); *and ȝet*='even though', 'even if'.

1014 *þat*: MS. ⁊. A correlative to *such* 1011 is required, and it is probable that ⁊ was miswritten for *þ*ᵗ. A copyist working rapidly might easily misread *þ*ᵗ as ⁊. So also in 1032, 1386.

1025 *Forþy wonderly þay woke*: they stayed up all night. The waking and drinking here mentioned were customary on St. John's day. The drinking went round the whole company, and was called St. John's Blessing or St. John's Draught.

1026 *Daunsed ful dreȝly*: caroles were often danced at great length. After the coronation dinner of Richard II, the remainder of the day and the whole evening was spent in dancing caroles.

1032 *wayued*: this verb is difficult to distinguish from *wayne* 'to bring (to)'; in the MS. *n* and *u* are indistinguishable, and the sense is not always made clear by the context. Previous editions here read *wayned*, but cf. 1976 *such worchip he wolde hym weue* (rhym. *leue*), where *weue* is from OE. *wǣfan* influenced in sense by the (probably cognate) ON. *veifa.* The two forms appear interchangeably in Middle English. Cf. the phrase in 1743 *wayueȝ vp a wyndow*; *weued vp a window* in *W. of Palerne* 2978; *wafte he vpon his wyndowe*, in *Purity* 453; *wefden vp* 'opened' Laȝamon 19003.

1049 *toun*: here in a general sense 'habitation of men'. This idiom in speaking of time and seasons is very old. In Old English there is: *Menologium* 8 se kalend us cymeð to tune; 138 cymeð Weodmonað on tun, and similarly several times in that poem; cf. also *Byrhtferð's Handboc* viii. 311 ff. and *Beowulf* 1134. In Middle English compare: Laȝamon's *Brut* 2496 'Averil eode of tune'; and similarly 24242 (where the older MS. has *to londe* for *to tune*); also Sisam's *Fourteenth Century Prose and Verse* xv *b* 1 'Lenten ys come wiþ loue to toune'. Translate the line: 'Before the holy days (Christmas week) had wholly passed from the dwellings of men.'

1053 *I ne wot in worlde*: the insertion of the *ne* is required by the sense, and is always found in this common alliterative formula; cf. *Pearl* 65; *Destruction of Troy* 12903; *William of Palerne* 314, 478, &c. It appears also in Icelandic, cf. *Volsungs Rímur* i. 12:

Vissa eg ei í verǫldu fyrr væri stærri halla.

1074 *spenne*: probably the same word as *spene* in *Wars of Alexander* 4162, of unknown origin. From the two contexts the sense appears to be 'ground, space of turf'; *in spenne* is a tag='there', like *in stedde*,

439, and others. It is probably from OE. *spind*, see *N.E.D. Spine*, sb.[2] and compare *Sward.*

1108 'Good sir, let us strike a bargain thus, [let us] answer honestly [when called on], whether, sir, nothing or something better fall to our lot.'

1139 ff. A good many descriptions of the hunting and brittling of deer resembling those which follow here exist in other medieval romances. The following especially should be compared: *The Parlement of Thre Ages* 1–103; *The Awntyrs off Arthure* 33–67; *Sir Tristram* 441–528; *Ipomadon*, 1st version in Koelbing's ed. 587–680: 2nd version 366–416. The following hunting descriptions were probably not in the French original, but were composed by the English poet and inserted upon the suggestion of some such passage as one that occurs in the parallel French romance *Le Chevalier a l'Epee*, where it is said that Gawain's host went out 'to view his woods'.

1140 *kenel*: all the hounds were in one large kennel, which would be 'x. fadmys of lengthe and v. of brede, if þere be many houndes'. —*Master of Game.*

1141 *þre bare mote*: the mote was a long note. The fourteenth-century horn had only one note, and different calls were made by combining notes of different duration. The notes used may be represented thus:

——	–	∪ ∪ –	∪ ∪ ∪ –
Mote,	trut,	trororout,	tronororout.

Three motes were blown at the uncoupling (unleashing) of the hounds.

1142 *braches*: the same kind of hounds as *rachcheȝ* 1362 &c.; scenting hounds hunting in a pack. They were small hounds, in build resembling the beagles of the present time. They were to be used as *taysours* (see 1150, *note*). Twici says, '*Touz ceaus* (*bestes*) *qe sunt enchaces sunt meuz de lymer; et touz ceaus enquillez sunt trovez de braches.*' That is, all beasts that are 'enchased' are moved by a limer, and all those that are 'hunted up' (the method used here) are found by braches. The braches are now unleashed, while those said to be unleashed in 1147 are doubtless the greyhounds.

1143 'And they whipped in and turned back [the hounds] that strayed away on other scents.'

1150 'This word "quest" is a terme of hunters of biyonde the see, and it is to mene whan a man gooþ to fynde of a deere and to harborow hym'—*harborow* means 'track to the lair'. So the *Master of Game.* But 'quest' was also used of the peculiar cry of hounds on scenting or viewing game (see *N.E.D.*).

1150 ff. The hunt is like that described by the *Master of Game* 'when þe Kyng wil hunte in forest or in park for þe hert with bowes and greyhoundes and stable' (*stablye* 1153). Men and hounds were stationed at various points around the district in which the game was to be hunted. Light greyhounds and other *taysours* (hounds for putting up and driving game) were slipped, and as they drove the deer the *stablye* or beaters belonging to the ring of stations directed their course to where the lord and his party stood ready to shoot them. The men of the *stablye* also tried to strike down the deer if they came near enough, and at any of the stations might be some of the larger greyhounds ('receivers') to pull the deer down. The stations where special preparations were made to kill the deer constituted the *resayt* (1168).

1156–7 The close season of the hart and buck was from September 14 to June 24. Hinds and does were hunted from September 14 to February 2. There is some uncertainty as to whether *meue* or *mene* should be read in 1157, as *u* and *n* are indistinguishable in the MS. *Meue* is the technical term for starting a hart (cf. the pp. *meuz* in Twici, *meued* in the *Master of Game*), and seems the likelier word to be used here. There was also in French a verb *mener* 'to chase hard' (Cotgrave), derived from *menée* the name of a hunting call used as a signal that the deer was in full flight. Twici says that it was blown only to the hart, the boar, and the wolf.

1167 'Whatever animal escaped the men who were shooting was pulled down and slain at the receiving stations, by the time they had been driven from the high ground and down to the waters; the men at the lower hunting-stations were so skilled, the greyhounds so huge which seized them at once and pulled them down right there, as fast as men might look.' The second part of the sentence is explanatory; the deer were quickly dispatched, because the men were so skilled and the dogs so powerful.

1169 *taysed*: a technical term for driving game. See Turberville, p. 246.

1169 *þe wattreȝ*: the hart when hunted usually made for a river, according to the old writers. Dame Juliana Berners in *The Boke of St. Albans* (E VII) says:

> For two causes the hert desirith to the Ryuer:
> Oon cause for the Ryuer descende he is ay
> For he payris of is myght, the sooth I the say;
> Another is to the water whi he gooth other whyle
> The howndes that hym sewen to begyle.

The cunning stag would come out of the water by the same way that he went in, 'and he shal ruse aȝein þe same waye þat he come, a bowe shoot or moore, and þan he shal ruse out of þe way.'—*Master of Game.*

1174 *abloy*: explained by Mrs. Wright, *Mod. Lang. Rev.*, xviii. 86, as derived from OFr. *esbloi*, p. p. of *esbloir* = Mod. Fr. *éblouir*. The change of the initial *es-* to *a-* is Anglo-Norman. Translate: 'The lord, carried away with joy, full oft did ride forth and alight.'

1183 '(He heard) a little noise at his door, [and heard it] quickly open.' It is tempting to amend *derfly* to *dernly* 'stealthily', assuming that the copyist had taken the *n* of the word as *u*, and substituted *f*; this gives slightly better sense, but is unnecessary. *Vpon* is infin. depending on *herde*. For the spelling with *u* compare *vpon* adj. 'open' *Pearl* 198, *Purity* 318, 453 (*wafte vpon*; see 1032 note).

1239–40 'It behoves of very necessity that I be your servant, and I must be.' The syntax is unsatisfactory, and the rhyme unusual; *schal* appears here in emphatic use to take the ending *-e* on the analogy of the regular verbs.

1250 *hit were littel daynté*: 'it would show little good breeding.'

1255 *garysoun oþer golde*: this phrase is a variation of *gold and gersum* 'gold and treasure', which is a common alliterative formula in Middle English, see e.g. *Wohunge of Ure Laverd* in *Old English Homilies*, first series, ed. Morris, 269; *St. Marherete* 3/3; Laȝamon's *Brut* 885, 940, &c.; *Rauf Coilȝear* 936. It is of Scandinavian origin: compare *Eddica Minora* (ed. Heusler and Ranisch) 36/16 *gulli ok gørsimum*, also 34/6, 79/10; *Vølundarkviða* 19 *gull rautt ok gørsimar*; *Bosa Rímur* vi. 53; vii. 76, and elsewhere in Icelandic poetry. In this text the Scandinavian loanword *gersum* has been replaced by the French *garysoun*.

1263–7 It is difficult to be sure of the exact sense and application of this passage, but we take it to be this: '"My lady", said the merry man, "may Mary repay you, for I have found in you a noble generosity; and people very commonly take their line of action from others (i.e. they are showing honour to Gawain because of what they have heard from others), but the honour which they apportion to me they exaggerate above my desert; it (the honour you accord to me) is [due to] the generosity of yourself who can only behave with courtesy (*or*, show nothing but kindness to me)".' The verb *nysen* means literally 'make foolish by over-refinement'; it is recorded (in the pp.) in *N.E.D.* from the fifteenth century (under *Niced*, v.). For the alternative senses of *wel conneȝ* cf. on one hand Chaucer, *Troylus and Creseyde*, v. 106, *as he that coude his good* (knew how to behave); and on the other, *Cursor Mundi* 17659 *All we cunde* (v. l. *coude*) *þe mekil grame*. The lady replying to Gawain protests (1268 ff.) that his merit is not exaggerated.

1281 'The lady behaved as though she loved him greatly'. Napier preferred to retain MS. *a*, regarding it as a reduced form of *ho* 'she', though unable to produce other instances of such a weakened form. The need for a correlative to *lyk* has led us to emend to *as*; the idiom does not usually include *lyk*, but a following conj. is indispensable, cf.

let as 1201, and the Norse idiom (which is the origin of the Middle English one) *láta sem*. Here *lyk as* = OE. *gelice swa*.

1284 *for lur þat he soȝt, &c.*: this is an explanation of the lady's thought added by the author, as is shown by the past tense *soȝt*. If it were part of the lady's thought (as it has been taken in previous editions) a present form *sekeȝ* would be required. Translate 1283–7: 'Even if I were the fairest of ladies', the lady thought, 'the less love-(making) would he bring with him now'—by reason of the harm he sought without delay, the blow which would strike him down, and needs must it be done. For the use of *lode*, cf. Orm. 3455.

1304 *fire* is probably for *firre* 'further', but the syntax is loose: 'I shall kiss at your commandment, as is the duty of a knight, and as a further reason, lest he displease you.'

1320 *hyndeȝ barayne*: 'As of þe hyndes some bene bareyn, and some be þat bere calfes; of þise þat bene bareyn here sesoun bygynneþ whan þe sesoun of þe hert failleþ, and lasteþ to lenton.'—*Master of Game*. See note to 1156.

1324 *querré*: used here of the collection of slain deer. Originally it was the reward of offal given to the hounds, called *cuirée* because fed to them on a hide, as described in 1369. As Twici says: *Et il se serra mangé sur le quir. E pur ceo est il apelée quyrrye.*

1325 *þe best boȝed þerto*: the nobles and gentry made it a point of honour to be skilled in breaking up deer. So Tristram gained honour at the court of king Mark, and when the Duke of Calabria's daughter from her pavilion saw Ipomadon 'dight the venyson' she

> 'thoght in hyr herte than
> That he was come of gentill men.' (*Ipomadon* 410.)

1328 *þe asay*: the position of the assay and the method of trial is described by Turberville (edition of 1576, p. 134): 'The chiefe huntsman (kneeling, if it be to a prince) doth holde the Deare by the forefoote, whiles the prince or chief cut a slyt drawn alongst the brysket of the deare, somewhat lower than the brysket towards the belly. This is done to see the goodnesse of the flesh, and howe thicke it is.'

1329 'Two fingers (breadth of fat) they found in the poorest of them all.'

1331 The *erber* was opened, emptied of its contents, filled with blood and fat, and then tied or sewn together again. So in *La Chace dou Cerf* (trans. Dryden): 'afterwards take off the flesh under the throat, cut out the *erbiere* and the throat, and the *erbiere* you ought to tie, this I wish to teach and advise you.' *The Boke of St. Albans* describes the operation with more detail:

> And ther shall ye take owt th'erber anoon;
> Then put owt the paunche, and from the paunche taas
> Away wightly the Rate sich as he haas;

Hoole it with a fyngre—do as I yow kenne—
And with the bloode and grece fillith hit thenne;
Looke threde that ye have and nedell therto,
For to sew it withall, or ye moore do.

1334 *and lere of þe knot*: former editors read *bere*, and Sir Israel Gollancz wishes to emend to [*þe l*]*ere* (in the introduction to the facsimile reproduction of MS. Cotton Nero A x edited by him for the E.E.T.S.). But the MS. itself has *lere* and no alteration is necessary. The meaning of *lere* is 'flesh', and it is to be taken with *out token* in the preceding line: 'they took out the bowels, swiftly throwing them out, and (also took out) the flesh of the knot.' *Knot* is a translation of the Old French term *neuz*, a name given to two pieces of flesh in the neck, and also to two knots of suet in the flanks. A knot of flesh in the neck appears here to be meant. Turberville describes the knots thus: 'Two knottes or nuttes whiche are to be taken between the necke and the shoulders, and twoo others whiche are in the flankes of the Deare.'

1337–8. Turberville describes the cutting out of the shoulder in detail, p. 134. *Haled hem by a lyttel hole*: cf. Turberville in the passage just referred to: 'And there (i.e. a little above the elbowe ioynt) he rayseth out the synew or muskle with his knife, and putteth his fore-finger of his left hand through under the sayd muskle to hold the legge by.'

1342 *avanters* were part of the numbles at the front of the deer. They are thus defined in *The Boke of Saint Albans* (f. E vij *verso*):

Oon croke of the Nomblis lyth euermoore
Under the throte bolle of the beste befoore
That callid is auauncers.

1347 *þat* is contrasted with the first *hit* (the carcase) in 1346, meaning what they have cut away from the carcase.

1355 *þe corbeles fee*: 'There is a little gristle which is vpon the spoone of the brysket (i.e. at the end of the breast bone) which we cal the Rauens bone, bycause it is cast vp to the Crowes and Rauens whiche attende hunters.'—Turberville. It was thrown into the branches of a tree (*kest in a greue*), as the author of the *Chasse dou Cerf* clearly states: 'Forget not the corbie's bone, put it high on a tree.'

1358 *Vche freke for his fee*: each man worked to prepare the venison on the understanding that some portion was his perquisite. The man who killed a deer marked it, and afterwards claimed the hide as his fee. The man who 'undid' the deer had the left shoulder (and sometimes the head). The right shoulder went by custom to the forester. The numbles, haunches, and sides belonged to the lord. The neck and chine usually were claimed by the *cacheres*.

1362 *prys*: the call blown when the deer had been taken (OFr.

prise 'a taking, capture'). Twici says: *Quant le Cerf est pris vous devez corneer quatre mootz. The Master of Game* says the chief personage of the hunt should blow then four motes, wait for a short interval (less than half an Ave Maria), then blow four motes a little longer than the first four. Then all the rest would blow: 'Trut, trut, trororow, trororow', followed by four motes. They would continue blowing thus all the way home, as is indicated in 1364.

1393–4. 'It may be such (i.e. from such a source) that it is the better gain of the two if you tell me where you won this same wealth by your wit'—showing that the lord knew that it was from his wife.

1406 *wat*; MS. *þat*. The copyist's error was due to carelessness: *w* in the fourteenth century no longer resembled *þ*, and could hardly be misread as such.

1412 ff. There are similar descriptions of boar-hunting in other medieval romances, notably in *The Avowynge of King Arthure* (ed. Robson, *Three Metrical Romances*, Camden Society, 1842), Stanzas III–XVII; in *Garin le Loherain*, Livre V, Caps. 2, 3, 4 (ed. P. Paris, vol. i. 224); and in *Guy of Warwick* (fifteenth century version, ed. Zupitza) 6417–60.

1419 'Bores lie moste commonly in the strongest holdes of Thornes and thicke Bushes.'—Turberville.

1422 *rehayted þe houndeȝ*: the huntsman would call the names of the hounds that first gave tongue on the scent, and urge the others to come up, shouting after this fashion: 'Oyez, a Beaumont, oyez, assemble a Beaumont!' (Hearken, to Beaumont, hearken, assemble on Beaumont!). Beaumont is a favourite hound's name in hunting treatises; cf. note to 1699.

1436 *þe blodhoundeȝ*: these are the 'lymers', larger hounds than the raches, led on a *liam* or leash to the place where they are to work. They are described by Gaston Phoebus in *La Livre de la Chace* as large black-and-tan hounds of a build and shape of head which resemble the modern bloodhounds. The large 'rennyng hound' in the *Master of Game* which is 'right good for þe wilde boor but not good for the hert' is probably the same dog used in a pack. The use of the lymer to find a boar is well described in *Garin le Loherain*, ed. P. Paris, p. 224.

1440 The last half-line lacks an alliterating letter, which in this text can usually be taken as an indication of corruption. C. Brett (*Mod. Lang. Rev.* viii. 160) suggested reading *sengler* or *sing(u)ler* for *wiȝt*, and *singler* may well be right: *wiȝt* is a not unlikely misreading of *singler* with the *n* and *er* represented by the usual contractions. *Singler* or *sengler* was the technical term for a boar when he has left the *sounder* or herd: 'quant il est de quatre annees il doit partyr hors de la soundre par age. Et quant il est party hors de la soundre qe il va soul; par cel encheson est il appele sengler.'—Twici. As, however, the text makes good sense as it stands in the MS. we have left it unaltered.

1442 *grymme*: this word can be pieced together from what remains in the original positions in which it is written and the offset on the opposite page. Of *ful*, *f* is fairly clear. This and *sparred* 1444 are due to Menner, *M.L.N.* xli. 6. *gronyed*: referring to the savage grunts of the angry boar; it is from OFr. *grognir*, possibly blended with OE. *grunian*. This verb in Middle English is confused with *grone* from OE. *grānian*. Cf. *The Master of Game*—'And for no strooke ne for wound þat men doon to hym [he] beplaynneth nat ne crieþ not, but whan he runneth vpon þe men he manesseth, strongly gronyng'; and also *The Avowynge of Arthur* xii: 'So grisly he (the boar) gronus' (*rhyming* stonis 'stones').

1446 *rechated*: originally the recheat was used to call the hounds back from a wrong scent; later, as here, to call the hounds to the hunters or to urge them on. Twici gives the call thus: 'Trourourout, trourourout, trourourout'. It was often preceded or followed by a single mote.

1451 *mute*: a pack of hounds, other than *rachez*. In *The Boke of St. Albans*, the apprentice to venery is told to speak of 'A mute of houndes, a kenell of rachys.' Of the number that made a *mute*, the French treatise *Roy Modus* makes a clear statement: 'Mute de chiens est, quant il y a douze chiens courans et ung limier, et si moins en y a, elle n'est pas dicte mute, et si plus en y a, mieux vault.'

1452 *of*: partitive = 'some of'.

1456 *scheldez*: 'þei (boars) haue herd skynne and stronge flessh, and specially vpon þe shoulder, þat is called þe shelde.'—*Master of Game*.

1457 MS. *browe*: the sense is greatly improved by the simple emendation to *browen* 'boar's flesh'. The usual form is *brawen*, but *ow* for *aw* is elsewhere exemplified in this MS.; cf. *drowe* 1647 for *drawe*.

1467 *schafted*: this word has given difficulty to editors. Morris suggested ? *sattled* 'set, sank'; Gollancz emended to *schifted*, which translators have rendered 'declined'. As Emerson points out (*J.E.G.Ph.* xxi. 389), the idea 'decline, set' can hardly be right, as the hunt goes on for some time after this. It had begun before dawn (1415), so that the rising rather than setting of the sun is referred to. The verb is evidently formed from the noun *schaft* 'a beam of the sun', which occurs in *Pearl* 982, *Patience* 455, and elsewhere in Middle English. The natural sense of *schafted* would be 'shone forth'; this might not refer to the first beams of the sun, but to the first clear light. Not all winter dawns in Cumberland are as clear as that described 1691 ff. Sunrise in Cumberland at the end of December is about 8.15 a.m., so that the time intended here may be two or three hours earlier than the *myd-ouer-under* (about 12 o'clock) in 1730, when the fox-hunt has been going on for a long time.

1495 *meré*: 'merry'. For this interpretation of the form compare 1263 *þe myry mon*; but the word may be *mere* adj. 'beautiful, fair', from OE. *mǣre*: cf. *þis mai mere* 'this fair maiden', rhyming with *chere* 'face' in *Johon* 9 (one of the lyrics of MS. Harley 2253, p. 145 ed. Böddeker).

1508 ff. The sentence is interrupted by a long parenthesis (1512–19) on the service of knights to love; the first part of the lady's question *what were þe skylle* must be carried over to 1523. The whole of the question which is the principal clause of the sentence then is: 'What might be the reason that never yet have I heard any words proceed from your head that in any way belong to love?'

1515 'To describe the endeavour of true knights, it is the inscribed title and text of their deeds, how . . .' The deeds of knights are compared to those in a book of romance: service of love is both its title and text.

1526 *ȝonke þynk*: the unvoicing of the final consonant is characteristic of West Midland dialect = 'a young thing'.

1543 *or* here means 'than': it is originally the same word as ME. *or*, *ar* 'before'. For the sense development, see *N.E.D.* (*Or*, adv.[1], senses C 2 and C 3).

1558 *ruþes hym*: 'bestirs himself' seems to be the sense. The word occurs only here and in *Purity* 896, 1208, where it is used of rousing up some one. The etymology of the word is obscure, but we suggest ON. *hryðja* '*shake' (cf. MHG. *rütten*), traces of which are seen in ON. (*h*)*ryðja* 'toss' and 'clear out', a blend of more than one original word.

1561–5 'But the lord dashed forward many a time, pursues his ferocious boar, that rushes over the slopes and bit asunder the backs of the best of his hounds where he stood at bay, till bowmen broke it and made him move on despite his defence.' *swyngeȝ bi þe bonkkeȝ* has also been taken to mean 'wheels round by the banks' which fits the context admirably; but there is no evidence that *swynge* had such a sense in Middle English.

1566 *felle*: for *fele* 'many' rather than 'cruel, deadly' (OFr. *fel*). Double consonants are often used in this MS. where a single consonant would be expected: cf. *walle* 1403, *stollen* 1659, *stedde* 439, &c.

1573 ff. 'Of him then were wearied the men so bold who stood about him, of harassing him from afar, but none dared approach him by reason of the danger'; *irked* (impersonal) has here two constructions, first with *with hym*, and then with the infin. *to nye*, which is characteristic of this author's syntax.

1581 *kachande his blonk*: 'urging on his horse'. OFr. *cach(i)er* and *chacier* were dialectal variants, both derived from Latin *captiare* and meaning 'to pursue, chase, hunt'. The sense 'catch, seize' of *cach* was developed in England through association with native *lacche*, and *chacier* was also adopted as *chase*. But in Middle English the more original sense of *cache* 'to drive, urge on' is often found as well. In this poem the verb is used in both senses (see glossary).

1593 It was not unusual for a bold hunter to kill a wild boar with his sword, though often a spear was used. Begon in *Garin le Loherain* uses his sword; as the boar rushes on him

> Begues l'attent, qui l'a petit douté,
> En droit le cuer li a l'espié branlé
> Outre le dos li a li fer passé.

So does Arthur in *The Avowynge*, after his spear is broken. And he thrusts his sword in at the neck just as the lord does.

1595 *ȝed ouer*: MS. *ȝedoun*. This emendation is due to Napier. It makes the description intelligible, as it hardly is if we understand that the boar goes down the water, and involves the alteration of only one stroke—*oů* for MS. *oū*.

1603 *brachetes*: this is the etymologically correct form, from OFr. *brachet*. The pl. in French was *brachetȝ*, *bracheȝ*, and in late Anglo-Norman final *ȝ* and *tȝ* became in sound voiceless *s*, still preserved in the traditional pronunciation of *oyeȝ* used by criers, often written *Oh yes!* From the resulting pronunciation of *brachetȝ* a new sing. *brach* was formed, and the plural became spelled *braches*, *bracheȝ*. These are the usual forms in this poem (see Glossary).

1607 Cf. *The Avowynge*:

> The hed of that hardy
> He sette on a stake.

1610 *rewardeȝ*: this is the correct technical term, as the hunting treatises show, e.g. *The Craft of Venery*: 'When the borre is taken . . . ye schull gyve to youre houndeȝ the bowels broyled with bred, and that is clepid reward, for it is not ete on non [h]ide—for as much as is eten on the [h]ide schall be called quyrrye'.

1612 *hastletteȝ*: the entrails of the boar. According to *The Craft of Venery* if the boar 'be undo as is ryght ye schall have xxxii hasteletts.'

1634 *let lodly þerat*: 'expressed horror thereat', i.e. Gawain exclaimed at the ugly and dangerous appearance of the boar, admiring the lord's prowess in slaying such a beast. Emerson (*J.E.G.Ph.* xxi. 393) also has this interpretation.

1648 *trestes alofte*: it is not necessary to insert *on* before *trestes*, as previous editors have done; *alofte* is quoted as a preposition 'upon' in *N.E.D.* The earliest example there quoted is dated 1509, but compare *þeralofte* 569, in which *alofte* takes the place of the preposition *upon.*

1655 *coundutes of Krystmasse*: the OFr. *condut* (Med. Lat. *conductus*) was a motet sung while the priest was proceeding to the altar. Here the *coundutes* are songs hailing the Christmas season; it is from the medieval *coundutes* that modern carols are descended. The *caroles* mentioned in this line were dancing songs.

1659 *Wyth still stollen countenaunce*: 'with looks of love privily bestowed.'

1671 *to schulde*: 'had to go to'. *to* is prob. the prep. 'to', but might be a verb 'go'—either an error for *te* (see *towen* in glossary and note to 88), or a form of *take*; cf. *totȝ* 'goes' rhyming *gotȝ*, in *Pearl* 513.

1680 'Now "third time, turn out best" let us remember in the morning'; they were to exchange their day's gain for the third time next day, but for the present they may forget it and think only of mirth. *þrid tyme, þrowe best* is a proverbial expression which is quoted also in *Seven Sages* 2062 'Męn sais þe þrid time þrowes best.' The modern equivalent is 'third time pays for all'.

1699 ff. Descriptions of fox-hunting are rare in medieval romance. There is a very brief one in Laȝamon's *Brut* (ed. Madden, ii. 451) introduced as a simile of Arthur's pursuit of Childric.

1699–1700 'Some hounds fell in the scent where the fox awaited; they trail often from one side to another, in the practice of their wiles.' The hounds finding that the fox's trail was involved by his doubling often cast to one side to find a loop of it which would lead to a clear trail. That the subject of *trayleȝ* is the hounds and not the fox is indicated not only by *her* 'their', but also by the description of fox-hunting in *The Craft of Venery*: 'Syre hunter, how schalt thou seche the fox? Y schall blow at the furst iij moteȝ & afturward y schall let myn houndeȝ out of coupull, & y schall sey "so houȝe" iij tymes al in hyȝe, & sey noght "sta houȝe", that is to sey "sta ho". And afturward trayle aftur—"cha.ha.ha.hoe". And afterwurd y schall seye "sa houȝe, hue amys, so ho hue, ho syre, hoe!" & yf eny hounde trayle of hym & hathe a name as Richere or Bemounde, ye schull seye "Oyeȝ, a Bemounde! Done oyeȝ huy a luy est, dount a luy est! avaunt a Bemound, avaunt! ho syres ho ho ho!" & draw all youre houndeȝ to hym.'

1700 MS. *a trayteres* is probably corrupt, but might possibly represent OFr. *al tretour, a tretours* (rare), 'in a detour'. Reading *a traveres* compare *Purity* 1473 'So trayled and tryfled a traverce wer alle.'

1701 *kenet*: 'There ben rennyng houndes some lasse and som moor, And þe lasse byn clepid kenettis, and þes houndes rennen wel t al maner game. Men clepin him heirers (i.e. harriers).'—M. of G.

1710 *strothe*: the sense of the word is 'patch of tall herbage *or* lov brushwood'. It is derived from ON. *storð*. Ekwall (*Anglia Beiblat* xxix. 200) points out medieval forms of Lancashire place-names with the same metathesis of the *or*.

1719 ff. So *The Master of Game*: 'The huntynge for þe fox is fair for þe good crie of þe houndis þat folowen so nye and wiþ so goo a wille. Alway þei senten of hym for he fleþ by þik spoies and also fo he stinkeþ euermore.'

1729 *lad hem bi lagmon*: this obscure phrase is also used by th Shropshire poet Audelay (p. 222, l. 114 in the E.E.T.S. edition). Th sense can only be guessed at: perhaps 'led them by devious ways' See Menner, *Phil. Quarterly* x. 163 f.

1738 *trased aboute hir tressour*: 'The fret in which the hair was confined forms a remarkable feature of the female coiffure in the reigns of Richard II and Henry IV', Madden. This fret can be seen in the picture of the lady visiting Sir Gawain (frontispiece). The *tressour* was the gold thread or ribbon of which the fret was made: to it the precious stones were attached. A lady in *The Awntyrs of Arthure* 369 has a similar headdress:

Her fax in perré was frettut and fold.

Also the lady Mildore in *Sir Degrevant* 635:

With topyes and trechoure Overtrasyd that tyde.

The *tressour* was in use earlier in France; cf. *Romaunt of the Rose* 568:

And with a riche gold tresour
Hir heed was tressed queyntly,

rendering *treceor* in the original.

1743 *wayueȝ vp*: see note to 1032.

1750 'Sunk in the deep gloom of dreams that noble knight was muttering like one that was troubled by many grievous thoughts of how . . .'

1752 An infinitive dependent on *schulde* has obviously been omitted by the copyist; *dele hym* has been inserted from the analogy of line 2418.

1755 A verb has been omitted in this line; probably it was *com* which the repetition of *comly com* caused to be dropped.

1786 *For alle þe lufeȝ vpon lyue*: the lady refers to the practice of swearing by God's love, Christ's love, &c., and includes all these oaths in one—'for all the loves there are, do not conceal the truth.' The expression is found also in Old French, e.g. *Perlesvaus*, Branch I, Cap. IX.

1814 *þat lufsum vnder lyne*: 'that lovely one under linen', i.e. that lovely lady. There were many conventional phrases in Middle English describing persons as 'fair under garment'. This same phrase occurs in *Sir Tristram* 1202, 2816; *Eger and Grime* 362 (in the Percy Folio MS.); and (applied to lords) in *Emare* 864. Some of the parallel phrases are: semely under serk (*Emare* 501); worthy under wede (*Emare* 250); geynest under gore (Lyrics of MS. Harley 2253, ed. Böddeker, 148/37); comelye under kell (*The Green Knight* 257, Percy folio MS.).

1833 'Embroidered only at the edges (*arounde*), adorned with work of fingers.' The ornaments added 'with fyngreȝ' were pendants of gold (2037–8 and 2395).

1836 *nay* 'said . . . not' is the past tense of *nie* (OFr. *nier*) formed on the analogy of *lay* past tense of *lie*. The same form occurs as a past tense in *Purity* 805:

And þay nay þat þay nolde neȝ no howseȝ.

(Napier.)

1853 *haþel vnder heuen*: cf. *Beowulf* 52 hæleð under heofenum, and *Salomon and Saturn* 59. Probably the Middle English phrase is the same one, *hæleð* being altered to *haþel* by the influence of *aþele* 'noble'. The expression also occurs in *Wars of Alexander* 4937.

1881 *þe more and þe mynne*: 'the more and the less, every one', a common alliterative tag in Middle English. It is found, e.g. in *Piers Plowman* (C) IV. 399; *York Mystery Plays* 41/28; *Florence of Rome* 549; *Minor Poems of the Vernon MS.* 725/7, 743/131; *Liber Cure Cucorum* 8/22; Gavin Douglas, *Aeneid* i. 87/24; and in many other northern and western poems. The phrase is of Scandinavian origin; cf. *Vǫluspá* i:

Hljóðs biðk allar helgar kindir,
Meiri ok minni mǫgu Heimdallar.

'For a hearing I pray all divine beings and the sons of Heimdall greater and lesser.' Also *Fornmanna sǫgur* viii. 250: 'ekki neyti hann matar meira né minna.'

1941 *chepeȝ*: this word does not alliterate, and moreover is plural though the verb is singular. It is evidently an error of the copyist. Probably the original had *ꝑchaȝ* or even *ꝑcheȝ*, i.e. *porchaȝ*, or *porcheȝ*, 'gain'.

1946 The end of the first half-line is with *þro*, which should therefore be construed with *þryȝt*, not with *þre cosses*, as previous editors have taken it. Translate: 'such precious things as you have pressed warmly upon me here, such three kisses so good.'

1962 *selly*: MS. *sellyly*. There are adverbs in this text ending in *-lyly*, but the double *ly* is not justifiable in the adj. form. Cf. the similar dittography in 2390.

1964 'I will give you myself for one of your men.' Note *ȝef* for alliteration: the usual forms of the verb 'to give' in the poems of this group have *g* not *ȝ*. The same variation for alliterative convenience is found in *The Wars of Alexander*—see glossary to Skeat's edition.

1975 'Gawain thanked the lord.'

1979 ff. The elaborate leave-taking was required by good breeding; the attention given to the observance of elaborate manners is characteristic of French romance, and this passage no doubt is closely dependent on the French original. Compare the leave-taking of Perceval in Gerbert de Montreuil's continuation of Chrestien's *Perceval* (ed. Williams, 1922, l. 1159 ff.).

1999 *þe day dryueȝ to þe derk*: not 'the day passes on to darkness', as it is the passing of night which is spoken of. *Day* here means the dawn, and *dryueȝ* has the sense 'makes its way (to)' as in 222. Translate 'The daylight comes up on the darkness'.

2004 *wapped*: Mr. C. T. Onions has pointed out to us a parallel use of the word in Lancashire records: *Liverpool Town Records*, 1565 (ed. J. A. Twemlow, 1918, vol. i, p. 292), 'the snowe dryvyng and wappyng to and froe'.

2008 'By each cock that crew he was reminded of the appointed hour.'

2018 'The rings of his rich coat of mail cleansed from rust.' Chain armour was rolled (*rokked*) to rub the rust off. Compare Laȝamon's *Brut* 22288 heo ruokeden burnen—they 'rocked' their mail-coats. The later MS. of the *Brut* has: 'hii rollede wepne.'

2022 *wypped*: probably 'wiped'. For the spelling with double *p*, see note to *felle* 1566. The form is normally that of *wyppe* v. 'to whip', but it would be difficult for Gawain to whip on pieces of armour; they had to be fastened on with care.

2023 'The gayest (from here) to Greece'; cf. *Pearl* 231 'No gladder gome heþen into Grece'.

2072 'He praised the porter, [who] was kneeling before the prince (i.e. Gawain) and [the porter] commended him to God, that He save Gawain, and wished him good day—and he went on his way, attended only by his man'. *gef* includes in its sense both the commending and wishing.

2079 'The clouds were high, but it was threatening under them'; *halt* for *halet* 'drawn up'.

2092 *note*: 'noted', originally the pp. of the ME. verb from OFr. *noter*. The form *ynote* (as in *Kyng Alysaunder* 59) is a clear connecting link. Weak verbs with stems ending in a dental frequently do not take an inflectional ending in the pp. in this dialect.

2102 *Hestor*: this form at first sight looks like a mistake for Hector, and it is probably the Trojan Hector who is intended. But

Hestor appears to be a genuine variant, occurring in several French romances, e.g. the *Roman de Merlin* (ed. Paris and Ulrich) and in the so-called Vulgate Arthurian romances (ed. H. Sommer). It has been suggested by Onions (*Notes and Queries*, 19 April 1924, p. 286) that the hero referred to is Lancelot's brother Hector des Mares. But this Hector was hardly important enough to be cited in such an example.

2111 *may þe knyȝt rede*: 'if the knight may have his will.'

2136 *þaȝe he be a sturn knape To stiȝtel, and stad with stave*: 'Though he be a grim fellow to deal with, and stands there with a club'. Such a mound dweller might ordinarily be expected to carry a club. Compare the description of the black man on the mound, armed with a club, in *The Lady of the Fountain* (Lady Charlotte Guest's translation of the *Mabinogion*, ed. Nutt, 1910, p. 170). There may be a reference to the club being a fitting weapon for him in line 384, when Gawayn says he will take a buffet 'Wyth what weppen so þou wylt'.

2167 'The clouds seemed to him grazed by the crags.'

2173 *forȝ*: *ȝ* stands for *s*. This is the earliest recorded occurrence of *fors* 'a waterfall' in English.

2177 *his riche*: probably 'his noble [steed]'. The line is awkward and may contain a corruption of something like *and hit riched to* 'drew it to'; cf. *The Destruction of Troy* 2370:

> And raght to my reyne, richet o lenght,
> Bound vp my blonke to a bogh euyn.

Also 1231, 6693, &c.

2195 *þat chekke hit bytyde!* 'which destruction befall!' *þat . . . hit* = 'which'. *chekke* originally referred to the checkmate at chess.

2199 ff. This is a highly dramatic treatment of a detail which was probably mentioned but casually in the original. The existing parallel romances leave out the whetting, except the account of Lancelot's adventure in *Perlesvaus*, where there is a bare mention of it.

2205 *þat gere, &c.* 'That contrivance, as I believe, is prepared as a salutation to meet me, [sir] knight, by the way. Let God work [his will]; [To say] "Alas!" helps me not a bit; though I lose my life, no noise shall make me afraid.' See add. notes, p. 117.

2219 'Yet he went on with the noise speedily for a time, and turned away [to go on] with his whetting, before he would come down.'

2223 *A deneȝ ax*: properly not the same weapon as the guisarm, as the Green Knight's axe is called in 288 and 2665. The Danish axe was the ordinary long-bladed battle-axe, which had no spike as had the guisarm. It was called 'Danish axe', and in OFr. *hache danoise* because it was a favourite weapon of the Scandinavian vikings who raided England and France.

2226 *bi þat lace*: '(measured) by that lace.' Cf. 217–20.

2230 The Green Knight used the handle of the axe as a staff as he walked. *stele* = 'handle', not 'steel'; *stalked* evidently means 'stalked (with long strides)', though this sense (due perhaps to association with ME. *stalke* 'stalk' n.) is not else found until the sixteenth century (see *N.E.D.*).

2274–6 These lines are evidently closely translated from the original. They are very near even to the reproof given to Lancelot in the parallel episode in the French *Perlesvaus*: 'Sire chevaliers, ainsint ne fist mie mes freres que vos ocistes, ainz tint le chief et le col tout quoi, et ainsint vos couvient-il feire.'

2275 *in kyngeȝ hous Arthor*: 'in king Arthur's house.' In Middle English, when two substantives in apposition are put in the genitive case, usually only the first of them takes the inflectional ending.

2290 *ryueȝ*: as *n* and *u* are indistinguishable in the manuscript, it is uncertain whether this verb is *ryue* 'cleave' or *ryne* 'touch', OE. *hrinan*. The interpretation *ryue* is supported by 2346.

2316 *spenne-fote*: *N.E.D.* has 'with feet close together', evidently connecting *spenne-* with ON. *spenna* 'to clasp'. This would be a clumsy way of jumping; the word more probably means 'with feet kicking out, in a convulsive leap', and is to be connected with M.Du. *spinnevoeten*, Low German *spinnefoten*, Modern Frisian *spinfoetsje* 'to move or kick with the feet convulsively.'

2318 Gawain had his shield slung on his back, and by a movement of his shoulders swung it in front of him so that he could use it for defence.

2325 *foo* 'fiercely' is parallel with *ȝederly*. 2329 *fermed* Menner.

2337 *rynkande*: MS. *rykande*, emended in previous editions to *raykande*. Napier's *rynkande* 'ringing' gives better sense, and assumes a more explicable error—the omission of the single stroke representing *n* over the *y*.

2345–6 'I threatened you with a single feinted blow—and did not rend you with a grievous gash—[which] with justice I offered you, &c.' The punctuation is dictated by alliteration and rhythm.

2387 'Let me win your good will.'

2399 Owing to the difficulty of rendering *at* in this line Sisam emends to '*at* þe grene chapel *of*'. But it is possible to translate the passage in the MS. thus: 'this will be an excellent token of the adventure of the green chapel in the dwellings (*or* company) of chivalrous knights'. A parallel use of *at* is in Laȝamon's *Brut* 3423 when Lear says *Ich wes at Gornoille*.

2445 *Bercilak de Hautdesert*: the correct reading of the name (*Bernlak* in former eds.) is due to Hulbert (*Manly Anniversary Studies in Lang. and Lit.*, Chicago, 1923, p. 12). The name *Bercilak* is the same as *Bertelak* (in the Middle English prose Merlin romance) and

Old French *Bertolais* (nom. case; the acc. was *Bertolai*, earlier *Bertolac*). None of the other knights bearing the name can be certainly identified with the Green Knight. The name *Bertolac* is of Celtic origin, probably from an original **Brettulākos*, a derivative of *Britto* 'a Briton' (so Max Förster). *Hautdesert* refers to the Green Chapel and means 'high (as being in the mountains) hermitage'. The latter element shows the Celtic origin of the name. The OFr. *desert* meant 'waste land, wilderness', but *disert* (from Latin *dēsertum*) in Celtic languages was used of a solitary place where an anchorite took up his abode. It is common in place-names, e.g. Killadysert ('cell hermitage') in County Clare, Disserth in Radnorshire.

2448 *Merlyn*: the famous wizard of Arthur's court. He fell in love with Morgan, who induced him to teach her his magic art. Merlin is first mentioned by Geoffrey of Monmouth in the *Vita Merlini* and in his *Historia Britonum*. The tradition of the *Vita* which represents Merlin as going mad and taking to the woods (whence he was called *Merlin Silvestris* = Welsh *Myrddin Wyllt*) seems to be the more original. It is supported by the oldest Welsh texts, the poems of the Black Book of Caermarthen (a MS. written towards the end of the twelfth century). According to this tradition Merlin was present at the battle of Arthuret (near Carlisle), which was fought *c.* 573 between the northern Welsh and the heathen Celts of Scotland; so he could not have been contemporary with King Arthur. His association with Arthur is probably due to Geoffrey's *Historia*, as is also his character of wizard; in the *Vita* and the Welsh poems he is a bard and prophet, but no wizard. In his *Historia* Geoffrey took this older tradition and grafted it on to Nennius' account of a youth named Ambrosius who prophecied to Vortigern. He calls him Merlin Ambrosius, and, enlarging on the statement that Ambrosius had no mortal father, represents Merlin to be the son of a nun and an incubus. In the Welsh poems he is called Myrddin or Merddin, and is the son of Morvryn, who appears to have been an ordinary mortal.

2452 *Morgne þe goddes*: Morgan is called 'goddess' by Giraldus Cambrensis also in *Speculum Ecclesiae*, distinctio II, cap. 9: 'Propter hoc enim fabulosi Britones et eorum cantores fingere solebant, quod *dea* quaedam phantastica, scilicet et Morganis, dicta corpus Arthuri in insulam detulit Avaloniam ad eius vulnera sanandum.' (Rolls ed. of *Giraldus*, IV. 51.) In a Paris MS. of the Vulgate *Lancelot*, not used by Sommer for his edition, she is called 'Morgain la deesse'. The passage is printed in Jonckbloet's *Roman van Lancelot* II. lxix. This appellation 'goddess' helps towards the identification of Morgan with the Celtic goddess called Morrigu or Morrigain in Middle Irish. She appears frequently in the Ulster cycle of epic poems, where she is identified with Bodb, the goddess of battle (the name is cognate with

OE. *beadu* 'battle'). She is the enemy of Cuchulainn and pursues him with her magic just as Morgan does Arthur and his knights. She appears in various forms, sometimes (as in *Táin Bó Cúalnge*) as a hag of the type described in this poem 947 ff. Phonology also points to an Irish origin of her name: the native Welsh form was *Morien.*

2460 The cause of Morgan's hatred of Guenever is given in *Le Livre de Lancelot de Lac* (ed. Sommer, *The Vulgate Version of the Arthurian Romances*, vol. iv, p. 124, and in *Le Livre d'Artus* (ed. Sommer, vol. vii, p. 135). Morgan had an intrigue with a knight named Guiomar, which was discovered and revealed by the queen. Morgan had to flee from court. To annoy Guenever and the knights of the table she built a chapel in a valley, from which no one who entered might escape who had been faithless in love. Several of Arthur's knights were made prisoners, but were released by Lancelot. It is perhaps the story of Morgan's chapel that suggested the introduction of Morgan into this poem. Madden points out that there is a passage in the *Prophecies of Merlin* which shows Morgan as a figure similar to that in ll. 951 ff.:

'Ha! dame,' fait Morgain, 'vous m'avez honnye, car l'on cuidoit que je fusse de jeune aage, et ilz ont veu ma chair nu et ridée, et ma mamelles pendants, et aussi la peau de mon ventre, dont la nouvelle sera comptée on maint lieu.' 'Morgain,' fait la Dame d'Avallon, 'je scay cartainement que par maintes fors avez este en vostre lict toute nue avec maint beau chevalier.' 'En nom Dieu,' fait Morgain, 'Se je y ay esté aussi me suis-je baignée, et oings tous mes membres, dont les chevaliers les troverent toutes fresches et dures.'

Morgan's aged appearance, while her half-brother Arthur is described as still a youth (line 86 ff.) is accounted for by a passage in another Merlin romance (*Le Roman de Merlin*, ed. G. Paris and J. Ulrich, p. 166):

'Et sans faille elle (i. e. Morgan) fu bele damoiselle jusques a celui terme que elle commencha aprendre des enchantemens et des charroies; mais puis que li animis fu dedens li mis et elle fu aspiree et de luxure et de dyable, elle pierdi si otreement sa biauté que trop devint laide, ne puis ne fus nus qui a bele le tenist, si'l ne fu enchantés.'

2464 The story of Uther and Igern is first told by Geoffrey of Monmouth (*Historia* viii. 19). Arthur's father is called Uther also in the earliest Welsh poems (in MSS. of the end of the twelfth century). The name is perhaps a Welsh form of Latin *Victor* (so Windisch). There is a tenth century addition to Nennius, which says that Arthur was called 'Mab Uter Britannice, filius horribilis Latine', but cf. the similar interpretation of Arthur's own name (note to 26). Like most early etymologies, these are of little account.

2480 The antecedent of *þat* is *Wowen.*

2494 ff. It was usual for knights in Arthurian romances to relate their adventures to Arthur upon returning from a quest. In *Suite de Merlin*, Merlin advises Arthur to make each knight swear before setting out on a quest to relate it faithfully on his return.

2511 Probably: 'For none may hide his (spiritual) harm, on the contrary it cannot be unfastened (got rid of).' For a similar figurative use of *happe* v., see 655. *vnhap* has usually been taken as a noun, and *hit* as a verb ('unless misfortune may befall—i. e. without misfortune ensuing'). Apart from the awkwardness of the superfluous *ne* (though this can be paralleled, cf. 1991), this does not suit the context. It is not the danger of ignoring the past, but the impossibility of doing anything of the kind, that is Gawain's point.

2514 ff. This decision has sometimes been taken as an indication that the poem was composed with reference to some order of knights. Some orders had collars which were worn much as Gawain wore the lace (2485). The legend at the end of the poem *Hony soyt qui mal pence* is the motto of the order of the Garter, but neither that order nor any other, as far as is now known, wore a green collar or band. In *The Green Knight*, the later romance based on *Sir Gawain*, the lace is white and is said to be the origin of the collar worn by the Knights of the Bath. There is no good evidence that any such reference was intended in *Sir Gawain*.

2523 *Brutus bokeȝ*: this term might be applied to any chronicles or romances of British times, not necessarily devoted to the legendary history of Brutus. In the romance of *Arthour and Merlin* the French source is called 'þe Brout' (3486, 3675, &c.), though Brutus's story was not told in it. In Welsh, *brud* is still used meaning generally 'chronicle'.

ADDITIONAL NOTES. 104, 107: for *on* (*in*) *stalle* 'standing upright' cf. *Bestiary* 661, 663, 671, 679.

2123 *as . . . halydam*: prob. originated as formula in serious oaths taken on some definite holy thing (esp. relics). To this use, where a particular 'halidom' was in mind, *þe* is probably due. The article appears in OE. (*on þam haligdome swerian*), but is not always present. Cf. *aðes swor on halidom*, Chron. A. D. 1131. The closest parallel is: 'My lordes, as help me God and halidome, master doctor here said . . .' (More, *A Dyaloge* (1529)). Here, though these are the words of a witness, the oath is casual.

2206: *renk* is hardly credible as addressed to the unseen knight, or as extension of *me* (cf. *wyȝeȝ . . . þay*, 1435). Possibly *me renk to mete* = '(is intended with the due ceremony) to mark out the field of combat for me', i. e. to announce the challenge in place of the trumpets of a more courtly setting. [Mr. Sisam's suggestion.] *renk* is then from OFr. *renc* (cf. *Sir Beues* p. 178, ll. 3793 ff.). *mete* is then OE. *mĕtan* (cf. *wicsteal metan*, *Exod.* 92). Compare also ON. *hasla vǫll*, 'mark out space for single combat (with hazel-wands)', which acquires sense 'challenge one to a duel'.

METRE

Sir Gawain is composed in stanzas consisting of unrhymed alliterative lines followed by five short rhymed lines. The number of unrhymed lines varies from 12 to 38. There is no trace of the quatrain arrangement of the unrhymed lines which is found in *Purity*, *Patience*, *St. Erkenwald*, *The Siege of Jerusalem*, and *The Wars of Alexander*.

The Long Alliterative Lines.

The structure of these lines is similar to that of the OE. alliterative verse, from which it has descended through an unbroken oral tradition.[1] During the centuries which separate *Sir Gawain* from OE. verse the character of the alliterative line underwent some changes. The main differences are these:[2]

(1) The rhythm is purely accentual in ME. The lift is not required to fall on a syllable that is long as well as accented. This disregard of length probably arose when vowels were lengthened in open syllables in ME.

(2) The ME. verse is richer in alliteration; see below p. 120.

(3) The richer alliteration allows more freedom in the treatment of unstressed elements without weakening the line unduly. The number of unstressed syllables is considerably greater in ME. lines. The minimum half-line of four syllables, frequent in *Beowulf*, is rare in *Sir Gawain*.

(4) In OE. verse the falling rhythm (types A and D) predominates, whereas in ME. more lines begin with weak syllables and end with weak syllables as well, a rising-falling rhythm (types C and AB).

(5) In ME. the first half-line may have three lifts instead of two: usually all three then take the alliteration. The origin of the three-lift type is uncertain. Since it is found only in the first half-line, its evolution was evidently to some extent dependent on OE. precedent, for OE. verse also used heavier types in the first half-line than in the second.

[1] Cf. l. 33 and note.

[2] Some knowledge of OE. metre is necessary in order to follow this account. The terminology here used is that of Sievers in the form adopted by Sweet in his account of OE. verse (*A.-S. Reader*, pp. lxxv ff.).

Of the OE. types A, B, and C are still in use in ME.:

A: 11 a *Tícius to Túskan.*
381 b *Gáwan I hátte.*

B: 46 a *Such gláum ande glé.*
571 b *of a dére társ.*

C: 37 b *vpon Krýstmásse.*
No clear example in the first half-line.

Type AB is common. It already existed in OE. as type A with an introductory syllable.

Examples:

20 a *And quen þis Brétayn was bígged.*
27 b *I áttle to scháwe.*

The three-lift types may be classified thus:

A: falling rhythm.

(i) With lifts all separated by unaccented elements:
26 *áy was Árthur þe héndest.*

(ii) With two lifts 'clashing', i. e. one following immediately after the other:
76 *smál séndal bisídes.*

B: rising rhythm.

(i) 209 *A spétos spárþ to expóun.*
(ii) 2 *þe bórȝ bríttened and brént.*

AB: rising-falling rhythm.

(i) 8 *Fro ríche Rómulus to Róme.*
(ii) 61 *þat dáy dóubble on þe déce.*

In the (ii) types (when the lifts are in juxtaposition) there is a slight rhythmic pause in place of an unaccented element. Usually the lifts so placed are the first and second.

The metre is sometimes obscured by the copyist's carelessness of final unaccented *-e*, which he dropped at will. It is usually not essential to the metre, but at times it is, and then the copyist leaves a half-line incomplete. Such are:

253 b *Árthour I hát*[*te*]. Cf. 381.
294 b *stíf on þis flét*[*te*], and so 568 b.
2379 b *cówardyse me táȝt*[*e*], and others.

The Rhymed Lines.

The first short line of the group of rhyming lines is known as the 'bob', and the following four as the 'wheel'. The bob contains one stress preceded by one or sometimes two unaccented syllables. Each line of the wheel contains three stresses and is metrically equivalent to a three-lift half-line of the alliterative type. The rhythm is varied, but predominantly falling. The 'clash of stress' which is common in the unrhymed alliterative verse is found in 2452 *Mórgne þe góddés*, and also in 35, 736, 1948. Usually two or all of the accented syllables alliterate in each line, but the alliteration is not regular.

Alliteration.

Most lines have two or three alliterating staves in the first half, one in the second half. The type in which there is only one stave in the first half-line (so frequent in OE.) is still used, but is comparatively infrequent. Examples of it are lines 25, 44, 311, 649, 1372, 1406, 1497, 2179, &c.

In addition to the increased number of staves in the first half-line, there are other elaborations that are rarely found in OE., as two alliterations in one line:

60 *Wyle* Nw *ȝer watȝ so ȝep þat hit was* nwe *commen*,

and also in 335, 377, 906, 1223, 1727, 1962, &c. Sometimes, no doubt, one of the alliterations is merely accidental.

Every lift in the line may alliterate:

2077 *þay* bo*ȝen bi bonkkeȝ þer* bo*ȝeȝ ar* bare,
þay c*lomben bi* c*lyffeȝ þer* c*lengeȝ þe* c*olde.*

So also 87, 179, 379, 794, 1254, 2980–2, &c.

To assist in the construction of such elaborate alliterations the poet avails himself of several licences, viz.:

Words beginning with *h* may alliterate with words beginning with a vowel, as in lines 5, 26, 789, 1242, &c. (very common). It is clear that initial *h* of words of Germanic origin was still pronounced from such combinations as 59 *a here*; 743 *a hundreth*; 1257 *my honde*; 2276 *my hede*, &c.; if *h* had not been pronounced the forms *an*, *myn* would have been used.

A voiceless consonant is sometimes made to alliterate with the corresponding voiced consonant, namely: *ch* with *j*, as in 86; *s* with *z*, as in 517; *f* with *v*, as in 1375, 1391. The poet also alliterates *sch* with *ch*, in 1081 and perhaps also in 160 (where the pronunciation of *scholes* is doubtful).

Sometimes the alliteration falls on an unaccented syllable, such as a verbal prefix (b*igyne*ȝ, 112, 1571, cf. 495, 1340; similarly in 392, 452, 1168, 1422); an unaccented preposition (987, 1693, 1741); an auxiliary verb (1943, 2053); a pronoun (2325). In recitation such syllables were probably given an artificial stress. Lines of this sort, however, may sometimes be suspected of having suffered slightly in transmission: at 112, for instance, it is possible that the author wrote *þe borde bigine*ȝ, for in addition to alliterating well, this is the older and more usual form of the idiom (cf. *Prol. to Canterbury Tales*, 52).

The alliteration may fall on the second element of a compound word, as in 311 (cf. 2457); *where*-so 395; *day*lyȝt 1137, 1180; *quere*fore 1294, &c.

In the second half-line the alliteration usually falls on the first lift, as in OE, but sometimes on the second lift, as in 161, 263, 1193, 1654, 2131, &c. Occasionally no stave at all is evident in the second half-line; this is usually, perhaps always, due to corruption of the text. Corruption is clear in 236, 343, 958, 1208, 1906; probable also in 1440 and 1941 (see notes); 971 also may be corrupt.

It is to be noticed that *wh* (OE. *hw*) alliterates with *w*, as *wh* had become identical in sound with *w* in the poet's dialect; so in 224, 398, 1573, &c. The spelling of *wh* as *qu* often obscures the alliteration with *w*, as in 255, 257, 1186, 1227, &c. The reverse spelling of *qu* as *wh* obscures the alliteration on *qu* in 877 and 2492. In 1518 the alliteration on *v* is obscured by the spelling of *v* as *w*.

A group of consonants is repeated in alliteration when possible though by custom only the first of them need be repeated. Thus *gr* 1006, *sl* 1182, *sn* 2003, &c., are repeated in alliteration, while elsewhere the first consonant only is repeated. But *sp*, *st*, *sch*, *sk*, as a rule alliterate only with the same group; cf. 269, 570, 979, 2167, &c.

LANGUAGE

Spelling.

The most notable peculiarities of spelling in *Sir Gawain* are:

1. The use of *ȝ*, which has its origin from two distinct letters; it is (A) the development of the special shape of OE. *ᵹ* = *g*, and (B) a form of *z*. A is used for four distinct but related sounds:

(i) Approximately the sound of modern *y* in *you*. Initially it is derived from OE. front spirantal *g*, as in *ȝonge*, *ȝeþe*; medially, it is a glide between vowels, as is shown by such spellings as *fayryȝe* 240, and the rhymes with *hyȝe* 83, *wyȝe* 249.

(ii) The voiceless equivalent (as in German *ich*) of the preceding, chiefly in *ȝt* from OE., ON. *ht*, *gþ*: *myȝt*, *sleȝt*.

(iii) The sound of *w* derived from OE., ON. back-voiced spirant *g*: *arȝe*, *saȝe*, &c. The pronunciation *w* is shewn by frequent spelling of the sound as *w*, as in *bawemen*, *lawe*, &c.; by the use of *ȝ* for etymological *w*, in *broȝeȝ* 305 (cf. *browe* 2306); and by rhymes: *innoȝe* 514: *blowe*; *lawe* 1396: *knowe*, &c.

(iv) A related voiceless sound, a back spirant with lip rounding, chiefly in *ȝt* after *a*, *o*, *u*, from OE., ON. *ht*, *gþ*: *laȝt*, *oȝt*, &c., less frequently from OE. *-hh-* or final *-h*: *þaȝ*, *laȝande*, &c.

B. *ȝ* = *z*. *z* was used (both alone and in the combination *tz*) in OFr. with the sound of *ts*: e.g. the pl. of *brachet* was *brachets*, spelled *brache*(*t*)*z*. This *ts* in OFr. became simplified in pronunciation to *ss* and then voiceless *s*, and ultimately *z* (voiced). On this development is based the use in this text of *tȝ* as voiceless *s* in *watȝ*, *hatȝ*, *gotȝ*, &c., and of *ȝ* as voiceless *s* in *forȝ*, and probably *hedleȝ*, &c. In the ending *-eȝ*, *ȝ* may have had the sound of *z* (voiced): *brondeȝ*, *torneȝ*, *elleȝ*, &c.; also in *Ȝeferus* 517.

2. Etymological *i* (*y*) in an unaccented syllable is often *e*; to distinguish this *e* it is marked with an acute accent in the edited text: *meré*, *bodé*.

3. *w* is used to represent a diphthong, probably [*iu*]. The sources of the sound are OE. *ēow*, *īw* (never *ēaw*), and OFr. *ǖ*: *hwe*, *remwe*. More rarely, *u* is found: *crue* 2008, &c.

4. *v*, *u* is sometimes found for etymological *o*: *vpon* 1183, *bluk*, *rysoun*. This may be due to Anglo-Norman influence.

5. A redundant *i* is often inserted beside *i* or *y*: *iisse* 732, *niyȝt*, *niyry*, &c.

6. Unaccented *e* is variously represented: *papure*, *etayn*, *lentoun* French influence); *aventurus* (W. Midl.).

7. *w* is sometimes written for *v*: *awenture*, *wouche*, &c. This peculiarity belonged mainly to northern and Scottish spelling.

Further peculiarities of spelling are described in dealing with the phonology.

Phonology.

In so far as the rhymes provide evidence, it appears that the dialect in which the poem was composed did not differ materially from the form in which we have it preserved:

(1) ME. *a* was rounded to *o* before a nasal consonant: *blonk* 2024, *bonk*, *wlonk*. The word *blonk* in the fourteenth century alliterative poems always has *o*, even in texts which otherwise do not show rounding of *a*, as in *The Wars of Alexander*. But rounding of *a* was not consistent: *hande*, *laȝande* 1207. The ending of the pres. part. usually did not show rounding in ME.[1] ME. *o* (by rounding of *a*) +*ng* is retracted to *u*; see p. xxiv.

(2) OE., ON. *ā* is usually rounded to *ǭ*, but not invariably: *brode*, *lode*, *Gode* 965; *lote* 639, 1917, *cote*; *strokeȝ* 416, *cnokeȝ*, *slokeȝ*. But *wape*, *skape* 2353; *hame* 1530, *game*, *schame* (cf. 1314 *game*, *dame*, and 2504 *schame*, *lame*).

(3) OE. *ǣ* (Anglian *ẹ̄*), is *ę̄*: *were* 318, *lere*; *slepes*, *kepes* 1682.

(4) *ẹ̄* is found for *ę̄* in *clene* 146, *grene*. The explanation is that in OMercian *ǣ* was raised to *ẹ̄* before the dental consonants *d*, *t*, *s*, *l*, *n*, *r*.[2]

(5) ME. *ę̄* was raised to *ī* before *ȝ* (= OE. *h* or front *g*): *syȝe* 83, *descrye*; *yȝe* 228, *studie*.

(6) OE. *ā* in combinations which yield *āw* in early ME. was not rounded to *ǭ*; the *āw* fell together with ME. *aw*; cf. rhymes *lawe*, *knowe*, *drowe*, 1643 ff.

(7) OE. *ēow*, *īw*, and French *ṻ* have fallen together as [*iu*], variously spelled: *hewe* 1471, *salue*, *remwe*.

[1] Though *-onde* is not infrequent in *The Destruction of Troy*.

[2] See Bülbring's article in the *Miscellany presented to Dr. Furnivall*.

(8) Double consonants have been simplified: *stedde* 440 (OE *stede*), *bledde*, *redde*; *þikke* 175, *quik*[*e*].

From the alliteration we perceive that:

(9) OE. *hw* became *w*: see pp. xxiii, 121.

(10) ME. *ch* perhaps became identical with *sch*: see p. 121.

(11) ME. *squ* became *sw*; see line 138.

These characteristics are found throughout the text, except tha (3) and (4) can only be tested in rhyme. Under (1) it may be furthe noted that rounded *o* is found even when the vowel is lengthened i an open syllable, as *nome* 9. (5) was not carried out consistently we find *heȝ* beside *hyȝ*; *dreȝ* and *dryȝ*, &c. (6) is illustrated by th confusion of *aw* and *ow* in spelling; though *aw* remains in sound, th normal Midland *ow* is often used, and is even extended to original *aw* in *drowe* 1647 (OE. *dragen*). (7) is indicated also by the interchang *ew* and *w* in spelling. As a result of (8) the copyist is often uncertai when he should use double consonants, sometimes putting a singl consonant where it should be double, as *biges* 9, *wonen* 1365, sometime double consonants where a single one should stand, as *felle* 1566 (se note), &c. (10) The confusion of *sch* and *ch* is also illustrated in th spelling: *schere* for *chere*, *scholes* 160 (see note), *cheldeȝ* 1611 fo *scheldeȝ*. (11) *squ* is spelled *sw* in *sware* 138; *swyereȝ* 824.

There are some minor discrepancies between the phonology of th rhyme and alliteration, and the spelling of the copyist. Original OE *hw* usually appears as *wh* or *w* (*while*, *wyle*; *why*, *wy*), and OE. *cw* as *qu* (*quene*). Occasionally, however, northern spellings are used In northern dialects OE *cw* and *hw* had both become [χw] in sound and by reason of this identity *qu* and *wh* were interchangeable i northern spelling. This northern confusion appears in *Sir Gawain* in forms like *quyle*, *quy*; and in *whene*, *whyssynes* for *quene* *quyssynes*, although the alliteration shows that the author's dialec did not identify *qu* with *wh*. In *leude* 1124, *ȝede* the copyist ma have substituted *eu* for *e*; but it is possible that to some extent h used *e* and *eu* as spelling equivalents, as *e* and *eo* were used in man ME. texts, and emendation of his spelling is therefore undesirable.

There remain some important phonological characteristics of *Sir Gawain* of which the rhyme and alliteration give no evidence; ye they were probably much the same in the original text. Thus:

(12) OE., ON. *y̆* is usually *i*, *y*, but also *u*. The proportion o *u*-spellings is about 1 : 7: e.g. *bur*, *fust*. ME. *i* of other origin is also sometimes (rarely) *u*: *hult*, *rudel*, *wruxled*.

(13) OE. *ēo*, *éo* is usually *e*, but also [*ö* > *ü*] spelled variously *u*, *uu* *eu*: *burne*, *buurne*, *leude*, &c.

(14) OE. *ēa*, *ǣ* when shortened are *a*: *grattest* (OE. **grĕattra*, *grēatost*, without mutation), *walt*, *clanly*, *hadet*; rarely *ǣ* (*ē*): *brad*.

(15) ME. *i* is sometimes lowered to *e*: *clengeȝ*, *renke*.

(16) ME. *er* became *ar* towards the end of the fourteenth century in he north. There are a few examples of this change in *Sir Gawain*: *tart* 1716 and perhaps *charre*, *marre*, *ȝarrande*.

(17) OE. *tį*, *sį* appear as *ch*, but where *ch* is derived from *sį* it probably stands for *sch*: *feche*, *foche*, *halche*.

(18) Voiced consonants when final are unvoiced: *habet*, *bront*, *onke*, *þinke*, &c. Usually the conventional spelling with the original consonant is retained; thus final *d* is still written when in sound it has become *t*. Since *d* could have this value when final, it was used also to express original final *t*, as in *neked*. For final *ȝ*, see *Spelling*, § (i) *b*.

(19) *ow* (OE. *ŏg*, AFr. *ou*) sometimes appears as *aw*, *au*: *bauleȝ*, *bawemen*, *enbrawden*; cf. 6, above.

The Scandinavian Element. ✗

Scandinavian words are numerous in *Sir Gawain*; doubtless they were plentiful also in the author's spoken dialect, but it is evident that many of them in the poem have been called into play by the needs of alliteration. Scandinavian words were often specially convenient for alliterative poets, as having initial sounds that were not common in native English words. Thus we find, among words beginning with *sk-*, *skayned* (not recorded elsewhere in English), and *skyfted* for English *schyfted*, for the sake of alliteration. Northern alliterative poets in search of synonyms—the constant need of the alliterative technique—took up many a Scandinavian word that would otherwise have been lost. Thus *tulk* is added to the traditional stock of words for 'man'; *carp* to the verbs of speaking, *cayre* to the verbs of going, proceeding. The purely alliterative use of some Scandinavian loan-words goes back to ON. alliterative use, as *mynne* 'less', which is found in ME. only in the alliterative phrase *more and mynne*, an anglicizing of ON. *meiri ok minni*. Such survivals of Scandinavian literary tradition are not frequent. For further examples see the notes to lines 165, 1053, 1255.

While the literary use of Scandinavian words in *Sir Gawain* is extensive, it is to be observed that few of the common syntactical words (prons., conjs., preps.) are of Scandinavian origin—fewer than in most texts of the north and the north midlands. There are only these: *þay*, pron.; *þayr*, poss. adj. (twice; the usual word is English *her*, *hor*); *þoȝ*, *þof* (twice; the usual word is English *þaȝ*); *-and*(*e* ending of the pres. part. (from ON. *-ande*).

The Scandinavian loan-words in *Sir Gawain* have often diverge remarkably from the original senses; in general the Scandinavia words changed more in meaning in ME. than French or native Englis words. In the main this was due to the completeness of the brea with Scandinavian tradition. Many Scandinavian words had n etymological associations for the Englishman, and so their sense development was nearly uncontrolled. Thus we have among numerou examples the phrase *on lyte* 'in delay, apart', ON. *hlíta* 'to trust' *neked* 'little', ON. *nekkvat* 'something'. Sometimes alliterative us seems to be the cause, as in *tulk* 'man', ON. *tulkr* 'spokesman' *carp* 'talk', ON. *karpa* 'boast'.

The Scandinavian settlers in England were both Danish and Nor wegian, but at the time of the settlements (ninth and tenth centuries they spoke dialects of Scandinavian that differed but little. It is onl occasionally possible to distinguish loan-words as specifically from Ol Norwegian or Old Danish. *bayn*, *boun*, *bone*, *caple*, *farand*, *grayþ*(*e lyre* (n.[1]), *scowtes*, *tayt* are Norwegian; *busk* 182, *dyȝe*, *giue*, *kay*, *in melle* are Danish.

A certain number of Scandinavian words were borrowed in the OE period; of those in *Sir Gawain* OE. forms are recorded of *calle*, *cost felaȝe*, *hitte*, *lawe*. But there was probably not much blending o Norse and English in the north of England before the Normar Conquest; the greater number of Scandinavian loan-words first appea in ME. Owing to the similarity of Norse and English the number o words in northern dialects blended from the two sources must have been large; but when the Norse and English forms had the same meaning and phonologically would give the same result in ME. i is impossible to be sure of Scandinavian influence. Clear example of blend-words are found, however: *derf*, *dreme*, *ȝayned*, *ȝaule*, *ȝette*, *vmbe*, &c.

The ON. forms are quoted in the glossary in the normal spelling of thirteenth-century Icelandic, which represents fairly closely the language used by the Scandinavian settlers in England. When the forms had changed in Icelandic the older form also is given. The prin cipal changes which differentiate Icelandic from ON. may be thus classified:[1]

(1) ON. had falling diphthongs like those of OE. Those with *ĕ̄* as the first element shifted the stress to the second element, and the

[1] These are given as chronological rather than dialectal differences, and are not confined to Icelandic alone among the later Scandinavian languages.

e became *j*. Thus Icelandic *jú*, *jó*, *já*, *jǫ*, *ja* go back respectively to ON. *éu*, *éo*, *éa*, *eo*, *ea*.

(2) *auh* became *ōh*, which became Icel. *ó*. The form **þóh* (and shortened *þoh*) was adopted in ME. as *þoȝ*.

(3) ON. *a* was rounded to *ǫ* before *u* or *w* in the next syllable in Icelandic, as in *vǫndr*; *Sir Gawain* has *wand* from the older Norse form **wandur*.

(4) ON. *e* in unaccented syllables became *i*: see *bonke*, &c.

(5) ON. *nk* became *kk* by assimilation. A preceding *u* often became *o*, and *i* became *e*: *hrunka* became *hrukka*, *hrokka*. Hence *runkled* belongs to an earlier stratum of loan-words than *rokked*.

(6) *ð* disappeared before *n*: **beiðna* became *beina*. Hence *bayþen* in *Sir Gawain* belongs to an earlier stratum of loan-words than ME. *bayne*.

(7) ON. *w* became *v*, as in *vǫndr*: see (3).

The sounds of ON. resembled those of OE., and those which were identical received the same treatment in ME. For example, ON. *á* was rounded to *o* just as was OE. *ā*: e.g. *broþe*; ON. *a* before a nasal consonant was equated with OE. *a/o* before a nasal consonant, and hence usually appears in *Sir Gawain* rounded to *o*. But the following sounds did not exist in OE.:

(1) ON. *au* appears as *au* in *Sir Gawain*: *ȝaule*, *glaum*, *lausen*.

(2) ON. *éu* is treated like OE. *ēo*, and so appears as *ę̄*: *meke*; or *ī* before front *g*: *dryȝ*, from *dreȝ*, ON. **dréugr*.

(3) ON. *ea* arose from fracture of short *e*, which had taken place when the Scandinavians settled in England (Noreen, *Altisländisches Grammatik*, 4th ed., § 95). ON. *ea* differed from OE. *ea* (which was *æ*+*a*) and gives *e* in ME., not *a*. Hence *derue* from ON. **dearfr*.

(4) ON. *gg* and initial *g* and *k* were always stops, and did not share changes of OE. *g*, *c* before original front vowels and in the combination *sc*. This often gives a good test of Scandinavian origin. Thus *giue* is from ON., *ȝef* from OE.; *agayn* (in form) is from ON., *aȝayn* from OE.; and *skyfte*, *kirke*, &c. are seen to be from ON. On the other hand medial *g* (except in *ng*) was a spirant, and treated like OE. *g*, as in *gayn*, ON. *gegn*.

Very few Norse endings are preserved in ME. The only common one is *-ande* of the pres. part. The reflexive ending *-sk* of the Scandinavian middle voice is preserved in the verb *buske*, though no longer felt to be an ending. Usually the reflexive *-sk* was dropped in ME., as in *þryue* from ON. *þrífask*. The adverbial comparative ending *-r* is preserved in *helder*. ON. adjs. are quoted in the glossary in the nom. sing. masc., which ends in *-r*, as does also the nom. sing. of strong masc. nouns. But it was the stem of the word, not the nom. sing., that was borrowed, so that this nominatival *-r* does not appear in ME. An apparent exception is *haȝer*, but see note to 352. Where final *-r* belongs to the stem of the word, it is of course kept in ME., as in *anger* from ON. *angr*.

The French Element.

The French element in *Sir Gawain* is also extensive. The technical terms used in the descriptions of Gawain's equipment (506 ff.), the castle (764 ff.), and the hunting in the third fitt account for a large proportion of the French loan-words: otherwise they are mostly domestic terms of the aristocratic household, or abstract nouns. The French forms borrowed are nearly always found to be Anglo-Norman—in so far as the Anglo-Norman forms are distinct from Central French. Some of the marked Anglo-Norman characteristics of the French loan-words in *Sir Gawain* are:

(1) *ei* (became *oi* in CFr.) is preserved in AN. and becomes *ai*, *ay* in *Sir Gawain*, as in *fai*(*þ*), CFr. *foi*. Where *oi* is found, it is original, not from earlier *ei*.

(2) Loss of pretonic *e* before a vowel: *gra*(*u*)*nte*, CFR. *greanter*, *chaunce*, CFr. *cheance*.

(3) *ca* (beside *cha*), where CFr. has only *cha*: *cache*, CFr. *chasser*; cf. *chasyng* 1143. Similarly *likkerwys* with *k* = CFr. *lecherous*.

(4) *w* (beside *g*, *gu*) where CFr. has *g*(*u*): *werre*, CFr. *guerre*; *Wawain* (beside *Gawain*).

These characteristics Anglo-Norman had in common with continental Norman and to some extent with other northern French dialects. The following are distinctively Anglo-Norman:

(5) *ẹ* for *ie*: *feersly*, CFr. *fiers*; *maner*(*e*), CFr. *maniere*.

(6) Confusion of *u* and *o*: *vrysoun*, CFr. *horson*, *bluk*, CFr. *bloc*.

(7) The development of *u* between *a* or *o* and a following *n* or *m* + cons. The diphthong *au* often became *ā* before *m* + labial or *n* + dental. Hence *countenaunce*, but *grante* beside *graunte*, and *chambre* beside *chaumbre*.

(8) Loss of *s* before a consonant: *a-belef*, CFr. *a beslif*. Initial *es-* becomes *a-*: *abloi*, CFr. *esbloi*; *aumail*, CFr. *esmaille*.

(9) Loss of pretonic *e* before a cons.: *coprounes*, CFr. *couperon*; *drury*, CFr. *druerie*.

(10) *ę̄* for *ai*, *ei*: *plesaunt*, *ese*, *des*, CFr. *plaisant*, *eise*, *deis*.

(11) -*eia*- becomes -*ia*-: *ryal*, CFr. *roial*.

(12) -*ee*- becomes -*eie*: *devaye*, AN. *deveier*, CFr. *deveer*.

(13) The use of aphetic forms. In late Anglo-Norman an initial unaccented syllable was often dropped: *chekke*, CFr. *eschec*; *dut*, CFr. *dedut*; *bate*, CFr. *debat*.

The following changes in French loan-words may be noted:

(1) The principal accent was shifted to the root syllable. Throughout the ME. period the words of French origin could be accented either in the English or the French way, but in *Sir Gawain* they are nearly always accented like native English words. French accent is used only for the sake of rhyme. This shifting of accent caused the final syllables to be weakened; from this some confusion in spelling arose. The endings -*oun*, -*ain*, for example, came to be pronounced like -*en*, and then the spellings -*oun*, -*ain*, were extended to words that had original -*en*, as *lentoun*, OE. *lencten*; *etayn*, OE. *eoten*. French endings -*ure*, -*ere* came to be pronounced alike and were confused: thus *papure*, *salure*, *cropure*, AN. *papere*, *salere*, *cropere*.

(2) AN. *üi* (later *ǖ*) became *ǖ*, later *eu*, *ew* [= *iu*], but *ī* also appears, especially before vowels, as in *nyȝe* (AN. *anüi*), *distryȝe*. *byle* shows a distinct change: *ui*, *oi* to *ī*.

(3) AN. *au* became *ā* before labials: *sauage*, *sanap*, *saf*, from *sauvage*, **sauvenap*, *sauf*.

(4) Intervocalic *v* in early borrowings was vocalized as *u* in northern English dialects: *aventure* becomes *aunter*.

(5) Palatal *l* and *n* are represented as *ly*, *ny*: *fylyoleȝ*, OFr. *filoele*, *gronye*, OFr. *grognir*; or as *ngn*, *syngne*.

French nouns and adjectives were generally adopted in the form of the accusative sing. (without ending), but not *feers* (occurring in *Sir Gawain* in the derivatives *feersly* and **fersnes*), which has the -*s* of the nom. sing. masc. Of verbs it was the stem that was borrowed. In some verbs there was a strong and a weak form according to the position of the accent; in ME. usually the strong form (as in the present sing.) was adopted, but sometimes the weak form (as in the 1 and 2 plur.). Of some verbs there are double forms in ME., as *byle*, *keuer*, *meue* from the strong stem, *boyle*, *kouer*, *moue* from the weak stem. French verbs in *Sir Gawain* are conjugated weak, except *nie*, pa.t. *nay*, on the analogy of *lie*, pa.t. *lay*.

Grammar.

The most frequent inflexional ending in the author's dialect was *-e*, which the copyist has often obscured, as rhymes and metre prove. Rhymes and metre, however, do not give complete evidence of the author's usage, affording tests as they do, only in the emphatic position at the end of the line. In positions where there was no such emphasis and pause it is likely that the author dropped normal historical *-e* more frequently than such tests would indicate. Even in rhyme his use of *-e* was not consistent;[1] hence though rhyme or metre prove the use of *-e* at the end of the line, we assume that in other positions in words of the same grammatical function it was often dropped.

Nouns. The inflexional endings are:

Sg. nom. acc. —, *-e*. Pl. *-eȝ*, *-es* (*-us*); *-ȝ*, *s* (after *n*, *r*).
gen. *-eȝ*, *-es* (*-us*), —.
dat. *-e*, —.

The *-e* of the nom. sg. is usually historical, as in *waþe* 2355, *blonk*[*e*] 1581, &c.,[2] but sometimes is analogical: *blaste* 784, *knyȝt*[*e*], &c. The ending of the gen. sg. is usually *-eȝ*, *-es*, but a form without ending (as in northern dialects) is also found: *Bretaygne* 25, *segge* 574, &c. The endingless form is found also in the pl. in *rach mouþes* 1907. This form of gen. merges into the attributive use of nouns in adjectival function, as *trwluf craftes* 1527.

OE. fem. pls. survive in: *halue* 2070, 2165; *hond*[*e*] 494; OE. neut. pls. in *chylder* 280; *þyng*[*e*] 952, 1080 (cf. 645). After numerals a sg. form may be used in a pl. sense: *myle* 770, *mote* 1141, *dame* 1316. The ending of the OE. weak gen. pl. survives in *nakryn* 118 (see note). *fotes* 574 is dative plural, beside *fote* 2229, &c.

Adjectives: the pl. usually has the ending *-e*: *wlonk*[*e*] 515, 1977; *innoȝe* 852, &c.; but cf. *fayn* 840. A weak form in *-e* is used after the definite article or a demonstrative: *best*[*e*] 37, *halue* 165, *ȝonge* 1315, *ilk*[*e*] 1981, &c., and perhaps *derue* 1047. Adjectives ending in *-li*(*ch*) form their compar. in *-lok*(*k*)*er* and superl. in *-lok*(*k*)*est*, which are descended from the late OE. development *-lucor*, *-lucost* of earlier *-licor*, *-licost*.

[1] See p. xxi.

[2] Examples of forms having the ending *-e* are usually in rhyme or in metrical position, which proves the existence of the ending; *-e* thus proved but not inserted in the text is indicated by square brackets.

Pronouns: the forms are recorded in the glossary. It is to be noted that the second person pl. is used for the sg. in addressing a superior, as by Gawain to the king, by the porter and guide to Gawain (except *þe* 2110); in courtesy between equals, as by Gawain to the lady (who deliberately uses at times the more familiar sg. in return), and by Bercilak as host, in contrast to the *þou*, *þe* of the Green Knight's rougher manner.

Note also that pronouns in *-self*, *-seluen* are not necessarily reflexive, but may refer to any one prominent in the speaker's thoughts, as 'himself', &c., is still used in Ireland. A good example is in 113 (see note).

Pronouns following prepositions are often treated as enclitics, and the prep. then has a strong stress, as in *tó þe* 359, 412, *ón me*, 1277, &c.

Verbs: the endings of both strong and weak verbs are:

INFINITIVE: *-e*, *-en*, —. The usual ending is *-e*: *here* 46, *cach*[*e*] 133, *nyme* 993 &c.; *-en* is rare, *bayþen* 327, and seven other instances. Verbs having stems ending in an unaccented syllable have no ending: *fulsun* 99, *sadel* 1128, &c., as also many verbs of French origin: *payne̢* 1042, *graunte̢* 1841. These verbs may also drop *-e*(*n*) of other inflexions. A few infins. in *-ne* (as *sene* 712) are due to earlier confusion of the uninflected infin. (OE. *sēon*) with the inflected (OE. *sēonne*).

INDICATIVE, PRESENT:

Sg. 1 *-e*.[1] Pl. *-en*, *-e*.[1]

2 *-es*, *-eȝ*.

3 *-es* (*-is*), *-eȝ*.

A northern pl. *-es*, *-eȝ* also occurs rarely: *dares* 315, *desyres* 1257, *hyȝes* 1351, *trayleȝ* 1700, *beres* 2523.

INDICATIVE, PAST: Strong verbs:

Sg. 1 and 3 no ending. Pl. *-en* usual; also *-e*.[1]

Weak verbs:

Sg. 1 and 3 *-e*.[1] Pl. *-en*, *-e*.[1]

2 *-es*, *-eȝ*.

SUBJUNCTIVE, PRES. AND PAST: Sg. and Pl. *-e*:[1] *greue* 1070, *ṣtod*[*e*] 1768; *drowe* 1647, *helde* 2129.

IMPERATIVE: Sg. no ending: *let* 414; *-e*: *lenge* 254; *-es*: *slokes* 412. Pl. *-e*: *layne* 1786; *-eȝ*: *foldeȝ* 359.

[1] Forms without ending are most (if not all) due to the copyist.

Present participle: *-ande*: *laȝande* 1207, &c.; three instances of *-yng*: *sykyng* 753, *forlancyng* 1334, *gruchyng* 2126.

Past participle: strong verbs *-en*, rarely *-e*: *fonge* 1315, *beholde* 1842. To the pp. of weak verbs analogical *-e* is frequently added.

Analogy has caused many changes in the strong conjugations. Most important of these is the levelling of the vowel *ę̄* of the pa. t. pl. of the fourth and fifth conjugations into the pa. t. sg.; see glossary under *bere*, *schere*, *stek*, *swere*; *breke*, *gete*, *giue*, *heue*, *se*, *sitte*, *speke*. Exceptions are *gafe* 1861, *forȝate* 1472, *forgate* 2031, pa. t. forms which preserve the historic vowel. Some strong verbs have changed their conjugation, as *steke* conj. 4 (from 5), *swere* 4 (from 6), *heue* 4 or 5 (from 6). Some strong verbs have also a weak pa. t. or pp.: see glossary under *blowe*, *falle*, *fle*, *fonge*, *laȝe*, *louke*, *ryse*, *schape*, *speke*. Others, originally strong, are conjugated weak, as *boȝe*, *loute*, *slepe*, &c.

Weak verbs adhere more closely to the OE. types. Those of the first class regularly shorten a long vowel in the pa. t. and pp., as *loute* (originally strong, see above), pa. t. *lut*, and similarly *dut*, *lante*, &c. Verbs of the OE. *lufian* class have not preserved the *-i-* of the present stem except in some forms of *louye* and *wonye*. The *-i-* is there extended to the pa. t. and pp. also. Many verbs of French origin in early ME. belonged to this class, exemplified in *Sir Gawain* by *fayly* and *gronyed*. Weak verbs having stems in *d* or *t* sometimes do not add any suffix in the pa. t. or pp., as *depaynt* 620 beside *depaynted* 649, *frayst* 324 beside *fraysted* 1679, *defende* 1156, *start* 1716, &c. *Were* has a strong pa. t. *were* (on analogy of *bere*) as well as historical weak *wered*.

GLOSSARY

In the Glossary completeness is aimed at. Intentional exceptions are: (i) references to common forms or uses have been much curtailed (marked *&c.*); (ii) variation between *ȝ*, *gh*; *i*, *y*; *th*, *þ*; *u*, *v*; and final *-eȝ*, *-es*, has often been disregarded; (iii) the inflected forms of nouns, adjectives, and weak verbs have only exceptionally been recorded (for their normal forms see pp. 130–2).

Etymologies. These are given as an aid in interpreting spellings, fixing meanings, and differentiating words of diverse origin and similar appearance. Though extremely brief, they are not solely repetitions of common material; several are here (often very tentatively) suggested for the first time, e.g. *burde*, *misy*, *ruþe*, *schynder*, *spennefote*, *wone*. For the better illustration of the forms of the text, the Old French forms cited are largely Anglo-French (usually without specification), the Old English forms Anglian. The marking of long vowels has not been attempted in Old French. In Old English the long vowels are marked as in *ān*; uncertain quantity or probable shortening in the Old English period is marked as in ARE, *ǣ̆r*; vowels lengthened in Old English (e.g., before *ld*) are marked as in BOLD, *báld*, when the forms of the text point to, or allow of the possibility of this lengthening. On the forms cited from Old Norse see p. 126; long vowels are marked as in *ár*.

Arrangement. In Glossary and Index of Names (i) **ȝ** in any function (see p. 122) has a separate alphabetical place immediately after **g**; (ii) **þ** has a separate place immediately after **t**, and here also is recorded rare initial **th**; (iii) the MS. distinction between initial **u**, **v** and **i**, **j** has not been observed—only **v** and **i** are used; (iv) initially **y** has its usual place, but medially and finally it will be found in the alphabetical place of **i**.

ABBREVIATIONS

AFr.	Anglo-French.
cf.	in etymologies indicates uncertain or indirect relation.
Dan., ODan.	Danish, Old Danish.
Du., MDu.	Dutch, Middle Dutch.
E., ME., OE.	English, Middle English, Old English.
E. D. D.	The English Dialect Dictionary.
Fr., OFr., ONFr.	French, Old French, Northern dialects of Old French.
Fris., OFris.	Modern Frisian dialects, Old Frisian.
from	is prefixed to etymologies when the word illustrated has an additional suffix or prefix not present in the etymon.
G.	German.
Goth.	Gothic.
HG., MHG., OHG.	High German, Middle High German, Old High German.
Icel.	Modern Icelandic.
infl.	influenced; influence.
L., Med.L.	Latin, Medieval Latin.
LG., MLG.	Low German, Middle Low German.
n.	see note.
N. E. D.	The Oxford (New) English Dictionary.
Norw.	Modern Norwegian dialects.
Nth., ONth.	Northumbrian dialect of Old English.
OIr.	Old Irish.
ON.	Old Norse, especially Old Icelandic.
OS.	Old Saxon (Old Low German).
prec.	preceding word.
Prov.	Provençal.
red.	reduction; reduced.
rel.	related.
Swed., OSwed.	Swedish, Old Swedish.
*	is prefixed to forms theoretically reconstructed, and to references to emendations.
+	between elements shows that a compound or derivative is first recorded in Middle English.

GLOSSARY

A

a, *indef. art.* a, one, any, some, 76, 208, 2421, &c.; (with materials), 571, 573, 879; **an** (before vowels), 27, 1808, &c. [OE. *ān.*]

abataylment, *n.* battlement, 790. [From OFr. *abatailler,* to fortify.]

a-belef, *adv.* obliquely, slantwise, 2486, 2517. [OFr. *à be(s)lif.*]

abide, *v. intr.* to stop, 2090; *imper.* wait! 2217; *trans.* await, 1900; endure, 1754. [OE. *abīdan.*]

abloy, *adj.* carried away (with joy), 1174 n. [OFr. *e(s)bloi,* pp.]

abode, *n.* stop, stay, 687. [Rel. to ABIDE.]

abof, aboue(n), *adv.* above, 2217; thereover, upon it, 153, 166, 856; in a higher seat, 73; at the head of the table, 112; *prep.* above, 184, 478, 765. [OE. *abufan.*]

about(t)e, *adv.* about, round about, 75, 217, 600, 949, 1427, 2233, &c.; *prep.* (round) about, around, 164, 189, 1986, 2187, 2517, &c.; concerning, 68. [OE. *abūtan.*]

absolucioun, *n.* absolution, 1882. [OFr. *absolucion.*]

achaufed, *pa. t.* warmed, 883. [OFr. *eschaufer.*]

acheue, *v.* to gain, accomplish, 1081, 1107; *acheue to,* make one's way to, reach, 1838, 1857. [OFr. *achever.*]

acole, *v.* to embrace, 1936, 2472. [OFr. *acoler.*]

acorde, *n.* agreement, 1384. [OFr. *acorde.*]

acorde, *v.* to reconcile, 2405; *refl.* consent, 1863; associate (with), 2380; *pp.* accorded, granted, 2519. *Intr.* to agree, resolve, 2514; match (in colour), 602; *a. to,* befit, 631; *a. of,* agree to, 1408. [OFr. *acorder.*]

adoun, *adv.* down, 254, 505, 2266, &c.; downwards, 2263. [OE. *of-dūne.*]

afyaunce, *n.* trust, 642. [OFr. *afia(u)nce.*]

aft(t)er, *prep.* after, behind, in pursuit of, 501, 543, 1165, 1188, 1742, &c.; for, 1215, 2093; along, 218; *adv.* afterwards, 255, 516, 1518, &c.; after the same fashion, 171; along, 1608. [OE. *æfter.*]

after, *conj.* after, 2525. [Reduced from OE. *æfter þam þe.*]

agayn, *adv.* in return, 386, 1638. [ON. *í gegn.*]

age, *n.* age; *in her first age,* in the prime of life, 54. [OFr. *age.*]

aghlich, *adj.* terrible, 136. [ON. *agi* + OE. *-lic.*]

agreued (*for*), *pp.* weighed down, overcome (with), 2370. [OFr. *agreuer.*]

aȝayn, *adv.* back, in return, again, 530, 1217, 1459, 2400, &c.; *prep.* against, 2116. [OE. *ongegn.*]

aȝayneȝ, *prep.* towards, to meet, 971; against, 1661. [Prec. + adv. *-es.*]

aȝleȝ, *adj.* without fear, 2335. [ON. *agi* + OE. *-lēas.*]

aȝt(e). See OGHE.

ay, *adv.* always, ever, 26, 167, 562, &c.; in each case, 73, 128, 190. [ON. *ei.*]

ayled, *pp.* troubled, 438. [OE. *eglan.*]

ayquere, *adv.* everywhere, 599, 629, 800, 952, 959, 1521; anywhere (*after neg.*), *660; **aywhere,** 745, 2181. [OE. *ǣghwǣr.*]

ayþer, *adj.* each (of two), both, 1356, 2180; *as pron.* *1357; *ayþer . . . oþer*, each (the) other, 841, 939, 1307, 2472. [OE. *ǣgþer*.]

al, *conj.* although, 143. [From AL, *adv.* with subj.]

alder, *adj. compar.* older, 948; elder, 972, 1317. [OE. *ældra*.]

alder-, alþer-, *intensive prefix in* **aldertruest, alþergrattest,** truest, greatest, of all, 1486, 1441. [OE. *alra*, gen. pl.]

alderes, *n. pl.* princes, kings, 95. [OE. (verse) *aldor*.]

algate, *adv.* at any rate, 141. [Cf. ON. *alla gǫtu*, all along, always.]

al-hal-day, *n.* All Saints' Day (Nov. 1), 536. [OE. *alra hălgena dæg*.]

alyue, *adj.* living, 1269. [OE. *on līfe*.]

al(le), *adv.* entirely, quite, everywhere, 75, 831, 1608, 1662, &c.; *al þeroute*, without any shelter, 2481; *expletive*, moreover, 1349. [OE. *al(l)*.]

al(le), *adj.* all, 7, 39, 50, 54, 1943, &c.; *pron.* all, everything, 48, 603, 836, &c.; all (the people), they (them) all, 242, 315, 1234, 1578, &c. [OE. *al(l)*.]

aloft(e), *adv.* up, above, at the top, 194, 572, 981, 1125, 1818, 2288; on horseback, 435, 2060; *as prep.* on, 1648. [ON. *á loft*.] See LOFT(E).

alosed, *pp.* praised, 1512. [OFr. *aloser*.]

als(e), *adv.* as, 1067; also, as well, 270, 1224, 1627, 2360, &c.; **alce,** 2492. [Reduced from next.]

also, *adv.* also, as well, 90, 1155, 2057. [OE. *al-swā*.]

alþer-grattest. See ALDER-.

aluisch, *adj.* elvish, 681. [From OE. *ælf*.]

alway, *adv.* always, 1482. [OE. *alne weg*.]

am, 1 *sg. pres.* am, 354, 624, 2509, &c. [OE. *eam, am*.]

amende, *v. intr.* to improve, 898. [OFr. *amender*.]

among, *prep.* among, 101, 466, 473, &c. [OE. *on mong*.]

amount, *(to)*, *v.* to amount to, mean, 1197. [OFr. *amo(u)nter*.]

anamayld, *pp.* enamelled, 169. [OFr. *enamailler*.]

and, *conj.* and, 354, 566, 1319, 1402; **ande,** 20, *46, 151, 270, 308, 323, 756, 788, 1426, 1668; *elsewhere abbrev. in MS., as* 1, 2277; if, 1271, 1393, 1509, 1647, 1996, 2129; *and ȝet*, even if, 1009. [OE. *and*.]

anelede, *pa. t.* puffed after, pursued, 723. [OFr. *aneler*.]

angarde, *n.* pride, vanity, 681. [OFr. *angarde*.]

anger, *n.* harm, *2344. [ON. *angr*.]

any, ani, *adj.* any (whatsoever), same, 24, 257, 337, 2470, &c.; *pron.* any one, any (people), 285, 300, 333, 1497; **anyskynneȝ,** of any kind, 1539 (OE. **ǣniges cynnes*). [OE. *ǣnig*.]

anious, *adj.* troublesome, 535. [OFr. *anuieus, anoious*.]

answare, *v.* to answer, 241, *1044, *1262; **onsware,** 275, 386. [OE. *an(d)swarian*.]

apende, *v.* to belong, 623, 913. [OFr. *apendre*.]

apere, *v.* to appear, 911. [OFr. *aper-*, accented stem of *apareir*.]

apert, *adj.* evident, plain, 154, 2392. [OFr. *apert*.]

apparayl, *n.* gear, adornment, 601. [OFr. *aparail*.]

aproched, *pa. t.* approached, 1877. [OFr. *aprocher*.]

aquoyntaunce, *n.* acquaintance, 975. [OFr. *acointaunce*.]

aray(e), *n.* array, dress, 163, 1873. **arayed, arayde,** *pp.* prepared, dressed, 1130, 1134; constructed, 783. [OFr. *arei, areier*.]

are, *adv.* before, 239, 1632, 1891. [OE. *ǣ̆r* (? late Nth. *ar*); ON. *ár*.]

arered, *pp.* retreated, drawn back, 1902. [OFr. *arerer*.]

ar(e)wes, *n. pl.* arrows, 1160, 1455. [OE. *ar(e)we.*]
arȝe, *adj.* afraid, 241. [OE. *earg.*]
arȝe (*wyth*), *v.* to be terrified, quail (at), 1463, 2271, 2277, 2301. [OE. *eargian.*]
aryȝt, oryȝt, *adv.* right well, in the right fashion, 40, 1911. [OE. *on riht, ariht.*]
arme, *n.* arm, 185, 582, 841, 1305, 2487, &c. [OE. *earm.*]
armed, *pp.* armed, 2335. [OFr. *armer.*]
armes, -eȝ, *n. pl.* arms, armour, 204, 281, 567, 590, 2104; knightly warfare, 95, 1513, 1541, 2437; heraldic arms, 631. [OFr. *armes.*]
ar(n), *pres. pl.* are, 207, 280, 1094, &c.; are, 1226. [OE. *aron.*]
arounde, *adv.* at the edges, 1833. [*a*- (OE. *on*) + ROUNDE, *adj.*]
arsoun(e)ȝ, *n. pl.* saddle-bows, 171, 602. [OFr. *arso(u)n.*]
art, *n.* art, 1543. [OFr. *art.*]
art, 2 *sg. pres.* art, are, 675, 2240, 2270, 2391. [OE. *eart.*]
as, *conj.* (even) as, like, in the way that, 49, 73, 149, 182, 199, 388, 847, &c.; as far as, 193; as if, as though, 201, 244, 1202, *1281, &c.; according as, 99, 1811, &c.; as (one who), (as) being, 321, 638, 1104, &c.; *with oaths*, so, 256, 2123; while, when, 703, 995, 1592, &c.; since, 324, 1547; see ÞERE. [Reduced from ALS.]
as, *adv.* (just) as, 896, 1021, 1425, &c.; *correl. with* AS, *conj.*, as 437, 2393, &c.; see **AS-TITE, AS-SWYÞE.** [As prec.]
asay, *n.* 'assay', 1328 n. [OFr. *assai.*]
ascryed, *pa. t.* shouted, 1153. [OFr. *escrier.*]
asyngne, *v.* to assign, 1971. [OFr. *as(s)igner.*]
aske, *v.* to ask (for), request, 273, 393, 756, 1691, &c.; *absol.* require, 530, 1327. [OE. *ăxian.*]
askeȝ, *n. pl.* ashes, 2. [ON. *aska*; OE. *axe.*]
askyng, *n.* request, 323, 349. [OE. *ăcsung.*]
asoyled, *pa. t.* absolved, 1883. [OFr. *assoillir.*]
aspye, *v.* to discover, 1199. [OFr. *espier.*]
as(s)ay, *v.* to make trial of, put to the proof, 2362, 2457. [OFr. *essayer.*]
as(s)aute, *n.* assault, 1, 2525. [OFr. *as(s)aut.*]
as-swyþe, *adv.* straightway, 1400. [AS + SWYÞE.]
as-tit, as-tyt, *adv.* straightway, 31; in a moment, 1210. [AS + TITE *adv.*]
at(e), *prep.* at, 1, 264, 464, 836, 2249, &c.; to, 929, 1671; of, from, 359, 391, 646, 1977, &c.; according to, 1006, 1546; *watȝ hym ate*, attacked him, 1474; *adv.* at, 1727. [OE. *æt.*]
athel, aþel, *adj.* noble, glorious, splendid, 5, 171, 241, 904, 1654, 2466. [OE. *æþel.*]
atyred, *pp.* attired, 1760. [OFr. *atir(i)er.*]
at(t)le, *v.* to intend, 27, 2263. [ON. *ætla.*]
atwaped, *pa. t.* escaped, 1167. [OE. *æt-*, away + WAPPE.]
avanters, *n. pl.* part of the numbles of the deer, 1342 n. [AFr. **avanter*, from *avant.*]
aue, *n.* the Ave Maria, 'Hail Mary', 757.
aumayl, *n.* enamel, 236. [OFr. *esmail*, **a(u)mail.*]
auen. See OWEN.
auentayle, *n.* movable front of a helmet, beaver, 608. [OFr. *aventaille.*]
auenture, aventure, awenture, *n.* adventure, marvellous event, 29, 250, 489, 2482; **auenturus**, *pl.* 95, 491. [OFr. *aventure.*]
auenturus, *adj.* perilous, 93. [OFr. *aventuros, -eus.*]
auinant, *adj.* pleasant, 806. [OFr. *avenant.*]
auyse, awyse, *v.* to devise, 45, 1389; to behold, contemplate, 771. [OFr. *aviser.*]

auncian, *adj.* old, aged, 1001, 2463; *as sb.* 948. [OFr. *a(u)ncien.*]
aune, 10. See OWEN.
aunt, *n.* aunt, 2464; *þy naunt*, thine aunt, 2467. [OFr. *a(u)nte.*]
aunter, *n.* adventure, strange event, 27, 2522, 2527. [As AUENTURE, but an older and more popular borrowing.]
auntered, *pp.* ventured, risked, 1516. [OFr. *aventurer.*]
auter, *n.* altar, 593. [OFr. *auter.*]
auþer. See OÞER, *conj.*
ax(e), *n.* axe, 208, 330, 2223. [OE. *æx.*]
away, *adv.* away, 1718, 2119. [OE. *on weg.*]
awharf, *pa. t.* turned aside, 2220. [OE. *ahweorfan.*]

B.

bade. See BIDE.
bay(e), *n.* baying of hounds about an animal making a stand; *byde (at) þe baye*, turn, stand at bay, 1450, 1582; the defensive position of the animal; *bode in his bay*, stood at bay, 1564. [OFr. *(a)bai.*]
baye, *v.* to bay, bark, 1142, 1362; bay at, 1603. [OFr. *baier.*]
bayn, *adj.* obedient, 1092, 2158. [ON. *beinn*, direct.]
bayst, *pa. t.* was dismayed, 376. [AFr. *abaiss-*, OFr. *esbaïr*, *esbaiss-.*]
bayþe(n), *v.* to grant, 327 n.; agree, 1404; consent, 1840. [ON. *beina*, older **beiðna.*]
bak, *n.* back, 143, 1563; *at his bak*, behind him, 1571. [OE. *bæc.*]
bak-bon, *n.* backbone, 1352. [Prec. + OE. *bān.*]
baken, *pp.* baked, 891. [OE. *bacan.*]
bald(e)ly, *adv.* boldly, vigorously, 376, 1362. [OE. *baldlīce.*] See BOLD.
bale, *n.* death, 2041; woe, 2419. [OE. *balu.*]
balé, *n.* belly, 1333. [OE. *bæl(i)g.*]
balȝ, *adj.* swelling with round smooth surface, *967 n., 2032, 2172. [OE. *balg*; Ekwall, *Pl. N. Lancs.*, p. 7.]
bande, *n.* band, 192. [OFr. *bande.*]
baner, *n.* banner (hung on trumpet), 117. [OFr. *ban(i)ere.*]
barayne, *adj.* barren, without fawn, 1320. [OFr. *baraigne.*]
barbe, *n.* barb (of arrow), 1457; cutting edge (of axe), 2310. [OFr. *barbe*, beard, barb.]
barbican, *n.* outwork, outer fortification of a castle, 793. [OFr. *barbacane.*]
bare, *adj.* bare, naked, exposed, 207, 746, 955, 961, &c.; without armour, 290; mere, 2352; downright, actual, 277; *þre bare mote*, three single notes, 1141; *adv.* without qualification, completely, 465; barely, 1066. [OE. *bær.*]
barely, *adv.* unconditionally, without fail, 548. [OE. *bærlīce.*]
baret, *n.* strife, fighting, 21, 353, 2115; trouble, sorrow, 752. [OFr. *barat.*]
barlay, *adv.* ? without resistance shown, 296 n. [Not known.]
barred, *pp.* barred, marked with parallel stripes, 159, 600. [From next.]
barres, *n. pl.* transverse bars adorning belt, 162. [OFr. *barre.*]
bastel, *n.* tower of castle; *bastel roueȝ*, roofs of towers, 799. [OFr. *bastille* (recorded later than in English).]
batayl, *n.* fight, 277. [OFr. *bataille.*]
bate, *n.* strife, fighting, 1461. [Shortened from DEBAT.]
baþed, *pp.* steeped, 1361. [OE. *baþian.*]
bauderyk, *n.* baldric, 621, 2486, 2516. [Cf. OFr. *baudrei*, MHG. *balderich.*]
bauleȝ. See BOWELES.
bawemen, *n. pl.* bowmen, archers, 1564. [OE. *boga* + *mann.*]
be-. See also BI-, BY-.
be, *prep.* by, 1788, 2271; according to, in, 1216; *be twenty*, twenty at a time, 1739. [OE. *be.*] See BI.
be, *v.* to be, 1071, 1240, 1393, 2179, &c.; *letteȝ be*, cease from, 1840; to bene, 141 (OE. *to bēonne*); be(n), *future 2 pl.* will be, 1646, 2111; be, *imper.*

1211, 2338; be, *subj. pres. sg.* (may) be, 448, 1242, 2107, &c.; *wheþer this be*, can this be? 2186; be(n), *pl.* 497, 2440, &c.; ben(e), *pp.* been, 613, 677, 1956, 2343, &c. [OE. *bēon.*]

beau, *adj.* fair; *beau sir*=OFr. *beau sire*, 1222.

becom, *v.* to become, 1279; **bycommes, bicumes**, is fitting (for), 471, 1491; **becom** (to), *pa. t. sg.* came, got (to), 460; **bicome**, *pl.* became, 6. [OE. *be-cuman.*]

bed(de), *n. dat. sg.* bed, 994, 1122, 1191, 1232, 1413, &c. [OE. *bedd.*]

beddyng, *n.* bedclothes, trappings of bed, 853. [OE. *bedding.*]

bede, *v.* to offer, 374, 382, 2322; **bede**, *pa. t.* 1824, 1834, 1860, 2248, 2352; bade, commanded, 1427 (*pl.*), 2012, 2024, 2090; see BIDDE. [OE. *bēodan*, already confused with *biddan.*]

bed-syde, *n.* bedside, 1193. [Earlier *beddes side*; see SIDE.]

belde, *n.* courage, 650. [OE. *béldo.*]

bele, *adj.* fair, gracious, 1034; see BEAU. [OFr. *bele*, fem.]

belleȝ, *n. pl.* bells, 195. [OE. *belle.*]

belt, *n.* belt, 162, 1860, 2377, 2485. [OE. *belt.*]

belted, *pp.* girt on, 2032. [From prec.]

bemeȝ, *n. pl.* rays, 1819. [OE. *bēam.*]

bench, *n.* bench, 280, 344; *upon bench*, at table, 337, 351. [OE. *benc.*]

bende, *n.* band, 2506, 2517. [OE. *bend.*]

bende, *pa. t.* bent; wrinkled (brows), 305; *pp.* in *b. by*, curved back in line with, 2224; *hatȝ much baret b.*, has directed (brought about) much strife, 2115. [OE. *bendan.*]

bene, *adj.* pleasing, fair, 2475; *adv.* pleasantly, 2402. [? OFr. *b(i)en*, adv.]

bent, *n.* grassy ground, field, 2233, 2338; *broȝt to bent*, drove to open ground, 1599; *on bent*, on (hunting) field, 1465; (of battle), 353, 2115; on the ground, there, 2148. [A special use of *bent*, grass; OE. *beonet.*]

bent-felde, *n.* the hunting field, 1136. [Prec. + FELD.]

ber, *n.* beer, 129. [OE. *bēor.*]

berde, *n.* beard, 306, 334, 845, 2228. [OE. *béard.*]

berdleȝ, *n.* beardless, 280. [OE. *béard-lēas.*]

bere, *v.* to bear, carry, wear, lift, 265, 637, 1616, 1913, 2066, 2261; have, possess, 1229; cast (light), 1819; *b. felaȝschip*, accompany, 2151; **beres**, *pres. pl.* bear (witness), 2523; **bere**, *pa. t.* 673, 2066, &c.; *bere on hym*, pressed on him, 1860; **born(e)**, *pp.* born, 752, 996, 2320, 2394; *b. open*, laid open, 2070. [OE. *beran.*]

bereȝ, *n. pl.* bears, 722. [OE. *bera.*]

berȝ, *n.* mound, 2172, 2178. [OE. *be(o)rg.*]

beseche, *v.* to implore, 341, 753, 776, 1881; **bisoȝt**, *pa. t.* 96, 1834, 1862. [OE. *be-* + *sēcan.*]

best, *adj. superl.* best, noblest, 73, 78, 259, 1563, 2101, &c.; *þe best*, the best man, 1645; those of highest rank, 550, 1325; the b. thing to do, 1216; *wyth þe b.*, among the b., as well as any, 986; *of þe b.*, from among the b. there were, (those) of the b. quality, 38, 863, 880, 1145; in the b. manner, 889, 1000. *Adv.* best, 73, 1005, 1680. [OE. *betst.*]

best, *n.* beast, 1359, 1377, 1436, 1603, 1631, 1901. [OFr. *beste.*]

beten, *pa. t. pl.* beat, 1437; *pp.* set (with stones, gold), embroidered, 78, 1833, 2028. [OE. *bēatan.*]

bette, *pp.* kindled, 1368. [OE. *bētan.*]

better, *adj. compar.* better, more valiant, 353, 793, 2278; *as sb.*, something better, 1109; *þe better*, 1393 n.; *adv.* better, 680, 1220, 1276, 1782, 1878 (see LERNE); *þe better*, the better (off), better, more, 410, 1035, 1084, 2096. [OE. *betera, bet(t)ra*, adj.]

beuerage, *n.* beverage, drink, 1112, 1409. [OFr. *bevrage.*]

beuer-hwed, *adj.* beaver-coloured, reddish brown, 845. [OE. *beofor* + *-hiwede.*]

bewté, *n.* beauty, 1273. [OFr. *beauté.*]

bi, by, *prep.* by, beside, along, over, according to, &c., 20, 67, 734, 1002 n., 1296, 1344, 2104, 2120, 2364, &c.; towards, 2310; measured by, 2226; *bi vche*, to each in turn, 1006; *adv.* by, 214; *conj.* by the time that, 1169; when, 2032. **bi þat,** *adv.* by that time, 597, 1868; thereupon, 2152; *conj.* by the time that, 443, 928, 1321, 1365, 1412; when, 1678, 1912, 2043. [OE. *bī.*]

bicause (*of*), *prep.* because (of), for, 1843. [BI + CAUSE.]

bicom(m)e, bicume. See BECOM.

bidde, bedde (1374), *v.* to ask, request, 1089; **bid,** exhort, command, 344, 370, 1374, 1603, 1999; **bede,** *pa. t.*, see BEDE; **boden** (form due to BEDE), *pp.* asked, 327. [OE. *biddan.*]

byde(n), bide, *v. trans.* to wait for, 376, 520, 2292; stand (and face), withstand, 290, 374, 1450; suffer, 2041; *intr.* wait, stay, stand firm, 1092, 1366, 1582, 1585; **bode,** *pa. t.* 785, 1564; **bade,** 1699. [OE. *bīdan.*]

bye, *v.* to buy, 79. [OE. *bycgan.*]

bifalle, befalle, *v.* to happen, 382, 1776. [OE. *be-fallan.*]

bifor(n)e, *prep.* before, 1126, 1675; in front, ahead, in presence, of, 108, 123, 347, 368, 694, 716, 1616, 1704, &c.; above, 914; in preference to, 1275, 1781; **before, byfor(n)e,** &c., *adv.* in front, 422, 1741; previously, 1405, 1577. [OE. *be-foran.*] See HERE.

big, *adj.* large, big, 554; **bigger,** *compar.* 2101; **bigly,** *adv.* mightily, 1141, 1162, 1584. [Uncertain.]

big(g)e, *v.* settle, found, 20; build, 9. [ON. *byggva.*]

bigyle, *v.* beguile, deceive, 2413, 2416, 2427. [OE. *be-* + OFr. *guiler.*]

bigyn(n)e, begynne, *v. intr.*, to begin, 1340, 1571, 1606; *trans.* 495; found, 11; *bigineȝ þe table*, sits at the head of the table, 112; **bygan,** *pa. t.* 661. [OE. *be-ginnan.*]

bigog, *interj.* 390, corruption of *bi God.*

bigrauen, *pp.* engraved, carved, 216. [OE. *be-grafan.*]

biȝonde, *prep.* across, beyond, 2200. [OE. *be-geóndan.*]

byȝt, *n.* fork (of the legs), 1341, 1349. [OE. *byht.*]

bihynde, *adv.* behind, 607, 1350, 1741; inferior, 1942. [OE. *be-hindan.*]

byholde, beholde, *v.* to see, behold, 232, 250, 1187; **beheIde,** *pa. t.* 794; **bihalden, -holde,** *pp.* beholden, obliged, 1842; in duty bound, 1547. [OE. *be-háldan*, hold, behold.]

bihoue (**by-, be-**), *v. impers.* to behove; as in *me bihoues*, I am obliged, (in duty) bound to, must, 324, 456 (*behoueus*), 1065, 1068, 1216, 1239, &c.; *bihoues*, (he) is to, 1754; **bihous,** *pres. sg.* 2296; **bihoued,** *pa. t.* 1771, 2040; **byhode,** 717; *burnes behoued to*, it was time for folk to go to, 1959. [OE. *be-hōfian.*]

bikenne, *v.* to commend, 1307; **bikende,** *pa. t.* 596, 1982. [OE. *be-* + KENNE.]

biknowe, *v.* to acknowledge, confess, 2385, 2495; **beknew,** *pa. t.* 903; **beknowen,** *pp.* cleared by confession, 2391. [Cf. OE *be-cnāwan*, know.]

bylde, *v.* to build, 509; **bult,** *pa. t.* dwelt, 25. [OE. **byldan*, in pp. *gebyld.*]

byled. See BOYLE.

biliue, bylyue, *adv.* quickly, 132, 1128, 1136, 1171, &c. [OE. **be līfe.*]

bynde, *v.* to bind, 1211; **bounden,** *pp.* 192, 2486; bound, trimmed, adorned (with attached ornament), 573, 600, 609, 2028. [OE. *bindan.*]

bischop, *n.* bishop, 112. [OE. *biscop.*]

bisemeȝ, *v. impers.* it is fitting (for) becomes, 1612, 2191; *bisemed*, (it) suited, 622, 2035. [OE. *be-* + SEME.]

bisied. See BUSY.

bysily, bisinesse. See BUSILY BUSYNESSE.

bisyde, *prep.* (*after its case*), beside, 109, 1030, 1657, 1777 (see LAY), 2172, 2265; *adv.* alongside, hard by, round about, 1083, 1582, 2088, 2230. **bisides**, **bisydeȝ**, *adv.* at the sides, round about, 76, 856, 2164. [OE. *be sīdan*, at the side; see SIDE.]

bisoȝt. See BESECHE.

bit(te), **bytte**, *n.* blade, cutting edge, 212, 426, 2224, 2310. [ON. *bit.*]

bite, *v.* to bite, 1598; *bite* (*of*, *on*), cut into, pierce, 426, 1162, 1457; **bot(e)**, *pa. t.* 426, 1162, 1563. [OE. *bītan.*]

bityde, *v.* to happen, befall, 1406; *pres. subj.* 1893, 2195, &c.; **bitidde**, *pa. t.* 2522. [OE. *be-* + *tīdan.*]

bytoknyng, *n.*; *in b. of*, as a symbol of, 626. [OE. **bitācnung.*]

bitwene, *prep.* between, 977, 1060, 1316, 1768, 2242, &c.; *adv.* at intervals, 611, 791, 795. [OE. *be-twēon-(an).*]

biwyled, *pp.* deluded, 2425. [OE. *be-* + *wīglian.*]

blake, *adj.* black, 958, 961. [OE. *blæc.*]

blame, *n.* blame, 1779; fault, 1488, 2506; *for bl.*, as a rebuke, 2500; *bout bl.*, unopposed, freely, 361. [OFr. *bla(s)me.*]

blame, *v.* to blame, 2368. [OFr. *bla(s)mer.*]

blande, *n.* mingling; *in blande*, (mingled) together, 1205. [ON. *í bland.*]

blande, *pp.* (*prob. wk.*), adorned, 1931. [ON. *blanda*, str. and wk.]

blasoun, *n.* shield, 828. [OFr. *blason.*]

blaste, *n.* blast, 784, 1148. [OE. *blǣst.*]

blaunmer, *n.* white fur, 856 n.; **blaunner**, 155, 573, 1931. [? OFr. **blanc de mer.*]

blawyng, *n.* blowing, 1601. [OE. *blāwung.*]

ble(e)aunt, *n.* a rich stuff, 879 n.; a mantle made of it, 1928. [OFr. *bliaut*, AFr. *bliaunt.*]

blede, *v.* to bleed, 441, 1163. [OE. *blēdan.*]

blenche, *v.* to start aside, swerve, 1715. [OE. *blencan*, deceive.]

blende, **blent**, *pp.* mingled, 1361, 1610; *pa. t.* streamed together, 2371 (cf. 2503). [OE. *ge-blęndan.*]

blended, *pp.* deluded, 2419. [OE. *blęndan.*]

blenk(e), *v.* to gleam, 799, 2315. [ON. *blekkja*, older **blenkja.*]

blered, *pp.* bleared, 963. [Cf. OE. *a-blered*, *blere*, bald.]

blesse, *v.* to bless, 1296; *refl.* cross oneself, 2071; **blessyng**, *n.* blessing, 370. [OE. *blětsian*, *blětsung.*]

blykke, *v.* to shine, gleam, 429, 2485; **blycande**, *pres. p.* 305. [OE. *blīcan*; *blician.*]

blynne (*of*), *v.* cease (from), 2322. [OE. *blinnan.*]

blysful, *adj.* delightful, 520. [From next.]

blys(se), *n.* happiness, joy, 18, 825, 1368, 2530, &c. [OE. *bliss.*]

blyþe, *adj.* merry, glad, 922, 1273, 1398, 2321, &c.; bright, gay, 155, 162; *adv.* 1684; **blyþely**, *adv.* gaily, merrily, 1311, 1834, 1990. [OE. *blīþe*, *blīþelīce.*]

blod(e), *n.* blood, 89, 317, 2315, &c.; kinship, 357; mettle, 286. [OE. *blōd.*]

blod-houndeȝ, *n. pl.* bloodhounds, 1436. [Prec. + OE. *húnd.*]

blonk, *n.* horse, steed, 434, 785, 1581, 2012, 2024, 2475; *pl.* **blonkkeȝ**, 1128, 1693. [OE. (verse) *blanca.*]

blossumeȝ, *n. pl.* blossoms, 512. [OE. *blŏsma.*]

blowe, *v.*[1] to bloom, 512. [OE. *blōwan.*]

blowe, *v.*[2] to blow, 1465; **blw(e)**, *pa. t.* 1141, 1362; **blowed**, 1913. [OE. *blāwan*, *blēow.*]

blubred, *pa. t.* bubbled, 2174. [Echoic.]

bluk, *n.* headless trunk, 440. [OFr. *bloc.*]

blunder, *n.* turmoil, trouble, 18. [From ME. *blundren*, daze, be dazed, rel. to 'blind'. Cf. ON. *blunda*, Norw. *blundra*, doze.]

blusch, *n.* gleam, 520. [From next.]
blusche, *v.* to glance, look, 650, 793; **blusschande**, *pres. p.* gleaming, 1819. [OE. *blyscan.*]
blwe, *n.* blue (stuff), 1928. [OFr. *bleu.*]
blwe, *pa. t.* See BLOWE.
bobbaunce, *n.* pomp, pride, 9. [OFr. *boba(u)nce.*]
bobbe, *n.* cluster, 206. [Unknown.]
bode, *n.* command, 852; offer, 1824. [OE. *bod.*]
bode(n). See BIDE, BIDDE.
bodi, body, *n.* body, 143, 353, 966, &c.; **bodé**, 357. [OE. *bodig.*]
boerne, boffet. See BORNE, BUFFET.
boȝe, *v.* to turn, go, 344, 434, &c.; **boȝed**, *pa. t.* 481, 1189, &c.; **boȝen**, *pres.* or *pa. t. pl.* 2077: *boȝe fro* (*of*), leave, 344, 1220. [OE. *būgan*, str.]
boȝeȝ, *n. pl.* boughs, branches, 765, 2077. [OE. *bōg.*]
boyle, byle, *v.* to boil, bubble, 2082, 2174. [OFr. *boillir.*]
bok(e), *n.* book, 690, 2521, 2523. [OE. *bōc.*]
bold(e), *adj.* bold, valiant, 272, 286, 1465, 2338, &c.; *as sb.* bold men, 21, 351; *adv.* boldly, quickly (?), 2476. [OE. *báld, bálde* (instanter).]
bole, *n.* tree-trunk, 766. [ON. *bolr.*]
bolne, *v.* to swell, 512. [ON. *bolgna.*]
bonchef, *n.* happiness, 1764. [OFr. *bonch(i)ef.*]
bone, *adj.*: *bone hostel*, a good lodging, 776. [OFr. *bon hostel.*]
bone, *n.* request, boon, 327. [ON. *bón.*]
bones, -eȝ, *n. pl.* bones, 424, 1344. [OE. *bān.*]
bonk(e), hill-side, slope, 710, 1571, 2172, &c.; **bonkkeȝ, -es**, *pl.* 14, 1562, &c.; *bi bonk*, on the slopes, 511; shore, bank, 700, 785. [ON. *bakki*, older **banke.*]
bor, *n.* boar, 722, 1441, 1448, 1590, 1606, 1616. [OE. *bār.*]
borde, *n.*[1] table, 481. [OE. *bord.*]
borde, *n.*[2] hem, embroidered strip, 159, 610. [OE. *borda.*]
bordeȝ. See BOURDE.
borelych, *adj.* strong, massive, 766, 2148, 2224. [Cf. OE. *borlīce*, excellently.]
borȝ. See BURȜ.
borne, boerne, *n.* stream, 731, 1570, 2174. [OE. *búrne.*]
borne, bornyst. See BERE, BURNYST.
bost, *n.* outcry, clamour, 1448. [Not known.]
bot, *adv.* only, but, 30, 280, 701, 763, 1795, &c.; *bot oure one*, alone by ourselves, 1230. [OE. *būton.*] See BOUTE.
bot, *conj.* (i) except, other than, but, 357, 565, 1054 (see NOLDE), 1267, 1553, 1887, &c.; *neuer bot, noȝt bot*, only, 547, 1833 (see NOBOT); (ii) unless, 716, 1300; *bot if*, unless, 1782, 1956; (iii) but, however, yet, 25, 85, 141, 2511 n., &c. [OE. *būton, būte.*]
bot(e). See BITE.
botounȝ, *n. pl.* buttons, bosses, 220. [OFr. *boton.*]
boþem, *n.* bottom, 2145. [OE *botm*, **boþm* (still NWM.).]
boþe, both(e), *adj. and pron.* both, 111, 192, 371, 582, 2352, &c.; either, 2070, 2165; *adv.* as well, too, 129, 155, 1580, &c.; both, 18, *144, &c. [ON. *báðir.*]
boun, *adj.* ready, 852, 1311, 1693; dressed, 2043; *boun to*, bound, setting out for, 548. [ON. *búinn, bún-.*]
bounté, *n.* worth, virtue, 357, 1519. [OFr. *bonté.*]
boure, *n.* bedroom, 853; ladies' bower, 1519. [OE. *būr.*]
bourde, borde, *n.* jest, 1212, 1409, 1954. [OFr. *bourde.*]
bourded, *pa. t.* jested, 1217; **bourdyng**, *n.* jesting, 1404. [OFr. *bourder.*]
bout(e), *prep.* without, 361, 1285, 1444, 2353. [OE. *būtan.*]

boweles, *n. pl.* bowels, intestines, 1609; **baule3**, *1333. [OFr. *bouel.*]
brace, *n. collective*, pair of arm-pieces, 582. [OFr. *brace.*]
brache3, **-es**, *n. pl.* hounds, 1142 n., 1563, 1610; **brachetes**, 1603 n. [OFr. *brachet.*]
brad, *pp.* grilled, 891. [OE. *brǣdan*, *brēdan.*]
bradde, *pa. t. intr.* reached, 1928. [OE. *brǣdan*, from *brād.*]
brayde, *v.* to draw, pull, 1584, 1609, 1901, 2319; seize, 621; **brayd(e)**, *pa. t.* pulled, 1339; flung, 2377; twisted, 440; spurted (*intr.*), 429; **brayde**, *pp.* pulled, 2069; **brayden**, **brawden**, linked, 580; embroidered, 177, 220, 1833. [OE. *bregdan*, pp. *brogden*, *bregden.*]
brayen, *v.* to bray, cry out, 1163. [OFr. *braire.*]
brayn, *n.* brain, 89. [OE. *brægn.*]
brayn, *adj.* mad, 286. [? Shortened from adjs. such as next.]
braynwod, *adj.* frenzied, 1461, 1580. [OE. *bræg(e)n* + *wōd.*]
braþ. See BROÞE.
braunch(e), *n.* branch, 265, 2177. [OFr. *branche.*]
brawen, **brawne**, *n.* (boar's) flesh, 1611; **browen**, *1457; *such a b. of a best*, such a quantity of flesh on any boar, 1631. [OFr. *brao(u)n.*]
bred, *n.* bread, 891, 1361, 1610. [OE. *brēad.*]
bredden, *pa. t. pl.* bred, were produced, multiplied, 21. [OE. *brēdan.*]
brede3, *n. pl.* planks, 2071. [OE. *bred.*]
brek, **breke(n)**, *pa. t.* broke, cut open, 1333; broke down, overcame, 1564; *intr.* burst forth, was uttered, 1764; foamed, 2082. [OE. *brecan.*]
brem(e), *adj.* brave, stout, 1155; fierce, 1142, *1441, 1580; wild, 2145; loud, 1601, 2200; *adv.* stoutly, 781; **bremlych**, *adv.* gloriously, 509; **brem(e)ly**, fiercely, 1598, 2233, 2319; quickly, 779. [OE. *brēme*, adj. and adv.]
brenne, *v.* to burn, 832, 875; *trans.* broil, 1609; **brent**, *pp.* 2; **brende**, refined (by fire), bright (gold), 195 (cf. ON. *brent gull*). [ON. *brenna.*]
brent, *adj.* steep, 2165. [Cf. OE. *brant.*]
bresed, *adj.* bristling, 305. [Not known.]
brest, *n.* breast, 143, 182, 955, 1339, 1741, 2371. [OE. *brēost.*]
breþer, *n. pl.* brothers-in-arms, 39. [ON. *brœðr*, pl.]
breue, *v.* to write down, 2521; declare, 465, 1393, 1488; announce (presence of game) by giving tongue, 1436. [Med.L. *breviāre*, OE. *brēfan.*]
brydde3, **-es**, *n. pl.* birds, 166, 509, 610, 746. [OE. *bridd*, young bird.]
brydel, *n.* bridle, 177, 434, 600, 1131, 2152. [OE. *brīdel.*]
bryg(g)e, *n.* drawbridge, 781, 821, 2069; *gen.* 779. [OE. *brycg.*]
bry3t, *adj. and adv.* bright, 117, 129, 212, 269, 2226, 2517, &c.; pure white, 155, 573, 856, 955; *compar.* 236; *superl.* fairest, 1283. [OE. *berht.*]
brymme, *n.* water's edge, 2172. [OE. *brymme.*]
bryné. See BRUNY.
bryng, *v.* to bring, 825, 925, 1112, 2024, 2530, &c.; **bro3t**, *pa. t. and pp.* 779, 853, 1120, 1519, 1990, 2145, &c. [OE. *bringan.*]
brit(t)en, *v.* to break up, destroy, 2, 680; cut (up), 1339, 1611. [OE. *brytnian.*]
brod(e), *adj.* broad, wide, 14, 845, 1162, 2233, &c.; long, 212; *adv.* with wide-open eyes, 446. [OE. *brād*; *brāde*, adv.]
bro3t. See BRING.
broke3, *n. pl.* streams, 2082. [OE. *brōc.*]
bronde, *n.* brand; piece of burnt wood, 2; sword, 561, 828, 1901, 2032, 2041, *2319 (*cf.* 1584, 1901); **bront**, 588, 1584. [OE. *bránd*, *brónd.*]
broþe, *adj.* fierce, 2233; **braþ**, *1909;

broþely, *adv.* 2377. [ON. *bráðr*, *bráðliga.*]

broþerhede, *n.* brotherhood, 2516. [OE. *brōþorræden*, with alter. of suffix due to OE. *-hād.*]

broun, *adj.* brown, 879; *as sb.* brown hide (of deer), 1162; bright, shining, 426, 618. [OE. *brūn.*]

browe, *n.* brow, forehead, 2306; *pl.* **broȝeȝ**, **-es**, eyebrows, 305, 961. [OE. *brū.*]

browen (*MS. browe*). See BRAWEN.

bruny, *n.* mail-shirt, 861, 2012, 2018; **bryné**, 580. [ON. *brynja.*]

brusten, *pp.* broken, 1166. [ON. *bresta*; OE. *berstan.*]

buffet, **boffet**, *n.* blow, 382, 1754, 2343. [OFr. *buffet.*]

bugle, *n.* bugle, 1136, 1141, 1465, 1913. [OFr. *bugle.*]

bukkeȝ, *n. pl.* bucks, 1155. [OE. *bucca.*]

bulleȝ, *n. pl.* wild bulls, 722. [Cf. ODan. *bul*; OE. *bula*, *bulluc.*]

bult. See BYLDE.

bur, *n.* onslaught, blow, 290, 374, 548; strength, 2261; violence, 2322. [ON. *byrr*, a following wind.]

burde, *n.* maiden, damsel, 613, 752, 942, 1373, &c.; lady, 961, 1283, &c. [OE. **byrde*, embroideress; cf. *byrdistre*, and ON. *byrða.*]

burde, *pa. t. subj. impers.*; *me burde*, I ought to, 2278, 2428. [OE. *gebyrian.*]

burȝ(e), **borȝ**(e), *n.* castle, city, 2, 9, 259, 550, 843, 1034, 1092, 2476. [OE. *burg.*]

burn(e), **buurne** (825), *n.* warrior, knight, man, 20, 73, 259, 272, 1582, 2320, &c; *voc.* sir (knight), 1071, 2284, 2322. [OE. *béorn.*]

burnyst, **bornyst**, *pp.* polished, 212, 582. [OFr. *burnir*, *burniss-.*]

burþe, *n.* birth, 922. [OE. *ge-byrd*, *byrþ-.*]

busy, *v. intr.* to be busy, bestir oneself, 1066; **bisied**, *pa. t. trans.* stirred, 89. [OE. *bysigian.*]

busyly, **bysily**, *adv.* earnestly, eagerly, 68, 1824. [From OE. *bysig.*]

busynes, *n.* solicitude, 1986: **bisinesse**, importunity, 1840. [OE. *bysignes.*]

busk, *n.* bush, 182, 1437. [ODan. *buske.*]

busk(**ke**), *v. intr.* to get ready, array, dress, 1220, 1693; *intr.* make haste (to), 509, 1136, 1411, 1448, 2284, 2476; *busken vp*, arise, 1128; *trans.* make, 2248. [ON. *búask*, refl.]

buttokeȝ, *n. pl.* buttocks, 967. [Obscure.]

C.

cace, **case**, *n.* chance, 907; occurrence, 1196; circumstances, affair, 546; *to vche a cace*, to everything she chanced to say, 1262. [OFr. *cas.*]

cach(**che**), **kach**, *v.* to catch; **caȝt**, **kaȝt**, *pa. t.* 643, 1011, 1118; *pp.* 1225, 2508. To chase, urge on, 1581, 2175; catch, seize, 368, 434, 1225, 1906 (MS.); take, 133, 1118, 1305; receive, get, 643, 1011, 1938, 2508; *caȝt vp*, raised, 1185; *intr.* in *kaȝt to*, laid hold of, 2376; *cach*, hasten, go, 1794. [ONFr. *cachier*, infl. by LAC(C)HE.]

cacheres, *n. pl.* dog-grooms, 1139. [Cf. OFr. *chacechien.*]

cayre, **kayre**, *v.* to ride, 43, *734, 1048, 1670, 2120. [ON. *keyra.*]

cakled, *pp.* cackled, 1412. [Cf. Dan. *kagle.*]

calle, **kalle**, *v. intr.* to call (out), shout, 807, 2212, &c., *c. on*, call to, 1701, 1743; *c. of*, crave, beg for, 975, 1882; call for, 1421; *trans.* to call, name, 456, 664, 964, 2278, &c.; summon, call, 1127, 1140, 1666, &c. [OE. (late) *ceallian.*]

can. See CON, *auxil.*

capados, *n.* a tunic of Cappadocian leather, 186, 572. [OFr. *capados*, Cappadocia.]

caple, *n.* horse, 2175. [Cf. ON. *kapall.*]

care, *n.* sorrow, grief, 557, 1254, 1979, 2384; trouble, 2495; *care of*, anxiety concerning, 2379. [OE. *caru.*]
care, *v.* to grieve for, 674; be concerned (for), 750, 1773. [OE. *carian.*]
caryeȝ, 734 (MS.) See CAYRE.
carneleȝ, *n. pl.* embrasures in the battlements, 801. [ONFr. *carnel.*]
carole, *n.* dance and song combined, 43, 473, 1026, 1655, 1886. [OFr. *carole.*]
carp, *n.* talk, conversation, 307, 1013; **karp**, mention, 704. [ON. *karp*, bragging.]
carp(p)e, karp, *v.* to speak, say, 263, 360, 377, 1088, 1221, 1979; converse, 696, 1225. [ON. *karpa*, brag.]
case. See CACE.
cast, kest, *n.* stroke, 2298; trick, 2413; ? fastening, 2376; *pl.* speech, utterances, 1295. [ON. *kast.*]
cast, kest, *v.*; **cast, kest**, *pa. t.* 228, 1649, 2317, &c.; *pp.* 64, 878, &c. To cast, throw, put, 621, 878, 1355, 1484, &c.; *kest . . . to*, cast (his eye) on, 228; *of k.*, cast off, 1147; to utter, 64; offer, make, 2242, 2275; *intr.* or *absol.* aim, 1901; cast about in mind, ponder, 1855; *c. vnto*, speak to, address, 249. [ON. *kasta.*]
castel, *n.* castle, 767, 801 (*attrib.*), 1366; **kastel**, 2067. [Late OE. *castel* from ONFr. *castel.*]
caue, *n.* cave, 2182. [OFr. *cave.*]
cauelaciounȝ. See KAUELACION.
cause, *n.* cause; *at þis c.*, for this reason, 648. [OFr. *cause.*]
cemmed, *pp.* combed, 188. [OE. *cemban.*]
cercle, *n.* circlet, 615 n. [OFr. *cercle.*]
chace, *n.* hunt, 1416, 1604. [OFr. *chace.*]
chaffer, *n.* trade, 1647; merchandise, 1939. [OE. *cēap + faru*; cf. ON. *kaupfǫr.*]
chalk-whyt, -quyte, *adj.* white as chalk, 798, *958. [OE. *cealc + hwīt.*]
chamber, chambre, *n.* private sitting-room or bedroom, 48, 833, 978, 1402, 1742 (*attrib.*), &c. [OFr. *chambre.*]
chamberlayn, *n.* chamberlain, groom of the chamber, 1310, 2011. [OFr. *chamberlain.*]
chapel(le), chapayle, *n.* (private) chapel, 63, 451, *705, 1070, 1876, 2186, &c. [OFr. *chapelle.*]
chaplayn, *n.* priest serving a chapel, *930, 2107. [OFr. *chapelain.*]
charcole, *n.* charcoal, 875.
charg, *n.* importance; *no charg*, it does not matter, 1940. [OFr. *charge.*]
charge, *v.* to take charge, possession of, 863; charge, enjoin, 451. [OFr. *charger.*]
chargeaunt, *adj.* onerous, toilsome, 1604. [OFr. *chargeant.*]
charyté, *n.* charity, kindliness, 2055. [OFr. *charité.*]
charre, *v. trans.* to turn back, 1143; *refl.* turn, go, 850; *intr.* return, 1678. [OE. *cerran, cærran.*]
charres, *n. pl.* affairs, business, 1674. [OE. *cerr, cærr.*]
chasyng, *n.* chasing, 1143 n. [From OFr. *chacier.*]
chastysed, *pa. t.* punished, 1143. [OFr. (rare) *chastiser.*]
chaunce, *n.* chance, fortune, 1406, 2068; adventure, 1081, 1838, 2399, 2496; *cheueȝ þat ch.*, brings it to pass, 2103; *for ch.*, in spite of anything, 2132. [OFr. *ch(e)ance.*]
chauncely, *adv.* by chance, 778. [From prec.]
chaunge, *v.* to exchange, 1107, 1406, 1678; change, 711 (see CHER), 2169; (clothes) 863. [OFr. *changier.*]
chaunsel, *n.* chancel, 946. [OFr. *chancel.*]
chauntré, *n.* singing of mass, 63. [OFr. *chanterie.*]
chef, *adj.* chief, principal, 1512, 1604; main (road), 778; **chefly**, *adv.* particularly, 850, 978; quickly, *883, 1940; **cheuely**, 1876. [OFr. *chef.*]
cheyer, *n.* chair, 875. [OFr. *chaere.*]

cheke, *n.* cheek, 953, 1204. [OE. *cē(a)c.*]
chek(k)e, *n.* checkmate; ill luck, 2195; fortune, 1107 (gain), 1857. [OFr. *eschec.*]
chelde3. See SCHELDE.
chemné, *n.* fireplace, 875, 977, 1667; **chymné**, 1030, 1402; **chymnees**, *pl.* chimneys, 798. [OFr. *chemenee.*]
chepe, *n.* trade; price, 1940; *pl.* goods (got in trade), 1941 n.; *hade goud chepe3*, had good bargains, 1939. [OE. *cēap.*]
chepen, *v.* to bargain, 1271. [OE. *cēapian.*]
cher(e), **schere**, *n.* (expression of) face, 334; *chaunge ch.*, turn this way and that, 2169 (*but not* 711); demeanour, behaviour, 1759, 2496; *made gret ch.*, behaved graciously, 1259; *bele ch.*, gracious company, 1034; mood, frame of mind, 711, 883; *mad ay god ch.*, remained cheerful, 562; *with ch.*, merrily, 1745. [OFr. *ch(i)ere.*]
cheryche, *v.* to treat kindly; salute graciously, 946; **cherysen**, *pres. pl.* receive kindly, entertain, 2055. [OFr. *cherir, cheriss-.*]
ches. See CHOSE.
cheualry, *n.* knighthood, 1512. [OFr. *chevalerie.*]
cheualrous, *adj.* chivalrous, 2399. [OFr. *chevalerous.*]
cheue, *v.* to acquire, get, 1271, 1390; bring about, 2103; *intr.* come (to an end), 63; *cheue to*, make your way to, 1674. [OFr. *chevir* and *achever.*]
cheuely. See CHEF.
cheuisaunce, **cheuicaunce**, *n.* winnings, gain, 1390, 1406, 1678; *ch. of*, obtaining, 1939. [OFr. *chevissance.*]
chylde, *n.* child, 647; **chylder**, *pl.* 280. [OE. *cild*, pl. *cildru.*]
child-gered, *adj.* boyish, merry, 86. [Prec. + GERE, manners.]
chymbled, *pp.* bound, wrapped up, 958. [Cf. ON. *kimbla.*]
chymne(es). See CHEMNÉ.
chyne, *n.* chine, backbone, 1354. [OFr. *eschine.*]
chyn(ne), chin, 958, 1204. [OE. *cinn.*]
chorle, *n.* man (of low birth), 2107. [OE. *ceorl.*]
chose, *v.* to choose, select, 863, 1271, 1310; *to chose of*, conspicuous among, 1512; pick out, perceive, 798; *chose þe waye* (*gate*), take one's way, go, 930, 1876; *hence intr.* make one's way, go, 451, 778, 946; *subj.* (that) you go, 451; **ches**, *pa. t. sg.* 798, 946; **chosen**, *pl.* 930; **chosen**, *pp.* chosen, 1275; undertaken, 1838; made his way, 778. [OE. *cēosan.*]
clad, *pa. t.* clothed, dressed, 2015; *pp.* covered, 885. [OE. (rare) *clǣþan*, pa. t. **clǣdde.*]
clayme, *v.* to claim, 1490. [OFr. *clamer*, 3 sg. *claime.*]
clamberande, *pres. p.* clustering, 1722; **clambred**, *pp.* 801. [ON. *klambra.*]
clanly, *adv.* clean; without omission, 393. [OE. *clǣn-līce.*] See CLENE.
clannes, *n.* purity, 653. [OE. *clǣn-nes.*]
clatered, *pa. t.* clattered, re-echoed, 2201; *pp.* fallen clattering down, 1722; **claterande**, *pres. p.* splashing, 731. [OE. *clatrian.*]
clene, *adj.* clean, pure, 885, 1013, 1883, 2393; bright, 158, 161; elegant, fair, 146, 154, 163, 854; *adv.* clean, 576, 2017, 2391; neatly, 792; completely, 1298. [OE. *clǣne.*]
clenge, *v.* to cling (to the earth), 1694, 2078; *cl. adoun*, shrink down (into the earth), 505. [OE. *clingan.*]
clepe, *v.* to call, 1310. [OE. *cleopian.*]
cler(e), *adj.* clear, bright, fair, 631, 854, 942, 1181, 1747, 2351, &c.; *as sb.*, fair lady, 1489; *adv.* in *cler quyt*, pure white, 885. [OFr. *cler.*]
clergye, *n.* learning; magical lore, 2447. [OFr. *clergie.*]
clerk, *n.* clerk, priest, 64; **klerk**, sage, wizard, 2450. [OE. *cler(i)c*; OFr. *clerc.*]

cleue, *v. intr.* to split, 2201. [OE. *clēofan*, trans.]
clyff(e), klyf(fe), *n.* cliff, (high) rock, 713, 1166, 1431, 1722, 2078, 2201. [OE. *clif.*]
cloyster, *n.* enclosure, wall, 804. [OFr. *cloistre.*]
clomben, *pa. t. pl.* climbed, 2078. [OE. *climban*, pa. t. pl. *clumbon.*]
close, *v.* to close, fasten, 572 n., 1742; enclose, cover, 186, 578; *pp.* contained, 1298; *closed fro*, free from, 1013. [From OFr. *clos*, n.]
closet, *n.* closed pew in the castle chapel for the lord and his family, 934, 942. [OFr. *closet.*]
cloþe, *n.* cloth, 2036; table-cloth, 885; *on clothe*, on the table, 125; **cloþeȝ, -es**, *pl.* clothes, 2015; coverings (for chair), 876; bedclothes, 1184; tablecloths, 1649. [OE. *clāþ.*]
cloudeȝ, *n. pl.* clouds, 505, 727; **clowdes**, 1696, 2001. [Cf. OE. *clūd*, mass of earth or rock.]
clusteres, *n. pl.* clusters, 1739. [OE. *cluster.*]
cnokeȝ, *2 sg.* knockest, dealest a blow, 414. [OE. *cnocian.*]
cofly, *adv.* promptly, 2011. [OE. *cāf-līce.*]
coȝed, *pa. t.* coughed, cleared his throat, 307. [OE. *cohhetan.*]
coynt, coyntly(ch). See KOYNT.
coke, *n.* cock, 1412; **kok**, 2008. [OE. *cocc.*]
colde, *adj.* cold, 727, 731, 818, 1732, 1844 (see HOT), &c.; grievous, 1982; **coolde**, the cold (snowy) ground, 2474; **colde**, *n.* (the) cold, 505, 747, 2001, 2015, 2078. [OE. *cáld*, n. and adj.]
cole(n), *v.* to cool; assuage, relieve, 1254. [OE. *cōlian*, intr.]
colour, *n.* colour, 1059; complexion, 944. [OFr. *colour.*]
com(me), cum, *v.* to come, arrive, 347, 594, 1073, 1476, &c.; *com ȝe*, if you go, 2111; **com(e)**, *pa. t.* 116, 502, *1755, &c.; **com(en)**, *p*[illegible] *c. to*, entered into, 1855; c[illegible] 907, 2491, &c.; **cum(m)en**, [illegible] 62, 533. [OE. *cuman.*]
comaunded, cumaunde, *v.* to bid, command, 366, 850, 1372; order, 992; **comaundeȝ**, *imper.* commend, 2411. [OFr. *comander.*]
comaundement, *n.* orders, bidding, 1303, 1501. [OFr. *comandement.*]
comended, *pa. t.* commended, praised, 1629. [OFr. *com(m)ender.*]
comfort, *n.* solace, pleasure, 1011, 1221, 1254. [OFr. *confort.*]
comfort, *v.* to comfort, 2513; solace, amuse, 1099. [OFr. *conforter.*]
comly, cumly, *adj.* fair, beautiful, noble, 934, 1366, 1732; **comlych**, 469, 539, 934, 1366, &c.; *quasi-sb.* fair knight, 674; fair lady, 1755; **comloker**, *compar.* 869; **comlokest**, *superl.* 53, 767, 1520; *quasi-sb.* fairest lady, 81; **comly(che)**, *adv.* fittingly, graciously, 648, 1307, 1629, 1794; **comlyly**, 360, 974, &c. [OE. *cy̆mlic, cy̆mlīce*, infl. by assoc. with ME. *becomen.*]
commen, -es, cummen. See COM.
compayny(e), companye, *n.* company, 556, companionship, 1011; (her) company, 1099; (polite) society, 1483; **compeyny**, retinue, 1912. [OFr. *compai(g)nie.*]
compas, *n.* measurement; proportion, 944. [OFr. *compas.*]
compast, *pa. t.* pondered, 1196. [OFr. *compasser.*]
con, *v.*[1] I know how to, can, 2283; *3 sg.* 2138, 2455; **conneȝ**, *2 pl.* 1267 n., 1483; **couth, couþe, cowþe**, *pa. t.* could, 45, 1125, 1299, 1486, 1937, 2273, &c.; knew their craft, 1139. [OE. *can, cūþe.*]
con, *v.*[2] *auxil. with infin. as equiv. of pa. t.*, did, 230, 362, 1598, 1666, &c.; can, 340, 1042. [Prec. confused with ME. *gan*, did.]
conable, *adj.* fitting, excellent, 2450.

[Reduction (Northern) of OFr. *covenable.*]

concience, *n.* conscience; mind, 1196. [OFr. *conscience.*]

confessed, *pp.* in *c. clene*, made clean by confession, 2391. [OFr. *confesser.*]

conysaunce, *n.* cognisance, badge, 2026. [OFr. *conissance.*]

conneȝ. See CON.

conquestes, *n. pl.* conquests, 311. [OFr. *conqueste.*]

constrayne, *v.* to compel, force, 1496. [OFr. *constreindre, constreign-.*]

contray, *n.* region, 713; *bi c.*, over the land, 734. [OFr. *contrée.*]

conueyed, *pa. t.* escorted, 596 n. [OFr. *conveier.*]

coolde. See COLDE.

coprounes, *n. pl.* ornamental tops, 797. [OFr. *couperon.*]

corbel, *n.* raven, 1355 n. [OFr. *corbel.*]

corner, *n.* corner, 1185. [OFr. *corn(i)er.*]

cors, *n.*[1] body, 1237. [OFr. *cors.*]

cors, *n.*[2] course (at dinner), 116; **cource**, 135. [OFr. *cours.*]

corsed, *pp.* and *adj.* cursed, 2374; **corsedest**, *superl.* 2196. [OE. *cūrsian*, from OIr. *cúrsagim.*]

corsour, *n.* courser (horse), 1583. [OFr. *corsier*, with altered suffix.]

co(u)rt, *n.* court, members of noble household, 43, 360, 400, 903, &c.; **ko(u)rt**, 1048, 2340; *to cort*, home, 1099. [OFr. *co(u)rt.*]

cortays(e), *adj.* chivalrous, courteous, gracious, 276, 469, 539, 1013, 1511, 1525; *quasi-sb.* gracious lady, 2411. **cortaysly**, *adv.* courteously, graciously, 775, 903. [OFr. *corteis.*]

cortaysy(e), *n.* courtesy, (manners and virtues of) chivalry, 263, 653, 1298, 1491, 1773. [OFr. *corteisie.*]

cort-fereȝ, *n. pl.* companions at court, 594. [OFr. *cort* + OE. *fēra.*]

cortyn, *n.* curtain, bed-hanging (*see frontis.*), 854, 1185, 1192, 1732; **cortayn**, 1476. [OFr. *cortine.*]

cortyned, *pp.* curtained, 1181. [From prec.]

coruon, *pp.* carved, 797. [OE. *ceorfan*, pp. *corfen.*]

cosyn, *n.* cousin; kinsman, 372. [OFr. *cosin.*]

cosse, *n.* kiss, 1300, 1946, 2351, 2360. [OE. *coss.*] See KYSSE.

cost, *n.* nature, quality, 546, 944, 1272, 1849; *pl.* manners, ways, disposition, 1483, 2360; observance (of religious duties), 750; *c. of care*, hardships, 2495. [Late OE. *cost* from ON. *kostr.*]

costeȝ, *pres. t.* coasts, passes by the side of, 1696. [From OFr. *coste*, n.]

cote, *n.* coat, 1921; tunic, 152, 335; coat-armour (see next), 637, 2026. [OFr. *cote.*]

cote-armure, *n.* coat armour, a vest of rich stuff, embroidered with heraldic devices, worn over the armour, 586.

coþe, *pa. t. sg.*, quoth, said, 776; ***quoþ**, 256, 309, 1779, &c. [OE. *cwæþ.*]

couardise, *n.* cowardice, 2508; **cowardise**, 2273; **coward(d)yse**, 2374, 2379. [OFr. *couardise.*]

couenaunt, **couenaunde**, *n.* agreement, compact, 393, 1384, 2328, 2340; *pl.* terms of the compact, 1123, 1408, 1642, 2242. [OFr. *covena(u)nt.*]

couerto(u)r, *n.* coverlet, 855, 1181; horse-cloth, 602 n. [OFr. *coverture.*]

couetyse, *n.* covetousness, 2374, 2380, 2508. [OFr. *coveitise.*]

coundue, *v.* to conduct, 1972. [OFr. *conduire.*]

coundutes, *n. pl.* 'conductus'; *c. of Krystmasse*, Christmas carols, 1655 n. [OFr. *conduite.*]

counse(y)l, *n.* counsel, 682; *to your c.*, to advise you, 347. [OFr. *co(u)nseil.*]

counseyl, *v.* to advise, counsel, 557. [OFr. *conseiller.*]

countenaunce, *n.* bearing; expression

of face, 335; custom, 100; favour, looks of favour, 1490, 1539, 1659. [OFr. *co(u)ntenance.*]

couples, *n. pl.* leashes, 1147. [OFr. *couple.*]

cource; court. See CORS, *n.*[2]; CORT.

couþ(e), cowþe. See CON.

couþe, *adj.* evident, plain to see, 1490. [OE. *cūþ.*]

coward(d)yse, &c. See COUARDISE.

couþly, *adv.* familiarly, 937. [OE. *cūþ-līce.*]

cowpled, *pa. t.* coupled, leashed together (in pairs), 1139. [OFr. *coupler.*] See COUPLES.

cowters, *n. pl.* elbow-pieces (of armour), 583. [OFr. **cout(i)ere* from *coute* elbow.]

crabbed, *adj.* crabbed; unconvivial, 502; perverse, 2435. [Obscure.]

craft, *n.* skill (in an art or pursuit), 1380; affairs, doings, 471; *pl.* (magic) crafts, 2447; (skilful) ways, dealings, 1527; pursuits, 1688. [OE. *cræft.*]

crafty, *adj.* cunningly made, 572. [OE. *cræftig.*]

craftyly, *adv.* with cunning art, 797. [OE. *cræftig-līce.*]

cragge, *n.* crag, 1430, 2183, 2221. [M.Welsh **crag*; cf. M.Breton *cragg.*]

crakkande, *pres. p.* echoing, ringing, 1166; **crakkyng**, *n.* (sudden) blaring, 116. [OE. *cracian.*]

craþayn, *n.* caitiff, villain, 1773. [Obscure.]

craue, *v.* to claim, 1384; ask for, 277 (*subj.*), 283; crave, beg (for), 812, 1300, 1670. [OE. *crafian*, demand.]

crede, *n.* creed, 643, 758. [OE. *crēda.*]

creped, *pa. t.* crept, 1192. [OE. *crēopan*, str.]

cresped, *pp.* curled, 188. [OFr. *crespe*; OE. *cirpsian*, v.]

crest, *n.* mountain-top, 731. [OFr. *creste.*]

creuisse, *n.* fissure, 2183. [OFr. *crevasse.*]

cry(e), *n.* shouting, 64; cry (for help), 775. [OFr. *cri.*]

crye, cri(e), *v.* to shout, call, 1088, 1445; lament, 760; *kryes þerof*, gives tongue at it (the line of scent), 1701. [OFr. *crier.*]

crystenmas(se), *n.* Christmas, 502; *quasi-adj.* 985; **krystmasse**, 37, 1655; **crystemas**, 283; **cristmasse, crystmasse**, 471, 683; *þat krystmasse*, those Chr. festivities, 907; *krystmasse euen*, Christmas Eve, 734. [OE. *crīsten*, adj. + *mæsse*; cf. OE. (late) *crīst-mæsse.*]

croys, *n.* cross, 643. [OFr. *crois.*]

croked, *adj.* crooked; *were neuer croked*, never went astray, never failed, 653. [From ON. *krókr*, n.]

cropure, cropore, *n.* crupper, 168, 602. [OFr. *crop(i)ere*, with altered suffix.]

cros, *n.* cross, 762 n. [ON. *kross*, from OIr. *cros.*]

croun, *n.* crown, 364; *þat bere þe c. of þorne*, Christ, 2529; crown of the head, 419, 616. [OFr. *coroune*; cf. ON. *krúna.*]

crowen, *pp.* crowed, *1412; **crue**, *pa. t.* crew, 2008. [OE. *crāwan.*]

cum, cum-. See COM, COM-.

curious, *adj.* skilfully made, of elaborate design, 855. [OFr. *curious.*]

D.

dabate, 2041. See DEBAT, *n.*

day(e), *n.* day, 44, 61, 1022, 1072, 1075, &c.; (life) time, 2522; daylight, 1126, 1999, &c.; *vpon d.*, by day, 47; *in daye*, ever, 80. [OE. *dæg.*]

daylyeden. See DALY.

daylyȝt, *n.* daylight, 1137, 1365. [DAY + LYȜT; cf. OE. *dæges liht.*]

daynté, dayntye, *n.* courtesy, courteous treatment, 1250, 1266, 1662, 1889; *adj.* charming, 1253;

delights, dainties, 121, 483, 998, 1401. [OFr. *deint(i)é.*]
dale, *n.* (bottom of) valley, 1151, 2005, 2162. [OE. *dæl.*]
daly, *v.* to trifle, make (courtly) love, 1253; **daylyeden**, *pa. t. pl.* 1114. [OFr. *dalier.*]
dalyaunce, *n.* courtly conversation, 1012, 1529. [OFr. **daliance.*]
dalt(en). See DELE.
dame, *n.* lady, 470; *pl.* 1316. [OFr. *dame.*]
dar, *pres. t.* dare, 287, 300, 1991; **durst**, *pa. t.* 1493, 1575. [OE. *dearr, dorste.*]
dare, *v.* to cower, 315, 2258. [OE. *darian.*]
daunsed, *pa. t.* danced, 1026; **daunsyng**, *n.*, 47. [OFr. *da(u)ncer.*]
dawed, *pa. t. subj.* would avail, 1805. [OE. *dugan.*]
debat, **dabate**, *n.* resistance, 1754, 2041, 2248. [OFr. *debat.*]
debate, *v.* to debate, argue, 68; **debatande**, *pres. p.* 2179. [OFr. *debatre.*]
debonerté, *n.* courtesy, 1273. [OFr. *deboneret(i)é.*]
dece, **des**, *n.* raised platform, dais (on which high table stood), 61, 75, 141, 222, 250, 445, 478, 1000. [OFr. *de(i)s.*]
ded, *adj.* dead; slain, 725, 2264. [OE. *dēad.*]
dede, *n.* deed, act, 1047, 1089, 1265 n., 1629; task, 1327; occupation, 1468; affair, 1662. [OE. *dēd.*]
defence, *n.* defence, 1282. [OFr. *defense.*]
defende, *v.* to defend, 1551, 2117; *pp.* forbidden, 1156. [OFr. *defendre.*]
degré, *n.* rank, 1006. [OFr. *degré.*]
deȝe, *v* to die, 996, 1163; **dyȝe**, 2460. [ON. *deyja, dø'ja.*]
dele, 2188. See DEUEL.
dele, *v.* to deal, mete out, 295, 397, 1266, *1752, 2285; (blows), 560; give, 1805; perform, 1968, 2192; **dalt(en)**, *pa. t.* and *pp.* 452, 1114, 2418, 2449; contended (in sport), 1668; *d. with*, behaved to, 1662. See DRURY, VNTYȜTEL. [OE. *dǣlan.*]
delful, **dulful**, *adj.* grievous, 560, 1517. [From DOEL.]
deliuer, *adj.* nimble, 2343; **deliuerly**, *adv.* quickly, 2009. [OFr. *de(s)livre.*]
delyuer, *v.* to assign, 851; *pp.* dealt with, over, 1414. [OFr. *de(s)livrer.*]
demay, *imper. refl.* be perturbed, 470; **dismayd** (*for*), *pp.* dismayed (at), 336. [OFr. *de(s)maier.*]
deme, *v.* to judge, consider, 240, 246, 1529; think fit, determine, 1082, 1089, 1668; tell, say, 1322, 2183. [OE. *dēman.*]
denayed, *pp.* refused, 1493. [OFr. *deneier.*]
deneȝ, *adj.* Danish, 2223 n. [OE. *denisc*; OFr. *daneis.*]
dep(e), *adj.* deep, profound, 741, 786, 1159, 1748; *adv.* 787. [OE. *dēop*; *dēope*, adv.]
depaynt(ed), *pp.* painted, 620; depicted, 649. [OFr. *depeindre*, 3 sg. pres. and pp. *depeint.*]
departe, *v.* to separate, 1335; *intr.* depart, 1983; **departyng**, *n.* parting, 1798. [OFr. *departir.*]
deprece, *v.*[1] to subjugate, 6; **deprese**, press, importune, 1770. [OFr. *depresser.*]
deprece, *v.*[2] to release, 1219. [OFr. *de(s)presser*, free from pressure; *de(s)priser*, free from prison.]
der(e), *n.* deer, 1151, 1157, 1322, 1324. [OE. *dēor.*]
dere, *adj.*[1] costly, precious, 75, 121, 193, 571; pleasant, 47, 1012, 1026, 2449; beloved, dear, 470, 754; noble, 2465; festal, 92, 1047; *as sb.* dear, 1492, 1798; noble, 678, 928 (Gawain dining alone). **derrest**, *superl.* noblest, 445; most excellent, 483. [OE. *dēore*; compar. *dēorra.*]
dere, *adj.*[2] grievous, 564. [OE. *dēor.*]
dered, *pa. t.* afflicted, hurt, 1460. [OE. *derian.*]
derely, *adv.* splendidly, 1559; plea-

santly, 1253; courteously, 817, 1031; neatly, 1327; deeply, 1842. [OE. *dēorlīce.*]

derf, derue, *adj.* doughty, 1000, 1492; stout, 1233; grievous, severe, 558, 564, 1047. [ON. *djarfr*, bold, infl. by sense of OE. *deorfan, derfan.*]

derfly, deruely, *adv.* boldly, 2334; quickly, 1183. [ON. *djarfliga.*]

derk, *adj.* dark, 1177, 1887; *n.* dark(ness), 1999. [OE. *de(o)rc.*]

derne, *adj.* private, 1012; **dernly,** *adv.* stealthily, 1188. [OE. *derne, dernlīce.*]

derworþly, *adv.* sumptuously, 114. [OE. *dēorwurþlīce.*]

des, *n.* See DECE.

deserue, disserue, *v.* to deserve, 452, 1779, 1803. [OFr. *deservir.*]

desyre, *v.* to desire, 1257. [OFr. *desirer.*]

destiné, *n.* fate, destiny, 564, 996, 1752, 2285. [OFr. *destinee.*]

deþe, dethe, *n.* death, 1600, 2105. [OE. *dēaþ.*]

devaye, *v.* to deny, refuse, 1497. [OFr. *deve(i)er.*]

deue, *v.* to stun, to strike down, 1286. [OE. *dēafian.*]

deuel, dele, *n.* Devil, 2188, 2192. [OE. *dēofol.*]

deuys, *n.* device (or *a deuys* = OFr. *a devis*, at one's desire, as many as desired), 617. [OFr. *devis.*]

deuise, *v.* to relate, 92. [OFr. *deviser.*]

deuocioun, *n.* devotions, 2192. [OFr. *devocion.*]

dewe, *n.* dew, 519. [OE. *dēaw.*]

diamauntez, *n. pl.* diamonds, 617. [OFr. *diamant.*]

dich, *n.* ditch, moat, 766, 786, 1709. [OE. *dīc.*]

dyȝe. See DEȜE.

diȝt, dyȝt, *v.* to appoint; *d. me þe dom*, adjudge me the right, 295; *d. hym*, went, 994; *pp.* set, 114; appointed, 678, 1884; dressed, 1689; prepared, 1559; made, 2223. [OE. *dihtan.*]

dille, *adj.* foolish, stupid, 1529. [OE. **dylle*, rel. to *dol.*]

dyn, *n.* noise, merrymaking, 47, 1159, 1183, 1308. [OE. *dyne.*]

diner, *n.* dinner (the chief meal of the day, begun about 2 o'clock), 928, 1559. [OFr. *diner.*]

dyngeȝ, *pres. t.* smites, *2105. [ON. *dengja*, wk.]

dyngne, *adj.* worthy, 1316. [OFr. *digne.*]

dynt, *n.* blow, 202, 1460, 2264, &c.; **dunt(e)**, 452, 1286. [OE. *dynt.*]

disceuer, discouer, *v.* to uncover, reveal, 418, 1862. [OFr. *descovrir*, 3 sg. *descuevre.*]

discrye, *v.* to behold, 81. [OFr. *descrier.*]

disches, *n. pl.* dishes, 122, 128. [OE. *disc.*]

disert, *n.* desert, merit, 1266. [OFr. *desert.*]

dismayd, 336. See DEMAY.

displayed, *pp.* displayed, 955. [OFr. *despleier.*]

displese, *v.* to displease, 1304; *impers. subj.* let it displease, 1839; *imper. pl. refl.* take offence, 2439. [OFr. *desplaisir, -plesir.*]

dispoyled, *pp.* despoiled, 860. [OFr. *despoill(i)er.*]

disport, *n.* entertainment, 1292. [OFr. *desport.*]

disserue. See DESERUE.

disstrye, *v.* to destroy, 2375. [OFr. *destruire.*]

dit, *pp.* closed, locked, 1233. [OE. *dyttan.*]

do, *v.* to do, 1089, &c.; **dos, dotȝ,** *3 sg.* 1308, 2211; *imper. pl.* 1533; **did(de),** *pa. t.* 998, 1327, &c.; **don(e),** *pp.* 478, 928, &c. To do, perform, make, 565, 1082, &c.; *do me* afford me, 1798; *dotȝ me drede*, makes me afraid, 2211; *didden hem vndo*, had them cut up, 1327; to put, set, 478; *do way*, cease from, 1492;

dos hir, goes, 1308; *pp*. over, 928, 1365. [OE. *dōn*.]
doel, *n*. grief. 558. [OFr. *doel*.]
dogge3, *n. pl*. dogs, 1600. [OE. (late) *docga*.]
do3ter, *n*. daughter, 2465. [OE. *dohtor*.]
do3ty, *adj*. doughty, 2264, 2334. [OE. *dohtig*.] See DU3TY.
dok, *n*. tail, 193. [Cf. Mod. Icel. *dokkr*.]
dole, *n*. part, 719. [OE. *dāl*.]
dom(e), *n*. judgement, doom, 295, 1216, 1968. [OE. *dōm*.]
dome3day, *n*. doomsday, 1884. [OE. *dōmes dæg*.]
donkande, *pres. p*. moistening, 519. [Cf. ON. *dǫkk*, pool; Swed. dial. *dänka*, to moisten.]
dor(e), *n*. door, 136, 1140, 1183, 1233, 1368. [OE. *duru, dor*.]
doser, *n*. wall-tapestry, 478. [OFr. *doss(i)er*.]
dote, *v*. to be foolish, dote, 1151, 1956. [Cf. MDu. *doten*.]
double, *adj*. double (-channelled), 786.
doub(b)le, *adv*. double, 2033; with twice the usual amount, 61, 483. [OFr. *double*.]
doublefelde, *adv*. with twice the usual amount, 890. [Prec. + OE. *-féld*, pp.; cf. *þriféldan*, &c.]
doun, *adv*. down, 817, 2309, &c.; *prep*. 2144. [OE. *of dūne, adūne*.]
do(e)s, *n. pl*. does, 1159, 1322. [OE. *dā*.]
doune3, **downe3**, *n. pl*. hills, 695, 1972. [OE. *dūn*.]
doute, *n*. fear, 246; *had doute*, was afraid, 442. [OFr. *doute*.]
douth(e), *n*. (assembled) company, 61, 397, 1365, 1415, 1956. [OE. *dugoþ*.]
douteles, *adv*. doubtless, 725. [DOUTE + OE. *-lēas*.]
dowelle, *v*. to remain, 566, 1075, 1082. [OE. *dwellan*.]
dra3e, *v*. to draw, lead, 1031; **drowe**, *pres. subj*. carry on (trade), 1647; **dro3(en)**, *pa. t*. drew, 335; closed, 1188; *intr*. withdrew, 1463; **drawen**, *pp*. 1233. [OE. *dragan*.]
dra3t, *n*. drawbridge, 817. [OE. **dræht*; ON. *dráttr*, older **drahtr*.]
draueled, *pa. t*. muttered (in sleep), 1750. [Cf. ON. *drafl*, tattle; *drafa*, to talk nonsense.]
drechch, *n*. trouble, annoyance, 1972. [Stem of OE. *dreccan*.]
drede, *v*. to fear, 2355; *intr*. be afraid, 2211. [OE. *drǣdan*.]
drede, *n*. fear, 315, 2258. [OE. *drēd*.]
dredles, *adj*. fearless, 2334. [From prec.]
dre3, **dry3e**, *adj*. unmoved, 335; enduring, 724; severe, 1460; heavy, 1750; *on dry3e*, aside, 1031; *adv*. forcibly, 2263; **dre3ly**, *adv*. unceasingly, 1026. [ON. *drjúgr*, older **drēug-*.]
dreme, *n*. dreaming, 1750. [ON. *draumr*, dream; OE. *drēam*, music.]
dreped, *pp*. slain, killed, 725. [OE. *drepan*, smite; ON. *drepa*, kill.]
dres(se), *v*. to arrange, array, 75, 1000, 2033; turn, direct, 445; *dresses hym vpon grounde*, takes his stand, 417; *dres me to*, proceed to, 474; *intr*. to prepare, 566; go, repair to, 1415; *dressed up*, got up, 2009. [OFr. *dresser*.]
dryftes, *n. pl*. (snow)drifts, 2005. [ON. *drift*.]
dry3e, *adj*. See DRE3.
dry3e, *v*. to endure, 560; *d. vnder*, withstand, survive, 202. [OE. *drē(o)gan*.]
dry3tyn, *n*. God, 724, 996, 1548, 1999, 2138. [OE. *dryhten*.]
drynk, *n*. drink, 497, 1684, 1935. [OE. *drinc*.]
drynk, *v*. to drink, 337; **dronken**, *pa. t. pl*. 1025, 1114, 1668; *pp*. as *adj*. drunk, 1956. [OE. *drincan*.]
dryue, *v*. to drive; **drof**, *pa. t*. 786, 1151, &c.; **dryuen**, **driuen**, *pp*. 558, 1047, &c. *Trans*. to drive, strike, 389, 523, 1047, 1159, 2005;

pursue (pastime), 1468; pass (the day), 1176; make, 558, 1020; *drof to*, hemmed in, enclosed, 786; *intr.* come, make one's way, 121, 222; rush, run, 1151; hurtle, 2263; *dryueȝ to*, comes up on, follows on, 1999. [OE. *drīfan.*]
droȝ(en). See DRAȜE.
droȝt, *n.* drought, 523. [OE. *drūgoþ*, **drūhþ-*.]
dronken. See DRYNK.
dropeȝ, *pres. t.* drops, 519. [OE. *dropian.*]
droupyng,**drowping**,*n.*drooping; deep gloom, 1748, 1750. [ON. *drúpa*, v.]
drowe. See DRAȜE, *v.*
drury(e), **drwry**, *n.* love, 1507, 1517, 1805; love-token, 2033; *dalt d.*, had love-dealings, 2450. [OFr. *druerie.*]
dubbed, *pp.* adorned, 75, 193; arrayed, 571. [OFr. *aduber.*]
dublet, *n.* doublet, jacket, 571. [OFr. *d(o)ublet.*]
duches, *n.* duchess, 2465. [OFr. *duchesse.*]
duȝty, *adj.* doughty, 724. [OE. *dyhtig.*] See DOȜTY.
duk, *n.* duke, 552, 678. [OFr. *duc.*]
dulful, **durst**. See DEL-, DAR.
dure, 110. See AGRAUAYN.
dust, *n.* dust, 523. [OE. *dūst.*]
dut, *n.* joy, 1020. [OFr. *dedu(i)t.*]
dut(te), *pa. t.* feared, 222, 784, 2257. [OFr. *douter.*]

E.

eft(e), *adv.* again, 700, 1340, 1404, 1668, 1875, 2295; afterwards, 898, 2388; then, 788, 1340; secondly, 641. [OE. *eft.*]
eftersones, **eftsoneȝ**, *adv.* again (immediately), 1640, (as a second instance), 2417. [OE. *eftsōna* with infl. of *æfter.*]
egge, *n.* edge, 212; weapon, 2392. [OE. *ecg*, edge, (verse) weapon.]
eke, *adv.* also, as well, 90, 1741. [OE. *ēac*; *tō-ēacan.*]
elbowes, *n. pl.* elbows, 184. [OE. *el(n)-boga.*]
elde(e), *n.* age; generation, time, 1520; *of hyghe e.*, in the prime of life, 844. [OE. *éldo.*]
elleȝ, **elles**, *adv.* on the other hand, 295; else, besides, 384, 1550, 2108; in other things, 1082; *oþer elles*, or else, 1529. [OE. *elles.*]
elnȝerde, *n.* measuring-rod an ell (45 in.) long, 210. [OE. *eln*+*gérd.*]
em(e), *n.* (maternal) uncle, 356, 543. [OE. *ēam.*]
enbaned, *pp.* provided with projecting horizontal coursings, 790 n. [Prov. *enbanar.*]
enbelyse, *v.* to adorn, grace, 1034. [OFr. *embelir*, *embeliss-.*]
enbrauded, *pp.* embroidered, 166, 879, 2028; **enbrawded**, 78, 856; **enbrawden**, 609. [OE. *ge-brogden* infl. by OFr. *broder.*]
enclyne, *v. intr.* to bow, 340. [OFr. *encliner.*]
ende, *n.* end, 63, 215, 660, 661, 1301, &c.; ending, result, 496; *vpon endeȝ*, at the ends, 2039. [OE. *énde.*]
endeles, *adj.* endless, 630; **endeleȝ**, *629. [OE. *énde-lēas.*]
endite, *v.* to direct; *to dethe e.*, do to death, 1600. [OFr. *enditer.*]
endured, *pp.* endured, 1517. [OFr. *endurer.*]
enfoubled, *pp.* muffled up, 959. [OFr. *afublir*, with altered prefix.]
englych, *adj.* as *n. pl.* the English, 629. [OE. *englisc*, adj.]
enker, *adv.* very; *e. grene*, bright green, 150, 2477. [ON. *einkar.*]
enmy, *n.* enemy, 2406. [OFr. *enemi.*]
enn(o)**urned**, ***inurnde**, *pp.* adorned, graced, 634, *881; set as adornment, 2027. [OFr. *aourner*, with altered prefix.]
enquest, *n.* enquiry, 1056. [OFr. *enqueste.*]
entayled, *pp.* carved; depicted (in embroidery), 612. [OFr. *entailler.*]

enterludeȝ, *n. pl.* dramatic or mimic displays (at a feast), 472. [AFr. **entrelude*; Anglo-Lat. *interludium.*]
entyse, *v.* to take, catch (infection), 2436. [OFr. *enticier.*]
entre, *v.* to enter, 221 (*trans.*), 934. [OFr. *entrer.*]
er(e), *adv.* before, 527, 1274; **er**, *prep.* ere, 197; *er þis*, ere now, 1892, 2528; *conj.* (*with subj.*) 92, 987, 2277, &c.; (*indic.*) 764. [OE. *ǣr.*]
erande. See ERNDE.
erbeȝ, *n. pl.* herbs, green plants, 517, 2190. [OFr. *herbe.*]
erber, *n.* first stomach (of ruminants), 1330. [OFr. (*h*)*erb*(*i*)*ere.*]
erde, *n.* land, region, 1544, 1808; *in erde*, in the world, actual(ly), 27, 140, 2416. [OE. *éard.*]
erly, *adv.* early (in the day), 567, 1101, 1126, 1474, 1689. [OE. *ǣr-līce.*]
ermyn, *n.* ermine, 881. [OFr. *ermine.*]
ernd(e), *n.* business, mission, errand, 257, 559, 809, 1051, 1067, 2303; *go myn ernde*, go as my messenger, 811; *an erande*, on a mission, 1808. [OE. *ǣrende*, ON. *erendi.*]
erraunt, *adj.* errant; *knyȝt erraunt*, knight journeying (on a mission), 810. [OFr. *errer*, travel.]
erþe, *n.* earth, ground, 4, 427, 728, 1137, 2098, &c. [OE. *eorþe.*]
ese, *n.* ease, 1676; *at þyn e.*, *in your e.*, at your ease, 1071, 1096; consolation, 1798; delight, 1539. [OFr. *aise, eise.*]
etayn, *n.* ogre, giant, 140, 723. [OE. *eoten.*]
ete, *v.* to eat, dine, 85, 91; **et(t)e**, *pa. t.* 113, 1135. [OE. *etan.*]
eþe, *adj.* easy, 676. [OE. *ē(a)þe.*]
eþe, *v.* to conjure, entreat, 379, 2467. [OE. *ge-ǣþan* from *āþ*, oath.]
eueȝ, *n. sg.* eaves, border (of a wood), 1178. [OE. *efes.*]
euel, *n.* evil, 1552. [OE. *yfel.*]
euen, *adj.* even; *even of*, fairly quit of, 1641; *adv.* in places of equal honour, 1004; straight, right, 1589, 1593; actually, indeed, 444, 2464. [OE. *efen*; *efne.*]
euen, *n.* eve (of a festival), 734, 1669. **euensong**, vespers, 932; **euentide**, evening, 1641. [OE. *ēfen*; *ēfen-song*, *-tīd.*]
euenden, *adv.* straight down, 1345. [EUEN *adv.* + DOWN.]
euer, *adv.* ever; always, 913, 1844, 2264, &c.; continually, 172, 1657; at any time, 52, 682, 1544, &c.; *for e.*, 293. **euermore**, *adv.* evermore, 1547, 2520; *for e.* 669. [OE. *ǣfre*; + *māre*, neut.]
euesed, *pp.* clipped, 184. [OE. *efsian.*]
excused, *pp.* excused, 2131, 2428. [OFr. *excuser.*]
exellently (*of*), *adv.* pre-eminently (among), 2423. [From OFr. *excellent.*]
expoun, *v.* to expound, 1540; describe, 209; *e. much speche of*, have much discussion concerning, 1506. [OFr. *expondre.*]

F

face, *n.* face, mien, 103, 445, 2503, &c.; surface, 524. [OFr. *face.*]
fade, *adj.* ? bold, 149. [Obscure.]
fader, *n.* father, 919. [OE. *fæder.*]
fage, *n.* deceit; *no fage*, in truth, *531 n.
fay, *n.* faith; *ma fay*, by my troth, 1495. [OFr. *fei.*]
faye, *n.* fairy, 2446. [OFr. *faie.*]
fayly, *v.* to fail, be at fault, 455, 641, 1067, 1295, 2356; lack opportunity, 278; *fayld neuer*, was nowhere incomplete, 658. [OFr. *faillir.*]
fayn, *adj.* glad, 386, 840; fain, desirous, 1067, 2019. [OE. *fægen.*]
fayr(e), *adj.* fair, comely, good(ly), 54, 181, 427, 803, 943, 1260, 1694, &c.; courteous, 1116; *þe fayrer*, the advantage, 99. [OE. *fæger.*]
fayr(e), *adv.* fairly; gracefully, courteously, well, 367, 622, 1046, 1556,

1961, 2229, &c.; deftly, 2309; *compar.* 1315. [OE. *fægre.*]

fayntyse, *n.* frailty, 2435. [OFr. *faintise.*]

fayryȝe, *n.* magic, 240. [OFr. *faierie.*]

fayþ(e), *n.* faith, plighted word, 1783; *in (god) f.*, in truth, 279, 381, 1535, &c.; *bi my (þi) f.*, on my (thy) honour, 2284, 2469. [OFr. *feid*, later *fei* = FAY.]

faythely, *adj.* truly, 1636. [From prec.]

faythful, *adj.* trustworthy, 632, 1679. [As prec.]

falce, *adj.* untrue, dishonest, 2382. [OE. *fals*, from L. *falsus.*]

fale, *adj.* pale, faded, 728. [OE. *fealu.*]

falle, *v.*; **fel(le)**, *pa. t.* 430, 1425, &c.; **falled**, 2243; **fallen**, *pp.* 1432, 2528. To fall (down), 507, 728, 1432, &c.; bend low, 1758; *f. to*, rally to, rush towards, 1425, 1702; *f. on*, fall on, 1904; *f. in*, hit on, 1699. To fare, 2378; happen, 2132, 2251, 2528; (*pa. subj.*) might befall, 1588; chance to be, 483; fall to one's lot, 2243, 2327; be fitting, right (for), 358, 890, 1303, 1358. [OE. *fallan.*]

falssyng, *n.* breaking of faith, 2378. [ME. *falsie*, v. from OE. *fals*, FALCE.]

faltered, *pa. t.* staggered, 430. [ON. *faltrask*, be cumbered.]

fange. See FONGE.

fannand, *pres. p.* fanning, waving, 181. [From OE. *fann*, n.]

fantoum, *n.* illusion, 240. [OFr. *fanto(s)me.*]

farand, *adj.* splendid, 101. [ON. *farandi*, fitting.]

fare, *n.* track, 1703; faring, fortune, 2494; fare, food, 694; feast, 537; behaviour, practices, 409, 2386; observances, 1116. [OE. *faru.*]

fare, *v.* to go, proceed, 699, 1231, 1973; *fareȝ wel*, farewell, 2149; **ferde(n)**, *pa. t.* 149, 703, 1282, 1433. [OE. *faran*, str.; pa. t. due to infl. of *fēran*. See FORFERDE.]

faste, *adj.* fast, binding, 1636. [OE. *fæst.*]

fast(e), *adv.* fast, securely, 782; pressingly, 2403; earnestly, 1042; vigorously, loudly, 1908; quickly, 1425, 1585, 1705, 2215. [OE *fæste.*]

faut(e), *n.* fault, faultiness, 1551, 2435, 2488. [OFr. *faute.*]

fautles, -leȝ, *adj.*, faultless, flawless, 640, 1761; **fautlest**, *superl.* in *on þe f.*, the most faultless, 2363. [Prec. + OE. *-lēas.*]

fawne, *v.* to fondle, stroke, 1919. [OE. *fagnian.*]

fawty, *n.* faulty, 2382, 2386. [From FAUTE.]

fax, *n.* hair, 181. [OE. *feax.*]

feblest, *adj. superl.* feeblest, least capable, 354. [OFr. *feble.*]

fech, *v.* to bring, 1375, 2013; obtain, 1857; **fette**, *pp.* 1084. [OE. *fetian*, *feccan.*] See FOCH, FOTTE.

fede, *v.* to fede, 1359. [OE. *fēdan.*]

fee, *n.* payment, 1622; portion of deer to which the huntsman is entitled, 1358; *corbeles fee*, the raven's fee, 1355 n. [OFr. *fe.*]

fe(e)rsly, *adv.* proudly, 329, 1323; fiercely, 832. [From OFr. *fers.*]

feȝt(yng). See FYȜT.

feye, *adj.* doomed to die; stricken by death, 1067. [OE. *fǣge.*]

felaȝe, *n.* companion (hound), 1702. [OE. *fēolaga* from ON. *félagi.*]

felaȝschip, *n.* love of fellow men, 652; company, 2151. [From prec.]

felde, *n.* field (of battle), 874. [OE. *féld.*]

felde, *v.* to fold, embrace, 841. [OE. **féldan*; cf. *-féldan.*]

fele, *adj.* many, 122, 890, 1653, 2417, &c.; **felle**, 1566; *as sb.* many (people), 428, 1588; **feler**, *compar.* more, 1391. [OE. *fela.*]

fele, *v.* to feel, perceive, 2193, 2272. [OE. *fēlan.*]

felefolde, *adj.* manifold, 1545. [OE. *fela-fáld.*]

felle, *adj.* bold, fierce, formidable, 291, 717, 847, 874, 2222; *as sb.* wild beast, 1585; **felly**, *adv.* fiercely, 2302. [OFr. *fel.*]
felle, *n.*[1] skin, 880, 943, 1359, 1737, 1944. [OE. *fell.*]
felle, *n.*[2] fell, precipitous rock, 723. [ON. *fjall, fell.*]
felle(n), **fel.** See FALLE.
femed, *pa. t.* foamed, 1572. [OE. *fǣman.*]
fende, *n.* fiend; *þe f.*, the devil, 1944, 2193. [OE. *fēond.*]
feng. See FONGE.
fer, *adv.* far, afar, 13, 714, 2092; **ferre**, 1093; **fyrre**, **fire**, *compar.* further; moreover, besides, 411, 1105, 1304, 2121, 2151; *fyrre passe*, proceed (with the business), 378. [OE. *feorr(an)*; *firr*, compar.]
ferde, *n.* fear; *for ferde*, in fear, 2130, 2272. [False division of OE. *forfǣred*, pp.; see next.]
ferde, *pa. t.* feared, 1588; *pp.* afraid, 1295, 2382. [OE. *fǣran, fēran.*]
ferde(n). See FARE, *v.*
fere, *adj.* proud, bold, 103. [OFr. *f(i)er.*]
fere, *n.*[1] companion, 695, 915; wife, 2411; peer, equal, 676; *in fere*, in company, ? with a force of men, 267 n. [OE. *gefēra.*]
fere, *n.*[2] company, 267 n. [OE. *gefēre*; *gefēran*, pl., as companions.]
ferk(ke), *v.* to go, ride, travel, 173, 1072, *1973, 2173; *ferkeȝ hym up*, gets up, 2013. [OE. *fer(e)cian.*]
ferly, *adj.* extraordinary, unusual, 716; *n.* a marvel, wonder, 23, 2414. [ON. *ferligr*, monstrous; OE. *fǣrlīc*, sudden.]
ferly, *adv.* wondrously, exceedingly, 388, 741, 1694; **ferlyly**, 796, 2494. [ON. *ferliga*; OE. *fǣrlīce.*]
fermed, *pp.* confirmed, *2329. [OFr. *fermer.*]
fermysoun, *n.* close-season, 1156. [OFr. *fermiso(u)n.*]
fersnes, *n.* pride, high courage, *646. [From OFr. *fer-s*, nom. sg.]
fest, *n.* feast, festival, 44, 537, 1036, 2401, &c. [OFr. *feste.*]
fest, *pa. t.* made fast, agreed upon, 2347. [OE. *fæstan*; ON. *festa.*]
festnéd, *pp.* made firm, bound, 1783. [OE. *fæstnian.*]
fete. See FOTE.
fèted, *pa. t.* behaved, 1282. [From OFr. *fait, fet*, action.]
fetled, *pp.* arrayed, 656. [From OE. *fetel*, girdle.]
fetly, *adv.* gracefully, daintily, 1758. [From OFr. *fait, fet*, adj.]
fette, 1084. See FECH.
fetures, *n. pl.* parts (of the body), 145, 1761. [OFr. *feture.*]
fyched, *pp.* fixed, established, 658. [OFr. *fich(i)er.*]
fyft, *adj.* fifth, 651. [OE. *fĭfta.*]
fiften, *adj.* fifteen, 44. [OE. *fĭftēne.*]
figure, *n.* figure, 627. [OFr. *figure.*]
fyȝed, *pa. t.* fitted, 796. [OE. *fēgan.*]
fyȝt, *n.* fight, 279. [OE. *fe(o)hte.*]
fyȝt, **feȝt**, *v.* to fight, 278, 717; **foȝt** *pa. t. pl.* *874; **feȝtyng**, *n.* fighting *in f. wyse*, in warlike fashion, 267 [OE. *fe(o)htan.*]
fyked, *pa. t.* flinched, 2274. [OE **fician*; cf. *befician.*]
fildore, *n.* gold thread or cord, 189 [OFr. *fil d'or.*]
fyled, *pp.* sharpened, 2225. [OE *fīlian*, file; or OFr. *afiler.*]
fylyoleȝ, *n. pl.* pinnacles, 796. [OFr *filloele.*]
fylle, *v.* to fulfil, carry out, 1405, 1934 [OE. *fyllan.*]
fylor, *n.* sharpening tool with whet stone, 2225. [Cf. OFr. *afiloir.*]
fylter, *v.* crowd together; contend, 986 [OFr. *feltrer*, press (felt).]
fylþe, *n.* impurity, 1013; defilement 2436. [OE. *fȳlþ.*]
fynde, *v.* to find, 123, 449, 660, 1053 &c.; obtain, 324; **fonde**, *pa. t. sg* 694 (had served), 716, 1875 (*subj.*)

pl. 1329; **founden,** *pl.* started, dislodged, 1704; **funde(n),** *pp.* 396, 640; **founden,** 1264. [OE. *findan.*]

fyndyng, *n.* finding, dislodgement, 1433. [From prec.]

fyn(e), *adj.* perfected; fully ratified, 1636; fine, superb, perfect, 173, 919, 1761; pure, sheer, 1239; *adv.* superbly, 1737; **fynly,** *adv.* completely, 1391. [OFr. *fin.*]

fyngreȝ, fyng(e)res, *n. pl.* fingers, 641, 1833; finger's-breadths (as measure), 1329. [OE. *finger.*]

fynisment, *n.* end, 499. [OFr. *finissement.*]

fyr(e), fire, *n.* fire, 832, 847, 1368, 1653, 1925; sparks, 459 (see STONFYR). [OE. *fȳr.*]

fire, fyrre. See FER.

fyrst, *adj. superl.* first, 54, 290, 2347, &c.; (*vp*)*on f.*, at first, in the beginning, 301, 528, 2019; first (of all), 9, 491, 1477, 1934; *as sb.* first day, 1072; *adv.* first(ly), 359, 568, 1422, 1592, 2524, &c.; before, 2227. [OE. *fyr(e)st.*]

fische, *n.* fish, 503, 890. [OE. *fisc.*]

fyskeȝ, *pres. t.* scampers, 1704. [? ON. **fjaska*, cf. Björkman, p. 137.]

fyue, *adj.* and *n.* five, 627, 632, &c.; group of five, 651. [OE. *fīf(e).*]

flaȝ(e). See FLE, FLYȜE.

flat, *n.* meadowland, 507. [ON. *flǫt* (in place-names in England).]

fle, *v.* to flee, flinch, 2125, 2130, 2272; **flaȝ(e),** *pa. t. sg.* (*pl. form*) 2274, 2276; **fled,** 1628. [OE. *flēon*, pa. t. pl. *flugon.*]

flesch(e), *n.* flesh, 943, 2313; (opposed to 'spirit'), 503, 2435; venison, 1363. [OE. *flǣsc.*]

flet(te), *n.* floor, 568, 859; (= hall) 294, 1374; *vpon f.*, in the hall, 832, 1653, 1925. [OE. *flett.*]

flete, *v.* to fleet, speed; *pa. t. pl.* (*sg. form*) 1566; **floten,** *pp.* having wandered, 714. [OE. *flēotan.*]

flyȝe, *n.* fly, 166. [OE. *flē(o)ge.*]

flyȝe, *v.* to fly, 524; **flaȝ(e),** *pa. t. sg.* (*pl. form*) 459, 2276 (*first*). [OE. *flē(o)gan*; see FLE.]

flynt, *n.* flint, 459. [OE. *flint.*]

flod, *n.* flood, stream, 2173; sea, 13. [OE. *flōd.*]

flokked, *pa. t.* assembled, 1323. [From OE. *flocc.* n.]

flone, *n.* arrow, 1161, 1566. [OE. *flān.*]

flor, *n.* floor (= hall), 834, 1932. [OE. *flōr.*]

flosche, *n.* pool, 1430. [Cf. OFr. *flache.*]

floten. See FLETE.

flowreȝ, *n. pl.* flowers, 507. [OFr. *flour.*]

fnast(ed), *pa. t.* snorted, panted, 1587, 1702. [OE. *fnǣstian.*]

foch(che), *v.* to get, take, 396, 1961. [Var. of FECH; cf. OE. *feotian* or *fatian.*] See FOTTE.

fode, *n.* food, 503. [OE. *fōda.*]

foyned, *pa. t.* thrust at; kicked, 428. [From OFr. *foi(s)ne*, fish-spear.]

foysoun, *n.* abundance, 122. [OFr. *foiso(u)n.*]

folde, *n.* earth, land, 23, 524, 1694; ground, 422; *vpon f.*, (tag) on earth, living, 196, 396, 642, 676, 1275, 2373 (there). [OE. *fólde.*]

folde, *v.* to fold; *f. to*, match, be like, 499; turn, go, 1363; pledge, grant, 359; **folden,** *pp.* plaited, tied, 189; enfolded, wimpled, 959; plighted, 1783. [OE. *fáldan*; here seems equated with both ME. *plihten* (plight), and *plīten* (fold).]

fole, *n.*[1] horse, 173, 196, 459 (*gen.*), 695, 803. [OE. *fola.*]

fole, *n.*[2] fool, 2414. [OFr. *fol.*]

folé, *n.* folly, 1545; **foly,** 324. [OFr. *folie.*]

folȝe, *v.* to follow, pursue, 1164, 1895; *þat f. alle þe sele*, to all of whom prosperity came, 2422; *folȝande*, in like manner, 145; *of f. sute*, of similar sort, 859. [OE. *folgian.*]

folk(e), *n.* people, men, 54, 816, &c.; throng, 1323. [OE. *folc.*]

fonde, *v.* to try, test, tempt, 291, 565, 986, 1549. [OE. *fóndian.*]
fonde(t). See FYNDE, FOUNDE.
fonge, **fange**, *v.* to take, receive, get, 391, 1265 n., 1363, 1556, 1622; welcome, entertain, 816, 919, 1315; **feng**, *pa. t.* derived, *646; **fonge(d)**, *pp.* 919, 1315. [OE. *fōn*, str.; ON. *fanga*, wk.]
foo, *adj.* hostile; forbidding, 1430; *adv.* fiercely, 2326. [OE. *fāh, fā-.*]
foo, *n.* foe, 716. [OE. *gefā.*]
for, *conj.* for, 147, 492, *1514, &c.; because, since, 258, 632, 1093, 1441, 1827, 1847. [OE. *for þam (þe).*]
for, *prep.* for (sake, purpose of), to be, as, 240, 479, 537, 1347, 1786, &c.; because of, through, 282, 488, 2125, &c.; (in return, exchange) for, 98, 287, 1055, &c.; in spite of, 1854, 2132, 2251; *for to,* in order to, so as to, to, 124, 1550, 1634, &c.; *for as much as*, in so far as, 356. [OE. *for.*]
forbe, *prep.* past; beyond, more than, 652. [OE. *for(a)n + be.*]
force, **forse**, *n.* necessity, 1239; strength, 1617. [OFr. *force.*]
forest, *n.* wild uncultivated land, forest, 741, 1149. [OFr. *forest.*]
forferde, *pa. t.* slew, killed, 1617; **forfaren**, *pp.* 1895. [OE. *forfaran*; see FARE, *v.*]
forfete, *v.* to transgress, 2394. [From OFr. *forfait, -fet*, n.]
forgat, *pa. t.* forgot, 2031. [OE. *forgetan*, with substitution of ON. *geta.*] Cf. FORȜATE.
forgoo, *v.* to give up, 2210. [OE. *forgān.*]
forȝ, *n.* force, waterfall, 2173. [ON. *fors.*]
forȝate, *pa. t.* forgot, 1472; **forȝeten**, *pp.* 1485. [OE. *forgetan.*]
forȝelde, *pres. subj.* repay, reward, 839, 1279, 1535, 2429. [OE. *forgéldan.*]
forlancyng, *pres. p.* throwing out, 1334. [Fr. *forlancer*, recorded later in Fr. than in E.]
forlond, *n.* foreland, promontory, 699. [OE. *for(e)- + lónd.*]
forme, *adj.* first, 2373; *n.* beginning, 499. [OE. *forma.*]
forme. See FOURME.
forne, *adv.* of old, 2422. [OE. *forne.*]
forolde, *pa. t.* had grown to great age, 1440. [OE. *for-áldian.*]
forred. See FURRED.
forsake, *v.* to deny, refuse, 475, 1826, 1846; forsake, 2380; **forsoke**, *pa. t.* 1826. [OE. *forsacan.*]
forsnes (MS.), 646. See FERSNES.
forst, *n.* frost, rime, 1694. [OE. *forst.*]
forth, *adv.* forth, forward, away, out, 66, 428, 1328, 1444, 1703, 2316, 2397, &c.; *forth dayeȝ* (= OE. *forþ dæges*), well on in the day, 1072. [OE. *forþ.*]
forþe, **forde**, *n.* ford, 699, 1617. [OE. *ford, *forþ.*]
forþi, **-þy**, *conj.* for this reason, and so therefore, 27, 240, 500, 631, 2110 &c. [OE. *forþī, -þy.*]
fortune, *n.* fortune, 99. [OFr. *fortune.*]
forward(e), *n.* agreement, covenant 1105, 1636, 2347; *watȝ not f.*, wa[s] not in our agreement, 1395; *pl. i[n] sg. sense*, 378, 409, 1405, 1934 [OE. *foreweard.*]
forwondred, *pp.* astonished, 1660 [*for-* intens. prefix + WONDER.]
fot(e), *n.* foot, 422; *of measure*, 2151 2225; **fete**, *pl.* 428, 1904; *vnder f.* under foot, 859; **foteȝ**, *d. pl.* 574 **fote**, *orig. gen. pl.* in *fowre f. large* 2225; *dat. pl.* in *on (his), to my f.* 329, 2229, 2276, 2363. [OE. *fōt.*]
fotte, *v.* to get, 451. [OE. *fettan*, va[r.] of *feccan*, with vowel of FOCH.]
foule, **fowle**, *adj.* evil, 717; poor i[n] quality, 1329; vile, 1944; *adv.* evilly, 2378. [OE. *fūl, fūle.*]
founde, *v.* to hasten, 1585, 2229 **founded**, **fondet**, *pa. t.* 2125, 213[0]; *pp.* journeyed, 267. [OE. *fúndian.*]
founden. See FYNDE.

fourche3, *n. pl.* fork of body; legs, 1357. [OFr. *fo(u)rche.*]
fo(u)rme, *n.* manner, fashion, 145, 1295, 2130. [OFr. *fo(u)rme.*]
fourty, *adj.* forty, 1425. [OE. *fēowertig.*]
fowre, **foure**, *adj.* and *n.* four, 1332, 2101, 2225. [OE. *fēower.*]
fox, *n.* fox, 1699, 1895, 1944 (*attrib.*), 1950. [OE. *fox.*]
frayn (*at*), *v.* to ask, enquire (of), 359, 703, 1046, 2494; to make trial of, 489, 1549. [OE. (*ge*) *frægnian.*]
frayst, *v.* to ask, 1395; ask for, seek, 279, 324, 391; (*with inf.*) 455; make trial of, 409, 503, 1679; **frayst(ed)**, *pp.* 324, 391, 1679. [ON. *freista.*]
fram, *prep.* from, 461. [OE. *fram.*]
fraunchis(e), *n.* generosity, 652, 1264. [OFr. *fra(u)nchise.*]
fre, *adj.* noble, courtly, good, 101, 803, 847, 1156, 1885, 1961; *as sb.* noble lady, 1545, 1549, 1783; **freest**, *superl.* noblest, 2422. [OE. *frēo*, free, noble (*verse*); lady (*verse*).]
frek(e), *n.* man, knight, 149, 241, 537, 651, 840, &c. [OE. *freca.*]
frely, *adv.* readily, courteously, 816, 894. [OE. *frēolīce.*]
fremedly, *adv.* as a stranger, 714. [From OE. *fremede*, alien.]
frende3, *n. pl.* friends, 714, 987. [OE. *frēond.*]
frenges, *n. pl.* fringes, 598. [OFr. *frenge.*]
frenkysch, **french**, *adj.* French, 13; *f. fare*, elaborately polite behaviour, 1116. [OE. *frencisc.*]
fres, *pa. t.* froze, 728. [OE. *frēosan*, pa. t. *frēas.*]
fresch(e), *adj.* fresh, clean, 2019; *as sb.* fresh meats, 122; **freschly**, *adv.* quickly, 1294. [OFr. *freis*; fem. *fresche*; cf. OE. *fersc.*]
fryth, *n.* a wood, woodland, 695, 1430, 1973, 2151. [OE. *fyr(h)þ*, *gefyrþe.*]
fro, *prep.* away from, from, 524, *1440, 1534, *1863, &c.; *foll. its case*, 1797, 2331. [ON. *frá.*]
fro, *conj.* (after the time) when, after, 8, 62. [Shortened from *fro þat.*]
frote, *v.* to rub, stroke, 1919. [OFr. *froter.*]
froþe, *n.* froth, 1572. [ON. *froða.*]
frounse, *v.* to pucker, 2306. [OFr. *fro(u)nc(i)er.*]
frount, *n.* forehead, 959. [OFr. *fro(u)nt.*]
fuyt. See FUTE.
ful, *adj.* full, 2005. [OE. *full.*]
ful, *adv.* fully, 44; very, quite, full, 41, 1820, 2455, &c. [OE. *ful.*]
fulsun, *v.* to help, 99. [ME. *fülstnen*; cf. OE. *fylstan.*]
funde(n). See FYNDE.
furred, *pp.* lined with fur, 880, 1737, 2029; **forred**, 1929. [OFr. *furrer*, *forrer.*]
fust, *n.* fist, hand, 391. [OE. *fȳst.*]
fute, **fuyt**, *n.* track, trail of hunted animal, 1425, 1699. [OFr. *fuite.*]

G.

gafe. See GIF, *v.*
gay(e), *adj.* gay, bright, fair, 74, 167, 791, 1003, *1208, &c.; *adv. or predic. adj.* 179, 935; *as sb.* fair lady, 970, *1213, 1822; fair knight, 2035; **gayest**, *superl.* 2023 n.; **gayly**, *adv.* gaily, 598, 1760. [OFr. *gai.*]
gayn, *adj.* ready, prompt; suited (to), 178; *at þe gaynest*, by the most direct route, 1973; *adv.* promptly, 1621; *n.* an advantage, a good thing, 1241, 2491. [ON. *gegn*, adj.]
gayn(e), *v.* to profit, be of use to, 584, 1829. [ON. *gegna.*]
gayne, *n.* gain, what you obtained, 2349. [OFr. *gaigne.*]
gaynly, *adj.* courteous, 1297; *adv.* courteously, 476. [From GAYN, adj.]
game. See GOMEN.
gargulun, *n.* throat of deer, includes gullet (*wesaunt*) and wind-pipe, 1335, 1340. [OFr. *garguillon.*]

garysoun, *n.* keepsake, 1807; treasure, 1255 n., 1837. [OFr. *gariso(u)n*, and unrelated ON. *gersumi.*]
garyteȝ, *n. pl.* watch-towers, turrets along the walls, 791. [OFr. *garite.*]
gart, *pp.* made, caused, 2460. [ON. *gøra*, *gǫrva*; neut. adj. as pp. *gǫrt.*]
gast, *pp.* afraid, 325. [OE. *gǣstan.*]
gate, *n.* way, road, 709, 778, 930, 1967, 2119; *bi g.*, on the way, 696; *haf þe g.*, pass, 1154. [ON. *gata.*]
gaudi, *adj.* bright green; *g. of grene*, verdant hue of green, 167. [From OFr. *gaude*, weld (a dye).]
geder(e), *v.* to collect, assemble, 1326, 1426, 1566, 1625; lift (with both hands) 421, 2260; *g. þe rake*, pick up the path, 2160. [OE. *gæderian.*]
gedereȝ (MS.), 777. See GORDEȜ.
gef. See GIF, *v.*
gemme, *n.* gem, 78, 609. [OFr. *gemme.*]
gentyle, **ientyle**, *adj.* of gentle birth, noble, 42, 639, 2185; kindly, 774; noble, excellent, 1022; *as sb.* gentle knight, 542. [OFr. *gentil.*]
gerdeȝ See GORDEȜ.
gere, *n.* gear; armour, 569, 584; doings, behaviour, 2205; *pl.* bed clothes, 1470. [ON. *gervi.*]
gere, *v.* to clothe, attire, 1872; *pp.* 179, 957, 2227; fashioned, 791, 1832. [From prec.]
geserne. See GISERNE.
gest, *n.* guest, 921, 1024, 1036, 1127, 2055. [ON. *gestr.*]
get, *n.*; *my get*, that I get, 1638. [From next.]
gete, *v.* to get, 1871; *pa. t.* 1571; **geten**, *pl.* seized, 1171; **geten**, *pp.* 1943; fetched, 1625. [ON. *geta.*]
gif, *v.* to give, grant, 288, 297, 1383, &c.; **gafe**, *pa. t.* 1861; **gef**, 370, 2349; wished, 668, 1029, 2068, 2073; **geuen**, *pp.* 920, 1500. [ON. *gefa*, *gifa.*] See ȜEF.
gift(e), **gyft**, *n.* gift, 68, 1500, 1822, 2030; *of (my) g.*, as (my) gift, 288, 1799, 1807. [ON. *gift.*]
gile, *n.* guile, 1787. [OFr. *guile.*]
gyld, **gilt**, *pp.* gilded, gilt, 569, 777, 2062. [OE. *gyldan.*]
gyng, *n.* company, 225. [ON. *gengi.*]
gyrdeȝ, **girdel.** See GORDEȜ, GORDEL.
giserne, *n.* battle-axe, 288 n., 375, 2265; **geserne**, 326. [OFr. *guiserne.*]
glad, *adj.* merry, glad, 495, 1079, 1926, 1955. [OE. *glæd.*]
glade, *v.* to gladden, cheer, 989. [OE. *gladian.*]
gladly, *adv.* gladly, with pleasure, 225, 370, 415; **gladloker**, *compar.* 1064. [OE. *glædlīce*, *-lucor.*]
glam, *n.* din, 1426; noise of merry-making, 1652. [ON. *glam(m).*]
glaum, *n.* noise of merrymaking, 46. [ON. *glaumr.*]
glauer, *n.* babel, 1426. [Cf. ME., modern dial. *glaver(en)*, chatter.]
gle, *n.* merriment, 46, 1652; gladness, 1536. [OE. *glēo.*]
gled(e), *n.* red-hot coal, 891, 1609. [OE. *glēd.*]
glem, *n.* splendour, 604. [OE. *glǣm.*]
gleme, *v.* to shine, 598. [From prec.]
glemered, *pa. t.* gleamed, 172. [OE. **glimerian*, related to prec.]
glent, *pa. t.* glanced; flinched, 2292; sprang, 1652; glinted, 172, 569, 604, 2039; looked, 82, 476. [ON. **glenta*; cf. Norw. *glenta.*]
glent, *n.* a glance, 1290. [From prec.]
glyde, *v.* to glide, 2266; hasten, 748, 935; **glod**, *pa. t.* came, 661. [OE. *glīdan.*]
glyfte, *pa. t.* glanced (sidelong) at, 2265. [See next.]
glyȝt, *pa. t.* glanced, looked, 842, 970. [Obscurely related are ME. *glis(t)en*, *gliȝ(t)en*, *glif(t)en*, assoc. together as equivalents of GLENT; cf. OE. *glisian*; ON. *gljá.*]
glyter, *v.* to glitter, 604, 2039. [ON. *glitra.*]
glod. See GLYDE.

glode, *n.* open space; patch, 2181; *on glode,* on the ground, 2266. [Obscure.]
glopnyng (*of*), *n.* dismay (at), *2461. [ON. *glúpna.*]
glorious, *adj.* glorious, 46, 1760. [OFr. *glorious.*]
gloue, *n.* gauntlet, glove, 583, 1799, 1807. [OE. *glōf(e).*]
glowande, *pres. p.* shining, *236. [OE. *glōwan.*]
go, *v.* to go, 448, 2150; depart, 1024, 1127; be (alive), 2109; *quasi-trans.* 811; **gos,** *3 sg.* goes, 935; **gotȝ,** 375, 1293; **gotȝ,** *imper. pl.* 2119; **goande,** *pres. p.* walking, 2214; **gon,** *pp.* 1872. [OE. *gān.*] See ȜEDE.
God(e), Godde, *n.* God, 326, 965, 1036, 1110, 2156, 2205, &c.; *gef hym G.,* wished him Godspeed, 2073; *vnder G.,* on earth, 2470. [OE. *god.*]
god(e), good(e), goud(e), *adj.* good, 109, 129, 381, 702, 1625, 1766, 2118, &c.; *for gode,* as a good knight, 633; *go(u)d day,* 'good-day', 668, 1029, 1290, 2073; *go(u)d moroun,* 'good morning', 1208, 1213; **go(u)dly,** *adv.* courteously, graciously, 273, 842, 1933, &c, [OE. *gōd,* adj.]
god(e), *n.* good thing, 1064; goodness, 1482; advantage, 2031, 2127; *for gode,* as my own, to keep, 1822; *pl.* goods (the fox-skin), 1944. [OE. *gōd,* n.]
goddes, *n.* goddess, 2452. [OE. *god* + OFr. *-esse.*]
godlych, *adj.* goodly, 584. [OE. *gōdlic.*]
gold(e), *n.* gold, 159, 211, 1255, 2150, &c.; *attrib.* 587, 620, &c.; *red g.,* 663; *attrib.* 857, 1817. [OE. *góld.*]
golde-hemmed, *adj.* bordered with gold, 2395. [Prec. and OE. *hemm,* border.]
gome, *n.* knight, man, 151, 178, 696, *2461, &c. [OE. (verse) *guma.*]
gomen, *n.* game, sport, pleasure, 273, 283, 692, 1014, 1536; **game,** 365, 1314, 1532; **gamneȝ, gomneȝ, -es,** *pl.* 495, 683, 989, 1319, 1894; the kill, 1635; [illusion, 2461]; process, 661; *in* or *with g.,* merrily, 1376, 1933. [OE. *gamen, gomen.*]
gomenly, *adv.* merrily, 1079. [OE. *gomenlīce.*]
gorde, *pp.* girt, 1851; **gurde,** 588, 597. [OE. *gyrdan.*]
gordeȝ (*to*), *v.* strikes (spurs into), 2062; ***gerdeȝ,** 777; **gyrdeȝ,** 2160. [Perh. same as prec.]
gordel, *n.* girdle, 2035, 2037, 2429; **girdel,** 1829, 2358; **gurdel,** 2395. [OE. *gyrdel.*]
gorger, *n.* gorget, neckerchief enfolding throat, 957. [OFr. *gorgiere.*]
gost, *n.* spirit, soul, 2250. [OE. *gāst.*]
gostlych, *adv.* like a phantom, 2461. [OE. *gāstlice,* spiritually.]
gotȝ, gos. See GO.
goud(e), goudly. See GOD(E)
gouernour, *n.* ruler, lord, 225. [OFr. *gouern(e)ur.*]
gouleȝ, gowleȝ, *n.* gules, red (in heraldry), 619; *red g.,* 663. [OFr. *goules*; Med. L. *gulæ,* ermine dyed red.]
goune, *n.* gown, 2396. [OFr. *goune.*]
grace, *n.* favour, mercy, gracious gift (of God or fortune), 920, 1215, 1258, 1837, 2480; *druryes greme and g.,* unhappiness and happiness in love-making, 1507. [OFr. *grace.*]
gracios, *adj.* beautiful, 216; **graciously,** *adv.* graciously, 970. [OFr. *gracious.*]
gray(e), *adj.* grey, 82, 1024, 1714. [OE. *grǣg.*]
grayes, *v.* withers, 527. [From prec.]
grayn, *n.* spike of axe, 211 n. [ON. *grein,* branch, division.]
grayþ(e), *adj.* ready, 448, 597, 2047. [ON. *greiðr.*]
grayþe, *v.* to get ready, 2259; dress, 2014; *pp.* arrayed, prepared, 151, 666, 876; set, 74, 109. [ON. *greiða.*]

grayþely, *adv.* readily, promptly, at once, 417, 1006, 1335, 1683; duly, as was right, 2292; pleasantly, 876, 1470. [ON. *greiðiliga.*]

grame, *n.* wrath; mortification, 2502. [OE. *grama.*] See GREME.

grant merci, graunt mercy, gramercy, thank you (*lit.* great thanks), 838, *1037, 1392, 2126. [OFr.]

gra(u)nte, *v.* to consent, 1110, 1861; *trans.* grant, 273, 921, 1841, &c. [OFr. *graanter, graunter.*]

grattest. See GRETE.

grece, gres, *n.* fat, flesh, 425, 1326, 1378, 2313. [OFr. *graisse, gresse.*]

gref, *n.* grief, 2502. [OFr. *gr(i)ef.*]

gre-hounde3, *n. pl.* greyhounds, 1171. [OE. *grīg-, grei-húnd.*]

grem(e), *n.* wrath, 312; grief, 1507; mortification, 2370; hurt, 2251; *with g.*, wrathfully, 2299. [ON. *gremi.*]

grene, *adj.* green, 150, 172, 451, 2239, &c.; *as sb.* green man, 464; **grene**, *n.* green (hue), 151, 167, 216, 549, 2227, &c.; verdure, 207. [OE. *grēne.*]

grenne, *v.* to grin, 464. [OE. *grennian.*]

gres(se), *n.* grass, 235, 527, 2181. [ODan. *græs* (æ = ę); OE. *græs.*]

gres. See GRECE.

gret(e), *adj.* great, large, big, 9, 139, 1171, 2369, 2470, &c.; **grett**, magnificent, 2014; *g. wordes*, boasts, 312, 325; *as sb.* great one, king, 2490; **grattest**, *superl.* 207, 1441; *þe g. of gres*, those that were fattest, 1326. [OE. *grēat.*]

gret, *pa. t.* greeted, 842, 1933. [OE. *grētan*, wk.]

grete, *v.* to weep, 2157. [OE. *grētan*, str.]

greue, *n.* grove, thicket, 207, 508, 1355, 1707, 1898, 1974. [OE. *grǣfa.*]

greue, *v.* to afflict; *subj.* let it trouble, 1070; to dismay, 2460; *intr.* be dismayed, 1442; take offence, 316. [OFr. *grever.*]

greue3, *n. pl.* greaves, 575. [OFr. *greves.*]

gryed, *pa. t.* cried in anguish, 2370. [Not known; cf. *XI Pains of Hell* (O. E. Miscell.) l. 160, *gryd and wept.*]

grymme, *adj.* grim, 413, 2260; *as sb.* fierce beast. 1442. [OE. *grimm.*]

gryndel, *adj.* fierce, 2338; **gryndelly**, *adv.* wrathfully, 2299. [? Back-formation from next.]

gryndel-layk, *n.* fierceness, *312. [ON. *grindill*, storm + *-leikr.*]

gryndel-ston, *n.* grindstone, 2202. [OE. *grindel* + *stān.*]

gryp(p)e, *v.* to grasp, 330; *g. to*, lay hold of, 421, 1335; *hit bi grypte*, by which (he) gripped it, 214. [OE. *grīpan, grippan.*]

grome, *n.* lackey, servant, 1127; man, 1006 n. [Cf. MDu. *grom*; OFr. *gromet.*]

grone, *v.* to groan, lament, 2157, 2502. [OE. *grānian.*]

gronyed, *pa.t.* grunted (fiercely), 1442 n. [OFr. *grognir* ? + OE. *grunian.*]

grounde, *n.* ground, 426, 526, 2294; region, 705; open land, 508; (*vp*)*on g.*, on earth, 1058, 1070, 2150; *dresses hym vpon g.*, takes up his stand, 417. [OE. *grúnd.*]

grounden, *pp.* ground, 2202. [OE. *grindan*, pp. *grúnden.*]

growe, *v.* to grow, 235. [OE. *grōwan.*]

gruch, *v.* to bear ill will, 2251; **gruchyng**, *pres. p.* reluctant(ly), 2126. [OFr. *gro(u)cher.*]

grwe, *n.* grain, jot; *no grwe*, not at all, 2251. [OFr. *gru*, a grain.]

gurde(l). See GORDE(L).

gutte3, *n. pl.* guts, 1336. [OE. *guttas.*]

ȝaynd, *pp.* met, greeted, 1724. [OE. *ge-gegnian.*]

ȝare, *adv.* fully, 2410. [OE. *gear(w)e.*]

ȝar(r)ande, *pres. p.* snarling, 1595; chiding, 1724. [OE. *gyrran*, **georran*, str.]

3ark(k)e, *v.* to ordain, 2410; set, 820. [OE. *gearcian.*]
3ate, *n.* gate, 782, 820, 2069. [OE. *gæt.*]
3aule, *v.* to yowl, howl, 1453. [Cf. ON. *gaula.*]
3e, *adv.* yea, yes, indeed, 813, 1091, 1381, 1498, 1729, 1940. [OE. *gæ*, *gē(a)*.]
3e, *pron.* you, 30, 265, 1820, &c.; **yow**, *acc.* and *dat.* (to) you, 130, 624, 1997, &c.; *reflex.* (for) yourself, 470, 1390, 2117; **your(e)**, *poss. adj.* your, 311, 347, 2450, &c.; **yowre**, 836, 1071, &c.; **3owre**, 1065, *1092; **youre3**, *pron.* yours, 1106, &c.; **yowre3**, 1037; **3oure3**, 1387. **3our-self**, *pron.* you yourself, 350; **yourself**, 1267; *by y.* beside you, 1522; **yowreself**, in *if y. lyke3*, if you like, 1964; **yourseluen**, you, 1548; *to y.* upon yourself, 350; **3orseluen**, in *of 3.*, of your own, *1394. [OE. *gē*, *ēow*, &c.]
3ed(en), *pa. t.* went, 815, 817, 1122, 1400, *1595 n., 1684; **3od**, 1146; was, 2333; *on fote 3.*, lived, 2363. [OE. *ēode.*]
3ederly, *adv.* promptly, 453, 1215, 1485, 2325. [From OE. *ēdre*, *ǣdre.*]
3ef, *v.* give, 1964 n. [OE. *gefan.*]
3e3e, *v.* to cry (as wares), 67; *3. after*, cry for, 1215. [OE. **gēgan*, rel. to ON. *geyja.*]
3elde, *v.* to yield; **3elde(n)**, *pa. t.* 67, 1595, 1981; **3olden**, *pl.* 820; *pp.* 453. To give back, return, 453, 1478 (reply), 1981, 2223, 2325; bring (back), 498; give, 67; repay one (for), 1038, 1263, 1292, 1963, 2056, 2410, 2441; *3. hym*, allowed him (to pass), 820; *refl.* surrender, 1215, 1595. [OE. *géldan.*]
3elle, *v.* to yell, 1453. [OE. *gellan.*]
3elpyng, *n.* vaunt; bold undertaking, 492. [OE. *gylpincg*, **gelping.*]
3ep(e), *adj.* brisk, bold, valiant, 105, 284, 1510; fresh, 60, 951; **3eply**, *adv.* promptly, 1981, 2244. [OE. *gēap*, cunning.]
3er(e), *n.* year, 498, 500, &c.; *þis seuen 3.*, these seven years, for ages, 1382; *3onge 3.*, New Year's tide, 492. [OE. *gē(a)r.*] See NW3ERE.
3eres-3iftes, *n. pl.* New Year's gifts, 67. [Prec. + OE. *gift* infl. by ON.; see GIFTE. Cf. ME. *3eres-3iues.*]
3ern(e), *adv.* eagerly, 1478, 1526; swiftly, 498. [OE. *géorne.*]
3erne, *v.* to long, 492. [OE. *géornan.*]
3ernes, *v.* runs, passes, 498; **3irne3**, 529. [OE. *(ge-)éornan*, *ge-írnan.*]
3et, *adv.* yet, still, 1122, 1894, 2219; *3et firre*, moreover, 1105; all the same, (and) yet, nevertheless, 297, 465, 1010, 1489, 1613, 2276, &c.; *conj.* though, 1009 n. [OE. *gēt.*]
3ette, *v.* to grant, 776. [Late OE. *gé(a)tan* after ON. *játta.*]
3if, *conj.* (*usually with subj.*), if, 406, 1061, 1774, &c.; if, 30, 272, 1484, &c.; iif, 2343; if only, 1799; whether, if, 360, 704, 1057, 2457; *bot if*, unless, 1054, 1782, 1956. [OE. *gif.*]
3irne3. See 3ERNES.
3isterday, *adv.* yesterday, 1485; *n. pl.* passing days, 529. [OE. *gestrandæg.*]
3od. See 3ED.
3ol, *n.* Yule, Christmas, 284, 500. [OE. *gēol*; ON. *jól*, n. pl.]
3olden. See 3ELDE.
3ol3e, *adj.* yellow, withered, 951. [OE. *geolu*, *geolw-*.]
3omerly, *adv.* in pain, piteously, 1453. [OE. *geōmer-līce.*]
3on, *adj.* that, yon, 2144. [OE. *geon.*]
3onde, *adv.* yonder, over there, 2440. [OE. *geónd.*]
3onder, *adv.* as *adj.* yonder, that, 678. [Cf. prec. and MLG. *gender.*]
3ong(e), **3onke**, *adj.* young, youthful, 89, 1526; *3. 3er*, New Year, 492; *as sb.* young(er) one, 951, 1317; *so 3.*, one so young, 1510. [OE. *geong.*]
3or-, **3our-**, **3ow(re)**, &c. See 3E.
3ore, *adv.* since long ago, a long while, 2114. [OE. *geāra.*]

H.

habbe(ȝ), haf(e). See HAUE.

hadet, *pp.* beheaded, 681. [OE. *hĕafdian.*]

haȝer, *adj.* skilful; well-wrought, 1738; (trained to arms), warlike, 352 n. [ON. *hag-r.*]

haȝþorne, *n.* hawthorn, 744. [OE. *hagu-þorn.*]

hay, *interj.* hey! hi! 1158, 1445. [Cf. Du. and Germ. *hei.*]

haylse, haylce, *v.* to greet, 223, 810, 829, 972, 2493. [ON. *heilsa.*]

hal, halle, *n.* castle, hall, 48, 102, 2329, &c.; *h. dor,* hall-door, 136, 458; *h. ȝateȝ,* main entrance (within castle wall), 1693. [OE. *hall.*]

halce. See HALS.

halche, *v.* to embrace, 939; enclose, 185; loop, fasten round, 218, 1852; fasten, 1613; *h. in,* be joined to, 657. [OE. *halsian.*]

halde, holde, *v.* to hold (up), 436, 2297, &c.; rule, 53, 904, 2056 (*see* HONDE); keep, fulfill, 409, 1677, 2129, &c.; maintain, 1125, 1274; contain, 124, 627; restrain, 698, 1043, 1158; consider, account, 28, 285, 1297, 2390, &c.; **helde,** *pa. t. subj.* 2129; **halden, holden,** *pp.* 259, 2270, &c.; bound, 1040; beholden, 1828. [OE. *háldan.*]

hale, halle, *v.* to draw, 1338; lift, 2079; loose (from bow), 1455; *intr.* rise, 788; come, go, pass, 136, 458, 1049 n. [OFr. *haler* or OE. **halian.*]

halȝe, *n.* saint, 2122. [OE. *hălga.*]

haliday, *n.* (religious) festival, 805, 1049. [OE. *hālig-dæg.*]

halydam, *n.* holy thing (*as* relic) on which oath could be taken, 2123. [OE. *hāligdōm.*]

half, halue, *adj. as sb.* half (part), 165, 185, 649, 1543; *adv.* 140, 2321. [OE. *half.*]

half, halue (*dat. and pl.*), *n.* side, direction, 698, 742, 1224, 1552, 2070, 2165; **halueȝ,** sides of venison, 1613; (*vp*)*on Godeȝ h.,* for God's sake, 326, 692, 2149. [OE. *half.*]

half-suster, *n.* half-sister, 2464. [OE. *half-* + *swustor.*] See SISTER-SUNES.

halle(d). See HAL; HALE.

halme, *n.* shaft, handle, 218, 330, 2224. [OE. *halm,* stalk.]

halowe, halawe, *v.* to shout (at), 1445, 1723, 1908, 1914. **halowing,** *n.* shouting, 1602. [OFr. *halloer.*]

hals, halce, *n.* neck, 427, 621, 1353, 1388, 1639. [OE. *hals.*]

halt, hame, han(de)-. See HALE, HOME, HONDE(SELLE).

hap, *n.* happiness, 48. [ON. *happ.*]

hapnest, *adj.* most fortunate, 56. [ON. *heppinn,* infl. by prec.]

happe, *v.* to wrap, clasp, fasten, 655, 864, 1224. [Prob. rel. to HASPE.]

hard(e), *adj.* hard, 732, 733, 789, 2199; *adv.* 2153; firmly, 655 (*compar.*), 1783. [OE. *heard, hearde.*]

harden, *v.* to encourage, 1428; *refl.* become severe, 521. [ON. *harðna.*]

hardy, *adj.* bold, 59, 285, 372; **hardily,** *adv.* certainly, *2390. [OFr. *hardi.*]

harled, *pp.* tangled, 744. [? Cf. HERLE.]

harme, *n.* injury, misfortune, 2272, 2277, 2390, 2511. [OE. *hearm.*]

harnays, *n.* armour, gear, 590, 2016. [OFr. *harneis.*]

harnayst, *pp.* clad in armour, 592. [From prec.]

hasel, *n.* hazel, 744. [OE. *hæsel.*]

haspe, *n.* door-pin, 1233. [OE. *hæpse.*]

hasp(p)e, *v.* to clasp, fasten, 281, 590, 607, 831, 1388. [OE. *hæpsian.*]

hast(e), *n.* speed, 780, 1569, 1756, 2218. [OFr. *haste.*]

haste, *v.* to hasten, 1165, 1424; *trans.* press (in pursuit), 1897. [OFr. *haster.*]

hasty, *adj.* pressing, 1051; **hastyly,** *adv.* hastily, 1135; quickly, 605. [OFr. *hasti.*]

hastletteȝ, *n. pl.* edible entrails, 1612. [OFr. *hastelet.*]

hat(t)e, *v.* am (is) called, 10, 253, 381, 2445; **hattes**, *2 sg.* 379, 401. [OE. *hătte*; passive of HETE.]
hatȝ. See HAUE.
hatte, *n.* hat, 2081. [OE. *hætt.*]
haþel, *n.* knight, 221, 234, 323, 829, 1853 n., &c.; master, 2065; Lord, 2056. [OE. *hæleþ*, infl. by *æþele.*]
hauberghe, hawbergh, *n.* hauberk, *203, 268. [OFr. *hauberc*, infl. by OE. *halsbeorg.*]
haue, haf(e), *v.* to have, 99, 1711, 2135, &c.; *1 sg.* 263, 406, &c.; **habbe**, 1252; **habbeȝ, -es**, *2 and 3 sg.* 327, 452, 626, *2339; **hatȝ**, 330, 2341, &c.; **hatȝ, hauen, haf, han**, *pl.* 17, 497, 1089, 1255, &c.; **haue, haf**, *subj.* 1944, 2287; *imper.* 496, 2143, 2288; **had(e)**, *pa. t.* 52, 72, 442, 657, &c.; *subj.* 680, 1815, 2394, &c.; *pp.* 1962. To possess, 836, &c.; take, 773, 1051, 1612, 1944, 2247, 2408; put, 1446; reach, 700; beget, 2466; *auxil.* have, 17, 327, 452, 1380, &c.; *pa. subj.* would have, 677, 680, 725, &c.; if . . had, 2263, 2394, &c. *Haf at þe*, have (*i.e.* strike) at thee, 2288. [OE. *habban, haf-.*] See NADE.
hauilouneȝ, *v.* doubles back, 1708. [From OFr. *havilon*, n.]
haunche, *n.* haunch, 1345, 2032. [OFr. *ha(u)nche.*]
hawtesse, *n.* pride, 2454. [OFr. *hautesse.*]
he, *pron.* he, 9, *438, 523, *1389, 1666, &c.; the one, 53, 256, 1242, &c.; **him, hym**, *acc. and dat.* (to, for) him, the one, 49, 237, 294, 399, *862, *865, *1906, &c.; *refl.* (for) himself, 8, 221, 303, 1104, 2305; *pleonastic*, 1423, 1444, 2154, &c.; **hymself, hym-, hisseluen**, himself, the same, this very one, him (in person), 107, 113, 164, 226, 902, 1046, 1298, &c.; *refl.* (to, for) himself, 285, 1198, 2031, 2051, &c.; **his, hys**, *adj.* his, its, 4, 447, 676, *2291, &c.; *þat . . hys*, whose, 913; *pron.* his own affairs, 1018. [OE. *hē*; *him*, dat.; *his*, gen.]
hed(e), *n.* head, 180, 286, 333, 1523, 1721, 2217, &c.; (arrow) 1162, 1459; (axe) 210, 217; (including antlers), 1154; lord, 253. [OE. *hēafod.*]
hedleȝ, *adj.* headless, 438. [OE. *hēafodlēas.*]
hef; **heȝ-**. See HEUE; HIȜ-, HYȜT.
hegge, *n.* hedge, 1708. [OE. **hecg.*]
helde, *v. intr. and refl.* to slant, sink west, 1321; bow, 972, 1104; turn, 2331; proceed, go, come, 221, 1523, 1692, 1922. [OE. *hĕldan.*]
helde, 2129. See HALDE.
helder, *adv.* rather; *þe h.*, the more for that, 376, 430. [ON. *heldr.*]
heleȝ, *n.* heels, 1899; (spurred) 777, 2062, 2153. [OE. *hēla.*]
helme, *n.* helmet, 203, &c. [OE. *helm.*]
help, *n.* aid, 987. [OE. *help.*]
help(p)e, *v.* to help, 2209; *subj.* 256, 1055, 2123. [OE. *helpan.*]
hem, *pron. dat. and acc. pl.* (to, for) them, 301, 870, 1613, &c.; **hom**, 99, 819, 1484, &c.; *refl.* 1130, 1254, 1910, &c.; **hemself**, them, 976; *refl.* themselves, 1085; **her**, *adj.* their, 54, 706, 976, *1129, &c.; **hor**, 130, 1265, 1516, &c. [OE. *heom, heora.*]
heme, *adj.* neat, 157; **hemely**, *adv.* 1852. [OE. *gehǣme*, customary.]
hemme, *n.* border, 854. [OE. *hemm.*]
hende, *adj.* courteous, gracious, courtly, 108, 405, 647, 904, 1633, 1731; *superl.* noblest, 26; *as sb.* courteous, gracious (one), 827, 946, 1104; *voc.* 1252. 1813; good sir, 2330; **hend(e)ly**, *adv.* 773, 895, 1639, &c. [OE. *gehende*, convenient.]
hendelayk, *n.* courtliness, 1228. [Prec. + ON. *-leikr.*]
heng(e), *v. wk.* to hang, 477, 983, 1357, 1614; *intr.* 117, 182, 478, 732, 1345, 1930. [ON. *hengja*, trans.]
henne, *adv.* hence, 1078. [OE. *heonane.*]

hent, *v.* to take, catch (up), receive, 605, 827; *pa. t. and pp.* 864, 1597, *1639, 2277, &c. [OE. *hentan.*]
hepes, **-eȝ**, *n. pl.* heaps; ruins, 1722; mêlée, 1590. [OE. *hēap.*]
her. See HO, HEM.
herber, *n.* lodging, 755, 812. [OE. *herebeorg.*]
herber, *v.* to lodge, 805, 2481. [OE. *herebeorgian.*]
here, *adv.* here, now, at this point, 23, 1056, 1243, *2187, 2385, &c.; **herebiforne**, before now, 2527; **herinne**, in this place, 300. [OE. *hēr*; *hērbeforan*, *-inne.*]
here, *n.*[1] company of warriors, host, 59, 2271. [OE. *here.*]
here, *n.*[2] hair, 180, 183, 190, 436, 1587. [OE. *hǣr*, *hēr.*]
here, *v.*[1] to hear (of), 46, 755, 2273, &c.; be told, 630; **herd(e)**, *pa. t.* 31, 690, 1897, &c.; *pp.* 515, 1135; *h. telle*, &c., 26, 263, 1144; *herande*, in the hearing of, 450. [OE. *hēran.*]
here, *v.*[2] to praise, 1634. [OE. *herian.*]
heredmen, *n. pl.* courtiers, 302. [OE. *hēord-*, *hīred-mann.*]
herk(k)en, *v.* to hear, listen (to), 592, 775, 1274, 1529, 1708. [OE. *hercnian.*]
herle, *n.* strand, 190. [Cf. MLG. *herle.*]
hersum, *adj.* devout, 932. [OE. *hērsum.*]
hert, *n.* heart, secret thoughts, courage, 120, 371, 467, 1594, 1781, 1855, &c. [OE. *heorte.*]
hertte, *n.* hart, 1154. [OE. *heor(o)t.*]
heruest, *n.* autumn, 521. [OE. *hærfest.*]
hes, *n.* obligation, *or* promise, 1090. [OE. *hǣs*, order; *behǣs*, promise.]
hest, *n.* bidding, behest, 1039, 1092. [Extended from prec.]
hete, *v.* to promise, 2121; **hyȝt**, *pa. t.* 1966, 1970, 2218, 2341; **hette**, 448; *pp.* 450. [OE. *hātan*; *hēt*, *hĕht.*]
hetes, *n. pl.* vows, assurances of knightly service, 1525. [From prec.]

het(t)erly, *adv.* fiercely, vigorously, suddenly, 1152, 1446, 1462, 1587, 2291, 2311, 2317. [Cf. OE. *hetol*, fierce; MLG. *hetter.*]
heþe, *n.* heath, 1320. [OE. *hǣþ.*]
heþen, *adv.* hence, away, 1794, 1879. [ON. *héðan.*]
heue, *v.* to lift, 1184, 2288; **hef**, *pa. t.* 826; made bristle, 1587; was uplifted, 120; **heuen**, *pl.* 1346. [OE. *hebban*, *hef-.*]
heuen, *n.* heaven(s), sky, 323, 647 (*gen.*), 2057, 2079, 2442; *vnder h.*, on earth, 56, 352, 1853 n. [OE. *heofon.*]
heuened, *pp.* raised, 349. [OE. *hafenian*, infl. by HEUE.]
heuenryche, *n.* heaven; *vnder h.*, on earth, 2423. [OE. *heofon-rīce.*]
heuy, **heué**, *adj.* heavy, grievous, 289, 496. [OE. *hefig.*]
hewe, *n.* See HWE.
hewe, *v.* to hew, cut, 1351, 1607; **hwen**, *pa. t. pl.* 1346, 1353; **hewen**, *pp.* hammered, made, 211; shaped, 789. [OE. *hēawan.*]
hyde, *n.* skin, 1332, 2312. [OE. *hȳd.*]
hyden, *v.* to hide, conceal, 2511; **hid**, *pa. t.* 1875. [OE. *hȳdan.*]
hider(e), *adv.* hither, here, 264, 1209, 1537, 2524, &c. [OE. *hider.*]
hyghe, *interj.* hi! 1445.
hyȝe, *n.* haste; *in h.*, suddenly, 245. [From next.]
hiȝe, **hyȝ(e)**, *v.* to hasten, speed, 299, 521, 826, 1152, 1351, 1462; *refl.* 1910, 2121. [OE. *hīgian.*]
hiȝ(e), **hyȝ(e)**, **heȝe**, (i) *adj.* high, tall, 137, 281, 1138, &c.; high (of special dignity), 108, 222, 250, 593, 1963, 2462, &c.; *h. kyng*, God, 1038, 1963; *h. tyde*, feast, 932, 1033; noble, 5, &c.; important, 1051; loud, 1165, 1417; mature, 844: (ii) *as sb.* height, high ground, 1152, 1169, 2004; *(vp)on h.*, on high, 1607, 2057; in heaven, 256, 2442; loudly, 67, 1602; to the highest pitch, 48; *h. and lowe*,

great and small, all, 302 ; all matters, 1040 : (iii) *adv.* high, 120, 223, 258, &c. ; loudly, 307, 468, 1445, 2212 ; *so h.*, to one so exalted, 349 : (iv) **herre**, *compar.* taller, 333 ; **hyȝest**, **heȝest**, greatest, 57 ; *adv.* highest (at table), 1001. [OE. *hēh* ; *hĕrra.*]

hyȝly, **heȝly**, *adv.* erect, 1587 ; highly, deeply, 949, 1547, 1828 ; devoutly, 755, 773 ; gaily, 983. [From prec.]

hiȝlich, *adj.* noble, splendid, 183. [OE. *hēalic*, infl. by *hēh.*]

hyȝt, *pa. t.* See HETE.

hyȝt, **heȝt**, *n.* height, 788 ; *on h.*, towering, 332 ; aloft, 421. [OE. *hēhþo.*]

hiȝtly, *adv.* fitly, 1612. [OE. *hyhtlīce.*]

hil(le), *n.* hill, 742, 2081, 2271, &c. ; castle-mound, 59. [OE. *hyll.*]

hym(self), &c. See HE.

hind, *n.* hind, 1158, 1320. [OE. *hind.*]

hypped, *pa. t.* hopped, 2232 ; *hypped aȝayn*, rebounded, 1459. [OE. **hyppan* ; cf. *hoppian.*]

hir, **his(seluen)**. See HO, HE.

hit, **hyt**, *pron.* it, 10, 187, 839, 1391, &c. ; *impers.* 73, 843 (he), 948 (she), 988, 1293, &c. ; *hit ar(n)*, there are, 280, 1251. **hitself**, *refl.* itself, 1847. [OE. *hit.*]

hit(te), *v.* to hit, smite, 2296 ; *pa. t.* 1455, 1459, 1594, 2153; *pp.* 2287 ; *h. to*, fell to, 427. [ON. *hitta.*]

ho, *pron.* she, 738, 948, *1872, &c. ; **hir**, *acc. and dat.* (to) her, 76, 1200, 1289, 1742, &c. ; **her**, 1002, 1477 ; *refl.* herself, 1193, 1735, &c. **hir**, *adj.* her, 647, 955, 1862, &c. ; **her**, 1778. [OE. *hēo*, *heō* ; *heore*, *hire.*]

hode, *n.* hood, 155, 2297, &c. [OE. *hōd.*]

hoge. See HUGE.

hoȝes, *n. pl.* hocks, 1357. [OE. *hōh.*]

holde, *v.* See HALDE.

holde, *n.* stronghold, castle, 771 ; possession, 1252. [OE. *gehāld.*]

holde, *adv.* loyally, 2129. [OE. *hólde.*]

holdely, *adv.* faithfully, carefully, 1875, 2016. [OE. *hóldlīce.*]

hole, *n.* hole, 1338, 1569, 2180, 2221. [OE. *hol.*]

holȝ, *adj.* hollow, 2182. [OE. *holh.*]

holyn, *n.* holly ; *h. bobbe*, holly branch, 206. [OE. *hole(g)n.*]

hol(l)e, *adj.* whole, intact, healed, 1338, 1346, 1613, 2296, 2484 ; amended, 2390 ; **holly**, *adv.* entirely, quite, 1049, 1257. [OE. *hāl.*]

holsumly, *adv.* healthfully, 1731. [OE. *hāl* + *-sum* ; cf. ON. *heilsamr.*]

holt, *n.* wood, 1320, 1697. [OE. *holt.*]

holtwode, *n.* wood, 742. [OE. *holtwudu.*]

hom. See HEM.

hom(e), **hame**, *n.* home, dwelling, 12, 408, 1924 ; *adv.* 2121 ; *to h.*, home, 1615, 1922 ; *at h.*, 268, 2451, &c. ; *fro hame*, 1534. [OE. *hām.*]

homered, *pa. t.* hammered ; struck, 2311. [From OE. *homor*, *hamor*, n.]

hond(e), *n.* hand, 206, 328, 494, 2249, &c. ; **hande**, 458, 1203 ; possession, 1270 ; *bi h.*, in person, 67 ; *tan on h.*, undertaken, 490 ; *out of h.*, straight away, 2285 ; *holden in h.*, govern, dispense, 2056. [OE. *hánd*, *hónd.*]

hondele, *v.* to handle, take hold of, 289, 570, 1633, 2505. [OE. *hondlian.*]

hondeselle, **hanselle**, *n.* gift(s) at New Year, 66, 491. [OE. *handselen.*]

hone, *n.* delay, 1285. [? Rel. to HOUE.]

honour, *n.* honour, 1038, 1228 ; honour shown, hospitality, 1963, 2056 ; *your h.*, worthy of you, 1806 ; honours, *pl.* 1813. [OFr. *honour.*]

honour, **honowr**, *v.* to honour, 830, 949, 1033, 2412, 2520 ; celebrate, 593. [OFr. *honourer.*]

hoo, *imper.* stop, 2330. [ME. *hǭ-*, v. from *ho !* interj. ; cf. E. *whoa !*]

hope, *v.* to hope, 2301 ; expect, think, 140, 352, 395, 926 ; *h. of*, hope for, 2308. [OE. *hopian.*]

hor. See HEM.

hore, *adj.* hoar, grey, 743. [OE. *hār.*]

horne, *n.* (hunting) horn, 1165, 1417, 1601, 1923, &c. [OE. *horn.*]
hose, *n. pl.* hose, 157. [OE. *hosa.*]
hors(s)e, *n.* horse, 175, 180, 1138, 1904 (*gen.*), &c.; **horce**, 1464; *on hors*, mounted, 2065. [OE. *hors.*]
hostel, *n.* lodging, dwelling, 776, 805; **ostel**, 253. [OFr. *hostel.*]
hot, *adj.*; *in h. and colde*, through thick and thin, 1844. [OE. *hāt.*]
houe, *v.* to tarry, halt, 785, 2168. [?]
houes, *n. pl.* hooves, 459. [OE. *hōf.*]
hound, hownd, *n.* hound, 1139, 1359, 1422, 1597, 1897, &c. [OE. *húnd.*]
hous, *n.* house, 285, 309, 2275, &c.; *in house*, under a roof, 2481. [OE. *hūs.*]
how(e), *adv.* how, in what way, what, 401, 414, 1379, 2436, &c. *how þat*, how, 379, 1752; **how-se-euer**, *adv.* however, 1662. [OE. *hū.*]
huge, hoge, *adj.* great, huge, 208, 788, 1536, 2420, &c. [OFr. *ahuge.*]
hult, *n.* hilt, 1594. [OE. *hilt.*]
hundreth, *adj.* and *n.* hundred, 743, 1144, 1543, 1597, 2294. [ON. *hundrað.*]
hunt, *v.* to hunt, 1320, 1677, 1943; **huntyng**, *n.* hunting, 1102. [OE. *huntian*; *huntung.*]
hunte, *n.*[1] hunt(ing array), 1417 (*or as next*). [From prec.]
hunt(e), *n.*[2] huntsman, 1147, 1422, 1604, 1701, 1910. [OE. *hunta.*]
hunter, *n.* hunter, 1144, 1165, 1428, 1697. [From HUNT, *v.*]
hurt, *n.* wound, 2484. [OFr. *hurte.*]
hurt, *v.* to hurt, wound, 1452, 1462, 1577, 2291, 2311. [OFr. *hurter.*]
hwe, hewe, *n.* hue, colour, shade of colour, 147, 234, 620, 707, 867, 1471, 1738, 1761. [OE. *hīw, hēow.*]
hwen. See HEWE.

I.

I, *pron.* I, 24, 253, 1962, &c.; **me**, *acc. and dat.* (to, for) me, 256, 292, 1035, 1214, 2112, 2213, &c.; *ethic dat.* 1905, 1932, 2014, 2144, 2459; *dat. absol.* 1067; *refl.* 474, 1271, 1964, &c. **my**, *adj.* my, 288, 408, &c.; **my(y)n**, *before vowels*, 257, 1067, &c.; **myn(e)**, *pron.* 342, 1816, 1942. **myself(e), -seluen**, myself, 1052, 1244, 1540. [OE. *ic, mē, mīn*; *mē selfan.*]
iapeȝ, *n. pl.* jests, 542, 1957.
iche. See VCHE.
ientyle; **i(i)f**. See GENTYLE; ȜIF.
iisse-ikkles, *n. pl.* icicles, 732. [OE. *īs + gicel*; cf. *īses gicel.*]
iles, *n. pl.* islands, 7, 698. [OFr. *ile.*]
ilyche, *adj.* the same, 44. [OE. *gelīc.*]
ilk(e), *adj.* same, very, 24, 819, 2397, 2461, &c.; *pron.* 1385, 1981; same (hue), 173, 1930. [OE. *ilca.*]
ille, *adv.* ill, 346; *n.* in *tas to i.*, take amiss, 1811. [ON. *illa*; *illr*, adj.]
in, *prep.* in, on, at, 7, 645, 1096, 1421, 2199, 2433, &c.; (in)to, 924, 1699; within, 764, 1198, &c.; *of time*, 22, 54, 1641, 1646, &c. [OE. *in.*]
in, *adv.* in, 136, 189, 2161, &c. [OE. *inn.*]
inmyddeȝ, -es, *adv. and prep.* in the middle (of), 167, 1004 n., 1932. [From OE. *on middan.*]
inne, *adv.*; *þer* (*þat*) .. *inne*, in which, 2196, 2440, 2509. [OE. *inne.*]
innermore, *compar. adv.* further in, 794. [OE. *innor + māre.*]
innoghe, **i(n)noȝ(e)**, **innowe**, *adj.* enough, 404, 730; say no more! 1948; many, in plenty, 77, 514, 826, 1401, 2123, &c.; *adv.* enough, 477, *803, 1496; exceedingly, 289, 888. [OE. *genōh, genōg-.*]
intent, *adj.*; *i. to telle*, bent on telling, 624. [OFr. *intent.*]
into, *prep.* into, 62, 435, 697, &c.; from here to, 2023. [OE. *inn tō.*]
inurned. See ENNOURNED.
inwyth, *adv.* within, 2182; *prep.* within, 1055. [OE. *in + wiþ.*]
ioy(e), *n.* joy, gladness, 646, 910, 1022, 1247, 2053, &c. [OFr. *joie.*]

ioyne, *v.* to join (with), encounter, 97. [OFr. *joindre, joign-.*]
ioyfnes, *n.* youth, 86. [OFr. *joefnesse.*]
ioyleȝ, *adj.* joyless, 542. [From IOY.]
ioly, *adj.* gay, 86; **iolilé**, *adv.* gallantly, 42. [OFr. *joli.*]
iopardé, *n.* peril, 1856; *in i. to lay*, to hazard (one's life), 97. [OFr. *ju (jeu) parti.*]
irke, *v. impers.*; *irked burneȝ to nye*, men tired of hurting, 1573. [?]
is, *3 sg.* is, 33, 754, 1319, &c. [OE. *is.*]
iuel, *n.* jewel; *fig.* 1856. [OFr. *joel.*]
iugged, *pp.* adjudged, assigned, 1856. [OFr. *jug(i)er.*]
iuste, *v.* to joust, 42; **iustyng**, *n.* 97. [OFr. *juster.*]
iwysse, *adv.* indeed, certainly, 1035, 1065, 1557, 2526, &c.; **iwy(i)s**, 252, 264. [OE. *mid* (or *to*) *gewisse.*]

K.

K. See also C.
kanel, *n.* pipe, wind-pipe; neck, 2298. [ONFr. *canel*, channel.]
kauelacion, *n.* cavilling, objection, 2275; ***cauelaciounȝ**, *pl.* triflings, 683. [OFr. *cavillacion.*]
kay, *adj.* left, 422. [ODan. *kei.*]
kene, *adj.* bold, 321, 482; bitter, 2406; **kenly**, *adv.* daringly, 1048; bitterly, 2001. [OE. *cēne, cēnlīce.*]
kenel. *n.* kennel; *attrib.* 1140. [ONFr. **kenil*; Fr. *chenil.*]
kenet, *n.* (small) dog, 1701. [ONFr. *kennet.*]
kenne, *v.* to teach, 1484; entrust, commend (= BIKENNE), 2067, *2472; **kende**, *pa. t.* taught, 1489. [OE. *cennan*; ON. *kenna.*]
kepe, *v.* to keep, hold, preserve, 1059, 2148, 2298; *subj.* let him keep, 293; to occupy, 1312; attend to, 1688; care for, 2016; care, be anxious (to), 546, 2142; *k. hym wyth carp*, engage in conversation with him, 307; *kepe þe*, take care, 372. [OE. *cēpan.*]
ker(re), *n.* thicket on marshy ground; *ker(re) syde*, side of the marsh, 1421, 1431. [ON. *kjarr*, older **ke(a)rr-.*]
kerchofes, *n. pl.* kerchiefs, coverings for the head and neck, 954. [OFr. *cuevrechief.*]
kest(en). See CAST, *n.* and *v.*
keuer, *v.* to recover, 1755; obtain, 1221, 1254; afford, give, 1539; *intr.* recover, survive, 2298; manage (to), 750, 804; *keuereȝ*, makes his way, 2221. [OE. *a-cofrian*, intr.; OFr. *(re-)covrer, -keuvre*, trans.]
kyd, kydde, *pp.* made known, shown, 263; *k. hym cortaysly*, shown him courtesy, 775; *k. þe vnmanerly*, treated thee discourteously, 2340; *as adj.* famous, 51; reputed, 1520. [OE. *cȳþan*, pp. *ge-cȳdd.*]
kylled, *pp.* killed, 2111. [ME. forms point to OE. **cyllan*, beat.]
kyn, *n.* kind; *gen. sg.*, in *alle kynnes*, of every kind, every kind of, 1886; *originally gen. pl.* in *fele kyn*, many kinds of, 890. [OE. *cynn.*]
kynde, *n.* nature, natural character, 321, 2380; kindred, offspring, 5; *of þe worldes k.*, among men, 261. [OE. *(ge)cýnd.*]
kynde, *adj.* natural, proper; seemly, courtly, 473. [OE. *(ge)cýnde.*]
kyndely, *adv.* duly, properly, 135 [OE. *(ge)cýndelīce.*]
kyng(e), *n.* king, 37, 364, 393, 992 (MS.), &c.; the king, Arthur, 57, 100, 2340, &c.; *kynges hous Arthor*, k. Arthur's house, 2275; *þe heȝe k.*, God, 1038, 1963. [OE. *cyning, cyng.*]
kyrf, *n.* cutting, 372. [OE. *cyrf.*]
kyrk, *n.* church, 2196. [ON. *kirkja.*]
kyrtel, *n.* kirtle, a coat or tunic reaching to the knees, 1831. [OE. *cyrtel.*]
kysse, *v.* to kiss, exchange kisses, 605, 974, 1303, 1501, 2472, &c.; **kyssed, kyst**, *pa. t.* 596, 1118, 1758, 2351, &c.; *pp.* 1869; **kyssyng**, *n.* kissing, 1489, 1979. [OE. *cyssan.*]

kyth, *n.* native land; land, 460, 2120. [OE. *cȳþþu.*]
knaged, *pp.* fastened, 577. [From ME. *knagg*, peg; cf. Swed. *knagg.*]
knape, *n.* fellow, 2136. [OE. *cnapa.*]
knarre, *n.* gnarled and twisted rock, crag, 721, 1434, 2166. [Cf. LG. *knarre*, knot.]
knawen. See KNOWE.
kneled, *pa. t.* knelt, 368, 818, 2072 n. [OE. *cnēowlian.*]
kneȝ, *n. pl.* knees, 577; knes, 818. [OE. *cnēo.*]
knyf, *n.* 1331; **knyffe,** *dat.* (*note rhyme*), 2042; **knyueȝ,** *pl.* 1337. [OE. (late) *cnīf*, prob. from ON. *knifr.*]
knyȝt, kniȝt, *n.* knight, 42, 51, 62, 96, 1272 (*voc.*), 1279, &c. [OE. *cniht*, servant.]
knyȝtyly, *adj.* knightly, chivalrous, 1511; **knyȝtly,** *adv.* courteously, 974. [From prec.]
knitte, knyt, *pa. t.* tied, sewed, 1331 n.; made (fast), 1642; **knit,** *pp.* knotted, bound, 1831; knit, entwined, 1849. [OE. *cnyttan.*]
knokke, *n.* knock, blow, 2379. [Stem of OE. *cnocian.*] See CNOKEȜ.
knokled, *adj.* knobbed, rugged, 2166. [From ME. *knok(e)le*, knob, knuckle; cf. OFris. *knokele.*]
knorned, *adj.* gnarled, 2166. [Obscure.]
knott(e), *n.* knot, 188, 194, 577, 2376, 2487; (part of deer), 1334 n.; rocky (wooded) hill, 1431, 1434; (*endeles*) *k.*, pentangle, 630, 662. [OE. *cnotta.*]
know(e), *v.* to acknowledge, recognize, 357, 937; know, 325, 400, 454, 546, 1095, 1484, &c.; **knew,** *pa. t.* 682, 1849; **knwe,** 460, 2008; **knawen, knowen,** *pp.* discovered, 1272; acknowledged (to be), 348, 1511; *k. for*, known to be, 633. [OE. *cnāwan.*]
koynt, *adj.* skilful; cunningly made, beautiful, 877; **coynt** (*of*), polite, gracious (in), 1525; **quaynt,** cunningly prepared, 999; **coyntly(ch),** *adv.* cunningly, elegantly, 578; gracefully, daintily, 934; **koyntly,** adroitly, 2413. [OFr. *cointe, queinte.*]
koyntyse (*of*), *n.* skill, cunning (in), 2447. [OFr. *cointise.*]
kort, kourt. See CORT.
kowarde, *adj.* cowardly, recreant, 2131. [OFr. *couard.*]

L.

lace, *n.* thong, 217, 2226; belt, 1830, 2487, 2505, &c. [OFr. *las.*]
lach(che), *v.* to catch; **leȝte,** *pa. t.* 1410; **laȝt, laght,** 127, 667, &c.; *pp.* 971, &c.; caught back, 156. To take hold of, 292, 936, 1029, *1906, &c.; take, get, 127, 234, 595, &c.; receive, 2061, 2499, &c.; accept, 1772; *l. at* (*to*), seize, 328, 433. [OE. *læccan.*]
lachet, *n.* lachet, 591. [OFr. *lachet.*]
lad(de). See LEDE, *v.*
lady, ladi, *n.* lady, 49, 346, 1187, 2030, &c.; **ladé,** 1810. [OE. *hlǣfdige.*]
laft. See LEUE, *v.*[1]
lagmon, 1729. See note.
laȝe, *v.* to laugh, 316, 988, 1207, 2514, &c.; *wk. pa. t.* 69, &c.; **loȝe,** 2389; **laȝyng,** *n.* 1954. [OE. *hlæhhan.*]
laȝter, *n.* laugh, 1217. [OE. *hlæhtor.*]
lay, *v.* to lay, 97, 156, 419; deliver, 1480; *l. vp*, put away safe, 1874; *l. hym bysyde*, put aside, parry, 1777; *refl.* lie down, 1190. [OE. *lecgan.*]
laye, *n.* lay; poem, 30. [OFr. *lai.*]
layk, *n.* sport, entertainment, 262, 1023, 1125, 1513. [ON. *leikr.*]
layke, *v.* play, amuse oneself, 1111, 1178, 1554, 1560; **laykyng,** *n.* playing, 472. [ON. *leika.*]
layne, *v.* to conceal, 1786, 1863; *layne yow* (*me*), keep your (my) secret, 2124, 2128. [ON. *leyna.*]
layt, *n.* lightning, 199. [OE. *lēget.*]
layt(e), *v.* to seek, 411, 449; wish to know, 355. [ON. *leita.*]
lakked, *pa. t.* found fault with, 1250; *impers.* in *you l.*, you were at fault, 2366. [From MLG. *lak.*]

lance. See LAUNCE, *v.*
lante, *pa. t.* gave, 2250. [OE. *lǣnan.*]
lappe, *n.* loose end or fold (of garment) 936, (of skin) 1350. [OE. *læppa.*]
lappe, *v.* to fold, wrap, embrace, 217, 575, 973. [From prec.]
large, *adj.* great, 210; wide, 2225. [OFr. *large.*]
larges(se), *n.* great size, 1627; generosity, 2381. [OFr. *largesse.*]
lasse, *adj. compar.* less, smaller, 1284, 1524, 2226; *adv.* 87, 1829, 1848, 2368; *see* NEUER. **lest,** *superl.* 355, 591. [OE. *lǣssa, lǣs(es)t.*]
lassen, *v.* to ease, 1800. [From prec.]
last(e), *adj. superl.* last, 1133; *as sb.* 1023; *at þe l.*, at last, finally, 1027, 1120, 2497, &c. [OE. *lætest.*]
last(e), *v.* to endure, last, live, 1061, 1235, 1665, 2510; **lested,** *pa. t.* 805; **lasted,** extended, 193. [OE. *lǣstan.*]
late, *adj.* late, 1027; **later,** *adv. compar.* less readily, 541. [OE. *læt.*]
laþe, *v.* to invite, 2403. [OE. *laþian.*]
laþe. See LOÞE.
laumpe, *n.* lamp, *2010. [OFr. *lampe.*]
launce, *n.* lance, 667, 2066, 2197. [OFr. *la(u)nce.*]
la(u)nce, *v.* to cut, 1343, 1350; (fling), utter, 1212, 1766, 2124; *intr.* fly, 526; dash, gallop, 1175, 1464, 1561. [OFr. *la(u)ncer.*]
launde, *n.* glade, lawn, field, 765, 1894, 2146, 2154, 2171, 2333. [OFr. *la(u)nde.*]
lausen, lawse, *v.* to undo, 2376; break(troth), 1784. [From ON. *lauss.*]
lawe, *n.*[1] law; style, 790; *bi. l.*, duly, 1643. [OE. *lagu*, from ON.]
lawe, *n.*[2] mound, knoll, 765, 2171, 2175. [OE. *hlāw.*]
lece; lede, *n.* See NEUER; LEUDE.
lede, *v.* to lead, conduct, 936, 947, 977; rule, 849; experience, have, 1927, 2058; *l. for*, set (risk) against, 98; **lad(d)e,** *pa. t.* 1729, 1927, &c.; *pp.* 1989. [OE. *lǣdan.*]
leder, *n.* leader, 679. [From prec.]
lee, *n.* protection, shelter; *in l.* in castle, 849 n.; comfortable place, 1893. [OE. *hlēo.*]
lef, leue (*wk.*), *adj.* dear, beloved, delightful, 909, 1111, 1133, 1924, 2054; **leuer,** *compar.* dearer, 1782; *þat l. wer*, whom it would delight more, 1251; **leuest,** *superl.* 49, 1809. [OE. *lēof.*]
leg(g)e *adj.* entitled to feudal allegiance; sovereign, 346, 545. [OFr. *l(i)ege.*]
leg(g)e, *n.* leg, 575, 2228. [ON. *leggr.*]
leȝten, 1410; **leke.** See LACH, LOUKE.
lel(e), *adj.* loyal, faithful, true, 35, 1513, 1516; **lelly,** *adv.* 449, 1863, 2124, 2128. [OFr. *leël.*]
leme, *v.* to shine, 591, 1119, 1137, 1180, 2010, 2226. [ON. *ljóma.*]
lemman, *n.* beloved one, lover, 1782. [OE. **lēofman*; early ME. *leofmon.*]
lende, *v.* to arrive; dwell, stay, 1100, 1499; **lent,** *pa. t.* took his place, 1002; *pp.* 2440; *is l.*, has gone, 1319. [OE. *lendan.*]
lene, *v.*; *l. with*, incline, 2255; *l. to*, lean on, 2332. [OE. *hleonian.*]
leng(e), *v.* to make stay, keep, 1672, 1683; *hym l.*, let him stay, 1893; *intr.* stay, 254, 411, 1068, 2446, &c. [OE. *lengan.*]
lenger. See LONGE, *adv.*
len(k)þe, *n.* length, 210, 1627, 2316; *on lenþe*, afar, 1231; for a long time, 232. [OE. *lengþu.*]
lentoun, *n.* Lent, 502. [OE. *lencten.*]
lepe, *v.* to leap, run, 292, 328, 981, 1131, 1709; **lopen,** *pp.* 1413; *lepeȝ hym*, gallops, 2154. [OE. *hlēapan.*]
lere, *adj.* empty; *as sb.* (something) worthless, 1109. [OE. *gelǣr.*]
lere, *n.* See LYRE, *n.*[1] and *n.*[2]
lern(e), *v.* to learn, 908, 918, 927, 1532; teach, 1878; *pp.* well instructed, skilful, 1170, 2447. [OE. *léornian.*]
lese, *v.* to lose, 2142; **lost,** *pp.* 69, 675. [OE. *(for)lēosan*; *losian.*]

lest, *conj.* (*with subj.*) lest, 750, 1304, 1773, &c. [OE. *þe-læ̅s-þe.*]
lest. See LASSE.
let(e), **lette**, *v.* (*pres.* and *pa. t.*) to let (fall), 817, 2309; let, allow, 248, 423, 468, 1063, 1733, 2387, &c.; *forming imper.* 360, 414, 1994, &c.; *l. se*, show (me), 299, 414; *l. be*, cease from, 1840; *l. one*, let be, 2118; cause to, 1084; utter, 1086; look and speak, behave, 1206, 1634; *l. as* (*lyk*), behave as if, pretend, 1190, 1201, 1281, 2257. [OE. *læ̅tan*, str.]
lette, *v.* to hinder, 2142, 2303; dissuade, 1672. [OE. *lettan*, wk.]
letteres, *n. pl.* letters, staves, 35. [OFr. *lettre.*]
lettrure, *n.* lore, science, 1513. [OFr. *lettreüre.*]
leþe, *v.* to soften, make humble, 2438. [OE. *geliþian, -leoþian.*]
leþer, *n.* skin; *l. of þe paunches*, tripe, 1360. [OE. *leþer.*]
leude, *n.*[1] man, knight, prince, 675, 851, 1023, 1306, 2499, &c.; **lede**, 38, 126, 258, *1516, &c.; **lude**, 133, 232, 449. [OE. (verse) *lēod*, m.]
leude, **lede**, *n.*[2] people, 833, 1113, 1124. [OE. *lēod*, f.; *lēode*, pl.]
leudleȝ, *adj.* companionless, 693. [From LEUDE, *n.*[1]]
leue, *adj.* See LEF.
leue, *v.*[1] to leave, 1583, 1870, 2154; leave off, 1502; laft, *pa. t.* gave up, 369; omitted, 2030. [OE. *læ̅fan.*]
leue, *v.*[2] to allow, 98. [OE. *lēfan.*]
leue, *v.*[3] to believe, 1784, 2128, 2421. [OE. *gelēfan.*]
leue, *v.*[4] to live, 1035, 1544. [OE. *lifian, leofian.*]
leue, *n.* leave, 133, 545, 971, 1218, 1670; leave-taking, 1288; *take* (*&c.*) *l.*, take leave, depart, 595, 993, 1118, 1556, 1960, 1978, &c. [OE. *lēaf*, f.]
leueȝ, *n. pl.* leaves, 519, 526. [OE. *lēaf*, neut.]
lewed, *adj.* ignorant, 1528. [OE. *læ̅wede.*]
lewté, *n.* loyalty, fidelity, 2366, 2381. [OFr. *le(a)uté.*]
liddeȝ, *n. pl.* eyelids, 2007. [OE. *hlid.*] See YȜELYDDEȜ.
lyf, **lif**, *n.* life(time), 87, 98, 545, 675, &c.; person, 1780; lyue, *dat.* 706, 2480, &c.; **lyues**, *pl.* 1516, 2112; *l. haden*, lived, 52; (*vp*)*on l.*, alive, on earth, 385, 1786, 2095; during life, 2054. [OE. *līf.*]
liflode, *n.* food, 133. [OE. *līflād.*]
lyft(e), *adj.* left (hand, &c.), 698, 947, 2146, 2487. [OE. *lyft.*]
lyfte, *n.* heaven(s), 1256. [OE. *lyft.*]
lyft(e), to lift, raise, 1878 (*fig.*), 2309; build, 12; *pa. t.* 369, 433, 446; *pp.* extolled, 258. [ON. *lyfta.*]
ly(ȝ)**e**, *v.* to lie (down, idle), 88, 1096, 1780, 1994; *imper.* 1676; **lygeȝ**, *3 sg. pres.* 1179; **lys**, **lis**, 1469, 1686; **leȝ**, *pa. t.* 2006; **lay**, 1195, 2088; was lodged, 37. [OE. *licgan, lig-*; *lygeȝ* prob. from ON. *liggja.*]
lyȝt, *adj.*[1] bright, 199; cheerful, 87; gay, 1119. [OE. *lē̆(o)ht*, adj.[1]]
lyȝt, *adj.*[2] light, active, 1119 (*or prec.*), 1464; *set at l.*, think light of, 1250. [OE. *lē̆(o)ht*, adj.[2]]
lyȝt, *n.* light(s), 992, 1649, 1685, 1989, 2010; dawn, 1675. [OE. *lē̆(o)ht.*]
lyȝt(e), **liȝt**(e), *v.* to dismount, 254, 329, 1175, 1583, 1906, 2176; come down, 1373, 2220; land (on), 423, 526; *pa. t.* 822; *pp.* in *is l.*, has arrived, 1924. [OE. *līhtan.*]
lyȝteȝ, *n. pl.* lights, lungs, 1360. [LYȜT, adj.[2] as sb.]
lyȝtli, *adj.* light (gleaming *or* of fine texture), 608. [OE. *leohtlic*, shining; light.]
lyȝtly, *adv.* lightly; swiftly, 292, 328, 423, 1131, 1830, 2309; easily, 1299. [OE. *lē̆(o)htlice.*]
lyk, *v.* to taste, 968 n. [OE. *liccian.*]
lyke, *adj.* like, 187; *as sb.* similar (events), 498; *adv.* in *lyk as*, as if, 1281. [OE. *gelīc*; *gelīce*, adv.]
lyke, *v.* to please, 87, 893, 1084, 1234,

&c.; *impers.* 289, 814, 976, &c.; *lyked ille*, it might displease, 346; *pers.* like, 694 (*and perhaps* 893, 1682, 2134). [OE. *līcian.*]
lykkerwys, *adj.* delicious, sweet, 968. [ONFr. **lekerous* (OFr. *lecheros*) with altered suffix.]
lym(m)e, *n.* limb, member, 139, 868, 1332. [OE. *lim.*]
lymp(e), *v.* to befall, 907; *subj.* falls to our lot, 1109. [OE. *limpan.*]
lynde, *n.* lime-tree; (*allit.*) tree, 526, 2176; **lynde-wodeȝ**, woods, 1178. [OE. *linde.*]
lyndes, *n. pl* loins, 139. [OE. *lendenu*; ON. *lendir.*]
lyne, *n.*[1] line, 628. [OFr. *ligne.*]
lyne, *n.*[2] linen (attire); *lufsum vnder l.*, fair lady, 1814n. [OE. *līn.*]
lyppe, *n.* lip, 962, 1207, 2306. [OE. *lippa.*]
lyre, *n.*[1] cheek, face, 943, 2228; **lere**, 318. [ON. *hlýr*, OE. *hlēor.*]
lyre, *n.*[2] flesh, 2050 (coat); **lere**, 418, 1334. [OE. *līra*; confused with prec.]
list, *n.* joy; *lif vpon l.*, brave sport, 1719. [ON. *lyst.*]
lyst(e), *pres. sg. impers.* it pleases (*yow l.*, you desire), 1111, 1502, 1784, 2133, 2142; *pa. t.* 941, 2049. [OE. *lystan.*]
lysten, *v.* to listen to, 30; *intr.* 2006. [OE. *hlysnan*; *hlystan.*]
lystyly, *adv.* cunningly, skilfully, 1190, 1334. [OE. *listelīce.*]
lyt(e), *adj.* little, 1777; *pl.* few, 701. [OE. *lȳt*, indecl.]
lyte, *n.* expectation; *on l.*, in delay, 2303; back (in fear), 1463. [From ON. *hlíta*, to trust.]
littel, **lyt(t)ẹl**, *adj.* little, small, 30, 1183, 1250, 1338, 1709, 1848; *adv.* 2007; *a littel*, a little, 418, 973, 1185, 2267, 2366; some way (away), 2146, 2171. [OE. *lȳtel*, adj.]
lyþen, *v.* to hear, 1719. [ON. *hlýða.*]
liþerneȝ, *n.* ferocity, 1627. [OE. *lȳþernes.*]
lyuer, *n.* liver, 1360. [OE. *lifer.*]
lo, loo, *interj.* lo! look, 1848, 2378, 2505; *we loo*, ah well! 2208. [OE. *lā.*]
lode, *n.* conveying goods; *on l.*, (in tow), with her, 969; *in his l.*, with him on his journey, 1284. [OE. *lād.*]
lodly, *adv.* horribly, (*let l.*, professed horror, 1634); offensively, 1772. [OE. *lāþlīce.*]
lofden. See LUF.
loft(e), *n.* upper-room, 1096, 1676; (*vp*)*on l.*, aloft, 788, 2261. [ON. (*á*) *loft.*] See ALOFTE.
loȝe, **loghe**, *adj.* low(lying), 1170; *as sb.* 302, 1040 (*see* HYȜE); *on l.*, down (to the hall), 1373; **lowe**, *adv.* low, 972, 2236; **loȝly**, *adv.* humbly, with deference, 851, 1960. [ON. *lágr.*]
loȝe, 2389. See LAȜE.
loke, *n.* look, 1480; *þe loke to*, a glance at, 2438. [From next.]
loke, *v.* to look, 223, 446, 970, 1172, 1194, 2146; (*with subj.*) see to it that, 448; appear, 199; *l. on* (*at*), look at, see, 479, 941, 950, 1063, 2333; *trans.* look after, guard, 2239; **lokyng**, *n.* staring, 232. [OE. *lōcian.*]
loken. See LOUKE.
lokkeȝ, *n. pl.* locks of hair, 156, 419, 2228. [OE. *locc.*]
lome, *n.* tool, weapon, 2309. [OE. *lōma.*]
londe, *n.* land, ground, country, 411, 1055, 2440, &c.; *pl.* countryside, 1561; *in* (*vpon*) *londe*, in the land, on earth, 36, 486, 679, 1802, 2058. [OE. *lónd.*]
long(e), *adj.* long, 139, 419, 796, 1195; *hym þoȝt l.*, he was impatient, 1620. [OE. *láng*, *lóng.*]
long(e), *adv.* a long while, 36, *88, 1554, &c.; **lenger**, *compar.* 1043, 2063, 2303. [OE. *lónge*; compar. adj. *lengra.*]
longe, *v.* to belong to, befit, 1524, 2381, 2515. [From OE. *ge-lóng*, adj.]
longynge, *n.* grief, 540. [OE. *longung.*]
lopen. See LEPE.

lord(e), *n.* lord, noble, ruler, 38, 316, 753, 850, *992, 2185, &c.; *oure l.*, 1055; husband, 1231, 1271, 1534, 1863. [OE. *hlāford.*]

lore, *n.* learning; *with l.*, learned, 665. [OE. *lār.*]

lortschyp, *n.* lordship, 849. [OE. *hlāfordscipe.*]

los, *n.* renown, 258, 1528. [OFr. *los.*]

losse, *n.* damage, 2507. [OE. *los.*]

lost. See LESE.

lote, *n.* sound, noise, 119, 1917, 2211; word, saying, speech, 639, 988, 1086, 1116, 1399, 1623, 1954. [ON. *lát* (*pl.*) behaviour, cries.]

loþe, *adj.* hateful; *þuȝt l.*, were loath, 1578. [OE. *lāþ.*]

loþe, laþe, *n.* offence (*or* injury), 2507; grudge, 127. [OE. *lāþ.*]

loude, *adj.* loud, 64. [OE. *hlūd.*]

loude, lowde, *adv.* loudly, aloud, 69, 1088, 1623, 1724, &c. [OE. *hlūde.*]

loue-, louy(e). See LUF, LUFLYCH, &c.

louke, lowke, *v.* to shut, 2007; *intr.* (be) fasten(ed), 628; *wk. pa. t.* 217, 792; **leke**, *str.* 1830; **loken**, *pp.* linked, 35 n.; fastened, 2487; shut, 765. [OE. *lūcan.*]

loupe, *n.*[1] loop, 591. [Obscure.]

loupe, *n.*[2] loop-hole, window, 792. [?]

loute, *v. intr.* to bow, bend, 1306, 1504; turn, go, 833, 933; *trans.* bow before, reverence, 248; **lut(te)**, *pa. t.* 2255; saluted, 2236; *l. with*, bent, 418. [OE. *lūtan*, str.]

louue, lowe, *v.* to praise, 1256; *to l.*, praiseworthy, 1399. [OFr. *louer.*]

lowande, *pres. p.* shining, 236 (MS.); brilliant, 679, 868. [ON. *loga.*]

lowe. See LOȜE, LOUUE.

lowkeȝ; lude. See LOUKE; LEUDE.

luf, *n.* love, 540, 1284, 1524, &c.; friendliness, 1086; sake, 1802; *for l.*, because of (my) l., 1733, 1810; *for alle lufeȝ vpon lyue*, for all loves there be, 1786 n. [OE. *lufu.*]

luf, louy(e), *v.* to love, 1780, 2095, 2099, 2421, 2468; be in l., 1795; **lou(i)ed**, *pa. t.* 87, 126, 1281; **lufed**, 2368; **lofden**, *pl.* 21. [OE. *lufian.*]

luf-lace, *n.* love-lace, girdle as love-token, 1874, 2438. [LUF + LACE.]

luf-laȝyng, *n.* loving laugh, 1777. [LUF + LAȜYNG.]

lufly(ch), louely(ch), *adj.* pleasing, gracious, fair, 38, 419, 433, 1218, 1480, &c.; **loueloker**, *compar.* 973; **louelokkest, loflyest**, *superl.* 52, 1187. **lufly(ch)**, *adv.* graciously, courteously, 254, 595, 981, 1002, 1606, &c. [OE. *luflic, -līce.*]

luflyly, *adv.* graciously, amiably, in seemly manner, 369, 2176, 2389, 2514. [From prec.]

lufsum, *adj.* lovely, 1814. [OE. *lufsum.*]

luf-talkyng, *n.* (art of) lovers' conversation, 927. [LUF + TALKYNG.]

lur, *n.* loss, disaster, 355, 1284; sorrow, 1682. [OE. *lyre.*]

lurk(k)e, *v.* to lie snug, 1180; *pp.* lurking, 1195. [Cf. Scand. dials. *lúr-* (extended *lurk-*) (i) doze, &c.; (ii) sneak off.]

lut(te). See LOUTE.

M.

ma fay, by my faith, 1495. [OFr. *ma fei.*]

mace. See MAKE.

mach, *v.* to match, 282. [OE. *gemæcca*, n.]

madame, *n.* lady, 1263. [OFr. *ma dame.*]

madde, *v.* to act madly, 2414. [From OE. *gemǣdd*, mad.]

maȝtyly, *adv.* powerfully, forcibly, 2262, 2290. [OE. *mæhtiglīce.*]

may(e), *v.* can, may, 380, 409, 926, 1795, &c.; *pl.* 70, 2396; **mowe**, *pl.* 1397; **myȝt**, *pa. t.* 79, 201, 1569, 1903, &c.; if . . might, *1858; *quat he m.*, what he was doing, 1087; **moȝt(en)**, 84, *872, 1871, 1953. [OE. *mæg*, &c.]

may, *n.* woman, 1795. [ON. *mær, meyj-*; OE. (verse) *mǣg.*]

mayme, *v.* to injure, 1451. [From ME. *maym*, OFr. *mahaym*, &c., maiming.]
mayn, *adj.* great, strong, 94, 187, 336, 497. [ON. *megn*; OE. *mægen-*.]
maynteine, *v.* to support, keep, 2053. [OFr. *maintenir*.]
mayster, *n.* lord, knight, 136; master, 1603, 2090. [OFr. *maistre*.]
maystrés, *n. pl.* arts, 2448. [OFr. *maistrie*; *maistrise*, sg.]
make, *v.* to make, do, commit; cause to be; 43, 1073, 1674, 2455, &c.; **mas**, *3 sg.* 106; **mace**, 1885; **make**, *subj. 1 pl.* let us make, 1105, 1681; **mad(e)**, *pa. t.* 71, 562, 687, &c.; created, 869; compelled, *1565; **maked**, 1142, 1324; *pp.* 1112; **made**, 982. [OE. *macian*.]
male, *adj.* male, 1157. [OFr. *ma(s)le*.]
male, *n.* bag, 1129, 1809. [OFr. *male*.]
malt, *pa. t.* melted, 2080. [OE. *mieltan*, *mæltan*; pres. is *malte* in this MS.]
mane, *n.* mane, 187. [OE. *manu*.]
maner, *n.* custom, 90; kinds, 484; way, 1730; *pl.* manners, 924. [OFr. *manere*.]
manerly, *adj.* seemly, 1656 [see prec.]
mansed, *pa. t.* threatened, 2345. [OFr. *manecier*, *manasser*.]
mantyle, *n.* mantle, robe, 153, 878, 1736, 1831. [OFr. *mantel*.]
marre, *v.* to destroy, 2262. [OE. *merran*.]
mas, **masse**. See MAKE; MESSE.
masseprest, *n.* priest, 2108. [OE. *mæsse-prēost*.] See MESSE.
mat(e), *adj.* daunted, 336; exhausted, 1568. [OFr. *mat*.]
matyneȝ, **matynnes**, *n. pl.* matins (first of the canonical 'hours', recited at midnight or before daybreak), 756, 2188. [OFr. *matines*.]
mawgref, *prep.* in *m. his hed* (extension of *his*, gen.), in his despite, do what he might, 1565. [Alteration (assoc. with GREF) of *maugreþ* from OFr. **malgred*, *maugré*.]
meȝelmas, *n.* Michaelmas (Sept. 29); *m. mone*, harvest moon (full at or near the equinox), 532. [Cf. OE. *Michaeles mæsse*; forms with *ch* treated as spirant, as OFr. *Mihiel*, used exclusively of the archangel.]
me(y)ny, *n.* company, household, court, 101, 1372, 1625, 1729, 1957, 2045, 2468, &c. [OFr. *mai(s)nee*.]
mekely, *adv.* humbly, 756. [ON. *mjúkliga*.]
mele, *n.* mealtime, 999. [OE. *mǣl*.]
mele, *v.* to speak, say, 447, 543, 974, 1280, 2295, 2336, 2373. [OE. *mǣlan*.]
melle, *n.* in *inn melle*, in the midst, on all sides, 1451. [ODan. *i melle*.]
melle, *v.* to mingle; stream (together), 2503 (cf. 2371). [OFr. *meller*.]
melly, *n.* contest, battle, 342, 644. [OFr. *mellee*.]
membre, *n.* limb, 2292. [OFr. *membre*.]
mended, *pa. t.* improved, 883. [Shortened from AMENDE.]
mene, *v.* to mean, 233; **menyng**, *n.* understanding, 924. [OE. *mǣnan*.]
menged, *pp.* mingled, 1720. [OE. *méngan*.]
mensk, *adj.* worshipful, 964. [ON. *mennskr*, human; cf. next.]
mensk(e), *n.* courtesy, honour (shown), 834, 2052; honour, fame, 914; *pl.* 2410. [ON. *mennska*, humanity, generosity.]
mensked, *pp.* adorned, 153. [From prec.]
menskful, *adj.* of worth, 1809; *as sb.* noble (knights), 555; (lady), 1268. [As prec.]
menskly, *adv.* courteously, 1983; worthily, 1312. [As prec.]
merci, **mercy**, *n.* mercy, 1881, 2106; *see* GRAUNT. [OFr. *merci*.]
mere, *adj.* noble, 924, 1495 (*but see* MERY). [OE. *mǣre*, *mēre*.]
mere, *n.* appointed place, 1061. [OE. *gemǣre*, landmark.]
mery, **meré**, **mi(y)ry**, **myry**, *adj.* merry, 497, 1086, 1447, 1691, 1891, 1915; gay, fair, 142, 153, 878, 1263,

1495, 1736; *mace hym m.*, makes merry, 1885; *without refl. pron.* 1313, 1681, 1953, 2468; *adv.* 1623. **meryly, muryly,** *adv.* gaily, playfully, 740, 2295, 2336, 2345. [OE. *myrge.*]

merk, *n.* appointed place, 1073. [ON. *merki*; OE. *gemerce.*]

merkke, *v.* to aim (a blow) at, 1592. [ON. *merkja*; OE. *me(a)rcian.*]

merþe, mirþe, myrþe, *n.* joy, pleasure, amusement, 40, 45, 541, 1007, 1656, 1763, 1871, 1952; *meue m.*, provide fun, 985; *make m.*, make merry, revel, 71, 106, 899, 982. [OE. *myrgþ.*]

meruayl(e), *n.* wonder, marvel, 94, 466, 479, 718, 1197, 2307; *had m.*, wondered, 233. [OFr. *merveille.*]

meschaunce, *n.* disaster, 2195. [OFr. *mescha(u)nce.*]

meschef, *n.*; *his m.*, the disaster (to himself), 1774. [OFr. *mesch(i)ef.*]

mes(se), *n.* meal, 999; food, 1004; *pl.* dishes of food, 999. [OFr. *mes.*]

messe, *n.* Mass, 1690; **masse,** 592, 755, 1135, 1311, 1414, 1558. [OE. *messe, mæsse*; OFr. *messe.*]

messequyle, *n.* time for Mass, 1097. [Prec. + WHYLE.]

mesure, *n.* stature, 137. [OFr. *mesure.*]

metail, *n.* metal, 169. [OFr. *metail.*]

mete, *adj.* equal; extending (to), 1736; **metely,** *adv.* duly, 1004, 1414. [OE. *gemēte*; cf. *gemetlīce.*]

mete, *n.* food, meal, 45, 474, 543, 887, 1312, 1414, &c.; *attrib.* 71 n.; *pl.* dishes, 121, 1952. [OE. *mete.*]

mete, *v.* to meet, 1061, 1753, 1932; greet, 834, 2206 n., 2235; **met(te,** *pa. t.* 703, 1723, 1984; *m. wyth*, 1370; *intr.* 1407, 1592; *pp.* 1720. [OE. *mētan.*]

methles, *adj.* immoderate, violent, 2106. [OE. *mǣþlēas.*]

meue, mwe, *v.* to move; arouse, 985; influence, 90; *intr.* move, pass (on), 1312, 1565, 1965; *m. to*, result in, 1197; interfere with, 1157. [OFr. *moveir*; *moev-, meuv-.*]

myddelerde, *n.* the world, 2100. [Cf. OE. *middangeard.*]

myddes: *in þe m.*, in the midst, 74. [Var. of INMYDDES.]

myd-morn, *n.* midmorning, nine a.m., 1073, 1280. [OE. *midd + morgen.*]

myd-nyȝt, *n.* midnight, 2187. [OE. *mid-niht.*]

myd-ouer-under, *n.* midday, 1730. [OE. *mid + ofer undern.*]

myȝt, *n.* power, 2446; *at my m.*, as far as I can, 1546; *for myȝteȝ so wayke*, because of (their) powers (that are) so weak, 282. [OE. *miht.*]

myȝt; **miyry.** See MAY; MERY.

myld, *adj.* gentle, 754. [OE. *milde.*]

myle, *n. pl.* miles, 770, 1078. [OE. *mīl.*]

mylk-quyte, *adj.* milk-white, 958 (MS.). [OE. *milc-hwīt.*]

mynde, *n.* mind, memory, 497, 1484; *in m. hade*, reflected, 1283; *gotȝ in m.*, is debated in my mind, 1293. [OE. *gemýnd.*]

mynge, *v.* to draw attention to (by giving tongue), 1422. [OE. *myndgian.*]

myn(n)e, *v.* to declare, 141; exhort, 982; remember, think of, 995, 1992; *m.* (*vp*)*on*, give one's mind to, 1681; be reminded of, 1800; *m. of*, have thought for, 1769. [ON. *minna*, remind; *minnask*, remember.]

mynne, *adj.* less; *þe more and þe m.*, all, 1881 n. [ON. *minni.*]

mynstralsye, mynstralcie, *n.* minstrelsy, 484, 1952. [OFr. *menestralsie.*]

mynt, munt, *n.* aim; feint, pretence at a blow, 2345, 2350, 2352. [From next.]

mynte, *v.* to aim, swing (axe), 2290; *pa. t.* 2274; **munt,** 2262. [OE. *myntan.*]

myre, *n.* mire, swamp, 749. [ON. *mýrr.*]

miry, mirþe. See MERY; MERÞE.

misboden, *pp.* ill-used, 2339. [OE. *misbēodan*, pp. *misboden.*]

mysdede, *n.* sin, 760, 1880. [OE. *misdēd.*]
misy, *n.* swamp, bog, 749. [Cf. Mod. Lancs. dial. *mizzy*; (?) OE. **mysig*, adj. rel. to *mos*, MOSSE.]
mislyke, *v.* to displease, 1810; *impers.* (*subj.*) 2307. [OE. *mislīcian.*]
mysses, *n. pl.* faults, 2391. [OE. *miss*, and *mis-* prefix.]
mist, *n.* mist, 2080. [OE. *mist.*]
myst-hakel, *n.* cloak of mist, 2081. [OE. *mist* + *hacele.*]
mo, *adj.* more (in number), 23, 730, 2322, 2324; *adv.* 770. [OE. *mā.*]
mode, *n.* heart, mood, 1475. [OE. *mōd.*]
moder, *n.* mother, 754, 2320. [OE. *mōdor.*]
moȝt(en). See MAY.
molaynes, *n. pl.* ornamented studs at each end of horse's bit, 169. [OFr. **molein*; cf. ME. *mollet*, OFr. *molete.*]
molde, *n.*; *vpon m.*, on earth, 137, 914, 964; in life, 1795. [OE. *mōlde.*]
mon, *n.* man, 57, 141, 2349, &c.; *voc.* 1746, 1800, &c.; *as pron.* one, 565, 1077, 1160, 1209, 1682, 2355, &c.; *vche* (*no*) *m.*, everybody, nobody, 84, 233, &c.; **men,** *pl.* men, people, 28, 45, 914, 1447, *1729, &c.; **menne,** *dat. pl.* 466. [OE. *mon(n).*]
mon, *3 sg.* must, 1811, 2354. [ON. *mun.*]
mone, *n.*[1] moon, 532, 1313. [OE. *mōna.*]
mone, *n.*[2] complaint, 737. [OE. **mān*, rel. to *mǣnan*, v.]
moni, mony, *adj. and pron.* many, 14, 284, 351, 454, 2448, &c.; *mony a*, (*with sg.*) many, many a, 710, 1217; (*without* a) 22, 38, 442, 1447, &c. [OE. *monig.*]
monk, *n.* monk, 2108. [OE. *munuc.*]
mor, *n.* moor, 2080. [OE. *mōr.*]
more, *adj. compar.* greater, larger, 649, 677, 1881, 2100; more, further, 130, 1308, &c.; *lasse ne m.*, (not) any, at all, 1524; *adv.* more, further, 333, 2316, &c.; *forming compar.* 503, 968, &c.; *no m.*, not in return, 560; no further, not again, 546, 2286, 2443, &c.; none the more for that, 2311. **most,** *superl.* greatest, most, 137, 141, 985, &c.; *adv.* 51, 638. [OE. *māra*, *mǣst* (late Nth. *māst*).]
morn(e), moroun, *n.* morning, morrow, 453, 740, 995, 1024, 1208, 1670, &c. [OE. *morgen*, dat. sg. *morne.*]
mornyng, *n.*[1] morning, 1691, 1747. [From prec.]
mornyng, *n.*[2] See MOURNE, *v.*
morsel, *n.* a bite, small meal, *1690. [OFr. *morcel.*]
mosse, *n.* moss, 745. [OE. *mos.*]
most(e). See MORE, and next.
mot, *pres. t.* may, 342; (*in wishes*) 387, 2053, 2120, 2239, 2378; must, 1965, 2510; **most(e),** *pa. t.* must, 1287, 1958. [OE. *mōt*, pa. t. *mōste.*]
mote, *n.*[1] a whit, 2209. [OE. *mot.*]
mote, *n.*[2] moat, 764; castle, 635, 910, 2052. [OFr. *mot(t)e.*]
mote, *n.*[3] moot, (single) note on hunting-horn, 1364; *pl.* 1141. [OFr. *mot.*]
mount(e), *n.* hill, 740, 2080; *bi m.*, *bi þe mountes*, among the hills, 718, 1730. [OFr. *mo(u)nt*, OE. *munt.*]
mounture, *n.* mount, horse, 1691. [OFr. *monteure.*]
mourne, *v.* to sorrow, 1795; **mo(u)rnyng,** *n.* sorrow, 543, 1800; *in m. of*, troubled with, 1751. [OE. *múrnan.*]
mouþ(e), muthe, *n.* mouth, 447, 1446, 1572, 1778, 1907; voice, 1428, 1447. [OE. *mūþ.*]
mowe. See MAY.
much(e), *adj.* great, powerful, 182, 2336; much, abundant, 558, 684, 899, 1017, 1506, &c.; **miche,** 569; *as sb.* much, 1255, 1992; *þus m.*, to this purpose, 447; *so m. spelleȝ*, go so far as to say, 2140; *adv.* much, greatly, to a great extent, 187, 726, 1265, 1795; **mych,** 1281; *for as m. as*, in so far as, 356. [OE. *mycel*, *micel.*]
muchquat, *n.* many things, 1280. [Prec. + WHAT.]

muckel, *n.* size, 142. [OE. *myc(e)lu.*]
muged, *pa. t.* drizzled, was damp, 2080. [Cf. Norw. *mugga*, and *Mug*⁴ in E.D.D.]
mulne, *n.* mill, 2203. [OE. *mylen.*]
munt; muryly. See MYNT(E); MERY.
mused, *pa. t.* were bemused (with love), 2424. [OFr. *muser.*]
mute, *n.* hunting-pack, 1451, 1720; baying of hounds, 1915. [OFr. *muete.*]
muthe; mwe. See MOUÞ; MEUE.

N.

naf, *v.* have not, 1066; **nade**, *pa.t.* 763; *subj.* 724. [OE. *nabban*; see HAUE.]
naȝt. See NIȜT.
nay, *pa. t.* denied, 1836 n. [OFr. *nier.*]
nay(e), *adv.* nay, 256, 279, 706, 1222, 1813, 2250, 2407, 2471. [ON. *nei.*]
nayleȝ, *n. pl.* nails, 603. [OE. *nægel.*]
naylet, *adj.* studded with nails, 599. [OE. *nægled.*]
nayted, *pp.* celebrated, enjoyed, 65. [ON. *neyta.*]
naked, *adj.* naked, bare, 420, 730, 962, 1740, 2498; *as sb.* bare flesh, 423; the ill-clad, 2002. [OE. *nacod.*]
nakerys, *n. pl.* kettledrums, 1016; **nakryn**, *gen. pl.* 118. [OFr. *nac(ai)re.*]
name. See NOME.
nar, *v.* are not, 2092. [OE. *naron.*]
nase, *n.* nose, 962. [OE. *nasu.*]
naunt. See AUNT.
nauþer, nawþer, nouþer, *adj.* (n)either, 1552; *adv.* in *ne . . nauþer*, nor . . either, 203, *659, 2367; *conj.* nor, 1552; *nauþer . . ne*, neither . . nor, 430, 1095, 1837, 2157, 2274. [OE. *nāwþor.*]
ne, *adv.* not, 488, 750, *1053, 2105, 2142, 2511, &c.; *with other neg.* 1991, 2236; *conj.* nor (*with neg.* or, and), 196, 400, 1087, 1812, 2340, 2431, &c. [OE. *ne.*]
nede, *adv.* of necessity, (*with* BIHOUE) 1216, 1771; **nedeȝ, -es**, needs, 1287, 1965, 2510. [OE. *nēde, nēdes.*]
nedeȝ, *n. pl.* needs, business, 2216. [OE. *nēd.*]
nedes, *v.* in *hit n.*, there is need of, 404. [From prec.]
neȝ(e), neghe, nieȝ, *adv.* near, close, *697, 929, 1671; nearly, 1922; *prep.* 1771 (see ÞRED). [OE. *nēh.*] See NER.
neȝe, negh(e), *v. intr.* to approach, 697, 1998; *watȝ neȝed*, had drawn (near), 929; *trans.* 1575; reach, 1054; touch, 1836. [From prec.]
nek, nec, *n.* neck, 420, 2255, 2310, 2484, 2498, 2506. [OE. *hnecca.*]
neked, *n.* little, 1062, 1805. [ON. *nekkvat*, something.]
neme. See NYME.
ner(e), nerre, *adv.* (*compar.*) near(er), 1305; close at hand, 1995; nearly, 729; *as prep.* nearer to, near, 237, 322, 556. **nexte**, *superl. as prep.* next, beside, 1780. [OE. *nēr*, (*nĕrra*, adj.), compar.; ON. *nær*, compar. and positive. OE. *nĕxt.*]
neuen, *v.* to name, call, mention, 10, 58, 65, 541. [ON. *nefna.*]
neuer, *adv.* never, 91, 223, 659, 706, 2216, 2320, &c.; not at all, 399, 470, 1487, &c.; none, 376, 430; *n. bot*, only, 547; *n. so*, no matter how, 2129; *n. þe lece*, none the less, 474, 541. [OE. *nǣfre*; cf. *nā þe lǣs.*]
newe; nexte. See NWE; NER.
nye, nyȝe, *n.* harm, 2141; bitterness, 2002; *hit were n.*, it would be hard, 58. [OFr. *anui.*]
nye, *v.* to annoy, 1575. [OFr. *anuier.*]
nieȝ. See NEȜE.
nif, *conj.* unless, 1769. [NE + (Ȝ)IF.]
nyȝt, *n.* night, 730, 751, 1177, 1887, 2347, &c.; **ni(y)ȝt**, 929, 1687; **naȝt**, 1407; *on nyȝteȝ*, at night, 47, 693. [OE. *niht, næht.*]
nikked, nykked, *pa. t.* in *n. hym (wyth) nay*, said no to him, 706, 2471. [OE. (once) *niccan* from *nic*, not I.]

nyme, *v.* to take, 993; *n. to þyseluen*, bring upon, 2141; nome, *pa. t.* 809; obtained, 1407; **neme** (*for*), took (to be), 1347; nomen, *pp.* taken on (himself), 91. [OE. *niman.*]

nirt, *n.* slight cut, 2498. [Cf. Norw. dial. *nerta*, v. and SNYRT.]

nys, *adj.* foolish, 323, 358. [OFr. *nice.*]

nyse(n), *v.* make foolish; (they) foolishly exaggerate, 1266. [From prec.]

no, *adj.* no, 201, 696, 1809, &c.; **non**, 438, 657, 1552; (*foll. noun*) none, 2106; see OÞER, WAY. [OE. *nān.*]

no, *adv.* no, 411, 2063, 2226, 2303, &c.; see MO, MORE. [OE. *nā.*]

nobelay, *n.* splendour; *þurȝ n.*, in his magnificence, 91. [OFr. *nobleie.*]

nob(e)le, *adj.* noble, 623, 675, 917, 1264, &c.; glorious, splendid, 118, 514, 853, 1858, 1873; *as sb.* 1750. [OFr. *noble.*]

nobot, *conj.* only, 2182. [Next + BOT.]

noȝt, *adv.* not (at all), by no means, 358, 694, 1472, 2257, &c.; not, 85, 134, 400, *2131, 2290, &c.; *noȝt bot*, only, 1833. [OE. *nāht, nōht.*]

noȝt(e), *n.* nothing, 680, 961, *1815, 1823, 1943; *neuer . . for n.*, never on any account, 1865; *n. bot*, nothing but, only, 1267. [As prec.]

noyce, noyse, *n.* noise, 118, 132, 134, 1423, 2200, &c. [OFr. *noise.*]

noke, *n.* angle, point, 660. [Cf. Norw. dial. *nōk*, hook, bent figure.]

nolde, *pa. t.* would (not), 1661, 1825, 1836, 2150, 2471; *n. bot if*, would not have it happen that . . not, 1054. [OE. *nolde.*] See WILLE.

nome, *n.* name, 10, 408, 937, 1347, 2443; **name**, 400, 2453. [OE. *noma, nama.*]

nome(n). See NYME.

non(e), *pron.* none, no one, 307, 352, 1790, 1823, 2170, 2511, &c. [OE. *nān.*]

noneȝ: *for þe noneȝ*, for the nonce, indeed, 844. [OE. *for þan ānum.*]

norne, nurne, *v.* to announce, propose; offer, 1823; urge, press, 1771; *n. hir aȝayneȝ*, refuse, 1661; *n. on þe same note*, propose same terms, 1669; call, 2443. [Cf. Swed. dial. *norna, nyrna*, inform (secretly).]

norþe, *n.* north, 2002. [OE. *norþ*, adv.]

not. See NOȜT.

note, *n.*[1] business, 358; *to þe n.*, in readiness, 420; *for þat n.*, for the purpose, specially, 599. [OE. *notu.*]

note, *n.*[2] (musical) note, 514; tenor, fashion, 1669. [OFr. *note.*]

note, *pp.* noted, 2092 n. [OFr. *noter.*]

noþyng, *n. as adv.* no whit, not at all, 2236. [OE. *nā(n)þing.*]

noumbles, *n. pl.* offal from back and loins of deer, 1347. [OFr. *no(u)mbles.*]

nouþe, nowþe, *adv.* now, 1251, 1784, 1934, 2466. [OE. *nū þā.*]

nouþer. See NAUÞER.

now(e), *adv.* now, still, 10, 494, 1998, 2304, &c.; in these days, 58; moreover, now, 299, 656, 776, 1242, &c.; *oþer n. oþer neuer*, 2216; *conj.* now that, 2296; since, 2420. [OE. *nū.*]

nowel, *n.* Christmas, 65. [OFr. *noel.*]

nowhere, *adv.* nowhere, 2164; **nowhare**, in no case, not at all, 2254. [OE. *nāhwǣr, -hwāra.*]

nurne. See NORNE.

nurture, *n.* good breeding, 919, 1661. [OFr. *nurture.*]

nwe, *adj.* new, fresh, novel, 118, 636, 1401; **newe**, 132, 1655; *adv.* newly, anew, 60, 599, 1668, 2223; **nweȝ**, *as sb. gen.* in *what n.*, whatever new thing, 1407. [OE. *nēowe*; *hwæt nēowes.*]

nw(e)ȝer(e), newȝere, *n.* New Year's tide, New Year's day, 60, 105, 284, 453, 1075, 2244, 2400, &c. [Prec. + ȜER(E); cf. ON. *nýjár.*]

O.

of, *adv.* off, 773, 983, 1346, &c. [OE. *of.*]

of, o (615), *prep.* of; from, out of, 183, 903, 1087, &c.; (consisting, made) of, 121, 159, &c.; by, with, 172, 1455, 2167, &c.; about, concerning, 93, 108, 927, &c.; for, 96, 975, 1032, 2308, &c.; *as equiv. of gen.* 63, 424, &c.; *partitive,* from, among, 25, 29, 38, 1816, &c.; in, as regards, 86, 143, 1478, 1940, 2238, &c.; in, on (*confused with* ON), 1329, 1457. [OE. *of.*]

offre, *v.* to offer, 593. [OFr. *offrir.*]

oft(e), *adv.* often, 18, 23, 65, 1123, 2482, &c. [OE. *oft.*]

oghe, *v.* to have, owe; ought, 1526; **aȝt(e),** *pa. t.* owned, 767, 843, 1775; had (*or* owed), 1941. [OE. *āgan*; *āhte.*]

oȝt, *n.* anything, 300, 1815 (MS.), 2215. [OE. *ā(wi)ht, ō(wi)ht.*]

okeȝ, *n. pl.* oaks, 743, 772. [OE. *āc.*]

olde, *adj.* old, 1001, 1124, 2182, 2183. [OE. *ald.*]

on, *adj.* one, a single, 30, 314, 2151, 2252, &c.; one, as opposed to 'other', 206, 771, 2312. [OE. *ān.*]

on, *adv.* on, away, 2219, 2300; (with *infin.* or *rel.*) on, 170, 173, 968. [OE. *on.*]

on, *prep.* (up)on, 4, 236, 372, 1589, 2232, &c.; (*postponed*; *orig. adv.*) 953; to, 1701, &c.; (think) of, 1800, 2052, &c.; at, 479, 491, 2180, &c.; in(to), 517, 683, 1722, 1730, &c.; a, a-, 385, 1102, 1143, 2363, &c.; *of time,* on, in, by, 47, 537, 1675, 1680, 1732, 1868, &c. [OE. *on.*]

on(e), *pron.* one (person *or* thing), 223, 442, 1340, 1964, 2416, 2439, &c.; *with superl.,* 137 n., 1439, 2363; some one, 2202, 2217; *þat on,* the one, 952, 954, 2412. [OE. *ān.*]

one, *adj.* alone, only, 2074; *a . . one,* a single, 2249, 2345; *al one, al hym* (*his*) *one,* alone, 749, 1048, 2155; *hym one,* 905; *oure one,* by ourselves, 1230, 2245. [OE. *āna.*]

oneȝ, ones, *adv.* once, 2280, 2512; formerly, 2218; *at oneȝ,* at the same time, together, 895, 1425, 1913; *at þys oneȝ,* at this very moment, 1090. [OE. *ānes.*]

onewe, *adv.* anew, 65. [OE. *on* + *nīwan.*]

on-ferum, *adv.* from a distance, 1575. [OE. *on* + *feorran.*]

only, *adv.* only, 356. [OE. *ānlic,* adj.]

on-stray, *adv.* out of his course, in a new direction, 1716. [OFr. *estraié,* ME. *astraie,* altered by assoc. with *a-, on-*; but cf. OFr. *strai.*]

onsware. See ANSWARE.

open, *adj.* open, 2070. [OE. *open.*]

or, *conj.*[1] or, 88, 661, 2183. [Reduced form of OÞER, *conj.*]

or, *conj.*[2] than, 1543 n. [Same as ARE.]

oryȝt. See ARYȜT.

oritore, *n.* oratory, chapel, 2190. [OFr. *oritur.*]

orpedly, *adv.* actively, 2232. [OE. *orpedlīce.*]

ostel. See HOSTEL.

oþer, *adj. and pron.* other (one), other kinds of, 24, 90, 190, 555, 655, 2342, &c.; *pl.* others, 64, 551, 1249, 1445, 2423, &c.; one another, 673. *An o.,* otherwise, 1268; *non o.,* nothing else, what I say, 1396; *þat o.,* the other, 110, 208, 386, 2389, 2412, &c.; latter, 1591; second, 1020, 2350; *of alle o.,* than any other, 944 n.; *ayþer o.,* each (the) other, 841, 939, 1307, 2472; *vch* (*on*) . . *oþer,* each . . the other, 98, 501, 628. [OE. *ōþer.*]

oþer, auþer, *adv. and conj.* or, or else, 96, 456, 591, &c.; either (foll. by *oþer, or*), 88, 702, 1772, 2216; else (prec. by *oþer*), 1956, 2293; *oþer oþer,* or any one else, 2102. [OE. *āhwæþer, ā(w)þer, ō-.*]

oþerquyle, *adv.* at other times, 722. [OÞER, *adj.* + WHILE, *n.*]

oþeȝ, *n. pl.* oaths, 2123. [OE. *āþ.*]

ouer, *adv.* above (them), 223; across,

2232; over there, 700. *Prep.* above, 76, 732, 1908, 2217, &c.; over, 182, 419, 957, 1758, &c.; over, across, 13, 1595, 1709, 1896, &c. [OE. *ofer.*]
oueral, *adv.* all over, entirely, 150; everywhere, 630. [OE. *ofer all.*]
ouerclambe, *pa. t.* climbed over, 713. [OE. *oferclimban.*]
ouergrowen, *pp.* overgrown, 2181, 2190. [OE. *ofer + grōwen*, pp.]
ouerȝede, *pa. t.* passed by, 500. [OUER + ȜEDE; cf. OE. *oferēode.*]
ouertake, *v.* to regain, 2387. [OE. *ofer* + ON. *taka.*]
ouerþwert, *adv.* athwart (his path), 1438. [OE. *ofer* + ON. *þvert.*]
ouerwalt, *pp.* overthrown, 314. [OE. *ofer + wæltan.*]
oure. See WE.
out, *adv.* out, 432, 458, 802, 1333, 1438, &c.; *hatȝ out*, removes, 1612. [OE. *ūt.*]
oute, *adv.* far and wide, 1511. [OE. *ūte.*]
outtrage, *n.* excess; *as adj.* exceeding strange, 29. [OFr. *outrage.*]
owen, *adj. and pron.* own, 408, 2359; **awen**, 836, 1036, 1488, 1519, 2301, &c.; **auen**, 293; **aune**, 10. [OE. *āgen.*]

P.

pay, *n.* pay, 2247. [OFr. *paie.*]
paye, *v.* to please, 1379; *pp.* satisfied, 2341; paid up, 1941. [OFr. *payer.*]
payne, *n.* hardship, 733. [OFr. *peine.*]
payne, *v. refl.* take pains; endeavour, 1042. [OFr. *se pener*, 3 sg. *peine.*]
paynte, *v.* to paint, 800; depict, 611. [OFr. *peindre*; *peint*, 3 sg., pp., sb.]
payre, *v.* to be impaired, fail, 650, 1456, 1734. [OFr. *empeirer.*]
payttrure, *n.* breast-trappings of horse, 168, 601. [Cf. OFr. *peitrel.*]
palays, *n.* a fence of pales, palisade, 769. [OFr. *pal(e)is.*]
pane, *n.* fur-lining, 154. [OFr. *pan(n)e.*]
paneȝ, *n. pl.* panels (of stuffs of varying colours), 855. [OFr. *pan.*]
papiayeȝ, *n. pl.* parrots, 611. [OFr. *papegai, papejaye.*]
papure, *n.* paper, 802. [OFr. *pap(i)er.*]
paradise, *n.* paradise, heaven, 2473. [OFr. *para(d)is.*]
paraunter, parauenture, *adv.* perhaps, 1009, 1850, 2343. [OFr. *par aventure.*]
pared, *pp.* cut, 802. [OFr. *parer.*]
park, *n.* park, 768. [OFr. *parc.*]
parte, *v.* to part, 2473. [OFr. *partir.*]
passe, *v.* to pass (by, away), proceed, 266, 378, 1998, 2129, &c.; *trans.* cross, 2071; surpass, 654; *watȝ passande*, surpassed, 1014; **passed**, *pa. t.* 715, &c.; **past(e)**, 1667; was over, 1280. [OFr. *passer.*]
passage, *n.* journey, 544. [OFr. *passage.*]
pater, *n.* the Pater Noster, 'Our Father', [757.
patroun, *n.* lord, 6. [OFr. *patron.*]
paumeȝ, *n. pl.* 'palms' (broad flat parts) of horns of deer, 1155. [OFr. *paume.*]
paunce, *n.* armour covering abdomen (properly *pauncer*), 2017. [OFr. *pancier, pauncer*; see next.]
pauncheȝ, *n. pl.* stomachs (of a ruminant), 1360. [ONFr. *panche.*]
pece, *n.* piece, 1458; (of armour), 2021. [OFr. *pece.*]
pelure, *n.* fur (esp. for lining or trimming), 154, 2029. [OFr. *pelure.*]
penaunce, *n.* penance, 2392; penitential fare, 897. [OFr. *pen(e)ance.*]
pendaunt, -aund, *n.* pendant, 168, 2038, 2431. [OFr. *pendant*, pres. p.]
penyes, *n. pl.* pennies, money, 79. [OE. *peni(n)g.*]
penta(u)ngel, *n.* five-pointed star, 620 n., 623, 636, 664. [Alteration of OFr. *pentacle*, Med. L., *pentācu-lum*, by assoc. with *angle.*]
pented, *pa. t.* had to do with, belonged, 204. [OFr. *apendre*, APENDE.]
peple, *n.* people, 123, 664. [OFr. *poeple.*]
pere, *n.* peer, equal, 873. [OFr. *per.*]

perelous, *n.* perilous, 2097. [OFr. *perillous.*]
perile, **peryl**, *n.* peril, 733, 1768. [OFr. *peril.*]
perle, *n.* pearl, 954, 2364. [OFr. *perle.*]
pernyng, *pres. p.* preening, 611. [See N.E.D. *Preen*; *Prune*, v.[1]]
persoun, *n.* person, 913. [OFr. *persone.*]
pertly, *adv.* openly, plainly, 544, 1941. [From OFr. *apert*, APERT.]
pes, *n.* peace, 266. [OFr. *pais*, *pes.*]
pese, *n.* pea, 2364. [OE. *pise*, *peose.*]
piched, *pp.* attached, 576; **pyched**, set up, erected, 768; **pyȝt**, *pa. t.* pitched, struck, 1456; was (fixed), 1734. [OE. **piccan*; cf. (late) *pīcan.*]
pyked, *adj.* with spikes, 769. [From OE. *pīc.*]
piked, *pp.* polished, 2017. [See N.E.D., *Pick*, v.[1]]
pynakle, *n.* pinnacle, 800. [OFr. *pinacle.*]
pine, **pyne**, *n.* pain, grief, trouble, 747, 1812, 1985; *pine to*, it was difficult to, 123. [OE. **pīn*; cf. next.]
pyne, *v. refl.* to trouble oneself, 1009, 1538. [OE. *pīnian*; cf. PAYNE.]
pyned, *pp.* enclosed, 769. [OE. *pýndan*, ME. *pinden* (pp. *pind*) and *pin(n)en*, partly infl. by *pinnen*, pin.]
pipe, *n.* pipe, 118. [OE. *pīpe.*]
pipe, *v.* to pipe, 747; **pypyng**, *n.* music of pipes, 1017. [OE. **pīpian.*]
pysan, *n.* armour for upper breast and neck, 204. [OFr. *pisa(i)ne* (sc. *gorgerette*), of Pisa.]
pité, *n.* pity, compassionateness, 654. [OFr. *pité.*]
pyth, *n.* toughness, 1456. [OE. *piþa.*]
pitosly, *adv.* piteously, 747. [From OFr. *pitous.*]
place, *n.* room, 123; place, dwelling, 398, 1052, 2240, &c. [OFr. *place.*]
play, *n.* play, sport, 1014, 1379, 1538. [OE. *plega.*]

play, *v.* to sport, amuse oneself, 262, 1664. [OE. *pleg(i)an.*]
playneȝ, *n. pl.* level lands, fields, 1418. [OFr. *plaine.*]
plate, *n.* steel plate, piece of plate armour, 204, 583, 2017. [OFr. *plate.*]
plede, *v.* to plead, 1304. [AFr. *pleder.*]
plesaunce, *n.* pleasure, 1247. [OFr. *plaisance*, *plesaunce.*]
plesaunt, *adj.* civil, 808. [OFr. *plaisant*, *plesaunt.*]
plese, *v.* to please, 1249, 1659. [OFr. *plaisir*, *ple(i)sir.*]
plyȝt, *n.* offence, 2393; danger, hostility, 266. [OE. *pliht.*]
plytes, *n. pl.* (evil) conditions, hardships, 733. [AFr. *plit*; OFr. *pleit.*]
poynt, *n.* (i) (sharp) point, 1456, 2392; point of angle, 627, 658: (ii) quality, 654; (good) condition, 2049; question, 902; *bryng me to þe p.*, come to the point with me, 2284. [OFr. (i) *pointe*; (ii) *point.*]
poynte, *v.* to describe (in detail), 1009. [OFr. *pointer.*]
polayneȝ, *n. pl.* pieces of armour for knees, 576. [OFr. *polain.*]
policed, **polyst**, *pp.* polished, 576, 2038; **polysed**, cleansed, 2393. [OF. *polir*, *poliss-.*]
pore, **pouer**, *adj.* poor, humble, 1538, 1945. [OFr. *pov(e)re*, *poure.*]
porter, *n.* porter (at the gates), 808, 813, 2072. [OFr. *port(i)er.*]
poudred, *pp.* powdered, scattered, 800. [OFr. *poudrer.*]
pray(e), *v.* to pray, beg, 254, 757, 1219, 1785, 2439, &c. [OFr. *preier.*]
prayere, *n.*[1] prayer, 759. [OFr. *preiere.*]
prayere, *n.*[2] meadow, 768. [OFr. *praiere.*]
prayse, *v.* to praise, 913, 1228, 1630, 1633, 2072; esteem, 1850; *to p.*, praiseworthy, 356. [OFr. *preis(i)er.*]
praunce, *v.* to prance, 2064. [Obscure.]
prece, **prese**, *v.* to press forward, hasten, 830, 2097. [OFr. *presser.*]

presense, *n.* presence, 911. [OFr. *presence.*]
prest, *n.* priest, 1877. [OE. *prēost.*]
prestly, *adv.* promptly, 757, 911. [From OFr. *prest.*]
preue, *adj.* valiant, 262. [OFr. *preu.*]
preué, *adj.* discreet, 902; **preuély**, *adv.* privately, 1877. [OFr. *privé.*]
preued, proued, *pp.* proved, 79; given proof of, shown, 1630. [OFr. *prover*, accented stem *proev-*, *preuv-*.]
pryde, *n.* pride, 681, 2038, 2437; *with p.*, splendidly, 587. [OE. *prȳdo.*]
prik, pryk, *v.* to pierce, stir (heart), 2437; to spur (*intr.*), gallop, 2049. [OE. *prician.*]
pryme, *n.* prime, first division of the day, 6–9 a.m., 1675. [OE. *prīm*, from L. *prīma* (*hōra*).]
prynce, *n.* prince, 623, 873, 2398, &c.; *gen.* 1014; *p. of paradise*, Christ, 2473. [OFr. *prince.*]
pryncece, *n.* princess, *1770. [OFr. *princesse.*]
pris, prys, *n.*[1] value, 79, 1277, 1850; excellence, 912, 1249, 1630; praise, 1379; *your p.*, politely for 'you', 1247; *o(f) prys*, precious, 615, 2364; noble, 1770, 2398; **prys**, *adj.* precious, 1945. [OFr. *pris.*]
prys, *n.*[2] capture; blast on horn when hunted animal is taken, 1362, 1601. [OFr. *pris(e)*, from *prendre.*]
prysoun, *n.* prisoner, 1219. [OFr. *priso(u)n.*]
profered, *pa. t.* offered, 1494, 2346, 2350. [OFr. *proffrir*, *proferer.*]
proude, prowde, *adj.* proud, haughty, 830, 1277, 2049, 2104, 2269; superb, splendid, 168, 601. [OE. *prūt*, *prūd*, from OFr. *prout*, *prou(d)*.]
proued, 1630. See PREUED.
prouince, *n.* realm, 6. [OFr. *province.*]
prowes, *n.* prowess, 912, 1249, 2437. [OFr. *pro(u)esse.*]
pure, *adj.* pure, 620; faultless, fair, noble, 262, 654, 664, 2398; sheer, 1247; *as adv.* faultlessly, 808; **purely**, *adv.* entirely, certainly, 802, 813. [OFr. *pur.*]
pured, *pp.* purified, refined, 633, 912, 2393; (of fur) trimmed, or cut down, so as to show one colour only, 154, 1737. [OFr. *purer.*]
purpose, *n.* purpose, 1734. [OFr. *purpos.*]
put, *v.* to set, put, 1277; *pp.* 902. [OE. *pŭtian*, *pȳtan.*]

Q.

qu-. See also WH-.
quaynt. See KOYNT.
quaked, *pa. t.* trembled, 1150. [OE. *cwacian.*]
queldepoyntes, *n. pl.* quilted coverings, 877. [OFr. *cuiltepointe.*]
quelle, *v.* to quell, end, 752; kill, 1324, 1449, 2109. [OE. *cwellan.*]
queme, *adj.* pleasant, 2109; goodly, 578. [OE. *cwēme.*]
quene, *n.* queen, 339, 469, 647; **whene**, 74, 2492. [OE. *cwēn.*]
querré, *n.* quarry, assemblage of game slain in chase, 1324. [OFr. *cuirée.*]
quest, *n.* searching of hounds after game (*calle of a q.*, call for a search to be made), 1421; baying of hounds (on scenting or viewing), 1150. [OFr. *queste.*]
quethe, *n.* utterance, 1150. [Stem of OE. *cweðan.*]
quik, quyk, *adj.*, alive, 2109; lively, restive, 177; *adv.* quickly, 975; **quikly, quykly**, *adv.* 1324, 1490. [OE. *cwic(u)*; *cwiclīce.*]
quyssewes, *n. pl.* thigh-pieces, 578. [OFr. *cuissel*, pl. *cuisseus.*]
quit-clayme, *v.* to declare settled; renounce, 293. [Pp. of next + CLAYME.]
quyte, *v.* to requite, repay, 2244, 2324. [OFr. *quiter.*]
quoþ. See COÞE.

R.

rabel, *n.* rabble, 1703, 1899. [Cf. OFr. *rabler*, make confused noise.]
race, *n.* headlong course, 1420; onslaught, 2076. [ON. *ras*, *rás*.]
rach, *n.* hound that hunts by scent, 1903, 1907 (*gen. pl.*); **rach(ch)eȝ**, *pl.* 1164, 1362, 1420, 1426. [OE. *ræcc*.]
rad, *adj.* afraid, 251. [ON. *hræddr*.]
rad, *adv.* promptly, 862. [OE. *hrade*.]
radly, *adv.* swiftly, promptly, 367, 1341, 1744, 1907, &c. [OE. *hrædlīce*.]
raged, *adj.* ragged, shaggy, 745. [ON. *raggaðr*; OE. *raggig*.]
raȝt. See RECH(E).
rayke, *v.* to wander; depart, 1076; *out r.*, make for the open, 1727; *rayked hir*, went, 1735. [ON. *reika*.]
rayled, *pp.* arranged, arrayed, 163, 603, 745, 952. [OFr. *reiller*.]
rayn, *n.* rain, 506. [OE. *regn*.]
rayne, *n.* rein, 457, 2177. [OFr. *reine*.]
rayse, *v.* to raise, 1916; bid rise, 821. [ON. *reisa*.]
raysoun. See RESOUN.
rak, *n.* drifting clouds, 1695. [Cf. ON. *rek(i)*, Norw. dial. *rak*, flotsam.]
rake, *n.* path, 2144, 2160. [OE. *racu*, water-course.]
ran. See RENNE.
rande, *n.* border, 1710. [OE. *rand*.]
rape, *v. refl.* to hasten, hurry, 1309, 1903. [ON. *hrapa*.]
rapely, *adv.* hastily, quickly, 2219. [ON. *hrapalliga*.]
rase, *v.*[1] to rush, 1461. [ON. *rasa*.]
rase, *v.*[2] to snatch, 1907. [Shortened from OFr. *arac(i)er*.]
rasor, *n.* razor, 213. [OFr. *rasor*.]
rasse, *n.* level; (?) smooth bank, 1570; cf. *Purity*, 446. [OFr. *ras*.]
raþeled, *pp.* entwined, 2294. [See N.E.D. s.v. *Raddle* v.[1], *Ratheled*.]
raweȝ, *n.pl.* hedgerows, 513. [OE. *rāw*.]
rawþe, *n.* ruth, grief; *r. to here*, grievous to hear, 2204. [Blend of OE. *hrēow*, ON. *hryggð*.]
rech(e), *v.* to reach; offer, give, 66, 1804, 2059, 2324; *intr.* extend, 183; *r. to*, come up to, merit (*or* presume to accept), 1243; **raȝt**, *pa. t.* offered, gave, 1817, 1874, 2297, 2351; *r. out*, reached out, 432. [OE. *rǣcan*.]
rechate, *v.* to blow the recall, indicating where hunters should assemble, 1446, 1466, 1911. [OFr. *rechater*.]
rechles, *adj.* care-free, joyous, 40. [OE. *recceléas*.]
recorded, *pa. t.* recalled, mentioned, 1123. [OFr. *recorder*.]
recreaunt, *adj.* confessing oneself vanquished, faint-hearted, 456. [OFr. *recrea(u)nt*.]
red(e), *adj.* red, 304, 663, 1205, 2036; *n.* 1695; (of face) 952; *on red*, against red background, 603. [OE. *rēad*.] See GOLD.
red(e), *v.* to advise; direct, 738; manage, deal with, 373, 2111 n.; **redde**, *pa. t.* advised, 363; *pp.* declared, 443. [OE. *rǣdan*, *rēdan*.]
redé, *adj.* ready, 1970. [From OE. *ge-rǣde*.]
redly, *adv.* fully, 373; **redyly**, promptly, 1821, 2324; willingly, 2059; rightly, 392. [OE. *gerǣdelīce*.]
refourme, *v.* to restate, 378. [OFr. *reformer*.]
refuse, *v.* to refuse, 1772. [OFr. *refuser*.]
rehayte, *v.* to encourage, 1422; exhort, 895; rebuke, rally, 1744. [OFr. *rehait(i)er*, *reheiter*.]
reherce, **reherse**, *v.* to repeat, 392; describe, 1243. [OF. *rehercer*.]
rekenly, *adv.* promptly, courteously, 39, 251, 821. [OE. *recenlīce*.]
rele, *v.* to reel, roll, 304; *refl.* swagger, 229; *intr.* turn suddenly, 1728; sway (in combat), 2246. [From OE. *hrēol*, a reel.]
relece, *v.* to release, 2342. [OFr. *relaicier*; *relesser*.]
remene, *v.* to recall, recount, 2483. [OFr. *remener*, bring back.]

remnaunt, *n.* remainder, rest, 2342, 2401. [OFr. *remena(u)nt.*]
remorde, *v.* to call to mind with remorse, 2434. [OFr. *remordre.*]
remwe, *v.* to remove; alter (mood), 1475. [OFr. *remuer.*]
renaye, *v.* to refuse, 1821, 1827. [OFr. *reneier.*]
renaude, *n.* Reynard, the fox, 1898, 1916 (*gen.*); **reniarde**, 1728; **reynarde**, 1920. [OFr. *Renart*, *Renard*; assim. to OFr. *Renaud.*]
rende, *v.* to rend, 1608; **rent**, *pa. t.* 1332; *pp.* 1168. [OE. *rendan.*]
renk, *n.* knight, man, 303, 2206 n., 2246, &c.; **renkkeȝ**, *pl.* 432, 862, 1134. [OE. *rinc*; ON. *rekkr*, older **renk-*.]
renne, *v.* to run, slide, flow, 731, 857, 1568, 1570; be current, 310, 2458; **ran**, *pa. t. pl.* 1420; **runnen**, 66, 1703; *pp.* 1727. [ON. *renna.*]
renoun, *n.* renown, glory, 231, 313, 2434, 2458, 2519; *of renoun*, noble, 2045. [OFr. *renoun.*]
repayre, *v.* to resort; be present, 1017. [OFr. *repairer.*]
repreued, *pa. t.* rebuked, 2269. [OFr. *repro(u)ver, repreuv-.*]
require, *v.* to ask, 1056. [OFr. *requerre*; 3 sg. *requier.*]
rered, *pp.* raised, 353. [OE. *rǣran.*]
res, *n.* rush, 1899. [OE. *rǣs.*]
resayt, *n.* reception; receiving stations, 1168 n. [OFr. *receite.*]
resayue, *v.* to receive, 2076. [OFr. *receivre.*]
rescowe, *n.* rescue, 2308. [Stem of OFr. *rescourre*, v.]
resette, *n.* refuge, shelter, 2164. [OFr. *recet*; cf. RESAYT.]
resoun, **raysoun**, *n.* reason; speech, statement, 227, 392; *bi r.*, correctly, 1344; by rights, 1804; **resounȝ**, *pl.* speech, 443. [OFr. *raison, resoun.*]
respite, *n.* respite, 297. [OFr. *respit.*]
rest, *n.* rest, 1990. [OE. *ræst, rest.*]
restaye, *v.* to stop, turn back, 1153; *resteyed to lenge*, bade remain and linger, 1672. [OFr. *resteir*; see N.E.D. s.v. *Stay*, v.[1]]
restore, *v.* to restore, 2283, 2354. [OFr. *restorer.*]
reue, *v.* to take away, 2459. [OE. *rēafian.*]
reuel, *n.* revelry, revelling, 40, 313, 538. [OFr. *revel.*]
reuel, *v.* to revel, 2401. [OFr. *reveler.*]
reuerence, *n.* honour, 1243; *at þe r.*, out of respect, 2206. [OFr. *reverence.*]
reuerenced, *pa. t.* saluted, 251. [OFr. **reuerenc(i)er.*]
rewarde, *n.* reward, 1804, 2059. [ONFr. *reward.*]
rewarde, *v.* to reward, 1610, 1918. [ONFr. *rewarder.*]
ryal, *adj.* royal, 905; **ryol**, splendid, 2036; **ryally**, *adv.* 663. [OFr. *rial.*]
ryalme, *n.* realm, 310, 691. [OFr. *rialme.*]
rybbeȝ, *n. pl.* ribs, 1343, 1356, 1378. [OE. *ribb.*]
richche, **rych(e)**, *v.* to direct, decide, intend, prepare, 360, 599, 1223, 2206; *refl.* prepare (oneself), dress, 1130, 1309, 1873; *refl. and intr.* make one's way, proceed, 8, 1898. [Prob. same as RUCH, but senses also due to OE. *reccan.*]
rich(e), **rych(e)**, *adj.* of high rank, noble, 8, 20, 39, 347, 905; wealthy, 1646; splendid, costly, rich, 40, 243, 513, 882, 2036, &c.; resounding, 1916; pleasant, 1744; high (feast), 2401; *as sb.* noble (steed), 2177 n.; *pl.* nobles, courtly folk, 66, 362; *adv.* richly, 159, 220, 872; **rychest**, *superl. as sb.* those of highest rank, 1130. [OE. *rīce*; OFr. *riche.*]
rychely, *adv.* richly, 163; with festive peal, 931; **richley**, in lordly fashion, 308. [OE. *rīclīce.*]
ride, **ryde**, *v.* to ride, 142, 160, 738, &c.; **rod(e)**, *pa. t.* 689, 821, *1466, &c.; **rydyng**, *n.* 1134. [OE. *rīdan.*]
ryd(d)e, *v.* to relieve (of the contest),

364; separate (combatants), 2246; *r. of*, clear away, 1344. [OE. *ryddan.*]

rygge, *n.* back, 1344 (*attrib.*), 1608. [OE. *hrycg.*]

ryȝt, *adj.* true, 2443; actual, very, 1703. [OE. *riht.*]

ryȝt, riȝt, *adv.* properly, 373; right, just, even, 667, 931, 1173, 1899, 1903, 2328, &c.; at all, 1790; *r. to*, as far as, 1341, 2162. [OE. *rihte.*]

ryȝt, riȝt, *n.* obligation, duty, 1041, 2342; justice, 2346; right, privilege (of the Christmas season), 274. [OE. *riht.*]

ryȝt, *pa. t.* directed; *refl.* proceeded, 308. [OE. *rihtan.*]

rimed, *pa. t. refl.* stretched himself, puffed himself out, 308. [OE. *rȳman.*]

rymeȝ, *n.* membranes, 1343. [OE. *rēoma.*]

rynk, *n.* ring, 1817, 1827; **ryngeȝ**, *pl.* rings of mail-shirt, 580, 857, 2018. [OE. *hring.*]

rynkande, *pres. p.* ringing, *2337; **ronge**, *pa. t. sg.* 2204; **r(o)ungen**, *pl.* 195, 1427, 1698; *trans.* rang (the bells), 931. [OE. *hringan*, wk.]

ryol. See RYAL.

rype, *adj.* ripe, 522. [OE. *rīpe.*]

rype, *v.* to ripen, 528. [OE. *rīpian.*]

rys, *n.* branch, twig; *bi rys*, in the woods, 1698. [OE. *hrīs.*]

rys(e), rise, *v.* to rise, stand up, get up (from bed), 306, 366, 1076, 1101, 1126, 1695, &c.; **ros**, *pa. t.* 1148, 1427, 1735; grew, 528; **rysed**, rose, 1313. [OE. *ārīsan.*]

rytte, *v.* to cut, 1332. [OE. **rittan.*]

ryue, *adv.* abundantly, much, 2046. [Late OE. *rȳfe*, **rīfe*, adj.]

ryue, *v.* to rip, cut (open), 1341, 2290; **roue**, *pa. t.* 2346. [ON. *rifa.*]

robe, *n.* robe, 862. [OFr. *robe.*]

roche, *n.* rock, 2199. [OFr. *roche.*]

roché, *adj.* rocky, 2294. [From prec.]

rocher, *n.* rock, 1427, 1432, 1698. [OFr. *roch(i)er.*]

rod(e). See RIDE.

rode, *n.* rood, cross, 1949. [OE. *rōd.*]

rof, *n.* gash, wound, 2346. [ON. *rof.*]

roȝ(e), rogh, ruȝe, rugh, *adj.* shaggy, 745; rough, rugged, 953, 1432, 1898, 2162, 2166, 2177, 2198; **roghe**, *adv.* roughly, 1608. [OE. *rūh*, *rūg-*.]

rokke, *n.* rock, 730, 1570, 2144, 2198. [Cf. OE. *stānrocc*; OFr. *ro(c)que.*]

rokked (*of*), *pp.* burnished, made clean (from) by rolling under pressure, 2018. [ON. *hrukka*, fold, in *hrukkask* (refl.) wrinkle; cf. Norw. *rukka.*]

rol(le), *v. intr.* to roll, 428; hang in loose folds, 953. [OFr. *rol(l)er.*]

romaunce, *n.* romance, 2521. [OFr. *roma(u)nz.*]

rome, *v.* to wander, make one's way, 2198. [ME. forms point to OE. **rāmian.*]

roneȝ, *n. pl.* bushes, 1466. [ON. *runnr.*]

ronge. See RYNKANDE.

ronk, *adj.* luxuriant, 513. [OE. *ronc.*]

ronkled, *pp.* wrinkled, 953. [Cf. ON. *hrukka*, **hrunka*, a wrinkle.]

ropeȝ, *n. pl.* cords, 857. [OE. *rāp.*]

rote, *n.* way; *bi rote*, on the way, 2207. [OFr. *rote.*]

rote, *v.* to decay, 528. [OE. *rotian.*]

roteȝ, *n. pl.* roots, 2294. [ON. *rót.*]

roue. See RYUE, *v.*

roueȝ, *n. pl.* roofs, 799. [OE. *hrōf.*]

roun, *v.* to take whispered counsel, 362. [OE. *rūnian.*]

rouncé, *n.* horse, 303. [OFr. *ronci.*]

rounde, *adj.* round; *þe Rounde Table*, 39, 313. 538, 905, 2458, 2519. [OFr. *roönd, round.*]

roungen. See RYNKANDE.

rous, *n.* fame, talk, 310. [ON. *hrós* or *raus.*]

roust, *n.* rust, 2018. [OE. *rūst.*]

rout, *n.* roar, 457. [Stem of ON. *rauta*, v.]

ruch(ch)e, *v. refl.* to turn (oneself), 303; proceed, 367. [OE. **ryccan*; cf. ON. *rykkja.*] See RICHCHE.

rudede, *pp.* reddened, fiery, 1695. [OE. *rudian.*]
rudel, *n.* curtain, 857. [OFr. *ridel.*]
ruful, *adj.* grievous, 2076. [OE. *hrēow* + *-full.*]
rungen; **runnen.** See RYNKANDE; RENNE.
runisch, *adj.* rough, violent, 457; **runyschly**, *adv.* 304, *432. [See note to 457.]
rurd(e), *n.* voice, 2337; noise, 1149, 1698, 1916, 2219. [OE. *réord.*]
rusched, *pa. t.* made a loud rushing noise, 2204; *r. on þat rurde*, went on with that rushing noise, 2219. [Echoic; cf. OFr. *russer*, OE. *hryscan.*]
ruþe, *v.* to bestir, 1558. [See note.]

S.

sabatounȝ, *n. pl.* broad-toed steel shoes, 574 n. [Prov. *sabató.*]
sadel, *n.* saddle, 164, 303, 437, 597, 2012, 2110. [OE. *sadol.*]
sadel, *v.* to saddle, 1128. [OE. *sadelian.*]
sadly, *adv.* steadily, firmly, 437, 1593; vigorously, 1937; sufficiently, long enough, 2409. [From OE. *sæd.*]
saf. See SAUE, WOWCHE.
sage, 531 (MS.). See FAGE.
saȝe, *n.* saying; prayer, 1202; *s. oþer seruyce*, word or deed, 1246; *pl.* words, 341. [OE. *sagu.*]
say, *v.* to say, tell, 84, 130, 1797, 1991, &c.; **sayn**, *pres. pl.* 1050; **sayd(e)**, *pa. t.* 200, 252, 673, &c.; *herde say*, heard tell, read in, 690. [OE. *secgan.*]
saylande, *pres. p.* sailing; flowing, 865. [OE. *seglian.*]
sayn. See SAY; SAYNT.
sayned, *pa. t.* blessed (with sign of cross), 761, 763, 1202. [OE. *segnian.*]
saynt, *adj.* Saint, 1644; **sayn**, *774, 1022, 1788. [OFr. *saint.*]
saynt, *n.* girdle, 2431; **sayn**, 589. [OFr. *ceint.*]
sake, *n.* in *for . . . sake*, for (one's) sake, 537, 997, 1862. [ON. *fyrir sakir.*]
sale, *n.* hall, 197, 243, 349, 558, 1005, 1372, 1651. [OE. *sæl*; OFr. *sale.*]
salue, *v.* to salute; wish good morning to, 1473. [OFr. *saluer.*]
salure, *n.* salt-cellar, 886. [OFr. *sal(i)ere*, with altered suffix.]
same, *adj.* same, 157, 1405, 1669; *pron.* in *of þe s.*, with the same, 881, 1640; (of) the same colour, 170. [ON. *samr.*]
same(n), *adv.* together, 50, 940, 1318; *al(le) s.*, (all) together, 363, 673, 744, 1345. [OE. *æt samne*; ON. *saman.*]
samen, *v. trans.* to gather, 1372; **samned**, *pa. t. intr.* came together, joined, 659. [OE. *samnian.*]
sanap, *n.* over-cloth to protect table-cloth, 886. [OFr. **sa(u)ve-nape.*]
sate. See SITTE.
saue(n), *v.* to preserve, keep safe, bring to salvation, 1879, 2040, 2139; *subj.* 1548, 2073. [OFr. *sa(u)ver.*]
saue, **saf**, *prep.* in *s. þat*, save that, 394, 2229. [OFr. *sauf.*]
sauer, *adj. compar.* safer (from temptation), 1202. [OFr. *sauf*, fem. *sauve.*]
sauered, *pp.* flavoured, 892. [OFr. *savourer.*]
sauerly, *adv.* with relish, 1937; to his liking, 2048. [From OFr. *savour.*]
saule, *n.* soul, 1916; **sawle**, 1879. [OE. *sāwol.*]
sawes, *n.* sauce, 893 n. [OFr. *sauce.*]
scade, **schadde.** See SCHEDE.
scaþe, *n.* injury, 2353; *hit is s.*, it is disastrous, 674. [ON. *skaði.*]
schaft(e), *n.* shaft (of arrow), 1458; handle, 2332; spear, 205. [OE. *scæft.*]
schafted, *pa. t.* beamed, 1467 n.
schaȝe, *n.* shaw, small wood, 2161 (see SIDE). [OE. *scaga.*]
schal, *v. 1 sg.* shall, will, 31, 288, 2094, &c.; shall be, 1544; *2 sg.* 374, 389, 675, &c.; *3 sg.* 374, 898, 925, 2487, &c.; *pl.* 255, 992, 1071, &c.; shall come, 2400; **schyn**, *pl.* (OE. *scylon*), 2401; *and schale*, and I will be, 1240.
schulde, *pa. t.* should, would, 238,

248, 398, 931, *1286, 2349, &c.; must go, 1671 n., 2084. [OE. *sceal*, *scólde*.]

schalk, *n.* man, 160, 424, 1454, 1776, 2061, 2268, 2372. [OE. *scealc*.]

scham(e), *n.* shame, 317, 2504; **schome**, 2372; *for schame*, for shame! 1530. [OE. *scamu*, *scomu*.]

schamed, *pa. t.* was embarrassed, 1189. [OE. *scamian*, impers.]

schankes, **schonkeȝ**, *n. pl.* legs, 431, 846; *vnder schankes*, on his feet, 160. [OE. *scanca*, *sconca*.]

schape, *v.* to make; give (account), 1626; contrive, 2138; *intr.* be arranged, 1210; **schop**, *pa. t.* appointed, 2328; **schaped**, **schapen**, *pp.* adorned, 1832; fashioned, 213, 662; arranged, 2340. [OE. *sceppan*.]

scharp, *adj.* sharp, 213, 1337, 2267, &c.; *as sb.* sharp blade, 424, 1593, 1902, 2313, 2332. [OE. *scearp*.]

schaterande, *pres. p.* dashing and breaking, 2083. [OE. **scaterian*.]

schaued, *pa. t.* scraped, cut away, 1331; **schauen**, *pp.* shaven, smooth, 1458. [OE. *scafan*, str.]

schawe. See SCHEWE.

schede, *v.* to sever, shed; *intr.* be shed, fall, 506, *956; **schadde**, *pa. t.* was shed, 727; **scade**, severed, 425. [OE. *scādan*, *scēadan*.]

schelde, *n.* shield, 205, 619, 637, 2061, &c.; **(s)cheldeȝ**, tough skin and flesh at shoulders, 1456 n.; slabs of boar's flesh, 1611, 1626. [OE. *scéld*.]

schemered, *pa. t.* shimmered, 772. [OE. *scimerian*.]

schende, *v.* to destroy, 2266. [OE. *scéndan*.]

schene, *adj.* bright, 662, 2314; *as sb.* bright blade, 2268. [OE. *scēne*.]

schere, *v.* to cut, 213; **scher**, *pa. t. pl.* 1337; **schorne**, *pp.* cut, 1378. [OE. *sceran*.]

schere. See CHER(E).

schewe, **schawe** (27), *v.* to look at, 2036; bring out for one, produce, 619, 2061; show, lay bare, declare, 27, 1378, 1626, 1880, 2256, 2498, 2504; offer, 315, 1526; *intr.* show, be seen, appear, 420, 507, 885. [OE. *scēawian*, *sceāwian*.]

schylde, *v.* to defend; *God schylde*, God forfend, 1776. [OE. *scíldan*.]

schyn. See SCHAL.

schinande, *pres. p.* shining, 269; **schon**, *pa. t.* 772, 956. [OE. *scīnan*.]

schynder, *v. trans. and intr.* cleave, burst asunder, 424, 1458, 1594. [OE. *syndrian*, infl. by words of similar sense in *sch*- (SCHEDE, *schiueren*, &c.).]

schyr(e), **schyree**, **schyire**, *adj.* bright, fair, white, 317, 506, 619, 772, 2083; *s. grece*, 425, 1378, 2313; *as sb.* (white) flesh, 1331, 2256; **schyrer**, *compar.* 956; **schyrly**, *adv.* clean, 1880. [OE. *scīr*.]

scho, *pron.* she, 969, 1259, 1550, 1555, 1556. [See *N. E. D.* s. v. *She*.] See HO.

scholes, *n. pl.* sollerets, shoes with long pointed toes, 160. [See note.]

schome, **schon**, **schonkeȝ**. See SCHAM, SCHINANDE, SCHANKES.

schore, *n.* shore; bank, 2083; steep rock, small crag, 2161; *vpon s.*, on the ground (by the river), 2332. [Cf. MDu., MLG. *schore*.]

schorne. See SCHERE.

schort, *adj.* short, 966. [OE. *scort*.]

schote, *v. trans.* to shoot (arrows), 1454; **schot**, *pa. t.* jerked, 2318; *intr.* shot, sprang, 317, 2314; **schotten**, *pl. trans.* 1167. [OE. *scēotan*, str.]

schowre, *n.* shower, 506. [OE. *scūr*.]

schouwe, **schowen**. See SCHWUE.

schrank(e), *pa. t.* shrank; flinched, winced, 2267, 2372; sank, penetrated, 425, 2313. [OE. *scrincan*.]

schrewe, *n.* villain, 1896. [OE. *scrēawa*, shrew-mouse; see *N. E. D.*]

schrof, *pa. t.* shrove, confessed, 1880. [OE. *scrīfan*.]

schuld(en). See SCHAL.

schulder, *n.* shoulder, 156, 1337, 1930, 2061, 2318, &c. [OE. *sculdor*.]

schunt, *n.* sudden jerk and swerve, 2268. [See next.]
schunt, *pa. t.* swerved, 1902; flinched, 2280. [Prob. rel. to OE. *scunian.*]
schwue, *v.* to thrust, 205; **schouwe,** *intr.* press, make one's way, 2161; schouwed, *pa. t.* 2083; **schowen,** *pl.* (OE. *scufon*), 1454. [OE. *scūfan.* str.]
scowtes, *n. pl.* jutting rocks, 2167. [ON. *skúti.*]
scrape, *v.* to scrape, paw the ground, 1571. [OE. *scrapian*; ON. *skrapa.*]
se, *v.* to see, look at, 226, 751, 963, 1160, &c.; sene (OE. *sēonne*), 712; *let se,* let me (us) see, 299, 414; **segh(e),** *pa. t.* 1632, 1705; **seȝ(e),** 672, 707, 1382, 1624, 1911, &c.; **syȝ(e),** 83 (*subj.*), 200, 1582. [OE. *sēon.*] See SEN(E).
sech(e), *v. trans.* to seek, look for, 266, 395, 549, 2169; *intr.* go, 1052; **soȝt,** *pa. t.* was making for, 1284, 1995; made (out) at, 1438; came, went, 685, 2493. [OE. *sēcan, sōhte.*]
seche. See SUCH.
sedeȝ, *n. pl.* seeds; seeding grasses and plants, 517. [OE. *sǣd.*]
seg(g)e, *n.* siege, 1, 2525. [OFr. *sege.*]
segg(e), *n.* man, knight, 96, 115, 226, 574 (*gen.*), 1882 (priest), &c.; in appos. to *he,* 763; *voc.* 394; *vch s.,* everybody, 1987; *pl.* men, people, 673, 822, 882, &c. [OE. (verse) *secg.*]
segh, seȝ. See SE, SEYE.
seye, *v.* to go, 1879; **seȝen,** *pp.* come, 1958. [OE. *sīgan*; *sǣgan,* trans.]
seker. See SIKER.
selden, *adv.* seldom, 499. [OE. *seldan.*]
sele, *n.* happiness, good fortune, 1938, 2409, 2422. [OE. *sǣl.*]
self, seluen, *adj.* same, very, 751, 2147; *as sb.* self, 2156, 2301; *þe burne(s) s., Krystes s.,* the knight (&c.) himself, 51, 1616, 2377. [OE. *self(a).*] See ȝE, HE, I, ÞAY, WE.
selly, *adj.* marvellous; excellent, *1962; strange, 2170; *as sb.* wonder, marvel, 28, 475; *pl.* 239; **sellokest,** *adj. superl.* 1439; **selly,** *adv.* exceedingly, very, 1194; **sellyly,** 963, 1803. [OE. *sel(d)-lic, -lucost*; *sellīce,* adv.]
selure, *n.* (ceiling), canopy, 76. [L. *cēlātura,* OFr. **cel(e)ure.*]
semb(e)launt, *n.* appearance, looks, 148; sign of his feelings, 468; (kindly) demeanour, manner, 1273, 1658, 1843. [OFr. *semblant.*]
semblé, *n.* company, throng, 1429. [Shortened from OFr. *assemblee.*]
seme, *adj.* seemly; fair, excellent, 1085; **semly(ch),** *adv.* becomingly, excellently, 865, 882, 888; pleasantly, sweetly, 916, 1658, 1796. [ON. *sœmr.*]
seme, *v.* to beseem, suit, 1929; *impers.* 679, 848; seem fitting, 73, 1005; seem, appear, 201, 235, 840, 866, 1827, 1847, &c.; *semed,* was to be seen, 1551. [ON. *sóma* (pa. t. subj. *sœmdi*) infl. by prec.]
semeȝ, *n. pl.* ornamental stitching about seams, *or* embroidered stuff laid over them, 610, 2028. [OE. *sēam.*]
semly, *adj.* seemly, fitting, 348, 1198; comely, fair, 685; *as sb.* in *þat s.,* that fair knight, 672; **semloker,** *compar. as sb.* one more fair, 83; **semlyly,** *adv.* becomingly, 622. [SEME + OE. *-lic, -lucor*; ON. *sœmiligr.*]
sen(e), *adj.* visible; plain to see, 148; plain, clear, 341; *used as pp. of* SE, seen, 197, 239, 468, 475. [OE. *gesēne,* adj. (late as pp.).]
sendal, *n.* a kind of thin rich silk, 76. [OFr. *cendal.*]
sende, *pa. t.* sent, 2362; *subj.* should send, 1837. [OE. *sendan.*]
sene. See SE.
sengel, *adj.* single, all alone, 1531. [OFr. *sengle.*]
serched, *pa. t.* searched, examined, 1328. [OFr. *cerchier.*]
sere, *adj.* separate, individual, 1985; various, 124, 889; several, 761, 822; *fele sere,* many and various (women), 2417; *adv.* in each case, 632 n.; *sere twyes,* on two separate occasions,

1522. [ON. *sér* (dat. sg.) for oneself, separately.]
serlepes, *adv.* separately, in turn, 501. [Prec. + OE. *-lēpes*, in *sundor-lēpes*.]
sertayn, *adv.* assuredly, indeed, 174. [OFr. *certain*, adj.]
seruaunt, *n.* servant, 976, 1240, 1971, 2139, &c. [OFr. *servant*.]
serue(n), *v.*[1] to serve (God), 724; wait on, 827, 851; *s. of* (*with*), serve with, 482, 888, 1640; *pp.* served (with food), 61, 85, 114; served (up), 135, 1006, 1559; *intr.* wait at table, 1651; *s. aboute*, wait on, 1986. [OFr. *servir*.]
serue, *v.*[2] to deserve, 1380. [Shortened from DESERUE.]
seruyce, seruyse, *n.* serving, service, 1246, 1985; (at table) 130; (in church), 940; *s. of þat syre &c.*, celebration of Christmas, *751. [OFr. *servise*.]
sese, *v.* to seize, take, 822, 1083, 1330, 1825, 2407. [OFr. *seisir*.]
sesed, *pp.* ceased; *watȝ s.*, had come to an end, 1, 134, 2525. [OFr. *cesser*.]
sesoun, *n.* season, 501, 516, 1382; due time, 1958, 2085. [OFr. *se(i)son*.]
sesounde, *pp.* seasoned. 889. [OFr. *saisonner, sesoner*.]
sete, *adj.* fitting, excellent, 889. [OE. *(*ge*)*sǣte*; cf. *andsǣte*.]
sete, *n.* seat, place at table, 72, 493. [ON. *sæti*.]
sete(n). See SITTE.
sette(e), *v.* to set, &c.; **sett(e),** *pa. t.* 422, 574, &c.; *pp.* 148. To set in a seat, 1083; set, put, 124, 1607, 2230, 2332, &c.; lay table, 1651; establish, found, 14; plant, 1593, 1937; make, 1883; do, 1246; *refl.* seat oneself, sit down, 437, 1193, 1479. *S. at lyȝt*, were to esteem lightly, 1250; *s. hym on*, rush at, 1589; *s. on*, called down on, 1721; apply (yourself) to, 372; *s. solace*, made merry, 1318; *s. in* (*þe*) *waye*, put on the right road, 1077, 1971. [OE. *settan*.]
settel, *n.* seat, chair, 882. [OE. *setl*.]
seuen, *adj.* 613, 1382. [OE. *seofon*.]
seuer, *v.* to sever (*or intr.*), 2312; *intr.* separate, 1958; depart (from), 1797; part (with), 1987. [OFr. *sevrer*.]
sewe, *n.* broth, stew, 124, 889, 892. [OE. *sēaw*.]
sidbordeȝ, *n. pl.* side-tables, 115 n. [OE. *sīd-* + *bord*.]
syde, *adj.* long, dangling, 2431. [OE. *sīd*.]
side, syde, *n.* side, flank, 110, 152, 771, 1338, 1356, 1632, 1830, &c.; *at* (*bi, in*) . . . *side*, at the side of, beside, 1421, 1431, 1697, 2144, 2161 (orig. with gen., cf. 589, 2486); *in no s.*, in no direction, 659, 2170. [OE. *sīde*.] See BISYDE.
syfle, *v.* to whistle, blow gently, 517. [OFr. *sifler*.]
syȝ(e). See SE.
syȝt, *n.* sight, 1721; *se wyth* (*in*) *s.*, set eyes on, 197, 226, 1705; *in siȝt*, to see, 28. [OE. *gesihþ, -siht*.]
syke, *v.* to sigh, 672, 753, 1796; **sykyngeȝ,** *n. pl.* sighs, 1982. [OE. *sīcan*.]
syker, seker, *adj.* sure; assured, 265; true, 403; trusty, 96, 111, 115, 2493; *in a s. wyse*, securely, 2048; *adv.* certainly, 1637. [OE. *sicor*.]
siker, *v.* to assure; *s. my* (*bi þi*) *trawþe*, give my (your) word, 394, 1673. [From prec.]
sylence, *n.* silence, 243. [OFr. *silence*.]
silk(e), sylk(e), *n.* silk, 854, 959, 1832, 5035, 2431; silken thing, 1846; *as adj.* 159, 164, 589. [OE. *seolc*.]
sylkyn, *adj.* silken, 610. [OE, *silcen*.]
sille, *n.* sill, flooring; *on s.*, in the hall; *cf.* FLET. [OE. *syll*.]
syluerin, *adj.* silver, 886; *as sb.* in *þe sylueren*, the silver (things), *124. [OE. *silfren*.]
symple, *adj.* plain (food), 503; of no great value, 1847. [OFr. *simple*.]
syn, *conj.* since, 919, 1892, 2440 (*with subj.*); *syn þat*, 2320; *as prep.* 24. [Reduction of SIÞEN.]

syng(e), *v.* to sing, 472, 509, 923. [OE. *singan.*]
syngne, *n.* sign, taken, 625, 2164, 2433. [OFr. *signe.*]
synne, *adv.* since then, 19. [Extended from SYN on anal. of ÞENNE, &c.]
synne, *n.* sin, 1774. [OE. *synn.*]
syre, *n.* lord, knight, 685, 751, 1083; **sir,** *as title before name,* 377, 552, 554, &c.; *polite voc.,* 276, 415, 477, 811, 1481, &c.; *beau sir,* 1222; *sir swete,* 2237. [OFr. *sire.*]
sister-sunes, *n. pl.* nephews, 111. [ON. *systra-synir.*] See HALF-SUSTER.
sitte, sytte, *v.* to sit (down, at table), 110, 906, 936, 1001, 2110, &c.; sit idle, 88; sit here, 290, 1531; be throned, 256, 2442; **sate,** *pa. t.* 339; **sete(n),** 242, 882, 940, 1003, 1402; *pp.* 1522; *sete on,* fitted, 865. [OE. *sittan.*]
syþe, *n.* scythe, 2202. [OE. *sigþe.*]
syþeȝ, *n. pl.* times, occasions, 632, 656, 761, 982; *bi s.,* at times, 17; **syþe,** *dat. pl.* 1868. [OE. *sīþ.*]
siþen, syþen, *adv.* afterwards, next, then, 6, 43, 115, 194, 791, 1559, &c.; since, 1094; *long s.,* since long ago, 1440; *conj.* since, 1, 1642, 2394, 2524; (*causal*) 358, 1234; now that, 2094. [OE. *siþþan.*] See SYN(NE).
skayned (*of*), *pp.* grazed (by), 2167. [ON. *skeina.*]
skere, *adj.* pure, 1261. [ON. *skær-r.*]
skete, *adv.* quickly, 19. [ON. *skjótt.*]
skyfted, *pp.* shifted, alternated, 19. [ON. *skifta.*]
skyl(le), *n.* reason, 1509; *bi þis s.,* as follows, 1296. [ON. *skil.*]
skyrteȝ, *n. pl.* skirts, lower part of flowing garment or covering, 601, 865. [ON. *skyrta.*]
skweȝ, *n. pl.* clouds, 2167. [ON. *ský,* earlier **skiuj-.*]
slade, *n.* valley, 1159, 2147. [OE. *slæd.*]
slayn, *pp.* slain, 729, 1854, 1950; **slowe,** *pa. t. sg.* slew, 1321. [OE. *slægen*; *slōgon,* pa. t. pl.]
slaked, *pa. t.* slackened; were stilled, 244. [OE. *slacian.*]
sleȝe, *adj.* (made with) cunning, 797, *893; **sleȝly,** *adv.* (made) warily, 1182. [ON. *slœgr.*] See VNSLEȜE.
sleȝt, slyȝt, *n.* skill, 1542; device, 1858; *for s. vpon erþe,* by any means, 1854; *sleȝteȝ of,* acts of practised skill in, 916. [ON. *slœgð.*]
slentyng, *n.* rushing flight, 1160. [ON. *sletta,* earlier **slenta.*]
slepe, *n.* sleep, 1095; *vpon slepe,* asleep, 244. [OE. *slēp.*]
slepe, *v.* to sleep, 1686, 1731, 1733, 1746, 2007; **sleped, slepte,** *pa. t.* 729, 1190. [OE. *slēpan.*]
sleper, *n.* sleeper, 1209. [OE. *slēpere.*]
slete, *n.* sleet, 729. [OE. **slīet-,* **slēt*; cf. MLG. *slōte.*]
slyde, *v. intr.* to glide, steal, 1209; **slode,** *pa. t. sg.* in *s. in slomeryng,* slept softly on, 1182. [OE. *slīdan.*]
slyȝt. See SLEȜT.
slypped, *pp.* slipped; escaped, 1858; fallen, 244; **slypte,** *pa. t.* were loosed, 1160. [Cf. MLG., MDu. *slippen.*]
slyt, *pa. t.* slit, 1330. [OE. **slittan.*]
slokes, *imper.* stop, enough! 412. [ON. *slokna*; cf. BAYÞEN, 327 n.]
slomeryng, *n.* slumber, 1182. [From OE. **slūmerian*; cf. *slūma.*]
slot, *n.* hollow above breast-bone at base of throat, 1330, 1593. [OFr. *esclot.*]
slowe. See SLAYN.
smal(e), *adj.* small, slender, 144, 1207; fine (in texture), 76. [OE. *smæl.*]
smartly, *adv.* promptly, 407. [From OE. *smeart,* sharp.]
smeþely, *adv.* gently, pleasantly, 1789. [From OE. *smēþe.*]
smyle, *v.* to smile, 1789; **smylyng** *n.,* 1763. [OE. **smīlan*; cf. OHG. *smīlan.*]
smyte, *v.* to smite, 205, 2260; **smeten,** *pa. t. pl. intr.* in *s. into merþe,* fell quickly to merry speech, 1763; **smyten,** *pp.* 407. [OE. *smītan,* smear.]
smolt, *adj.* gentle, 1763. [OE. *smolt.*]

smoþe, *adj.* gentle; courteous, 1763; **smoþely**, *adv.* 407. [OE. *smōþ.*]
snayped, *pa. t.* nipped cruelly, 2003. [ON. *sneypa.*]
snart, *adv.* bitterly, 2003. [ON. *snarr*, neut. and adv. *snart.*]
snaw(e), *n.* snow, 956, 2003, 2088, 2234, 2315. [OE. *snāw.*]
snyrt, *pa. t.* snicked, cut lightly, 2312. [Cf. ON. *snerta*, str.]
snitered, *pa. t.* (snow) came shivering down, 2003. [Cf. Norw. dial. *snitra*, shiver with cold.]
so, *adv.* so, thus, in this way, this, that, 36, 200, 680, 998, 1108, 1259, 1847, 2281, &c.; then, 218; (that being) so, *1304, 2296; to such an extent, so, 59, 89, *282, 1048, 1728, 1848, 2140, &c.; so too, 2365; such, 1761, 2454; *intensive*, so, 103, 258, &c.; *neuer so*, no matter how, 2129; *half so*, 2321; *so . . . to*, so as to, 291; *so þat*, *so . . . þat*, 60, 717, 1414, &c.; without *þat*, 139, &c.; *so . . . as*, as (so) . . . as, 199, 592, 1510, &c.; as . . . as if, 612, 1883; *with indef. prons.* &c., *384, 1107, 1109, 1167, 1406, 1409, 1851. [OE. *swā.*]
soberly, *adv.* soberly, with propriety, 940, 1278; without exaggeration, 2051. [From OFr. *sobre.*]
soft(e), *adj.* soft, gentle, unwarlike, 271, 510, 516; *adv.* softly, 1929; in comfort, 1121, 1687; **sof(t)ly**, gently, quietly, 1193, 1479; in a whisper, 915. [OE. *sōfte.*]
soȝt. See SECHE.
soiorne, *n.* sojourn, stay, 1962. [OFr. *sojo(u)rn.*]
soio(u)rne, *v.* to stay, 2409; lodge, stable, 2048. [OFr. *sojo(u)rner.*]
solace, *n.* pleasure, delight, 510, 1085, 1318; kindness, 1985; *with s.*, joyously, 1624. [OFr. *solas.*]
somer, *n.* summer, 510, 516. [OE. *sumor.*]
son, sun, *n.* son, 113, 1064. [OE. *sunu.*]
sone, *adv.* at once, quickly, 433, 521, 534, 807, 935, 1289, 1309, 1872, 1906; soon, 884, 1421, 1704, 2085, 2171; *s. as*, as soon as, 864. [OE. *sōna.*]
song, *n.* song, 1654. [OE. *sáng, sóng.*]
sop, *n.* morsel of food, light meal, 1135 (*cf.* 1690). [OE. *sopp.*]
soper, *n.* supper, 1400, 1654. [OFr. *soper.*]
sore, *adj.* painful, grievous, 1793, 2116, 2346. [OE. *sār.*]
soré, *adj.* (was) grieved, 1896, 1987. [OE. *sārig.*]
sorȝe, *n.* sorrow, 2383, 2415; imprecation, 1721. [OE. *sorg.*]
sostnaunce, *n.* sustenance, food, 1095. [OFr. *sostenance.*]
soþ(e), *adj.* true, *and n.* (the) truth, a fact, 348, 355, 1385, 1488, 2457, &c.; *by his s.*, on his word, 1825, 2051; *for s.*, truly, 403, 2094; indeed, 415, 1222, 1793, 2302, &c.; *adv.* with truth, 84; certainly, 2110. **soþly**, *adv.* with truth, 673; truly, 976, 1095, 2362. [OE. *sōþ, sōþlīce.*]
soþen, *pp.* boiled, 892. [OE. *sēoþan*, pp. *soden*; ON. *soðinn.*]
souerayn, *n.* sovereign; liege lady, 1278. [OFr. *soverain.*]
sounde, *quasi-sb.* in *al in sounde*, in safety, 2489. [*in* repres. *ge-* in OE. *ge-súnd*, adj.; cf. FERE.]
sounder, *n.* herd of swine, 1440. [OE. *sunor.*]
soundyly, *adv.* soundly, 1991. [OE. *gesúndlīce.*]
soure, *adj.* sour, unpleasant, *or* sore, 963. [OE. *sūr*; *sūr-ēge*, bleared.]
sourquydrye, *n.* pride, 311; **surquidré**, 2457. [OFr. *surcuiderie.*]
sowme, *n.* number, 1321. [OFr. *summe.*]
space, *n.* space, short while; *in space*, soon after, 1418; soon, straightway, *1199, 1503. [OFr. *(e)space.*]
spare, *adj.* sparing; *vpon s. wyse*, without undue pressing, tactfully, 901. [OE. *spær.*]
spare, *v.* to spare, 1935. [OE. *sparian.*]

sparlyr, *n.* calf (of leg), 158. [OE. *spær-līra.*]

sparred, *pa. t.* sprang, *1444 (1442 n.).

sparþe, *n.* battle-axe, 209. [ON. *sparða.*]

spech(e), *n.* speech, conversation, 314, 410, 918, 1292; *pl.* expressions, words, 1261, 1778. [OE. *sp(r)ēc.*]

specially, *adv.* particularly, 2093. [From OFr. (*e*)*special.*]

specialté, *n.* partiality; fondness, 1778. [OFr. (*e*)*specialté.*]

spede, speed, *n.* success; profit, 918; speed (*good s.*, at great speed), 1444. [OE. *spēd.*]

spede, *v. trans.* to prosper, bless, 762, 1292, 2120; further, get done, 2216; *intr.* in *spedeȝ better*, will be better off, 410; **sped(ed),** *pa. t. refl.* sped, hastened, 979, *1444. [OE. (*ge*)*spēdan.*]

spedly, *adv.* with good result, to our good fortune, 1935. [OE. *spēd-līce.*]

speke(n), *v.* to speak, 226, 544, 1242, 2302, &c.; **spek(ed),** *pa. t.* 1288, 2329; **speken,** *pl.* 1117; **spoken,** *pp.* agreed upon, 1935. [OE. *sp(r)ecan.*]

spelle, *n.* speech, words, 1199; *expoun in s.* describe, 209; *deme hit with s.*, say which, 2184. [OE. *spell.*]

spelle, *v.* to say, 2140. [OE. *spellian.*]

spende, *v.* to spend; lose, 2113; utter, 410. [OE. *spéndan.*]

spenet (*on*), *pa. t.* were fastened, clung (to), 158; **spend,** *pp.* fastened, 587. [ON. *spenna.*]

spenne, *n.* green-sward, ground; *in spenne*, there, 1074. [See note.]

spenné, *n.* spinney; (?) thorn-hedge, 1709, 1896. [OFr. *espinei.*]

spenne-fote, *adv.* striking out with the feet, 2316 n. [Stem of OE. *spinnan*, kick + *fōt.*]

spere, *n.* spear, 269, 983, 2066, 2143; *gen.* 2316. [OE. *spere.*]

sperre, *v.* to strike, 670. [OE. *sperran.*]

spetos, *adj.* cruel, 209. [Shortened from OFr. *despitous.*] See SPYT.

spyce, *n.* spice, 892, 979. [OFr. (*e*)*spice.*]

spye, *v.* to look out for, 2093; get a sight of, 1896; inquire, 901 (cf. *York Plays*, xxi. 23). [OFr. (*e*)*spier.*]

spyt, *n.* doing harm, 1444. [Shortened from OFr. *despit.*]

spoken. See SPEKE.

sponeȝ, *n. pl.* spoons, 886. [OE. *spōn*, chip; ON. *spón-n*, chip, spoon.]

sporeȝ. See SPUREȜ.

sprenged, *pa. t.* sprang; (day) broke, 1415, 2009. [OE. *sprengan.*]

sprent, *pa. t.* leapt, 1896. [ON. *spretta*, earlier **sprenta.*]

sprit, *pa. t.* sprang, 2316. [OE. *sprytian*, *spring, sprout.]

sprong, *pa. t. sg.* sprang, 670; **sprange,** *pl.* 1778. [OE. *springan.*]

spureȝ, *n. pl.* spurs, 158, 670; **sporeȝ,** 587. [OE. *spura, spora.*]

spured, *pp.* asked, 901; **spuryed** (*after*), 2093. [OE. *spyrian* (*æfter*).]

stabeled, *pa. t.* put in a stable, 823. [OFr. (*e*)*stabler.*]

stabled, *pp.* established; agreed upon, 1060. [OFr. (*e*)*stablir.*]

stablye, *n.* ring of beaters, 1153 n. [OFr. *establie.*]

stad, *pp.* placed; put down (in writing), 33; present, 644; standing there, 2137. [ON. *steðja*; pp. *staddr.*]

staf, *n.* staff, 214; **staue,** *dat.* club 2137. [OE. *stæf.*]

staf-ful, *adj.* cram-full, 494. [Rel. obscurely to prec.]

stayne, *v.* to colour, 170. [ON. *steina.*]

stalke, *v.* to walk cautiously, 237; stalk, 2230. [OE. *stalcian.*]

stal(l)e, *n.* standing; *in s.*, standing up, 104, 107. [OE. *stall*; *in stalle.*]

stalworth, *adj.* stalwart, 846; *as sb.* 1659. [OE. *stǣlwyrþe.*]

stange, *n.* pole, 1614. [ON. *stǫng.*]

stapled, *pp.* fastened, *or* strengthened, with staples, 606 n. [ME. *stapel*, staple; prob. same as OE. *stapol*, post.]

starande, *pres. p.* staring; blazing, 1818. [OE. *starian.*]
start(e), *v.* to start (aside), flinch, 1567, 2286; leap forward, 2063; *pa. t.* sprang, 431; swerved, 1716. [OE. **stertan*; cf. *styrtan.*]
statut, *n.* statute; solemn agreement, 1060. [OFr. *statut.*]
staue. See STAF.
sted(e), *n.* steed, 176, 281, 670, 823; *on stedes to ryde*, among knights, 260. [OE. *stēda.*]
sted(de), *n.* place; *in (þis) s.*, here, there, 439, 2213, 2323. [OE. *stede.*]
stek. See STOKEN, *pp.*[2]
stel(e), *n.*[1] steel, weapon (of steel), 211, 426, 570, 575; *as adj.* 580. **stel-bawe,** *n.* stirrup-iron, 435 (cf. 2060). **stel-gere,** *n.* armour, 260. [OE. *stēle*; + OE. *boga*; + ON. *gervi.*]
stele, *n.*[2] stem, haft, 214, 2230. [OE. *stela.*]
stele, *v. intr.* to steal, 1710; **stel,** *pa. t. sg.* 1191; **stollen,** *pp.* as *adj.* stealthy, sly, 1659. [OE. *stelan.*]
stem(m)ed, *pa. t. intr.* stopped, halted, 230, 1117. [ON. *stemma.*]
steppe, *v.* to step, 435, 570, 2060; *wk. pa. t.* 1191. [OE. *steppan*, str.]
steropes. See STIROP.
steuen, *n.*[1] voice, 242, 2336. [OE. *stefn*, f.]
steuen, *n.*[2] appointment, tryst, 1060, 2194, 2213, 2238; appointed day, 2008. [ON. *stefna*; OE. *stefn*, m.]
stif(fe), styf, *adj.* stiff; unweakened, 431; unflinching, 294; stout, strong, firm, 176, 214, 846, 2099, &c.; fearless, bold, 104, 322, 823, 2369, &c.; *s. and strong*, brave (story), 34; *superl.* 260, 1567; *adv.* vigorously, 671; **stifly,** *adv.* strongly, 606; fearlessly, 287; undaunted, 1716. [OE. *stīf.*]
stiȝtel, styȝtel, *v.* to order, control; deal with, 2137; rule, be master, 2213; *s. in stalle*, stand, 104; *s. þe vpon*, limit yourself to, 2252. [OE. **stiht-lian*; cf. *stihtan.*]
stille, *adj. and adv.* (stand) still, 2252, 2293; without stirring, undisturbed, 1367, 1687, 1994; secret(ly), 1188, 1659; privately, 1085; between ourselves, 2385; silent (and motionless), 301 (*compar.*), 1996. **stilly,** *adv.* softly, secretly, 1117, 1191, 1710. [OE. *stille, stillīce.*] See STON.
stirop, *n.* stirrup, 2060; **steropes,** *pl.* 170. [OE. *stig-rāp.*]
styþly, *adv.* stoutly, undismayed, 431. [OE. *stīþ-līce.*]
stoffed, *pp.* stuffed, 606 n. [OFr. (*e*)*s-toffer.*]
stoken, *pp.*[1] shut, 782. [OE. **stecan* in *bestecan*, perh. same as next.]
stoken, *pp.*[2] stuck; set down (in writing), 33; *s. of*, full up, fully provided with, 494; *s. me*, imposed on me, 2194; **stek,** *pa. t. intr.* clung, fitted close, 152. [OE. **stecan.*]
stollen. See STELE, *v.*
stonde, *v.* to stand, 107, 1058, 2252, &c.; stand and take from, 294, 2286; **stod(e),** *pa. t.* 170, 237, 432, 1951, &c.; waited, 2063; went and stood, 322; *subj.* would have been present, 1768; *stondande alofte*, standing out, clear-set (*or* shining), 1818. [OE. *stándan, stóndan.*]
ston(e), *n.* stone, 789, 2166; (stony) ground, 2230, 2282 (*pl.*); pavement, 2063; gem, 162, 193, 1818, 2027, &c.; *stylle as þe s.*, stock-still, 2293. **ston-fyr,** *n.* sparks struck out of stones, 671; **ston-stil,** *adj.* in stony silence (and stockstill), 242. [OE. *stān.*]
stor(e), *adj.* mighty, 1923; strong, severe, 1291. [ON. *stórr.*]
stori, *n.* story, 34. [OFr. (*e*)*storie.*]
stoundeȝ, *n. pl.* times, 1517; *bi s.*, at times, 1567. [OE. *stúnd.*]
stouned, stowned, stonyed, *pa. t.* astonished, amazed, 301, 1291; *pp.* 242. [OFr. *esto*(*u*)*ner.*]
stoutly, *adv.* proudly, valiantly, vigorously, 1153, 1364, 1614, 1923. [From OFr. (*e*)*stout.*]

stray. See ON-STRAY.

strayne, *v.* to restrain, manage, 176. [OFr. *estreindre, estreign-.*]

strayt, *adj.* tight, close-fitting, 152. [OFr. (*e*)*streit.*]

strakande, *pres. p.* sounding call (on horn), 1364 n., 1923. [Not known.]

straunge, *adj.* strange, 709, 713. [OFr. (*e*)*strange.*]

streȝt, *adj.* straight, 152. [OE. *streccan,* pp. *streht.*]

strenkþe, *n.* strength, 1496. [OE. *strengþ.*]

stryde, *v.* to stride, 1584, 2232; *s. alofte,* stride into the saddle, 435, 2060. [OE. *strīdan.*]

strye, *v.* to destroy, 2194. [Shortened from OFr. *destruire.*]

stryf, *n.* resistance, 2323. [OFr. (*e*)*strif.*]

strike, stryke, *v.* to strike, 287, 331, 2099, 2305; **stroke,** *pa. t. intr.* was struck, sprang, 671. [OE. *strīcan.*]

stryþ(þ)e, *n.* stance, 2305; *stif on þe s.,* standing firm, 846. [(?) Rel. to OE. *stride,* stride, pace.]

strok(e), *n.* stroke, blow, 287, 294, 1460, 2252, 2286, 2323, 2327, 2341. [OE. **strāc,* rel. to STRIKE.]

stroke, *v.* to stroke, 334, 416. [OE. *stroccian,* rather than *strācian*; cf. rhyme 416, and 965 n.]

stronge, *adj.* strong, 34 (see STIF), 1028, 1618. [OE. *strang, strong.*]

strothe, *n.* small wood; *attrib.* or *gen.* 1710 n. [ON. *storð.*]

stubbe, *n.* stock, stump, 2293. [OE. *stybb, stubb.*]

study, *n.* study, silent thought, 2369. [OFr. (*e*)*studie.*]

studie, *v.* to look carefully (to discover), 230; watch intently, 237. [OFr. (*e*)*studier.*]

stuffe, *n.* stuff, 581. [OFr. *estoffe.*]

sture, *v.* to brandish (to try its weight), 331. [OE. *styrian.*]

sturn(e), *adj.* grim, of forbidding appearance, stern, 143, 334, 846, 2099, 2136; serious, 494; *as sb.* grim knight, 214; **sturnely,** *adv.* 331. [OE. *styrne,* **stiorne*; *styrnelīce.*]

sturtes, *n. pl.* 171 n. [OE. *steort,* tail.]

such(e), seche (1543), *adj.* and *pron.* such, so great, of the same kind, 92, 239, 396, 1631, 2528, &c.; such (as), as great (as if), 1166, 1721; with *þat,* 1011, 1426, 1658; *þat* omitted, 46, 1321, 1393 n. [OE. *swelc, swylc.*]

sue, *v.* to follow, pursue, 501, 510, 1467, 1705; **sweȝ,** *3 sg.* 1562. [OFr. *suir.*]

suffer, *v.* to suffer, permit, 1967; submit, 2040. [OFr. *suffrir.*]

sum, summe, *adj.* some, 28, 93, 1301, 1527, 2119, &c.; *pron.* 247, 891, 1328, &c. **sumquat,** *n.* something, 1799; *adv.* somewhat, 86. **sumquyle,** *adv.* once upon a time, 625; **sumwhyle,** sometimes, 720, 721. **sumtyme,** *adv.* formerly, 2449. [OE. *sum.*] See WHAT, WHYLE.

sumned, *pp.* summoned, 1052. [OFr. *sumondre,* infl. by OE. *somnian.*]

sun. See SON.

sunder, *adv.* in *in sunder,* asunder, 1563. [OE. *on-sundran*; ON. *í sundr.*]

sunder, *v. trans.* separate, 1354; **sundred,** *pa. t. intr.* 659. [From prec.; cf. ON. *sundra,* OE. *syndrian.*]

sunne, *n.* sun, 520, 1467, &c. [OE. *sunne.*]

sure, *adj.* trusty, 588; **surely,** *adv.* securely, 1883. [OFr. *s(e)ur.*]

surfet, *n.* transgression, 2433. [OFr. *surfait, surfet.*]

surkot, *n.* surcoat, flowing outer robe of rich stuff, 1929. [OFr. *surcote.*]

surquidré. See SOURQUYDRYE.

sute, *n.* suit; *of a sute, of folȝande s.,* to match, 191, 859; swete, in *of his hors s.,* to match his horse, 180; *in swete,* following suit, 2518. [OFr. *seute, suite.*]

swange, *n.* middle, waist, 138, 2034. [ON. *svangi.*]

swap, *v.* to strike a bargain, swap, 1108. [Same as ME. *swappen,* strike.]

sware, *adj.* squarely built, 138. [OFr. (*e*)*square*, n.; (*e*)*squarré*, adj.]
sware, *v.* to answer, 1108 n., 1756, 1793, 2011. [ON. *svara.*]
sweȝ. See SUE.
sweȝe, *v.* to sink; **sweȝe,** *pa. t. str.* stooped, 1796; **sweyed,** *wk.* fell, rushed, 1429. [See *N.E.D* s.v. *Sway.*]
swenge, *v.* to rush, hasten, 1439, 1615; come suddenly, 1756. [OE. *swengan.*]
swere, *v.* to swear, 403, 2051, 2122; **swere,** *pa. t.* 1825. [OE. *swerian.*]
swete, *adj.* sweet, lovely, 1204; *as sb.* fair lady, 1222; (*sir*) *swete*, good sir, 1108, 2237; *adv.* sweetly, 1757. **swetely,** *adv.* with delight, 2034. [OE. *swēte*; *swētelīce.*]
swete. See SUTE.
sweþle, *v.* to wind, wrap, 2034. [From OE. *sweþel*, wrapping.]
sweuenes, *n. pl.* dreaming, 1756. [OE. *swefn*, often pl. with sg. sense.]
swyer, *n.* esquire, 824. [OFr. *esquier.*]
swyft(e), *adv.* swiftly, 1354, *1825. [OE. *swift*, adj.]
swyn, *n.* swine, boar, 1439, 1467, 1562, 1589, 1615, 1628, 1632. [OE. *swīn.*]
swynge, *v.* to rush, 1562 n. [OE. *swingan.*]
swyre, *n.* neck, 138, 186, 957. [OE. *swīra.*]
swyþe, *adv.* greatly, 1866; earnestly, 1860; hard, 1897; quickly, 8, 815, 1424, 2034, 2259; **swyþely,** very much, 1479. [OE. *swīþe, swīþlīce.*]
swoghe, *adj.* swooning, dead (silence), 243. [OE. *ge-swōgen.*]
sworde, *n.* sword, 2319. [OE. *swurd.*]

T

ta. See TAKE.
tabil, table, *n.* (i) table, 112, *884, &c.; *hyȝe t.*, high table on dais, 108, 2462; *see* ROUNDE: (ii) projecting cornice-moulding, 789. [OFr. *table.*]
tacche, tach(ch)e, *v.* to attach, fasten, 219, 579, 2176, 2512. [OFr. *atachier.*]
taȝtte. See TECHE.
tayl, *n.* tail, 191, 1726. [OE. *tægl.*]
tayles, *n. pl.* notches (on stick), tally of deer slain, 1377. [OFr. *taille.*]
taysed, *pp.* harassed; driven, 1169. [See *N.E.D.* s.v. *Teise*, v.[2]]
tayt, *adj.* merry, 988; nimble, 1377. [ON. *teitr.*]
take, *v.* to take, 682, 1823, &c.; **tas,** *3 sg.* 2305; **tan,** *pl.* 1977, 1920; **take, ta(s),** *imper.* 413, 897, 1390, 2357, &c.; **tok(en),** *pa. t.* 709, 1333, 2243, &c.; **taken,** *pp.* 2448; **tan(e),** 1396, 1978, &c.; **tone,** 2159. To take, accept, receive, 709, 828, 897, 1690, 1811, &c.; capture, 1210; detect, 2488, 2509; acquire, 2448; assign, 1966; commit, 2159; *t. to yourseluen*, take upon yourself, 350; *t. to myself*, presume, 1540; *take at*, (I) will take from, 383; *tan*, circumstanced, 1811; *tan on honde*, undertaken, 490. [ON. *taka.*]
takles, *n. pl.* equipment, gear, 1129. [MLG. *takel.*]
tale, *n.* talk, speech, word(s), 638, 1236, 1301, 2133; account, report, 1057, 1626, 2124; story, 93, 1541, 2483. [OE. *talu.*]
talenttyf, *adj.* desirous, 350. [OFr. *talentif.*]
talk, *n.* speech, 1486. [From next.]
talk(ke), *v.* to talk, speak (of), 108, 2133, 2372; **talkyng,** *n.* conversation, 917, 977. [OE. **talcian*, rel. to TALE.]
tame, *adj.* tame, 2455. [OE. *tam.*]
tapit, *n.* tapestry, figured cloth; as wall-hanging, 858; as carpet, 77, 568. [OE. *teppet*; OFr. *tapit.*]
tap(p)e, *n.* tap, knock, 406, 2357. [Echoic; cf. OFris. *tap*; OFr. *taper*, v.]
tary, *v.* to delay, 624, 1726. [See *N.E.D.* s. v. *Tarry.*]
tars, *n.* Tharsia (Turkestan); silk of Tharsia, 571, 858. [OFr. *Tarse.*]
tas. See TAKE.
tassel, *n.* tassel, 219. [OFr. *tassel.*]
teccheles, *adj.* spotless, irreproachable, 917. [From next.]

tech, *n.* spot, stain, guilt, 2436, 2488. [OFr. *teche.*]
teche, *v.* to teach, 1527, 1533; inform, 407; show (the way), direct, 401, 1069, 1966, 2075; show, 1377; **ta3tte,** *pa. t.* 1485. [OE. *tǣcan.*]
tel. See TIL.
telde, *n.* tent; dwelling, house, 11, 1775. [OE. *téld.*]
telde, *v.* to erect, set up, 795, 884, 1648. [OE. *teldian*, set up tent.]
telle, *v.* to tell, relate, 26, 31, 272, 480, 643, &c.; recite, 2188; speak of (it), 291, 2130, 2501; say to, tell, 279, 380, &c.; *t. of*, tell, speak of, 165, 1514, 1656, &c.; *telle3*, tells them of it, 2494; **tolde,** *pa. t.* 1951. [OE. *tellan*; *tálde.*]
teme, *n.* theme, 1541. [OFr. **teme.*]
tender, *adj.* susceptible, liable, 2436. [OFr. *tendre.*]
tene, *n.* harm, trouble, 22, 547, 1008; *as adj.* troublesome, rough, 1707; dismal, ill, 2075. [OE. *tēona.*]
tene, *v.* to torment, harass, 1169, 2002; *intr.* suffer torment, 2501. [OE. *tēonian*, *tēnan.*]
tente, *v.* to attend to, mind, 1018, 1019. [From OFr. *atente*, n.]
tenþe, *adj.* tenth, 719. [ME. *ten* + *-þe.*]
terme, *n.* appointed place, 1069; appointment, 1671; *pl.* expressions, terms, 917. [OFr. *terme.*]
teuelyng, *n.* labour, deeds, 1514. [Prob. from ON. *tefla*, play (at tables); but see *N.E.D.*]
th-. See þ-.
tyde, *n.* time; (*at*) *þat t.*, then, 585, 736, 2168; *þat . . . þat t.*, when, 2086; *hy3e t.*, festival, 932, 1033. [OE. *tīd.*]
tyde, *v.* to befall; *yow tyde3*, is due to you, 1396. [OE. *tīdan.*]
tyffe, *v.* to prepare, make ready, 1129. [OFr. *tiffer*, adorn.]
ty3t, *v.* to arrange; intend, 2483; *pp.* spread, 568; *t. to*, hung on, 858. [OE. *tyhtan*; in ME. infl. by *dihtan.*]
til(le), tyl, *prep.* to, 673, 1979; until, 734, 1280; *til þat*, until, 697, 991, **til, tel** (1564), *conj.* until, 85, 532, 1581, &c.; *with subj.* 449, 2287. [ON. *til*; OE. (rare Nth.) *til.*]
tyme, *n.* time, period, occasion, 22, 41, 991, 1069, 1156, &c.; *at þis t.*, on this occasion, now, 1510, *1810, 2091, &c.; *at þat t.*, then, 1409. [OE. *tīma.*]
tymed, *pp.* timed, 2241. [From prec.]
tyrue, *v.* to strip off, 1921. [See *N.E.D.* s. v. *Tirve*, v.¹ and v.²]
tit(e), *adv.* quickly, 299, 1596. [ON. *títt.*] See AS-TIT.
tytel, *n.* description, 480; **tytle,** symbolism, 626. [OFr. *title.*]
tytelet, *pp.* inscribed, 1515. [OFr. *titler.*]
titleres, *n. pl.* ticklers (the hounds pressing him), 1726. [Cf. OE. *tinclian*, ON. *kitla.*]
tyxt, *n.* text, very words, 1515; romance, 1541. [OFr. *texte*, *tixte.*]
to, *prep.* to, 8, 292, 413, 1377, 1446, &c.; (in)to, 2, 680, 1855, 2313; at, 1455, 2333, 2438; (hold) of, 421, 433, 1335, 2376; on(to), 228, 728, 958, 2332; towards, 340, 1482; down (up) to, as far as, 138, 222, 786, 1341, 1928, &c.; until, 71, 1177, 1887; for, 420, 548, 932, 1247, 1558; as, 1811; *with inf.* 43, 58, 141, 472, 1130, 1388, &c.; as to, 291; *for to*, 863, &c.; in '*split*' *inf.*, 88, 1540, 1863. *Adv.* to them, 579; up, to the spot, 1454, 1903; *þat . . . to*, to which, 1671 n., 2097. [OE. *tō.*]
to, *adv.* too, 165, 719, 1529, 1827, 2300. [OE. *tō*; orig. same as prec.]
to-day, *adv.* to-day, 397, 470. [OE. *tō dæg.*]
to-fylched, *pa. t.* tore down, 1172. [?]
togeder, *adv.* together, 362, 481, 743, 1011, 1613, &c. [OE. *tō·gædere.*]
to3t, *adj.* stout, 1869. [OE. **toht*, taut, rel. to *tēon*; in ME. infl. by *tōh.*]
to-hewe, *v.* to cut down; slay, 1853. [OE. *tō-hēawan.*]
tok(en). See TAKE.

token, *n.* token, sign, indication, 1527, 2398, 2509; teaching, 1486; *tytelet t.*, inscribed title, 1515. [OE. *tācn.*]
tokenyng, *n.* indication; *in t.*, as a sign that, 2488. [OE. *tācnung.*]
tole, *n.* weapon, 413, 2260. [OE. *tōl.*]
tolke. See TULK.
tolouse, *n.* fabric of Tolouse, 77.
to-morn(e), *adv.* to-morrow morning, 548, 756, 1097, 1965. [OE. *tō mor(g)ne.*]
tone. See TAKE.
tonge, *n.* tongue, 32. [OE. *tunge.*]
toppyng, *n.* forelock of horse, 191. [Cf. OE. *topp*, top; *toppa*, tuft.]
to-raced, *pp.* pulled down, 1168. [OE. *tō-* + RASE, v.² or OFr. *raser*, tear.]
tor(e), *adj.* hard, difficult, 165 n., 719. [ON. *tor-*; cf. TORUAYLE.]
torches, *n. pl.* torches, 1119, 1650. [OFr. *torche.*]
toret, *adj.* turreted, 960. [From OFr. *torete*, n.]
tornaye, *v.* to double back, 1707; **tournaye**, tourney, joust, 41. [OFr. *to(u)rneier.*]
torne, *pp.* torn, 1579. [OE. *toren*, pp.]
torne, t(o)urne, *v. trans.* to turn, 457; *intr.* turn, 1200; return, 1099; wend, 2075; *turned towrast*, might go awry, come to no good, 1662; *turned tyme*, time that came to pass, 22. [OE. *turnian*; OFr. *to(u)rner.*]
tortors, *n. pl.* turtle-doves, 612. [L. *turtur.*]
toruayle, *n.* hard task, 1540. [ON. *torveldi*, infl. by OFr. *travail.*]
tote, *v.* to peep, 1476. [OE. *tōtian.*]
toun, *n.* dwellings (of men), court, 31, 614, 1049 n. [OE. *tūn.*]
tourn-. See TORN-.
toward(e), *prep.* towards, 445, 1189; *to hir warde*, 1200. [OE. *tōweard*, *tō hire weard.*]
towch, *n.* touch; burst of music, 120; allusion, hint, 1301; *pl.* (terms of) agreement, 1677. [OFr. *touche.*]
towche, *v.* to touch; treat of, 1541. [OFr. *toucher.*]
towen, *pp.* journeyed, 1093. [OE. *tēon*, pp. *togen.*] See VMBETEȜE.
to-wrast, *pp.* twisted awry; amiss, 1663. [OE. *tō-* + *wrǣstan.*]
towre, *n.* turret, 795. [OFr. *tour.*]
trayle, *v.* to (follow a) trail, 1700 n. [From ME. *traile*, a trail.]
trayst, *adj.*; *þat be ȝe t.*, be sure of that, 1211. [ON. *traustr*, assim. to *traiste*, v. (ON. *treysta*).]
trayteres (MS). See TRAUERES.
traytor, *n.* traitor, 1775. [OFr. *traitre*, acc. sg. *traitor.*]
trammes, *n. pl.* cunning devices, machination, 3. [OFr. *trame*, woof.]
trante, *v.* to practise cunning, dodge, 1707. [From TRAUNT.]
trased, *pp.* twined, 1739. [Uncertain; cf. OFr. *tresce*, a tress.]
trauayl, *n.* (toilsome) journey, 2241. [OFr. *travail.*]
trauayle, *v.* to travel (toilsomely), 1093. OFr. *travailler.*]
traueres, *adv.* in *a traueres*, across, backwards and forwards, *1700 n. [OFr. *a travers.*]
traunt, *n.* (cunning) practice, 1700. [Uncertain; cf. MDu. *trant*, step.]
trawe, trowe(e), *v.* to believe (in), be sure, think, 70, 94, 373, 813, 1396, &c.; *t. me þat*, take my word for it, 2112; *trawe of*, trust with regard to, 2238. [OE. *trēowan*, *truwian.*]
trawþe, trauþe, traweþ (403), *n.* fidelity, 626, 2470; truth, 1050, 1057; plighted word, 394, 1545, 1638, 1673, 2287; compact, 2348. [OE. *trēowþ.*]
tre, *n.* tree, 770. [OE. *trēo.*]
treieted, *pp.* tricked out, adorned, 960. [OFr. *tre(s)geter.*]
tresoun, *n.* treason, 3. [OFr. *tresoun.*]
tressour, *n.* fret enclosing hair, 1739 n. [OFr. *tress(e)or.*]
tresteȝ,-es, *n. pl.* trestles, 884, 1648. [OFr. *trestel*, acc. pl. *trestez.*]
trewe-. See TRWE, TRWLY.

tricherie, trecherye, *n.* treachery, 4, 2383. [OFr. *tricherie, trecherie.*]

tried, tryed, *pp.* tried (for crime), 4; *adj.* of proven quality, fine, 77, 219. [OFr. *trier.*]

trifel, tryfle, *n.* trifle, small matter, 108, 1301; detail (of ornament), 165, 960; *neuer bot t.*, not a bit, 547. [Cf. OFr. *trufle.*]

tryst, *v.* to believe, 380; *þerto ȝe t.*, be sure of that, 2325. [OE. * *trȳstan*, or ON. **trýsta*, rel. to TRAYST.]

trystyly, *adv.* faithfully, 2348. [From ME. *tristi*, rel. to prec.]

trystor, tryster, *n.* hunting station, 1146, 1170, 1712. [OFr. *tristre*, acc. sg. *tristor.*]

trochet, *pp.* provided with 'troches', the tines of a deer's horn; (towers) provided with ornamental pinnacles, 795. [OFr. *troche.*]

trowe(e). See TRAWE.

true, *n.* truce, 1210. [OE. *trēow.*]

trumpe, *n.* trumpet, 116, 1016. [OFr. *trompe.*]

trusse, *v.* to pack, 1129. [OFr. *trusser.*]

trwe(e), truee, *adj.* faithful, 1845; true (to one's word), trusty, honest, 638, 1514, 1637, 2354; true, accurate, 392, 480, 1274; **trewest,** *superl.* truest, most honourable, 4; *adv.* honestly, 2354. [OE. *trēowe.*]

trwly, truly, trewely, *adv.* faithfully, 2348; with belief, 2112; truly, rightly, 380, 401, 406, 1785, 2444. [OE. *trēowlīce.*]

trwluf, trweluf, *n.* true love, 1527 (*gen.*), 1540; **trulofeȝ,** *pl.* true-love knots, 612. [OE. *trēowlufu.*]

tulé, tuly, *adj.* made of rich red stuff (usually silk), such as was imported from Toulouse, 568; *as sb.* 858. [?]

tulk, tolke, *n.* man, knight, 3, 41, 638, 1093, 1775, 1811, 1966, 2133. [ON. *tulkr*, spokesman.]

turne. See TORNE.

tusch, *n.* tusk, 1573, 1579. [OE. *tŭsc.*]

twayne, tweyne, *adj.* two, 962, 1864. [OE. *twēgen.*, masc.]

twelmonyth, *n.* twelvemonth, year, 298; *as adv.* a year hence, 383; a year ago, 2243. [OE. *twelf mōnaþ.*]

twelue, *adj.* twelve, 128. [OE. *twelfe.*]

twenty, *adj.* twenty, 1739 (see BE), 2112. [OE. *twentig.*]

twyges, *n. pl.* twigs, branches, 746. [ONth. *twicg.*]

twynne, *adj.* double; *in t.*, in two, 425, 1339. [ON. *tvinnr*; OE. *getwinn.*]

twynne, *v.* to be separated, depart, 2512. [From prec.]

twynnen, *pp.* (were) twined, plaited, 191. [ME. *twīnen*, v. from OE. *twīn*, n.]

twy(e)s, *adv.* twice, 1522, 1679. [OE. *twiga* + adv. *-es.*]

two, *adj.* two, 128, 770, 1019, 1316, 2352, &c.; *in two*, 1351. [OE. *twā.*]

Þ

þad. See ÞAT.

þaȝ(e), *conj.* (*with subj.*), though, even if, 350, 1391, 2112, 2136, 2282, &c.; (with *wonder*), 496, 2307. [OE. *þē(a)h*, unaccented *þæh, þah.*]

þay, *pron. pl.* they, 50, 1019, 1452, &c.; **þayr,** *adj.* their, 1359, 1362; **þayres,** *pron.* theirs; their affairs, 1019. [ON. *þeir*; gen. *þeira.*]

þanne. See ÞENNE.

þar, *3 sg. pres.* need, 2355. [OE. *þearf.*]

þare, þore, *adv.* there, 463, 667, 1889, 2173, 2356, 2508. [OE. *þǣr, þāra.*]

þat, þad (686), *adj.* that, the, 9, *1069, 1775, 2256, &c.; *þat ilk(e)*, that (same), 24, 1256, 2358, &c.; *as def. art.* (*before* ON, OÞER, &c.), 110, 173, 771, 1385, 2412, &c. [OE. *þæt*, neut.]

þat, *conj.* that, 83, 131, 234, 726, 1045, 1111, &c.; so that, 120, 869, &c.; seeing that, 1209; after *so, such*, 60, 316, *1014, 1427, &c.; *with subj.* that, to (*with inf.*), 371, 380, &c.; so that, in order that, 133, 345, 380, 2073, &c.; *þat . . . were*, that there would be, 131; *pleonastic with other conj. or interrog.* (q.v.), 379, 1752, &c. *See also the preps.* (*as* BI, TIL, &c.). [OE. *þæt, þætte.*]

þat, *pron.* that, it, 70, 264, 1805, 2112, &c.; at that, moreover, 142, 717; of that, 1211. See BI, WITH. [OE. *þæt.*]

þat, *rel. pron.* that, which, who(m), 3, 22, 836, *877, *1032, 1171, 1312, 2529, &c.; to whom, 1251; (time) when, *996; that which, what, 291, 391, *1386, &c.; she whom, 969; (that) he that, 926; at what, 2372; *þat . . . hym, hys, hit*, whom, whose, which, 28, 912, 2105, 2195; *þat . . . þat tyde*, when, 2085; *with postponed prep.* (q.v.), 165, 170, 1780, 2196, 2465, &c. [Substitution of prec. for OE. *þe.*]

þe, *def. art.* the, 1, 2057, 2069, 2153, &c.; *generic*, 235, &c.; *with abstract sb.* (*as* OFr.), 1528, 2134, 2206, &c.; *with part of body*, 621, 962, 2255, &c. [Late OE. *þe* (for *se*).]

þe, *adv. with compar.* the, so much (the), for that, 87, 376, 541, 1035, 1284, &c. [OE. *þȳ, þĕ.*]

þe. See þOU.

þede, *n.* country, 1499. [OE. *þēod.*]

þeder. See þIDER.

þef, *n.* thief, 1725. [OE. *þēof.*]

þen, þen(n)e, *adv.* (i) then, next, in that case, 116, 250, 462, 619, 1076, 1870, 2033, 2248, 2288, &c.; **þanne**, 301: (ii) than, 24, 236, 337, 730, &c. [OE. *þanne, þænne, þon.*]

þenk(ke), *v.* to take heed, 487; remember, 1680; *þ. of* (*on, vpon*), be mindful of, remember, 534, 2052, 2397; **þoȝt(en),** *pa. t.* 1023; intended, 331, 1550. [OE. *þencan*; *þŏhte.*] See þYNKEȜ.

þer(e), *adv. demonstr.* there, 3, 44, 109, 240, &c.; *indef.* 232, 852, &c.; *þer(e) as*, where, 432, 731, 1432, 1897; *rel.* where, when, 160, 334, 349, 694, 1875, &c.; whereas, 839; *þer . . . inne*, in which, 2440; *with preps.* it, them, &c.: **þeraboute,** engaged on it, 613; round it, 2485; thereabouts, 705; **þerafter,** behind, after it (that), 671, 1021, 1342, 1826; **þer-alofte,** on it, 569; **þer-amongeȝ,** with it, 1361; **þerat,** 909, 1463, 2514; **þerbi,** on them, 117; **þer-byside,** 1925; **þerfore,-forne,** therefore, for that reason, 103, 1142, 2279, &c.; (?) (in exchange) for it, 1107; **þerinne,** in it, there, 17, 21, 1652, 1767; **þerof,** of it, to it, 480, 547, 2523, &c.; **þeron,** 570; **þeroute,** out (of it), 1140, 2044; out-of-doors, 518, 2000, 2481; **þertylle,** to it, 1110, 1369; **þerto,** to it (them), 219, 576, &c.; at it, 650; in that, 2325; to this end (*or* moreover), 757; *as . . . þerto*, as . . . (to do), 1040; **þervnder,** 185, 2079; **þerwyth,** (together) with it, thereupon, 121, 980, 1610. [OE. *þǣr, þēr.*]

þes(e). See þIS.

þeweȝ, *n. pl.* manners, knightly conduct, 912, 916. [OE. *þēawas*, pl.]

þy, þyseluen, &c. See þOU.

þider, þeder, *adv.* thither, 402, 935, 1424, 1735, 1910. [OE. *þider.*]

þiderwarde, *adv.* in that direction, 1186. [OE. *þiderweard.*]

þyȝe, *n.* thigh, 579, 1349. [OE. *þē(o)h.*]

þik(ke), *adj.* thick, stout, 138, 175, 579, &c.; *adv.* thick(ly), densely, 612, 769, 795, 801, 1702; continually, 1770. [OE. *þicce.*]

þyng, þing, *n.* thing, matter, 93, 1512, 1802; **þynk,** creature, 1526; **þyng(e),** *pl.* 652, 1080; **þyngeȝ, þinges,** 645, 1809, 1945. [OE. *þing.*]

þynk(k)eȝ, þinkkeȝ, *2 sg. pres.* you seem to, 2362; *impers.* it seems good to, 1502; seems to, 1111, 1241, 1793, &c.; **þink,** in *me þynk*, &c., I think, 348, 1268, 2109, 2428; **þoȝt, þuȝt,** *pa. t. impers.* it seemed to, 49, 692, 1245, 1620, 2491; (*merging into*) *pers.* thought (it), 803, 848, 945, 1578, &c. [OE. *þyncan*, pa. t. *þŭhte.*]

þis, þys, *adj.* this, the, 20, 1112, 1394, *1442, 1514, &c.; *pron.* 100, 1385, 2398, &c.; *er þis* (OE. *ǣr þissum*), ere now, 1892, 2528. **þis(e), þyse, þes(e),** *pl.* these, the, 42, 654, 656, 1386, 1445, 1514, &c.; *pron.* these (folk, things), 114, 1103, 2420, 2422; *þis seuen ȝere*, this many a day, 1382. [OE. *þis*, neut.]

þof, þoȝ, *conj.* even though, 69, 624. [ON. *þó*, older **þoh*.]

þoȝt, *n.* thought, 645, 1751, 1867, 1993. [OE. *þŏht*.]

þoȝt(en). See **þENK, þYNKEȜ.**

þoled, *pa. t.* suffered, allowed, 1859; endured, 2419. [OE. *þolian*.]

þonk(e), *n.* thanks, 1380; *made a þ.*, gave his thanks, 1984; **þonkkeȝ,** *pl.* thanks, 1980. [OE. *þonc*.]

þonk(ke), *v.* to thank, 773, 939, 1031, 1080, 1975, 2020, &c. [OE. *þoncian*.]

þore. See **þARE.**

þorne, *n.* thorn, 1419, 2529. [OE. *þorn*.]

þo, *adj. pl.* those, the, 39, 68, 466, 1419, &c. [OE. *þā*.]

þose, *adj. pl.* those, 495; *pron.* 963. [OE. *þās*.]

þou, þow, *pron.* thou, 277, 1485, 1676, &c.; **þe,** *acc. and dat.* 254, 258, 324, 2110, 2286, &c.; *refl.* 372, 396, 413, 2252, 2341, 2351; *halde þe þe hode*, h. that hood of thine, 2297. **þi(n), þy(n),** *adj.* thy, 255, 394, 1071, 2303, 2467, &c.; **þiself,** *nom.* thyself, 395; **þyseluen,** *refl.* 2141; *þyn awen seluen*, 2301. [OE. *þū, þē, þīn*.]

þrast, *n.* thrust, 1443. [Stem of OE. *þrǣstan*, v.]

þrawen, þrowen, *pp.* bound tight, 194; thrown, laid, 1740; well-knit, muscular, 579. [OE. *þrāwan*, twist.]

þre, *adj.* three, 1066, 1141, 1443, 1713, 1946. [OE. *þrēo*.]

þred, *n.* thread; *so neȝe þe þred*, so near to the limit, *i.e.* to a definite offer of love, 1771. [OE. *þrǣd*.]

þrepe, *n.* importunity, 1859; contest, 2397. [From next; cf. ON. *þrap*.]

þrepe, *v.* to quarrel; contend, 504. [OE. *þrēapian*, rebuke.]

þresch, *v.* to thrash; smite, 2300. [OE. *þerscan*, late *þrescan*.]

þrete, *n.* force, compulsion, 1499. [OE. *þrēat*.]

þrete, *v.* to threaten, 2300; **þrat,** *pa. t.* urged, pressed, 1980; attacked, 1713; **þreted,** *pp.* reviled, 1725. [OE. *þrēatian* with changed conjug.]

þrich, *n.* thrust; rush, 1713. [Stem of OE. *þryccan*, v.] See **þRYȜT.**

þrid, þryd, *adj.* third, 1021, 1680, 2356. [OE. *þridda*.]

þrye, *adv.* thrice, 763; **þryes, þryse,** 1412, 1936. [OE. *þria*; + adv. *-es*.]

þryȝt, *pa. t.* thrust, 1443; *pp.* pressed on, 1946. [OE. *þryccan*.]

þrynge, *v.* to press, make one's way, 2397; **þronge,** *pa. t.* 1021. [OE. *þringan*.]

þrynne, *adj.* threefold, three; *on þ. syþe*, thrice, 1868. [ON. *þrinnr*.]

þryuande, *adj.* abundant, hearty, 1980; **þryuandely,** *adv.* 1080, 1380. [Pres. p. of next.]

þryue, *v.* to thrive; *so mot I þ. as I am*, on my life I am, 387. [ON. *þrifask*.]

þryuen, *adj.* fair, 1740. [ON. *þrifinn*, pp. of prec.]

þro, *adj.* intense, steadfast, 645; oppressive, 1751; fierce, 1713 (*as sb.*), 2300; *as adv.* earnestly, heartily, 1867, 1946; *as þro*, equally crowded with delight, 1021; **þroly,** *adv.* heartily, 939. [ON. *þrár*; *þráliga*.]

þrote, *n.* throat, 955, 1740. [OE. *þrote*.]

þrowe, *n.* time; *a þrowe*, for a time, 2219. [OE. *þrāg*.]

þrowe, *v.* in *þrid tyme þ. best*, third time turn out best, third time pays for all, 1680 n. [OE. *þrāwan*.]

þrowen. See **þRAWEN.**

þuȝt. See **þYNKEȜ.**

þulged, *pa. t.* was patient (with), 1859. [OE. *geþyldgian*.]

þurȝ(e), *prep.* through(out), over, 243, 691, 772, 1005, 1418, &c.; because

of, for, by (means of), 91, 998, 1258, 1617, &c.; *þ. alle oþer þynge(ȝ)*, (for this) beyond all else, 645, 1080; *adv.* through, 1356. [OE. *þurh.*]
þurled, *pa. t.* made a hole in, pierced, 1356. [OE. *þyrlian.*]
þus, *adv.* thus, so, in this way, 107, 529, 733, 1177, &c. [OE. *þus.*]
þwarle, *adj.* intricate, 194. [(?) Rel. to OE. *þweorh*; cf. mod. Lancs. dial. *wharle-knot* (E.D.D.).]
þwong, *n.* thong, lace, 194, 579. [OE. *þwong.*]

V

vayle, *n.* veil, 958. [OFr. *veile.*]
vayres; *in vayres*, in truth, truly, 1015. [OFr. *en veires.*]
valay, *n.* valley, 2145, 2245. [OFr. *valee.*]
vale, *n.* vale; *by hylle ne be v.*, in no circumstances, 2271; *in vale*, in the land, by the way, 2482. [OFr. *val.*]
vch(e), *adj.* each, every, 101, 233, 501, 634, 980, 1014, &c.; **iche**, 126, 1811; *vche a*, every, 742, 997, 1262, 1491. **vchon(e)**, *pron.* each one, every one, 657, 1028; *in appos. to sb.*, 829, 1113, 1413; *v.* (*in*) *oþer*, (in) each other, 98, 657. [OE. *ǣlc*, (rare) *ylc.*]
veluet, *n.* velvet, 2027. [Cf. Med. L. *velvetum.*]
venysoun, *n.* venison, 1375. [OFr. *veneisun.*]
venquyst, *pa. t.* won victories, 2482. [OFr. *veintre*; pa. t. *venquis.*]
ver, *n.* spring-time, 866 n. [L. *ver.*]
verayly, *adv.* verily, 161, 866, 1342, 1375, 2245. [From OFr. *verai.*]
verdure, *n.* verdure, green, 161. [OFr. *verdure.*]
vertue, *n.* (knightly) virtue, *634, 2375. [OFr. *vertu.*]
vertuus, *adj.* precious (stones), *2027. [OFr. *vertuous.*]
vesture, *n.* vesture, raiment, 161. [OFr. *vesture.*]
vewters, *n. pl.* keepers of deer-hounds, 1146. [OFr. *veutrier, veutre.*]
vgly, *adj.* gruesome, 441; threatening, 2079; evil-looking, 2190. [ON. *uggligr*, causing apprehension.]
vyage, *n.* journey, 535. [OFr. *viage.*]
vylany(e), *n.* lack of (chivalrous) virtues, 634, 2375; discourtesy, 345. [OFr. *vilainie.*]
vilanous, *adj.* boorish, ill-bred, 1497. [OFr. *vilenneus.*]
visage, *n.* appearance, 866. [OFr. *visage.*]
vyse, *n.* vice, 2375. [OFr. *vice.*]
vmbe, *prep.* about, round, 589, 1830, 2034. [Blend of OE. *ymb(e)* and ON. *umb.*]
vmbe-clyppe, *v.* to embrace, surround, 616. [OE. *ymb(e)-clyppan.*]
vmbe-folde, *v.* to enfold, 181. [VMBE + FOLDE.]
vmbe-kesten, *pa. t.* cast about, searched all round, 1434. [VMBE + CAST.]
vmbe-lappe, *v.* to enfold, overlap, 628. [VMBE + LAPPE.]
vmbe-teȝe, *pa. t.* surrounded, 770. [VMBE + OE. *tēah*, pa. t. of *tēon.*]
vmbe-torne, *adv.* round in a circle, 184. [Blend of OFr. *en tur(n)* and ME. *umbe-trin* (Orm.); cf. MLG. *umme trint*, Dan. *om trind.*]
vmbe-weued, *pa. t.* enveloped, 581. [OE. *ymbe-wǣfan.*]
vnbarred, *pp.* unbarred, 2070. [OE. *on-*(*un-*) + OFr. *barrer.*]
vnbene, *adj.* inhospitable, dreary, 710. See BENE.
vnbynde, *v.* to undo, cut in two, 1352. [OE. *on-*, *un-bindan.*]
vnblyþe, *adj.* unhappy, mournful, 746. [OE. *unblīþe.*]
vncely, *adj.* ill-fated, *or* disastrous, 1562. [OE. *unsēlig.*]
vnclose, *v.* to open, 1140. See CLOSE.
vncouple, *v.* to uncouple, unleash, 1419. See COWPLED.
vncouþe, *adj.* strange, 93, 1808. [OE. *uncūþ.*] See COUÞE.

vnder, *prep.* under, 202, 748, 1831, 2487, &c.; in (clothes, &c.), 260, 1814; on 160 n.; *adv.* underneath, 868 n.; down, 2318; at their feet, 742; below, on his heels, 168. [OE. *under.*]
vndertake, *v.* to take in, perceive (what are), 1483. [OE. *underniman* with substitution of TAKE.]
vndo, *v.* to undo; *didden hem v.*, had them cut open, 1327. [OE. *on-, undōn.*]
vneþe, *adv.* hardly, 134. [OE. *unēaþe.*]
vnfayre, *adj.* hideous, 1572. [OE. *unfæger.*]
vnhap, *n.* mishap, 438. [ON. *úhapp.*]
vnhap, *v.* to unfasten, 2511 n. See HAPPE.
vnhardel, *v.* to unleash hounds, 1697. [From OFr. *hardel*, leash.]
vnlace, *v.* to unlace; cut up (boar), 1606. [From OFr. *lacer.*]
vnleuté, *n.* disloyalty, 2499. See LEUTÉ.
vnlyke, *adj.* unlike, different, 950. [OE. *ungelīc.*]
vnlouked, *pa. t.* opened, 1201. [OE. *on-, unlūcan*, str.]
vnmanerly, *adv.* discourteously, 2339. [From OFr. *man(i)ere.*]
vnmete, *adj.* monstrous, 208. [OE. *un(ge)mǣte.*]
vnrydely, *adv.* in rough confusion, 1432. [OE. *unrȳdelīce.*]
vnslayn, *adj.* not slain, 1858. See SLAYN.
vnslyȝe, *adj.* unwary, 1209. See SLEȜE.
vnsoundyly, *adv.* disastrously, 1438. See SOUNDYLY.
vnsparely, *adv.* unsparingly, 979. [OE. *un- + spærlīce.*] See SPARE.
vnspurd, *adj.* unasked, without asking, 918. See SPURED.
vntyȝtel, *n.* unrestraint, lightheartedness; *dalten vnt.*, revelled, 1114. [ME. *untühtle* (Laȝ. 24655), lack of discipline; *cf.* OE. *tyht.*]
vnto, *prep.* to, 249. [OE. **untō.*]
vntrawþe, *n.* perfidy, 2383, 2509. [OE. *untrēowþ.*]
vnþryuande, *adj.* unlucky (does no good to the user), 1499. See ÞRYUANDE.
vnworþi, *adj.* of no worth, 1835; unworthy, 1244. [From OE. *unweorþe.*]
voyde, *v.* to make empty; vacate, leave, 345; get rid of, 1518; *v. out*, clear out, 1342; *voyded of*, free from, 634. [OFr. *voidier.*]
vp, *adv.* up, 369, 884, 1131, 2260, &c.; up from table, 928; out of bed, 1128, 2009; open, 820, 1341, 1743; away safe, 1874; *vp to*, 789, &c.; *vp and doun*, 229. [OE. *up(p).*]
vpbrayde, *pp.* pulled up, 781. [Prec. + BRAYDE.]
vphalde, *v.* to uphold, 2442. [VP + HALDE.]
vplyfte, *v. intr.* to lift up, rise, 505. [VP + LYFTE.]
vpon, *prep. equiv. of* ON; upon, on, 159, 164, 431, 581, &c.; to, 2252; at, 793, 2039, &c.; in, 901, 1272, 1605, &c.; into, 244; (*time*) at, in, on, 37, 92, 301, 982, &c.; by, 47; *adv.* on (them), 1649; on (him), 2021 n.; *þat ... vpon*, by whom, 2466. [OE. *upp-on.*]
vpon, *v.* to open, 1183 n. [OE. *openian*, infl. by VP, open.]
vpryse, *v.* to rise up, 1437; **vpros,** *pa. t. sg.* 367; **vprysen,** *pl.* 1126. [OE. *upp arīsan.*]
vrysoun, *n.* embroidered covering on helmet, 608. [OFr. *horson.*]
vse, *v.* to use; have dealings with, 2426; show, practise (a virtue), 651, 1491, 2106. [OFr. *user.*]
vtter, *adv.* out, into the open, 1565. [OE. *ūtor, ŭtter.*]

W

wade, *v.* to wade, 2231; **wod,** *pa. t.* stood (in water), 787. [OE. *wadan.*]
wage, *n.* pledge, earnest, 533; *pl.* wages, payment, 396. [ONFr. *wage.*]
way(e), way, road, 670, 1077, 1876, 2479, &c.; *on his w.*, 670, 1028, 1132,

2074; *went his* (*hir*) *w.*, departed, 688, 1557; *bi non way*(*es*), by no means, 1045, 2471. [OE. *weg.*]
way, *adv.* away; *do w.*, enough of, 1492. [Shortened from AWAY.]
wayke, *adj.* weak, 282. [ON. *veikr.*]
wayne, *v.* to bring, send, 264, 2456, 2459 (*me* ethic). [OE. in *be-wægnan.*]
wayte, *v.* to look, 306, 1186, 2163, 2289. [ONFr. *wait(i)er.*]
wayth, *n.* (meat gained in) hunting, 1381. [ON. *veiðr.*]
wayue, *v.* to wave; *w. vp*, swing open, 1743; *pa.t.* swept from side to side, 306; *w. hom*, waved it at them, 984; *pp.* offered, shown, 1032 n. [ON. *veifa*, AFr. *waiver.*]
waked, *pp.* kept awake, revelled at night, 1094; **woke,** *pa. t.* 1025. [OE. *wacian*, infl. by *wæcnan.*]
wakened(e), **wakned,** *pa. t. intr.* woke up, 1200; would wake up, 1194 (*subj.*); was aroused, arose, 2000, 2490; *trans.* kindled, 1650; *pa. t.* awakened, 119. [OE. *wæcn(i)an*, intr.]
wakkest, *adj. superl.* weakest, most insignificant, 354. [OE. *wāc*, compar. *wăccra.*] See WAYKE.
wal, walle, *n.* wall, 783, 787, 809. [OE. *wall.*]
wale, walle, *adj.* choice, 1403; excellent, fair, 1010, 1712, 1759. [For ME. *to wale*, inf. of next.]
wale, *v.* to choose, 1276; take, 1238; find, 398. [ON. *velja*, pa. t. *valdi.*]
walke, *v.* to walk, 2178; be spread abroad, 1521. [OE. *walcan.*]
wallande, *pres. p.* welling up warm, 1762. [OE. *wallan.*]
walour, *n.* valour, 1518. [OFr. *valour.*]
walt. See WELDE.
walt, *v.* to toss, fling; *pa. t.* 1336. [OE. *wieltan*, *wæltan.*]
walter, *v.* to welter; roll in streams, 684. [Rel. to prec.; cf. MLG. *waltern.*]
wande, *n.* wand, branch; *vnder w.*, in the wood, 1161; **wandeȝ,** *gen.* stave's, 215. [ON. *vǫndr.*]
wane, *adj.* lacking, 493 n. [OE. *wana.*]
wap, *n.* blow, 2249. [As next.]
wappe, *v.* to rush, 1161, 2004. [Echoic.]
war, *adj.* (a)ware; *watȝ w. of*, perceived, 764, 1586, 1900; *war!*, ware! (hunting cry), 1158; **ware,** on my guard, 2388; **warly,** *adv.* warily, 1186, 1900; **warloker,** *compar.* more carefully, 677. [OE. *wær*, *wærlīce*, *-lucor.*]
warde, *adv.* See TOWARDE.
ware, *v.* to deal, 2344; spend, employ, 402, 1235. [OE. *warian.*[2]]
waryst, *pp.* cured, recovered, 1094. [ONFr. *warir*, *wariss-.*]
warme, *adj.* warm, 506, 684. [OE. *wearm.*]
warme, *v.* to warm, 1762. [OE. *werman.*]
warne, *v.* to warn, 522. [OE. *warenian.*]
warp, *v.* to cast; utter, 2253; **warp,** *pa. t.* uttered, 224 n., 1423; cast, put, 2025. [OE. *weorpan*; ON. *varpa.*]
warþe, *n.* shore, river-side, 715. [OE. *waroþ*, *wear(o)þ.*]
waschen, *pp. intr.* washed, 72; **wesche,** *pa. t.* 887. [OE. *wascan.*]
wast, *n.* waist, 144. [OE. **wæ(c)st.*]
waste, *n.* waste, uninhabited land, 2098. [ONFr. *wast*, adj.]
wat. See WHAT.
water, *n.* water, 715, 727, &c.; **watter,** 2231; **wattreȝ,** *pl.* 1169; *warme w.* tears, 684. [OE. *wæter.*]
watȝ, *pa. t. sg.* was, 4, 603, 652, *1315, &c.; **was,** 169, 726, &c.; had been, 2016, 2488; *with intr. pp.* had, 1, 62, 461, 1413, &c.; **wer(en),** *pl.* were, 78, 320, 1138, 1328, &c.; **wer(e),** *pa. t. subj.* would, (should) be, *58, 165, 1251, 1545, 1773, 2131, &c.; was, 92, 131, 143, 281, &c.; might be, 1509; *as hit were*, *2171; *if hit w.*, if only, 1799. [OE. *wæs*, *wǣron*, *wǣre.*]
waþe. See WOÞE.
wax, *v.* to grow, 518, 522; increase, 997; **wex,** *pa. t.* grew, became, 319. [OE. *weaxan*, *wĕox.*]
waxen, *adj.* of wax, 1650. [OE. *weaxen.*]

we, *interj.* ah! alas! 2185; *we loo*, ah well, 2208. [OE. *wǣ*; *wǣ lā*, *wel lā*.]
we, *pron.* we, 255, 378, 1681, &c.; **oure,** *adj.* our, 378, 1055, 1230, &c.; **vus,** *acc. and dat.* (to) us, 920, 925, 1210, &c.; **vs,** 2246. [OE. *wē*, *ūre*, *ŭs*.]
wede, *n.* garment, *987, 2358; raiment, 1310; *heȝ wede*, armour, 831; *pl.* raiment, clothes (and armour), 151, 271, 508, 861, 2013, 2025. [OE. *wǣd*, *ge-wǣde*.]
weder, *n.* weather, 504; *pl.* storms, 2000. [OE. *weder*; *gewider*, storm.]
weȝed, *pa. t.* brought, 1403. [OE. *wegan*, str.]
wel, *adv.* well, 188, 679, &c.; without doubt, clearly, 70, 270, 1820, &c.; certainly, 1847; fully, 1094; very much, 1276, 2095, &c.; very, 179, 684; *wel conneȝ*, 1267 n.; *wol þe wel*, wish thee well, 2469; *w. worþ þe*, good fortune betide thee, 2127. [OE. *wel*.]
wela, *adv.* very, 518, 2084. [OE. *wellā*.]
welcum, -com, *adj.* welcome, 252, 814, 835, 1237, *2240; *superl.* 938. [OE. *wilcuma*, n.; ON. *velkominn*.]
welcum, *v.* to welcome, 819, 1477, 1759. [OE. *wilcumian*; see prec.]
welde, *n.* control; *to haue at yowre wylle and w.*, to use as you please, 837. [OE. *gewáld*, infl. by next.]
welde, *v.* to wield, 270; possess, use, 835, 1528, 1790, 2454, &c.; **walt,** *pa. t.* possessed, 231; spent, 485. [OE. *wéldan*, *wǽldan*.]
wele, *n.* wealth, riches, 7, 1270, 1394, 1820; costliness, 2037, 2432; joy, delight, 50, 485, 997, 1371, 1767, 2490; *w. oþer wo*, 2134. [OE. *wela*.]
wel-haled, *adj.* pulled up properly, drawn tight, 157. [WEL + HAL(L)E.]
welkyn, *n.* heavens, 525, 1696. [OE. *wolcen*, *welcn*, cloud.]
welneȝ(e), *adv.* almost, 7, 867. [OE. *wel-nēh*.]
wende, *n.* turn, 1161. [OE. *wend*.]
wende, *v.* to turn, 2152; *intr.* go, 559, 1053, 1102, &c.; **wende,** *pa. t.* in *w. in hys hed*, went to his head, 900; **went(en),** 72, 493, 688, 887, 1143, 1718, &c.; *pp.* in *watȝ w.*, came, 1712. [OE. *wendan*.]
wene, *v.* to expect, think, 2404; *w. wel*, know well, 270, 1226; **wende,** went, *pa. t.* 669; *w. haf*, thought to have, 1711. [OE. *wēnan*.]
wener, *adj. compar.* more lovely, 945. [ON. *vænn*.]
wenge, *v.* to avenge oneself, 1518. [OFr. *venger*.]
weppen, *n.* weapon, 270, 292, 368, 384, 1586, 2222. [OE. *wǣpn*.]
wer, were(n). See WATȜ, WERRE.
werbelande, *pres. p.* blowing shrill, 2004. [OFr. *werbler*.]
werbles, *n. pl.* warblings, shrill tremulous notes, 119. [OFr. *werble*.]
were, *v.*[1] to ward off, 2015; defend, 2041. [OE. *werian*.[1]]
were, *v.*[2] to wear, 2358, 2510, 2518; **were,** *pa. t.* 1928; **wered,** 2037. [OE. *werian*.[2]]
werk(e), *n.* work, 494; *wylyde w.*, intrigue, 2367; **werk(k)eȝ,** *pl.* deeds, 1515; workmanship, 1817, 2432; embroidery, 164, 2026; designs, 216. [OE. *we(o)rc*.]
werne, *v.* to refuse, 1494, 1495, 1824; **wernyng,** *n.* resistance, 2253. [OE. *wernan*.]
werre, *n.* strife, fighting, 16, 726; **were,** 271, 1628. [ONFr. *werre*.]
werre, *v.* to fight, 720. [From prec.]
wesaunt. *n.* oesophagus, 1336. [OE. *wāsend*, *wǣsend*.]
wesche. See WASCHEN.
west, *adj.* west, 7 n. [OE. *west*, n.]
weterly, *adv.* clearly, 1706. [ON. *vitrliga*, wisely.]
weue, *v.* to offer, show (honour), 1976; give, 2359. [OE. *wǣfan*, *wave, equated with WAYUE.]
wex. See WAX.
wharre, *v.* to whirr, 2203. [Echoic.]
what, *interrog. pron.* what, 238, 462, 1487, &c.; **quat,** 233, 563, 1087, &c.;

what! 309; lo! behold! 1163, 2201–4; *indef.* what(ever), 1073, 1082; *adj.* what, 460, 1047. **what-so,** *pron.* whatever, 1550; **quat-so,** 255, 382; *what* (*wat*) ... *so*, 384, *1406, 1407, &c.; *quat* ... *so*, 1107, 1851; **quat-so-euer,** 1106. [OE. *hwæt*; *swā-hwæt-swā.*]

whederwarde, *adv.* whither, 1053; **whiderwarde-so-euer,** wherever, 2478. [OE. *hwider*; *swā-hwider-swā.*]

when, quen, *interrog. adv.* when, 1194; *indef. and rel.* when(ever), 20, 72, 517, 650, 1098, 1727, 1753, 1857, 2437, &c. **when-so,** whenever, 1682. [OE. *hwanne, hwænne.*]

whene. See QUENE.

wher(e), *interrog. adv.* where, 224, 311, 398, 399, 1394; **quere,** 1058; *indef.* (*with subj.*), wherever, 100; *rel.* in *where* ... *þerinne*, where, 16; **where-so,** wherever, 395; **quere-so,** 1227, 1490; **where-euer,** 661; **were-so-euer,** 1459; **quere-so-ever,** 644. [OE. *hwǣr*; *swā-hwǣr-swā.*]

wherfore, querfore, *interrog. adv.* wherefore, 1294; *rel.* in *wh.* ... *þerfore*, and so, 2278. [Prec. + OE. *fore.*]

whette, *v.* to sharpen, whet, 1573; **whette,** *pa. t. intr.* made a grinding noise, 2203; **quettyng,** *n.* grinding (his axe), 2220. [OE. *hwettan.*]

wheþen, queþen, *interrog. adv.* whence; *from queþen*, 461; *indef.* (*with subj.*) from wherever, 871. [ON. *hvaðan*; ODan. *hueden.*]

wheþer, *adv.* however, all the same, 203. [OE. *hwæþere.*]

wheþer, queþer, *interrog. adv.* whether; *introd. dir. question*, 2186; *qu.* ... *so*, whether (= if), 1109. [OE. *hwæþer.*]

why, wy, quy, *adv. interrog.* why, 623; *interj.* why! (*incredulous*), 1528; why! well then, 2300. [OE. *hwī.*]

whiderwarde. See WHEDERWARDE.

whil(e), wyle, quyl(e), quel (822), *conj.* while, as long as, 60, 351, 805, 814, 1035, 1469, 1852, 2025, &c.; until, 1180, 1435; *quyle þat*, as long as, 1115; *prep.* until, 536, 1072, 1075, 1097, 1730. [OE. *þā-hwīle-þe.*]

whyle, quile, *n.* time, 1235; *adverbially*, 30, 1195, 2369; *a wh.*, a moment, 134, 1996; *any qu.*, any length of time, 257, 2058; *in a wh.*, presently, 1646; *þe qu.*, at present, 1791; *þe seruise* (*&c.*) *qu.*, during the service time, 940, 985. [OE. *hwīl*, (*þā*)*hwīle.*]

whyrlande, *pres. p.* whirling, 2222. [OE. *hwyrftlian*; ON. *hvirfla.*]

whyssynes, *n. pl.* cushions, 877 (*allit. with* qu). [OFr. *cuissin.*]

whyte, *adj.* white, 1573; **quit(e),** 1205 (*as sb.*), 2364; **quyt(e),** 799, 885, 2088. [OE. *hwīt.*]

who, quo, *interrog. pron.* who, 231, 682, 1112, 2213; *indef.* whoever, 355. **who-so, quo-so,** *indef.* whoever, 209, 1849; *interrog.* who (it might be), 306. [OE. *hwā, swā-hwā-swā.*]

wich, *adj.* what, 918. [OE. *hwilc.*]

wyde, *adv.* wide, 820. [OE. *wīde.*]

wyf, *n.* woman, 1001, 1495; wife, 1098, 2351, 2359, 2361, 2404. [OE. *wīf.*]

wyȝe, wyghe (1487), *n.* man, knight, 249, 314, 581, 1039, 2074, &c.; person, one, 131, 384, 1087, &c.; (of God), 2441; *voc.* sir (knight), 252, 1508, 2127, &c.; *pl.* men, persons, 1167, 1403, &c. [OE. (verse) *wiga.*]

wyȝt, *adj.* valiant, 261; fierce, 1591; *as adv.* loud, 119; ardently, 1762; **wyȝtly,** *adv.* swiftly, 688. [ON. *vígr*, neut. *vígt.*]

wiȝt, *n.* creature, 1440; *þat wyȝt*, she, 1792. [OE. *wiht.*]

wyke, *n.* corner, 1572. [ON. *munn-vík.*]

wil, wyl(le), *1 & 3 sg. pres.* will, &c., 130, 1547, &c.; **wol,** 2469; **wyl(t),** *2 sg.* 273, 384, &c.; **wyl,** *pl.* 30, 1090, &c.; **wolde, woled,** *pa. t.* 85, 1508, &c. *Pres.* wish (for), desire, 384, 1822, 2469, &c.; intend to, will, 130, 1102, &c.; *merging into auxil. of future*, will, 30, 549, 2512, &c.; *I wyl to*, I mean to go to, 2132. *Pa. t.*

wished (to), would (wish), 85, 271, 347, 1127, 2478, &c.; *wolde of his wyte*, was like to go out of his senses, 1087. [OE. *wil(l)e, wyl(le)*; *wolde.*]

wylde, *adj.* wild, 119, 741, 1423, 1467, 1628, 2000, 2163, 2479; restless, 89. [OE. *wilde.*]

wylde, *n.* wild beast, 1167, 1586, 1900; *pl.* wild creatures, 1150, 2003. [OE. **wild, wilder*, pl. *wildru*; cf. MHG. *wilt.*]

wylé, wyly, *adj.* wily, 1728; *as sb.* 1905. [From next.]

wyleȝ, *n. pl.* wiles, 1700, 1711, 2415, 2420. [OE. *wīgel*; ONFr. *wīle*, OFr. *guīle.*]

wylyde, *adj.* guileful; *w.werke*, intrigue, 2367. [From ME. *wīle*; see WYLEȜ.]

wyldrenesse, *n.* wilderness, 701. [OE. *wildeornes*; see WYLDE, *n.*]

wylle, *adj.* wandering, perplexing, 2084. [ON. *villr.*]

wylle, *n.* desire, pleasure, (good) will, 255, 1665, 2158, 2387; *of w.*, in temper (of mind), 57, 352; *at his (&c.) wylle*, to his pleasure, 836, 1371, 1952; at his good pleasure, 887, 1039, 1081, 1214; *bi ȝowre w.*, by your leave, 1065; *with (a) god w.*, gladly, 1387, 1861, 1969, 2430. [OE. *willa.*]

wylnyng, *n.* desire, 1546. [OE. *wilnung.*]

wylsum, *adj.* bewildering, leading one far astray, 689. [WYLLE, *adj.* + OE. *-sum*; cf. ON. *villusamr.*]

wylt, *pp.* strayed, escaped, 1711. [ON. *villask.*]

wymmen, *n. pl.* women, 1269, 2415, 2426. OE. *wīf-men, wimmen.*]

wyn(e), *n.* wine, 129, 338, 900, 980, 1025, 1403. [OE. *wīn.*]

wynde, *n.* wind, 516, 525, 784, 2004; *as wroth as w.*, 319. [OE. *wind.*]

wynde, *v.* to wind (back), return, 530; **wounden**, *pp.* wound, bound round, 215. [OE. *windan.*]

wyndow, *n.* window, 1743. [ON. *vindauga.*]

wynne, *adj.* delightful, lovely, 518, 1032, 2430, 2456. [Next in compounds as *wynn-wyrt*, pleasant herb.]

wynne, *n.*[1] joy, 15, 1765. [OE. *wynn.*]

wynne, *n.*[2] gain, 2420. [OE. *gewinn.*]

wynne, *v.* to gain, win, get, 70, 984, 1106; win over, bring (to), 1550; bring, 831, &c.; *refl.* in *wynne me*, find my way, get, 402; *intr.* get with effort (to), reach, 1569; come, go, 1537, 2044, 2050, 2215 (*subj.*); **wan**, *pa. t. sg.* 70, 2231 (came); **wonnen**, *pl.* brought, 831; **wan**, got, 1394; **won(n)en**, *pp.* won, brought, 1379, *1386, 1550, 2091, 2415; *watȝ w.*, had come, 461, 1365. [OE. *ge-winnan*, ON. *vinna.*]

wynnelych, *adj.* pleasant, 980. [OE. *wynnlic.*]

wynter, *n.* winter, 504, 530, 726, 1382; *gen.* 533; *pl.* years (with numeral), 613. [OE. *winter.*]

wynt-hole, *n.* wind-hole, windpipe, 1336. [OE. *wind* + *hol.*]

wyppe, *v.*[1] to whip, slash, 2249. [Cf. ON. *svipa*, MDu. *wippen*, and ME. variation *wap, swap.*]

wyppe, *v.*[2] to wipe, polish, 2022 n [OE. *wīpian.*]

wyrde, *n.* fate, 1752, 2418; *þe wyrde* Fate, 2134; *pl.* as *sg.* 1968. [OE. *wýrd.*]

wys (*vpon*), *adj.* wise (in), 1605. [OE. *wīs.*]

wyse, *n.* manner, fashion, 185, 267, 901, 2014, &c.; *on fele w.*, in many ways, 1653; *in no w.*, by no means, 1836. [OE. *wīse.*]

wysse *v.* to guide, direct, 549, 739 (*subj.*). [OE. *wissian.*]

wysty, *adj.* desolate, 2189. [OE. *wēstig.*]

wit, wyt, *v.* to know, learn, 131, 255, 1864; *wyt at*, learn from, 1508; **wot**, *1 sg. pres.* 24, 354, 1053, &c.; **wot**, *pl.* 1965; **wyst**, *pa. t. sg.* 1087, 1712, 2125; **wysten**, *pl.* 461, 1552 (were aware of), 2490, &c.; *wyt ȝe wel*, be assured, 1820. [OE. *witan*; *wāt*, sg.; *wiste*, pa. t.]

wyt(**e**), **wytte**, *n*. (right) mind, 1087; sense, reason, 677; intelligence, understanding, cleverness, 402, 1394, 1533, 2096; *pl*. reason, wits, 2459; consciousness, 1755; *fyue wyttez*, five senses, 640, 2193. [OE. (*ge*)*witt*.]

wyte, *v*. to look, 2050. [OE. *wītan*.]

with, **wyth**, *prep*. with; (i) (= OE. *mid*) with, having, among, 38, 106, 116, 364, 375, 816, &c.; in, amid, 9, 50, 538, &c.; by, through, 32, 78, 681, 949, &c. (ii) (= OE. *wiþ*), with, against, 97, 262, 1253, &c.; at, 1573, 2301; *wyth þis* (*þat*), thereupon, 316, 1305. *Adv*. wherewith, 2223. [OE. *mid*, *wiþ*.]

wythhalde, *v*. to hold back, check, 2268; **withhelde**, *pa. t*. 2291; **wythhylde**, 2168. [OE. *wiþ* + *háldan*.]

withalle, *adv*. entirely; withal, 1926. [OE. *mid alle*, ON. *með ǫllu*.]

withinne, **wythinne**, *adv*. in, inside, within, 153, 573, 606, 880, 1192, 2029; inwardly, 2370; *prep*. *1435, 1732, 1742; *follows sb*. 804, 1386, 1388. [OE. *wiþinnan*.]

withoute(n), *prep*. without, 127, 315, 345, 873, &c. [OE. *wiþūtan*.]

wyttenesse, *n*. witness, testimony, 2523. [OE. *gewitnes*.]

wlonk, *adj*. noble, 1977, 1988 (*as sb*.); glorious, lovely, 515, 581, 2022, 2432; *superl*. 2025. [OE. *wlonc*.]

wo, *n*. woe, 1717, 2134. [OE. *wā*.]

wod. See WADE.

wode, *adj*. mad, 2289. [OE. *wōd*.]

wod(**e**), *n*. wood, forest, 764, 1106, 1415, 1711, 1718, 2152; *in* (*bi*) *wod*, in the wood(s), 515, 1628, 2084. [OE. *wudu*.]

wodwos, *n. pl*. satyrs, trolls of the forest, 721. [OE. *wudu-wāsa*.]

woȝe, **wowe**, *n*.[1] wall, 858, 1180; *bi woȝez*, on the walls, 1650. [OE. *wāg*.]

woȝe, *n*.[1] wrong, sin, 1550. [OE. *wōh*.]

woke. See WAKED.

wol(**ed**), **wolde**. See WIL.

wolues, *n. pl*. wolves, 720. [OE. *wulf*.]

wombe, *n*. paunch, 144. [OE. *wámb*.]

won(**e**), *n*. pleasure, will, 1238; multitude, host, 1269. [ON. *ván*, hope, fair prospect, &c.] See WONE.

wonde, *v*. to shrink from, fear, 563; neglect (through fear), 488. [OE. *wándian*.]

wonder (*of*), *n*. wonder, amazement (at), 147, 238; *have w*., be amazed, 147, 467, 496; prodigy, marvel, wondrous deed (*or* tale), 16, 480, 2459; *of Arthurez wonderez*, from among the marvellous tales concerning A., 29; *predic*. (a) wonderful (thing), 1322, 1481; *adv*. wonderfully, 2200. [OE. *wundor*; *wundrum*, adv.]

wondered, *pa. t. impers*.; *hym w*., he was surprised, 1201. [OE. *wundrian*, pers.; ON. *undra*, pers. and impers.]

wonderly, *adv*. marvellously, 778, 1025. [OE. *wunder-līce*.]

wone, *n*. dwelling, abode, 257, 739, 764, 906, 997, 2490; *pl. in sg. sense*, 685, 1051, 1386, 2198, 2400. [ON. *ván*; see note to 257.]

wone, *v*. to remain, dwell, live, 257, 814, 2098; **wonyes**, *2 sg*. 399; **wonde**, *pa. t. sg*. 701; **woned**, *pl*. 50, 721; **wonyd**, **wonde**, **wont**, *pp*. 17, 1988, 2114. [OE. *wunian*.]

wont, *n*. lack (of good things), 131. [ON. *vanr*, neut. *vant*.]

wont, *v. impers*. there lacks; *er me w*. ere I have to go without, lose, 987; *neked wontez of*, it wants little (time) till, 1062; *yow wonted*, you lacked, fell short of, 2366. [From prec.]

worch(**e**), *v*. to work, make; do, 1039, 1546; *absol*. act, do, 238, 2253; *w. bi*, act according to, 2096; *let God worche*, let God act (as He will), 2208; **wroȝt**, *pa. t. and pp*. made, 399; wrought, devised, brought (about), 3, 22, 2344, 2361; acted, 677, 1997 (*pl*.) [OE. *wyrcan*, *worhte* (late *wrohte*).]

worchip, worschyp, *n.* honour, honourable treatment, 1032, 1267 n., 1521, 1976, 2441; honour (conferred by possession), 984, 2432. [OE. *weorþ-, wurþ-scipe.*]

worchip, *v.* to honour, 1227. [From prec.]

word(e), *n.* word, 224, 314, 2373; a thing to say, 1792; fame, 1521; *pl.* words, speech, conversation, 493 n., 1012, 1423, 1766, 2269; *grete w.*, boasts, 312, 325. [OE. *wórd.*]

worie, *v.* to worry, 1905. [OE. *wyrgan.*]

worlde, *n.* world, 261, 504, 530 n., 2000, 2479; *alle þe w.*, all men, 1227; *in (þis) w.*, in the world, 871, 2321, &c.; *of (in) þe w.*, in the world, 50, 238, &c. [OE. *woruld.*]

worm, *n.* dragon, 720. [OE. *wyrm.*]

worre, *adj.* worse; *þe w.*, the worst of it (in a fight), 1588, 1591. [ON. *verri* infl. by next.]

wors, *adj. compar.* worse, 726; **worst,** *superl.* worst, 1792, 2098. [OE. *wyrsa, wyrsta.*]

wort, *n.* plant, 518. [OE. *wyrt.*]

worth, *adj.* worth, 1269, 1820. [OE. *weorþ(e), wyrþe.*]

worþe, worth(e), *v.* to become, be made (done), 1202; (*as future of* '*be*'), will be; *me worþeȝ þe better*, I shall be the better off, 1035; *worþeȝ to*, shall be(come), 1106, 1387; *me schal w.*, it shall be done to me, 1214; *subj.* let it be (done), 1302; be (*with pp.*), 2374; *wel w. þe*, may good fortune befall you, 2127; *w. hit wele oþer wo*, come what may, 2134; **worþed,** *pa. t.* came (to pass), was made, 485; *subj.* would fare, 2096; *pp.* become, been made, 678. [OE. *weorþan*, str.]

worþy, worthé (559), *adj.* worthy; of value, 1848; honoured, noble, 559, 1537; *as sb.* noble lady, 1276, 1508; becoming, fitting, 819; *worþyest*, most excellent, 261; *adv.* courteously, 1477. [OE. *wyrþig*, merited, infl. by *wyrþe*, worth(y).]

worþily, worþyly, *adv.* in honour, gloriously, 72, 1988; courteously, 1759; with honour, 1386; becomingly, 144. [OE. *weorþlīce*, infl. by prec.]

worþilych, *adj.* honoured, glorious, 343. [OE. *weorþlic*; as prec.]

woþe, *n.* danger, 222, 488, 1576; **waþe,** 2355. [ON. *váði.*]

wouen, *pp.* woven, 2358. [OE. *wefan.*]

wounded, *pp.* wounded, 1781. [OE. *wúndian.*]

wounden. See WYNDE.

wowche, *v.* to vouch; *I w. hit saf*, I would vouchsafe (freely grant) it, 1391. [OFr. *voucher sauf.*]

wowes, 1180. See WOȜE.

wowyng, *n.* wooing, (unlawful) love-making, 2367; *þe w. of*, your temptation by, 2361. [From OE. *wōgian.*]

wrake, *n.* distress, 16. [OE. *wracu.*]

wrang, *adj.* (in the) wrong, 1494. [ON. *rangr*, older *vrangr.*]

wrast, *adj.* strong; loud (noise), 1423. [OE. *wrǣst.*]

wrast, *pp.* turned, disposed (to), 1482. [OE. *wrǣstan*, twist.]

wrastel, *v.* to wrestle, strive, 525. [OE. *wrāstlian, wrǣstlian.*]

wrathed, *pa. t.* angered, grieved; afflicted, 726; *impers.* in *you w.*, you were angry, 1509; *pp.* brought to disaster, 2420. [From OE. *wræþþu*; cf. *gewrǣþan.*]

wreȝande, *pres. p.* denouncing, 1706. [OE. *wrēgan.*]

wro, *n.* nook, 2222. [ON. *(v)rá.*]

wroȝt(en). See WORCH.

wroth(e), wroþe, *adj.* angry, wroth, 319, 1660; displeased, 70; fierce, 525, 1706, 1905; **wroþely,** *adv.* fierce(ly), 2289; **wroþeloker,** *compar.* more harshly, 2344. [OE. *wrāþ*; *wrāþlīce, -lucor.*]

wroth, *pa. t.* writhed; stretched himself, 1200. [OE. *wrīþan.*]

wruxled, *pp.* wrapped, clad, 2191. [OE. *wrixlan*, wind to and fro, alternate; cf. related *wrigels, wrēon.*]

Y

y3e, *n.* eye, 198, 228; **y3en,** *pl.* 82, 304, 684, 962. [OE. *ē(a)ge.*]
y3e-lydde3, *n. pl.* eyelids, 446, 1201. [Late OE. *ēge(h)lid.*]
ymage, *n.* image, 649. [OFr. *image.*]
your-, yow(re). See 3E.
yrn, *n.* iron, 215; weapon, 2267; *pl.* (pieces of) armour, 729. [OE. *īren.*]

INDEX OF NAMES

Adam, 2416.
Agrauayn a la dure mayn, Agravain of the hard hand, 110 n.
Aywan, see *Ywan.*
Anglesay, Anglesey, 698. OE. *Anglesēg.*
Arthur(e), King Arthur, 26, 85, 330, 491, 904; *Arþur*, 2297, 2466; *Arthour*, 253, 275; *Arþour*, 250; *Arþer*, 467, 536; *Arthure3*, gen. 29; *Arþure3*, 309, 2102, 2329, 2464; *Arthurus*, 2522; *kynge3 hous Arthor*, 2275 n.

Barsabe, Bathsheba, 2419.
Bawdewyn, Bischop, 112 n.
Bercilak de Hautdesert, 2445 n.
Byduer, Sir, Bedivere, 554 n.
Boos, Sir, Bors, 554 n.
Bretayn, Britain, 14 n., 20; *Bretaygne*, gen. 25.
Brutus, founder of Britain, 2523 n., 2524; *Felix Brutus*, 13 n.

Camylot, Camelot, 37 n.
Clarence, þe duk of, 552 n.
Cryst, Christ, 643; *Kryst*, 596, 674, 839, 869, 2067, &c.; *cros Kryst*, 762 n.; *vnder Krystes seluen*, on earth, 51.

Dalyda, Delilah, 2418.
Dauyth, David, 2418.
Doddinaual de Sauage, Sir, 552 n.

Ennias, Aeneas, 5.
Errik, knight of Round Table, 551 n.

Felix, see *Brutus.*
French flod, English Channel, 13.

Gaynour, see *Guenore.*
Gawayn (Sir), 838, 842, 989, 1044, 1110, 1208, *1376, 1926, 2149, 2235, 2475, &c.; *Gawayne, Sir*, 1619; *Gawayne3*, gen. 1807; *Gawan (Sir)*, 109, 339, 377, 405, 633, 876, 1293, &c.; *Gawen (Sir)*, 463, 476, 993; *Gauayn*, 1103; *Gauan*, 398, 421, 692; *G*: (MS.) 1179, 2280, 2299, 2429, 2491; *Sir G*: 1624, 1686, 1872, 2396. *Wawan*, *343, 559; *Wawen (Sir)*, 96, 1010, 1477, 1481; *Wowen (Sir)*, 1226, 1302, 2479; *Wowayn*, 2189. See 109 n.
Gile, saynt, St. Giles (Aegidius), 1644.
Gilyan, sayn, St. Julian l'Hospitalier, 774 n.
Grece, Greece, 2023.
Gryngolet, Gawain's horse, 597 n., 748, 777, 2047, 2063, 2160, 2480,
Guenore, Guenever, 74 n.; *Gaynour*, 2460; *Gwenore*, 109; *Wenore*, 945.

Index of Names

ȝeferus, Zephyrus, the West Wind, 517.

Hautdesert, see *Bercilak.*
Hestor, Hector of Troy, 2102 n.
Holy Hede, 'Holyhead', 700 n.

Jesus, 774.
Jon, sayn, St. John, 1718; *sayn Joneȝ day*, Dec. 27th, 1022.

Kryst, see *Cryst.*

Langaberde, eponymous hero of the Langobards; founder of Lombardy, 12.
Launcelot, Lancelot, 553.
Lyonel, Lionel, 553.
Logres, England, 691 n., 1055.
Lucan þe gode, knight of Round Table, 553.
Lumbardie, Lombardy, 12.

Mador de la Port, 555.
Mary, the Virgin Mary, 737, 754, 1263, 1268; as oath, marry! 1942, 2140; *Maré*, 1769.
Merlyn, Merlin the wizard, 2448 n.
Morgne la Faye, Morgan le Fay, 2446; *Morgne þe goddes*, 2452.

Norþe Waleȝ, North Wales, 697.

Peter, St. Peter; as oath, 813.
Port, see *Mador.*

Reynarde, Reniarde, Renaud(e), see glossary.
Rome, 8.
Romulus, founder of Rome, 8.

Salamon, Solomon, 625, 2417.
Samson, 2417.
Sauage, see *Doddinaual.*

Tars, Tharsia; see glossary.
Ticius, 11 n.
Tyntagelle, Tintagel (Cornwall), 2465.
Tolouse, see glossary.
Troye, Troy, 1, 2525.
Tuskan, Tuscany, 11.

Vryn, Urien, 113 n.
Vter, Uther Pendragon, 2465 n.

Waleȝ, see *Norþe Waleȝ.*
Wawan, Wawen, see *Gawayn.*
Wenore, see *Guenore.*
West Iles, British Isles, 7 n.
Wyrale, Wirral, district between Dee and Mersey, Cheshire, 701. OE. *Wīrheal(as).*
Wowayn, Wowen, see *Gawayn.*

Ywan Vryn son, Iwain, 113 n.; *Aywan*, 551; see also 109 n.

PRINTED IN
GREAT BRITAIN
AT THE
UNIVERSITY PRESS
OXFORD
BY
JOHN JOHNSON
PRINTER
TO THE
UNIVERSITY